# Radio's Second Century

# Radio's Second Century

Past, Present, and Future Perspectives

EDITED BY JOHN ALLEN HENDRICKS
FOREWORD BY MICHAEL BROWN

**Rutgers University Press**
New Brunswick, Camden, and Newark, New Jersey, and London

Library of Congress Cataloging-in-Publication Data

Names: Hendricks, John Allen, editor.
Title: Radio's second century : past, present, and future perspectives / edited by John Allen Hendricks.
Description: New Brunswick, New Jersey : Rutgers University Press, [2020] | Includes bibliographical references and index.
Identifiers: LCCN 2019024573 (print) | LCCN 2019024574 (ebook) | ISBN 9780813598475 (hardback) | ISBN 9780813598468 (paperback) | ISBN 9780813598482 (epub) | ISBN 9780813598499 (mobi)
Subjects: LCSH: Radio broadcasting.
Classification: LCC PN1991.5 .R366 2020 (print) | LCC PN1991.5 (ebook) | DDC 384.54—dc23
LC record available at https://lccn.loc.gov/2019024573
LC ebook record available at https://lccn.loc.gov/2019024574

A British Cataloging-in-Publication record for this book is available from the British Library.

This collection copyright © 2020 by Rutgers, The State University of New Jersey
Individual chapters copyright © 2020 in the names of their authors
All rights reserved

No part of this book may be reproduced or utilized in any form or by any means, electronic or mechanical, or by any information storage and retrieval system, without written permission from the publisher. Please contact Rutgers University Press, 106 Somerset Street, New Brunswick, NJ 08901. The only exception to this prohibition is "fair use" as defined by U.S. copyright law.

∞ The paper used in this publication meets the requirements of the American National Standard for Information Sciences—Permanence of Paper for Printed Library Materials, ANSI Z39.48-1992.

www.rutgersuniversitypress.org

Manufactured in the United States of America

# Contents

Foreword by Michael Brown     vii
Preface     xi

### Part I   Contemporary Radio: Social and Digital Media

1. Digital Radio: Audio Listening from AM to FM to XM ... and Beyond     3
   JOHN ALLEN HENDRICKS AND BRUCE MIMS

2. Audience Research and Web Features of Radio Stations in a Time of Uncertainty     22
   LU WU AND DANIEL RIFFE

3. The Parasocial Nature of the Podcast     39
   LAITH ZURAIKAT

4. Social Media Analytics, Radio Advertising, and Strategic Partnerships     53
   JOSEPH R. BLANEY

### Part II   Programming Matters: Localism, Personalities, and Audiences

5. The Shrinking Electronic Town Square: Localism in American Talk Radio     67
   DAVID CRIDER

| | | |
|---|---|---|
| 6 | The Fandom of Howard Stern and Its Relationship to His Success: The "King of All Media" and a Dynamic Audience<br>RACHEL SUSSMAN-WANDER KAPLAN | 82 |
| 7 | *The War of the Worlds* Broadcast: Fake News or Engaging Storytelling?<br>JOHN F. BARBER | 96 |
| 8 | Unpredictable Programming: A Freeform Approach to Building Audiences<br>EMILY W. EASTON | 119 |

**Part III  Social Issues: Contemporary Overtones**

| | | |
|---|---|---|
| 9 | Air to the Kingdom: Religion and the Soul of Radio<br>MARK WARD SR. | 137 |
| 10 | "A More Inclusive Public Service": Can NPR Serve All of America?<br>JOHN MARK DEMPSEY | 154 |
| 11 | The Sound of Yellow Rain: Resisting Podcasting's Sonic Whiteness<br>ANJULI JOSHI BREKKE | 173 |

**Part IV  International Perspectives: Modern Paradigms**

| | | |
|---|---|---|
| 12 | Canadian Community/Campus Radio: Struggling and Coping on the Cusp of Change<br>ANNE F. MacLENNAN | 193 |
| 13 | Revenge of the Nerds: How Public Radio Dominated Podcasting and Transformed Listening to Audio<br>BRAD CLARK AND ARCHIE McLEAN | 207 |
| 14 | Reproducing Analog Pathologies in the Digital Radio Landscape: The Case of Greece<br>MICHAEL NEVRADAKIS | 231 |
| 15 | Almost 100 Years of Women in Radio: Where Are We Now?<br>SIMON ORDER | 255 |
| | Acknowledgments | 273 |
| | About the Editor | 275 |
| | Notes on Contributors | 277 |
| | Index | 283 |

# Foreword

*Radio's Second Century* is an important addition to radio scholarship. It reminds us that radio remains a vital and important medium as a technology, as a source of audio, and as a worldwide cultural force. *Radio's Second Century* provides a foundation for understanding radio's direction as it begins a second century of providing information and entertainment for a diversity of audiences.

The early 1900s were years of experimentation for radio as scientists and amateur enthusiasts developed the technology and its various uses. The emergence of radio broadcasting one hundred years ago as a popular mass medium was somewhat of a surprise. Most of the organizations and scientists who developed radio did not envision broadcasting as the primary use of the technology. Rather it was used to conduct business and connect with ships at sea and was viewed as point-to-point communication rather than broadcasting one message to many people. Radio's lack of privacy was a concern for those who used it for business, but the availability of radio signals for anyone with a receiver drove amateurs to begin transmitting to anyone willing to listen. This, in turn, fueled interest among average people who wanted to hear what was broadcast into the "ether." These activities were the foundation for radio broadcasting and shaped its role as a mass medium. The emergence of radio broadcasting came in the early 1920s. Frank Conrad's broadcast from KDKA in 1920 is often cited as the milestone that marks the beginning of broadcasting. By 1922 Waldemar Kaempffert (p. 40), who later would become the first science editor for the *New York Times*, said, "No one dreamed of broadcasting's possibilities. . . . Somehow the world with all its diameter of eight thousand miles, seems to shrivel into a little ball which can be held in the hand." And no one dreamed that radio broadcasting would become such a prominent part of our lives.

Uncertainties about the direction of radio framed the beginning of radio's second century as well. Digital technologies disrupted the place radio broadcasting assumed in American audio culture, and the future of radio broadcasting seemed somewhat in doubt. The cover of *Wired* magazine in March 2005 declared "THE END OF RADIO (as we know it)" with a picture of a portable radio exploding as a bullet passes through. Radio broadcasting did not die but certainly was recast in a more complex media environment, one that continues to attract audiences and scholars. Contemporary radio uses digital delivery systems and maintains a multimedia web presence. Podcasts are among new ways to reach audiences who can be much more difficult to define, and they organize themselves in different ways. New and more complicated advertising efforts are required. Radio has found new life in old programming strengths such as talk radio and local content but has also found innovative ways to reach and reconfigure audiences. Social issues such as race, gender, religion, and the role of public service continue to be sources of concern as they do in broader society. Kaempffert suggested one hundred years ago that radio shrunk the world, and digital technologies have shrunk it further. Radio has always been international. One hundred years ago radio amateurs or "DXers" were receiving signals from all over the world, but today's digital technology has increased international participation and exchange with an ease previously unattainable. Understanding radio today requires a strong understanding of radio's international use. *Radio's Second Century* addresses the new, exciting, complicated, problematic, and promising world of radio today. It provides an entry into the current radio milieu and provides content and ideas about how to address the opportunities and ideas presented by radio as it enters its second century.

*Radio's Second Century* points to a diverse and open field for those who wish to study radio and those who have an interest in learning what we know about the technology, programming, social issues, and international use of radio. It points to the opportunities and obstacles as radio gets defined in a much more diverse and complicated audio environment. It helps us understand the diversity of ways that radio provides a conduit between, and interacts with, industry and culture; and for scholars the book points to the variety of opportunities to study radio from different perspectives. *Radio's Second Century* shows us that radio is a lively medium and fertile academic ground.

As someone involved in ongoing discussions about the future of radio with groups like the Broadcast Education Association, Popular Culture Association, and Radio Studies Forum and at numerous conferences, I have heard concerns for what might be lost, excitement over what is to come, bewilderment about technological change and digital opportunities, but always a sense that radio will find its place going into its second one hundred years. Scholars within the Radio and Audio Media Division of the Broadcast Education Association wanted to mark a hundred years of radio broadcasting, and *Radio's Second Century* does so. It represents the new direction radio takes as both a practice and a source of scholarly concern. *Radio's Second Century* is a well-written, well-organized, valuable set of articles. In the past when I put together materials for my students to read, I gathered a sample of different book chapters and journal articles. *Radio's Second Century* is organized this way in a nice package that provides excellent guidance as we move radio into the future.

Michael Brown<br>
Emeritus Professor<br>
University of Wyoming

## Reference

Kaempffert, W. (1922). Radio simply explained. In G. Squire (Ed.), *The easy course in home radio* (pp. 1–50). New York: Martin H. Ray and Review of Review Co.

# Preface

Despite seismic shifts both internally and externally, radio enters its second century of serving the news, information, and entertainment needs of listeners around the world as a very robust and vital media industry in America and around the globe. Jacobs Media's *Tech Survey 2018* revealed that 92 percent of Americans aged eighteen and older listen to AM/FM radio, 66 percent listen to radio music apps, 61 percent listen to streaming audio, 25 percent listen to satellite radio, and 23 percent listen to podcasts. Although Baby Boomers (born between 1946 and 1964) and Gen Xers (born between 1965 and 1980) are the dominant listeners of radio composing 81 percent of the audience, it is worth noting that 15 percent of Millennials (born between 1981 and 1996) compose the radio audience (Jacobs Media, 2018).

Moreover, UNESCO asserts, "Radio is the mass media reaching the widest audience in the world" (2014, para. 1). There are more than forty thousand radio stations worldwide. A 2018 study by Deloitte Global indicated that nearly three billion people globally listen to radio weekly and more than 85 percent of adults listen to radio in the developed world (Stuart, 2018). Deloitte Global asserts,

> Unlike some other forms of traditional media, radio will continue to perform relatively well with younger demographics. In the United States, for example, we expect that more than 90 percent of 18–34-year-olds will listen to radio at least weekly in 2019, and they will listen to radio for an average of more than 80 minutes a day. (Stuart, 2018, para. 1)

Thus, despite numerous challenges, the radio industry remains vibrant, although it is definitely facing some competition from new disruptive technologies. This book investigates perennial topics that continue to assist in keeping the radio industry relevant while also exploring vanguard topics that are forcing the radio industry to adopt rapid change.

Research from both American and international perspectives of the radio industry is evaluated, and the book is divided into four sections. The first section of the book examines contemporary radio issues by focusing on digital, Internet, and social media issues. In the opening chapter, John Allen Hendricks and Bruce Mims describe to the reader how the radio industry is experiencing a paradigm shift. They examine and explain how disruptive technological advancements such as smartphones, connected cars, and audio streaming services are influencing listener behaviors and altering the contemporary radio landscape. In Chapter 2, Lu Wu and Daniel Riffe explore the broad question of how radio news operations have been responding to the increasing pressures for an expanded online presence. They discover that environmental uncertainties don't incentivize radio stations to actively collect audience data and conduct audience research; instead, ownership and resources allocation play a large role in determining radio stations' website features. Laith Zuraikat, in Chapter 3, explores the parasocial nature of podcasts and how listeners of these programs can develop a false sense of a relationship and connection with the hosts of their preferred shows. He looks at how this relationship compares to, and has been influenced by, the parasocial relationship that can develop between traditional radio hosts and their audience, as well as how the podcast could serve as a natural evolution of the parasocial effect of audio-based entertainment and mediums. Part I concludes with Joseph R. Blaney offering a glimpse into how small and large commercial radio companies have navigated use and analysis of their social media presence. He notes a particular need for systematic collection and analysis of social media data, better professional development for those responsible for social media (rather than assigning the duties as an afterthought), and better cooperation between industry and academe in identifying gaps in social media opportunities.

The second section looks at issues related to programming such as localism, personalities, and audiences. Chapter 5 studies localism in talk radio and finds that local content continues to be lacking in smaller markets, regardless of who owns the stations. David Crider finds that talk radio has placed a premium on discussions of national politics, sacrificing the unique concerns of local communities. In Chapter 6, Rachel Sussman-Wander Kaplan focuses on the strong sense of fandom surrounding *The Howard Stern Radio Show*, as Stern has attributed his success to his loyal audience. The theoretical foundation for this chapter comes from the literature on the nature of fandom, identity and fandom, and fan relationships with stars. She argues Stern has mastered the parasocial relationship, cultivating a kinship between Stern and listeners of the show. Chapter 7 offers an interesting perspective on and some needed context for the famous radio broadcast/incident *The War of the Worlds*. John F. Barber notes this radio drama is often called a hoax for its use of fictional news reporting style and break-in news announcements to move the narrative forward. But other radio dramas used this trope previously, and Barber examines each for inspiration and prototypes leading up to *The War of the Worlds* as engaging radio storytelling. And Emily W. Easton, in Chapter 8, explores how freeform radio stations approach the challenge of maintaining a consistent station identity while relying on highly decentralized programming strategies developed by individual DJs. She contextualizes how freeform's unique approach evolved within the wider context of American music radio programming and how one freeform station built their audience by selecting experienced DJs who could successfully draw on personal programming philosophies and educating those DJs on the station's expectations of delivering strange, but accessible, music.

The third section discusses social issues that are permeating the contemporary radio industry. Mark Ward Sr. observes that religious radio is the third largest format by station count, which suggests the genre holds a solid foothold in the medium's second century. In Chapter 9, Ward examines religious radio's past and present economic, technical, and regulatory changes, revealing how genre audiences make use of a shared sense of media content to build communities. Chapter 10 takes a close look at the venerable National Public Radio and asserts that NPR is not a truly national service in terms of geography, audience demographics, and content programming. But, after studying NPR's history and its current proposals for broadening its audience, John Mark Dempsey reveals that there are potential strategies for NPR to reach a wider, more inclusive audience. Anjuli Joshi Brekke, in Chapter 11, highlights how trends in podcasting continue mainstream radio's privileging of white aural preferences as standard while undermining and exoticizing the stories of people of color. The intimacy of podcast sound design, mobility of listening, and shareability impact how this "sonic whiteness" is experienced and taken up by listeners. Brekke discusses ways online networked culture may be leveraged to disrupt the hegemony of sonic whiteness.

The final section of the book examines radio from an international perspective. Anne F. MacLennan tracks the development of Canadian community broadcasting over the last century. In Chapter 12, the challenges of Canadian community, campus, and Native stations are tracked and analyzed through license renewal application documentation. The regulatory obligations, financial challenges, and other difficulties that she argues are significant to consider for the future of these stations in light of the current federal regulatory reassessments. Brad Clark and Archie McLean argue that public broadcasters in the United States and Canada have largely laid the foundation for podcasting's mass appeal and emergence in popular culture. Their analysis, in Chapter 13, examines thirty of the most listened to podcasts, and it is clear that the best features of public radio form the template for a range of on-demand audio products featuring elements of documentary, radio drama, interviews, and live storytelling. At the same time, this chapter shows that features once unique to podcasts are increasingly migrating to public radio programming as part of an evolving reciprocal relationship between audio formats. Michael Nevradakis asks, how can a transition to digital radio be implemented in an environment where the analog radio landscape has never effectively been regulated? He also asks, can digital forms of radio delivery provide a space for alternative voices and news content that are excluded from the FM dial? Chapter 14 examines the case of Greece, where broadcast regulation has long been haphazard and closed off to new voices without deep pockets. Last, Simon Order examines gender parity in the world of radio in a "Where are we now?" approach. In Chapter 15, he highlights the early days of women in radio in the United States and moves forward to a modern international representation of women via the Global Media Monitoring Project. He also traces key gender parity developments at the British Broadcasting Corporation in the United Kingdom and more recent debate in Australia. By way of illuminating contrast, this chapter also dives into the world of Indian community radio where female participation is at quite a different stage. Globally, gender parity in the production of broadcast media and the content of media, including radio, has improved but still has a significant way to go.

## References

Jacobs Media. (2018). *Tech Survey 2018: Radio navigates the digital revolution*. Retrieved from https://jacobsmedia.com/ts2018-results/

Stuart, D. (2018, December 11). Radio: Revenue, reach, and resilience. TMT predictions 2019. *Deloitte Insights*. Retrieved from www2.deloitte.com/insights/us/en/industry/technology/technology-media-and-telecom-predictions/radio-revenue.html

UNESCO. (2014). *UNESCO office commemorates World Radio Day 2014*. Retrieved from https://en.unesco.org/news/unesco-office-commemorates-world-radio-day-2014

**Radio's Second Century**

# Part I
# Contemporary Radio
Social and Digital Media

# 1
## Digital Radio

• • • • • • • • • • • • • • • • • • •

Audio Listening from AM to FM
to XM . . . and Beyond

JOHN ALLEN HENDRICKS
AND BRUCE MIMS

Similar to all new technological inventions, no single discovery or moment can be declared as the sole reason for radio's existence and success. The development of radio was contingent upon several technological discoveries such as James Clark Maxwell's theory of "invisible radiant energy similar to light" and Heinrich Hertz's experiment proving Maxwell's theory (Head & Sterling, 1990, p. 34). It also took Guglielmo Marconi's curiosity and persistence to build upon Hertz's discoveries through "endless experiments with different shapes, sizes, and types of antennas, ground systems and other components gradually improv[ing] the performance of his pioneering wireless system" (Head & Sterling, 1990, p. 35). This experimentation led to a Nobel Prize in physics for Marconi for his work in wireless telegraphy (Head & Sterling, 1990). Continuing to build upon all wireless telegraphy research, by 1906 Lee de Forest invented the "tube," or Audion, with diodes that allowed for weak signals to be amplified (Head & Sterling, 1990). Also, in 1906 Reginald Fessenden transmitted what has been called the first "broadcast" (Head & Sterling, 1990).

By the end of 1920, the first radio station, KDKA, went on the air in Pittsburgh, Pennsylvania, and was operated by Westinghouse. At or around the same time as KDKA's formation, other radio stations such as KCBS (San Francisco), KQW (San Jose), and WHA (Madison) were also being built (Smith, 1985). KDKA broadcast the voting results of the 1920 presidential election, and more people began listening to this new invention. Smith (1985) notes, "As mail came in from listeners, the pioneer radio station operators responded by setting up regular schedules of transmissions, programming for a general audience. They evolved from radio station operators into radio station broadcasters" (p. 18). Collectively, all of these inventions contributed to the start of the radio broadcasting industry. By the end of 1922, more than 480 radio stations had been licensed by the U.S. Department of Commerce (Smith, 1985). Radio steadily grew as the primary entertainment source for Americans for nearly two decades—until the mass medium of television was invented in the late 1930s and early 1940s (Smith, 1985).

From its humble beginnings, radio has continually experienced competition from new technological advances that attract the attention of the audience. When television was invented and became mainstream, drama and variety programming migrated from radio to television. Television displaced radio as the evening home entertainment option and became a source for local advertising (Sterling & Kittross, 1990). Sterling and Kittross assert, "Of concern to all other mass communication media, as well as operators of any means of recreation or entertainment, was the impact of television. Two media that felt the immediate brunt were radically changed—radio and the movies" (p. 309). The external competition did not end with the invention of television. It has continued with the invention and emergence of many new technologies, especially satellite radio and audio delivery services via the Internet. Biagi (2017) asserts, "The choices consumers make over the next ten years about how they want to receive radio programming ultimately will determine whether the competition for listeners will lead to expansion or contraction of the radio business" (p. 120).

Technology's constant evolution has changed the way in which people "listen" to radio stations and audio, ranging from the eight-track and cassette tape players to portable radios and iPods to modern-day technologies such as the Internet and satellites. Traditional, or legacy, radio required listeners to have an AM/FM receiver in their home or automobile to hear the programming produced in studios by professionals. In the second decade of the twenty-first century, that model has now changed completely, with listeners no longer restricted to only programming emanating from an AM or FM signal. The Internet, smartphones, and satellites have provided listeners, or consumers, with an impressive array of venues for listening to "audio" now rather than just "radio." When asked whether traditional radio, music streaming, and podcasting were morphing into one new medium called "audio" rather than "radio," John Rosso, president for market development at Triton Digital, replied, "Most certainly. It's also just common sense. All these are forms of audio. The only difference really is how you access them—and it's a minor difference. It is all one medium, growing and evolving, and reaching ever-larger groups of consumers" (Ely, 2018b, para. 21).

Despite the technological changes causing a paradigm shift in radio and audio listening, radio listenership remains healthy. The 2018 Jacobs Media *Tech Survey* indicated that 92 percent of those surveyed listened to traditional AM/FM radio, citing access to popular music and personalities as well as the convenience of listening in automobiles, while Nielsen found similarly that 93 percent of Americans listened to AM/FM radio ("Audio Today," 2018). The survey had more than 64,000 respondents who were 58 percent female and 41 percent males and more than 70 percent of the respondents were forty-five years or older. Only 10 percent were twenty-five to thirty-four years old, and 16 percent were thirty-five to forty-four years old. Of the survey respondents, 81 percent were Baby Boomers or Generation Xers, while only 15 percent of the respondents were Millennials.

Although radio listenership indeed remains robust in the second decade of the twenty-first century, the fact remains that listener habits are changing and listeners are migratory. And, it is important to remember that wherever the listeners go, the advertising dollars soon follow. Triton Digital's John Rosso asserts, "Podcasting is finding its audience, which is clear from the research. The question in my mind is how quickly advertisers will follow the rapidly growing audience. Podcasting has proven to be a very effective medium for direct-response advertisers, and I believe it will also perform well for marketers who want to use it for branding and high-end marketing" (Ely, 2018b, para. 16).

As noted, listening is becoming less about "radio" and more about "audio" as new technologies allow listeners to consume programming "on demand" based upon preferences and the ability to time shift with smartphones, smart speakers, and the connected car (see Figure 1.1). Goldthwaite (2018) suggests, "Radio remains the dominant media in the car, and the rising popularity of voice-activated devices such as Amazon Echo, Google Home, and Apple's HomePod are fueling a new audio renaissance that harks back to an era when families gathered to listen to FDR's fireside chats and shows like *The Lone Ranger* and Jack Benny" (para. 2).

Likewise, not only has twenty-first-century technology provided consumers with audio online programming on platforms via (1) traditional radio station programming, (2) audio streaming services such as Pandora and Spotify, and (3) podcasting, but there has also been a proliferation of new technologies that will influence listener patterns. For example, it is estimated that by 2022 almost 900 million "voice-assistant-enabled devices" will be in use (Goldthwaite, 2018). In 2018, Edison Research found that 43 million people owned a smart speaker ("The Smart Audio Report," 2018). Goldthwaite observes, "These next-generation radios are no longer designed just for passive listening—they're smart, interactive tools that enable us to live our lives in different ways" (para. 4).

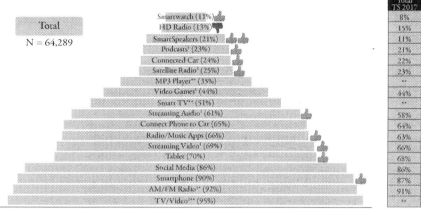

¹ Weekly or more   ² 1+ hour per day   ³ Paid & trial users   * Any platform/device   ** Wording Change

FIG. 1.1   Media pyramid 2018. ("Techsurvey 2018." © Jacobs Media)

## Internet Radio

To follow the listeners, traditional radio stations have migrated their signals beyond the AM and FM bands to the Internet. They now stream their over-the-air broadcast signal online to compete with listening alternatives such as pureplay webcasts and podcasts by giving consumers convenient access to programming. Consumers can also use an app that is defined by Tech Terms (2018) as, "short for 'application,' which is the same thing as a software program. While an app may refer to a program for any hardware platform, it is most often used to describe software that enables program delivery, including the broadcasts of AM and FM stations, to mobile devices such as smartphones and tablets" ("Tech Terms: App," 2018, para. 1).

Broadcasters ushered in the twenty-first century with a fresh and optimistic outlook for web radio development. In the midst of the dot-com boom of the early 2000s, AM and FM station operators seized opportunities to explore—and exploit—the capabilities of disseminating their programming over the World Wide Web. Since that time, steady growth in the numbers of both webstreaming stations and listeners has occurred. But, as is often the case with emerging technologies, there were those broadcasters who refused to adapt.

Consider that in 1994, just six years shy of the beginning of the twenty-first century, fewer than sixty stations had begun streaming their signals over the web (Raphael, 2000). The radio broadcasting community struggled to reach consensus on the need for and value of webcasting. One of the early scholarly studies to inquire into the streaming phenomenon shed light on the then-prevalent practice by broadcasters of publishing station websites but opting against utilizing those sites as the launching point for audio streams. Results of the content analysis of station websites conducted by Lind and Medoff (1999) included the observation that "although radio is an audio medium, stations' web sites do not utilize audio to any great extent" (p. 209). They concluded with a poignant recommendation for broadcasters: either shed reluctant attitudes about webstreaming and adopt a proactive, goal-oriented vision about providing an aural presence or risk the loss of audience to one of the proliferating number of "pure-plays," the emerging term identifying nonbroadcast, Internet-only audio content providers.

Arbitron, the preeminent audience measurement service of that era, reported in 1999 that listener enthusiasm for online radio was well poised for growth in the upcoming twenty-first century. Almost two in three (63 percent) online users—representing 30 percent of all Americans—claimed awareness of radio webcasting in 1999, twice the number recorded in the previous year (Arbitron, 1999). Its follow-up 2000 survey of online listenership indicated that half of the respondents listened either at home or at work to radio webcasts (Arbitron, 2000). Similar growth patterns in the number of radio station websites that offered audio webstreams were observed. Of the more that 12,000 licensed commercial radio stations operating that year, an estimated 4,300 licensees streamed their signals along the web (BRS Media, 2000), an increase of 39 percent over the previous year ("Radio Webcasts," 2000). In a listening environment where Arbitron speculated that one in every three office workers nationwide experienced electrical interference in receiving terrestrial AM and FM signals (Komando, 1999), the promise of relief from reception difficulties that web radio could deliver loomed large with radio audiences.

Multiple opportunists emerged to assist stations with their streaming activities. Table 1.1 aggregates information gleaned from the websites of nine media networks in October 2000. The data facilitate cross-comparisons of the varied financial and technical arrangements each network offered to assist broadcasters in establishing a webstream presence. The providers, and their corporate ownership, indicated within parentheses, included BRS Media (BRS Media, Inc.), Broadcast.com (Yahoo!), BroadcastAmerica.com (Broadcast America), GlobalMedia.com (Global Media, Inc.), RDG.com (Radio Data Group, a consortium founded by the radio broadcasting corporations Infinity Broadcasting, Clear Channel Communications, and Colfax Communications), RadioWave.com (Motorola), Real Broadcast Networks (RealNetworks.com), WarpRadio.com (WarpRadio, Inc.), and WebRadio.com (Interactive GEO).

Present-day operators largely have settled into one of two distinct modes of operation. Station ownership typically dictates where a station's steam originates. In some instances a station appears on an entity of its corporate parent, such as iHeartMedia's iHeartRadio.com. In other circumstances a station stream may launch from an aggregator directory. One example is TuneIn, a popular site utilized by smaller-market broadcasters that directs listeners to content streamed over the Securenet Systems platform. It bears observing that station relationships with platforms remain fluid: In mid-2018 group owner Entercom announced the

## Table 1.1
## Media Networks: Service Considerations

| Service considerations | BRSMedia.com | Broadcast.com | BroadcastAmerica.com | GlobalMedia.com | RDG.com | RadioWave.com | RBN.com | WarpRadio.com | WebRadio.com |
|---|---|---|---|---|---|---|---|---|---|
| Provides website-development assistance to station | N/A | Yes | N/A | Yes | Yes | N/A | N/A | N/A | Yes |
| Station advertising space available on service provider's website | No | No | Yes | No | No | No | No | No | No |
| Transfers listener from station website to service provider website | No | Yes | Yes | Yes | No | No | No | No | No |
| Station can stream additional audio content to its program audio stream | N/A | Yes | N/A | Yes | Yes | N/A | Yes | N/A | Yes |
| Streams message to listener prior to delivery of station audio | No | Yes | Yes | No | No | N/A | If desired | No | N/A |
| Commercial messages on webstream can be segregated from on-air messages | Yes | N/A | N/A | Yes | No | Yes | Yes | N/A | N/A |
| Listener can link to station website from service provider's website | Yes | Yes | Yes | Yes | Yes | No | Yes | Yes | Yes |
| Approximate number of streamed broadcast station signals | N/A | 600 | 200 | 250 | 200 | N/A | 250 | 300 | 126 |

NOTE: N/A indicates this information was not available on the provider's website.

exit of its stations from TuneIn. Webstreams from the stations of Entercom, the second-largest U.S. commercial broadcaster, have migrated to the site Radio.com, which Entercom acquired in its 2017 merger with CBS Radio ("Entercom to Exit," 2018).

An impediment to station webstreaming emerged early in the twenty-first century to roadblock the information superhighway for broadcasters. Growth stalled in both the number of stations that streamed and audience size, largely the result of legalities pertaining to broadcasters' use of the music industry's intellectual property. By webstreaming the copyrighted recordings of copyrighted music compositions, broadcasters infringed on the intellectual property rights of both record labels and songwriters alike. This formidable, hot-button issue was fueled by the actions of commercial and noncommercial broadcasters. Thus, public radio, religious, and college radio broadcasters also shouldered the responsibility alongside commercial broadcasters for licensing the use of copyrighted content (McClung, Mims, & Hong, 2003).

In order to better understand the implications of this issue, a review of the basics of the Copyright Act of 1976 as they pertain to music is helpful. Two related, yet separate, forms of protection for the creators of musical performances fixed in sound recordings are addressed by the act: "Section 102 . . . identifies various categories of works that are eligible for copyright protection. These include 'musical works' and 'sound recordings.' The term 'musical works' refers to the notes and lyrics of a song, while a 'sound recording' results from 'the fixation of a series of musical, spoken, or other sounds'" (United States Copyright Office, 2002a, pp. 4–5).

The first performing rights society (PRS), the American Society of Composers, Authors, and Publishers (ASCAP), was formed in 1914 for the purpose of collecting and disbursing royalty payments for the public performance of music compositions to its copyright-holding members ("ASCAP Music Organization," n.d.). ASCAP collects royalty payments on behalf of its members for every broadcast of live or recorded compositions within its repertoire. In the modern era ASCAP and two other PRSs, Broadcast Music, Incorporated (BMI) and SESAC (known formerly as the Society for European Stage Authors and Composers), represent the public performance copyright interests of more than 420,000 composers, songwriters, and publishers.

The recorded music industry likewise relies on copyright law to protect against unlawful use of its intellectual property in preserving its financial interests. Sounds fixed in music recordings reflect the unique creative talents of artists, technicians, and engineers, with an estimated value in the billions of dollars. As products of commerce, however, the sounds fixed in music recordings compose an industry whose worldwide sales top forty billion dollars annually ("About RIAA.org," 2019). Copyright law differentiates the legal protections available to holders of composition copyrights and sound recording copyrights. Holders of musical work copyrights receive the exclusive privilege of controlling the public performance of their compositions, including its conveyance via radio broadcasting. The law obligates commercial and noncommercial stations alike to compensate copyright holders whenever protected compositions, live or recorded, are broadcast (Copyright Law of 1976). However, there is no similar legal mechanism within the law for protecting the interests of the record labels. As the situation currently exists, radio stations owe nothing when recordings are played over AM and FM terrestrial broadcasts.

The obligations for making royalty payments are different when stations stream their audio over the Internet. Congressional passage of the Digital Performance Right in Sound Recordings Act of 1995 affirmed the legal distinctions between the activities of broadcasting and streaming. At issue was the method of dissemination: The former was recognized as an analog technology whereas the latter utilized digital technology. Unlike analog recordings, which degrade whenever copied and recopied, digital recordings retain their pristine audio quality from one generation of the recording to the next, and so on. In short, webstreams could deliver sound that equated with CD-based sonic purity.

Why, Congress reasoned, would consumers purchase CDs when webstreams delivered sound quality equivalent with that of the original recording? Thus, to further clarify the distinctions, Congress enacted the Digital Millennium Copyright Act (DMCA) in 1998. Radio station webstreaming, in the opinion of the Congress, constituted an activity that summoned protection of the financial interests of the record labels. In short, stations now were obligated to pay royalties to songwriters when recordings were broadcast terrestrially and make additional payments both to songwriters as well as to record labels when webstreaming (United States Copyright Office, 2002b, p. 8). This obligation to render additional payment caught broadcasters off guard and unprepared. Industry trades questioned whether station operators could afford to meet this unanticipated expense burden (Albiniak, 2002; Johnston, 2002). Connolly (2002) viewed the issue as surmountable, observing that "no, it's not the end of Webcasting" (p. 17).

The Recording Industry Association of America, termed the RIAA, responded to the situation. Under the direction of Congress, RIAA established SoundExchange and charged it with a single-purpose mission: "The organization collects and distributes digital performance royalties on behalf of nearly 175,000 recording artists and master rights owners accounts and administers direct agreements on behalf of rights owners and licensees" ("About SoundExchange," 2019, para. 1). For the better part of the twenty-first century the structure and order SoundExchange imposes on the royalty collection and distribution processes has helped ensure that broadcasters' webstreams do not infringe on the intellectual property rights of copyright holders. To date, the organization, headquartered in Washington, D.C., has disbursed more than five billion dollars in royalties.

Intellectual property issues also come into play when broadcasters stream commercials that utilize the talents of unionized voice actors and announcers.

SAG-AFTRA represents their financial interests under this rationale: "SAG-AFTRA brings together two great American labor unions: Screen Actors Guild and the American Federation of Television and Radio Artists. Both were formed in the turmoil of the 1930s, with rich histories of fighting for and securing the strongest protections for media artists. Our members united to form the successor union in order to preserve those hard-won rights and to continue the struggle to extend and expand those protections into the 21st century and beyond" ("About: Mission Statement," 2019, para. 1). Thus, the DMCA obligates radio stations to make royalty payments for both the terrestrial and the online dissemination of content—notably commercial advertisements—that utilize union-member talent. An expense-reducing practice adopted early on by broadcasters that has carried forward to the present is that of separating the commercial segments from the programming. Under this practice, whenever terrestrially broadcast commercials contain copyright protections, they are deleted from the simultaneous webstream and are substituted with "safe" content, notably public service announcements (PSAs) provided to stations by the Ad Council.

## Satellite Radio

Satellite radio shares a close timeline of development alongside station webstreaming. Both delivery systems have their origins in the 1990s digital revolution, and both began to gain traction with listeners at approximately the same time in the early 2000s. Initially, two operators developed platforms for delivering radio programming via satellite. XM Satellite Radio was the first to debut, in late 2001. Sirius Satellite Radio soon followed, entering into a competitive audio landscape already occupied not only by XM but also by commercial and noncommercial AM and FM radio stations. Both satcasters operated on a subscription model, initially charging fees of about ten dollars per month. In return, listeners received, depending upon the service, approximately one hundred channels of music and talk programming. XM's channel lineup veered slightly more toward the music universe, with the service offering seventy music stations, in comparison with the sixty music channels Sirius advertised. Music channels on both services operated commercial-free. Overall, the services directed the totality of the content to listeners of all ages and interests (Dennison, 2004, pp. 466–467).

Each service required the listeners to use proprietary receivers, and while devices became available for home, office, and mobile listening, two realities soon asserted themselves: (1) the potential subscriber pool was not large enough to support two satcasters and (2) the future of the service would reside with the mobile audience. Merger discussions between the two companies ensued, culminating in a deal announced in mid-2008. About the pairing, Reuters reported, "Neither XM nor Sirius has ever posted a net profit, and have recorded billions of dollars in losses building their operations" ("Sirius Completes," 2008, para. 6).

Consolidation of the assets of XM and Sirius was completed in late 2008 when the Sirius management team in place at that time assumed all responsibility for operations. The resulting company reported a subscribership at the time of the merger completion at 18.5 million persons ("Sirius Completes," 2008). A workforce reduction immediately ensued; XM channel programmer Marlin Taylor observed that "many talented XM programmers were discharged" (Taylor, 2018, p. 203).

Approximately ten years post-merger, SiriusXM's chief executive officer reported to stockholders in 2018 that "for SiriusXM, 2017 was a record-setting year. We achieved strong financial and operational performance while forging new paths for future value creation. Today, we are better positioned than ever to leverage our unparalleled content, our relationships with car makers, our ability to scale, our business strength, and our balance sheet to capitalize on the growth opportunities in front of us" (Meyer, 2018, para. 1).

The subscriber base, he stated, had grown to almost 33 million listeners. The company's financial performance is strong, and the company continues to innovate new content strategies ("Annual Report," 2017). SiriusXM announced in September 2018 that it would acquire Pandora. The satellite radio operator planned to pay $3.5 billion for the webstreaming pureplay that, in recent years, had faced stiff competition from streamers Spotify and Apple Music (Porter, 2018). Pureplay webstreaming is "a distinct class of webcasters whose predominant form of business and revenue generation is the streaming of sound recordings under a government license" ("SoundExchange," 2009, para. 4).

## Music Streaming Services

Music streaming services provide music and other programming via the Internet and are not associated with a traditional AM or FM radio station. Harris (2018), very simply, defines streaming music services as "a way of delivering sound—including music—without requiring you to download files from the internet" (para. 1). Music streaming services are rapidly growing in popularity among consumers. Wilson (2018) asserts, "With the rise of streaming music, people are listening to their favorite songs and compositions in their homes, offices, or any other location where their devices can connect to the internet" (para. 1). Further underscoring the prevalence of music streaming services, McIntyre (2018) states, "Streaming owns the music industry, and now that the format has established itself as the current savior and future of the business, many competitors in the space are focused on signing up as many users as possible" (para. 1).

Devices such as computers, smartphones, and smart speakers are used to listen to programming that is "streamed" on these services. There is no requirement to "download" a file to listen to the music, but some music streaming services allow both streaming and downloading to offer consumers specific music on

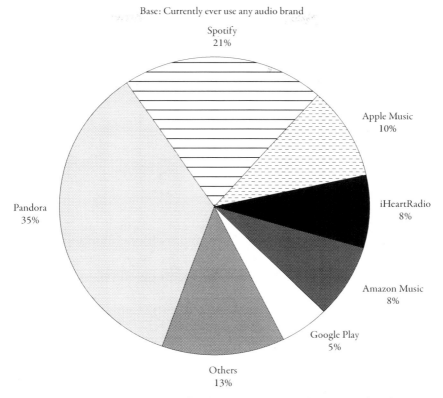

FIG. 1.2 Audio brand used most often. ("Infinite Dial 2018." © Edison Research and Triton Digital)

demand. Harris (2018) explains, "The way the streaming process works is that the audio file is delivered in small packets so the data is buffered on your computer and played pretty much straight away. As long as there is a steady stream of packets delivered to your computer, you'll hear the sound without any interruptions" (para. 4).

Spotify, Pandora, and Apple Music are the most popular and pervasive music streaming services. Edison Research found in its *Infinite Dial 2018* study that 85 percent of the respondents surveyed were aware of Pandora, 65 percent were aware of Spotify, and 60 percent were aware of Apple Music and Amazon Music (see Figure 1.2). Pandora and Spotify possess the largest share of audio streaming listeners between the ages of twenty-five and fifty-four, with 39 percent of respondents listening to Pandora and 18 percent listening to Spotify (see Figure 1.3). Spotify is in the lead, with 87 million subscribers and 200 million active monthly listeners in 78 countries and more than 40 million songs ("Spotify: Quick Facts," 2018). Pandora reports 6.8 million subscribers, 68.8 million active users, and 4.81 billion total listener hours ("Pandora Reports," 2018). Following Spotify and

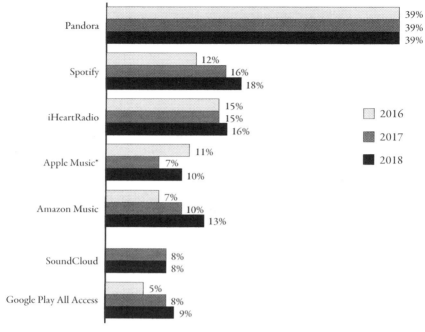

FIG. 1.3 Listened in the last month to.... (25–54) ("Infinite Dial 2018." © Edison Research and Triton Digital)

Pandora is Apple Music, reporting 36 million global subscribers (Liptak, 2018). These three audio streaming services command 66 percent of the audio brands most often used, with 35 percent using Pandora, 21 percent using Spotify, and 10 percent using Apple Music (Edison Research, 2018). Kiger (2018) found that "streaming music subscribers listen to a more diverse array of artists—and more music in general—on digital platforms" (para. 1).

## Podcasting

A podcast is a digital audio file that can be downloaded or streamed via the Internet, ranging from music to news to dramatic storytelling. More specifically, the Internet Advertising Bureau (IAB) defines podcasting as "an episodic series of digital audio files which a user can download and listen to. It is often available for subscription, so that new episodes are automatically downloaded via web syndication to the user's own local computer, mobile application, or portable media player" ("Podcast Playbook," 2017, p. 3).

Originally, podcast audio files used MP3 technology and were downloaded and listened to using the popular Apple iPods. In 2003, at Harvard University's Berkman Center for Internet & Society, Dave Winer and Christopher Lydon collaborated on a method that "streamlined a method of both uploading audio files to the Internet and downloading them to a computer or mobile device" (Walsh, 2011, para. 1). In 2004, Ben Hammersley (2004), a technology reporter for the *Guardian*, observed, "MP3 players, like Apple's iPod, in many pockets, audio production software is cheap or free, and weblogging an established part of the internet; all the ingredients are there for a new boom in amateur radio" (para. 1). Hammersley pondered what this new technology might be called: "But what to call it? Audioblogging? Podcasting? GuerillaMedia?" (para. 2). And by 2005 *The New Oxford American Dictionary* had designated "podcast" as its Word of the Year ("Oxford Dictionary Names," 2005).

By 2019 podcasting had become a very popular medium to consume audio entertainment content, thus affecting and altering the business model for the twenty-first-century radio industry. In 2006 Berry presciently observed,

> Podcasting is not only a converged medium (bringing together audio, the web and portable media devices) but also a disruptive technology and one that has already forced some in the radio business to reconsider some established practices and preconceptions about audiences, consumption, production and distribution. Whilst Audible was established to provide speech content for these devices, the automation, free access and the radio-like nature of Podcasts contribute to the disruptive nature of the new medium. It is an application of technology that was not developed, planned or marketed and yet its arrival does challenge established practices in a way that is not only unprecedented but also unpredictable. (p. 144)

Indeed, established practices and preconceptions have been changed as a result of the development and adoption of podcasting. The listenership numbers rival those of traditional, legacy radio by all metrics such as growing dollars spent on podcast advertising and increasing numbers of listeners to podcasts.

Podtrac Inc., a podcast and advertising measurement company, demonstrates the popularity and reach of podcasting. By November 2018, NPR (National Public Radio) had 18.58 million unique monthly audience members, iHeartRadio had 13.75 million, and *This American Life/Serial* (also an NPR-produced program) had 8.5 million. Interestingly, all three of these podcasts are produced by traditional radio programming sources. Edison Research's annual study, *The Infinite Dial 2018*, found that 44 percent of the American population (or 124 million) aged twelve years or older listened to a podcast, and that number has steadily increased since 2006 (see Figure 1.4).

Monthly listenership of podcasts among the twelve- to fifty-four-year-old demographics has steadily increased from only 9 percent in 2008 to 26 percent in 2018, a 17 percent increase (see Figure 1.5). From 2014 to 2018, among the

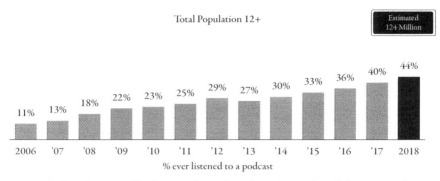

FIG. 1.4  Podcast listening. ("Infinite Dial 2018." © Edison Research and Triton Digital)

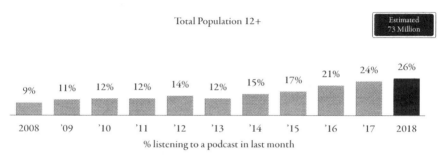

FIG. 1.5  Monthly podcast listening (2008–2018). ("Infinite Dial 2018." © Edison Research and Triton Digital)

twelve- to twenty-four-year-old age group, there was a 10 percent increase in listenership, a 15 percent increase among twenty-five- to fifty-four-year-olds, but only a 7 percent increase among the fifty-five and older demographic (see Figure 1.6). When consumers listen to podcasts, nearly 70 percent are listening on smartphones, tablets, and portable devices, compared to only about 30 percent listening on a computer. Nearly 50 percent of podcasts are listened to at home, nearly 30 percent in the automobile (Edison Research, 2018).

The IAB predicts that podcasting's future is robust: "The podcast industry is healthy and growing at a fast pace. New content is being delivered daily and there are thousands of new listeners every month. Podcast producers continue to see exponential year over year growth with no signs of slowing down. The continued rise of smartphone ownership, lower data fees, and the ease of consuming podcasts on the go, all provide an ideal environment for podcasts to find new listeners" ("Podcast Playbook," 2017, p. 9). Regarding the positive trajectory of podcasting's growth, Edison Research (2018) concurs with the IAB: "Podcasting continues its steady growth, with even more significant gains in the vehicle. After remaining fairly steady for several years, the number of

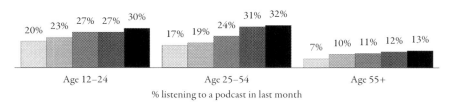

FIG. 1.6 Monthly podcast listening (2014–2018). ("Infinite Dial 2018." © Edison Research and Triton Digital)

podcasts consumed by weekly listeners has also gone up—matching the medium's increased Share of Ear" (p. 64).

## Conclusion

The radio industry continues to evolve and adapt in response to consumers' increasingly intimate relationship with modern technology. Without doubt, listeners are steadily migrating from traditional AM/FM radio to the new digital platforms offered by the Internet, smartphones, and smart speakers. Jacobs Media president Fred Jacobs states, "We are continuing to see increasing digital platform usage for all forms of audio, particularly the emergence of Amazon's Alexa, Google Home and the rise of smart speakers, whose ownership has nearly doubled in just one year" ("Highlights from Jacobs Media," 2018, para. 3). Furthermore, Paul Jacobs, vice president and general manager of Jacobs Media, states, "In addition to the boom in smart speaker penetration, many forms of digital media, including podcasting, satellite radio, streaming audio and streaming video all show increases in the number of regular users year-over-year" ("Highlights from Jacobs Media," 2018, para. 5). Explicitly, podcasting continues to experience rapid growth in terms of both listener numbers and cultural relevance, and this will pose perhaps the biggest challenge for the radio industry.

Internet giant Google launched Google Podcasts in 2018, and this new service is sure to assist in the development and growth of an already robust digital audio platform. Regarding the growth of podcasting, Zack Reneau-Wadeen, product manager of Google Podcasts, asserts, "It will continue to become more successful. It has been growing steadily in terms of the number of people listening, up to 50 million each week in the U.S. and almost as many internationally" (Ryan, 2018, p. 23). Google's massive position in the Internet market gives the tech giant the potential to compete head-on with Apple in terms of podcast delivery via apps. Concerning Google's podcast app, Barrett (2018) states, "Its very existence amounts to a sea change in the podcasting world. The majority of people who listen to podcasts do so on an iPhone, largely because Apple launched a dedicated Podcast app all the way back in 2012, and gave it prime real estate on the home screen. A Podcast app with the full weight of Google behind it could rapidly close that gap just by existing" (para. 14).

The rapid rise of disruptive technology that is creating a fragmented media landscape has not gone unnoticed by other observers of the radio industry. In one radio industry blog, the *Televisory*, the following observation was noted:

> It was first the TV, then recorded music, followed by streaming and now the rise of digital that is hurting the radio industry. Though radio is reaching more people, money is not flowing the way it should have been. This struggle of the industry reflects in the "Chapter 11" filings of iHeartMedia and Cumulus, the two giants within the industry, which together owns more than 11% of the U.S. radio stations and represent 25% of the radio ad market. iHeartMedia, which owns around 850 radio stations and is one of the most popular streaming platforms in the world is laden with $20 billion in debt. Cumulus with 445 radio stations had a debt of $2.4 billion when it filed for bankruptcy. Several other radio station operators are also saddled with excessive debt on their balance sheets. ("Is the Radio Broadcasting Industry in the U.S. Dying?," 2018, para. 6)

Due to consumers' increasing adoption of digital audio technology and the corresponding weak economic performance of the traditional AM/FM radio industry, there certainly exists an environment where businesses must evolve and adapt or cease to exist. Larry Miller, director of the Music Business program at New York University–Steinhardt, predicts the following: "Unless the industry is set to make peace with a long and inevitable decline, radio needs to invest in strong and compelling digital services. If it does, radio can look forward to a robust future built on the strong foundation it already has in the marketplace, leveraging the medium's great reach, habitual listenership, local presence, and brands. If it doesn't, radio risks becoming a thing of the past, like the wax cylinder or 78 RPM record—fondly remembered but no longer relevant to an audience that has moved on" (Miller, 2017, p. 31). It is not just Miller (2017) who has dire predictions for the radio industry. Recent headlines in leading industry publications have been discouraging. *Variety* published the following headline: "Traditional Radio Faces a Grim Future, New Study Says" (Aswad, 2017). *Forbes* published this headline: "Radio's Big Challenge: Finding Its Way Forward in This New Digital World" (Ely, 2018a). Ultimately, the radio industry's greatest weakness during an extraordinary period of emerging disruptive technologies and an increasingly fragmented media landscape might very well be its own leadership. Gordon Borrell, a leading industry analyst who founded Borrell Associates, when asked about the biggest threat to radio, asserted, "Straight up, the biggest threat to radio is myopic leadership. We're in a period of remarkable growth and opportunity, yet so many leaders believe their job is to defend 'radio'" (Ely, 2018a, para. 8).

## References

About: Mission Statement. (2019, January). SAG-AFTRA. Retrieved from www.sagaftra.org/about

About RIAA. (2019, January). RIAA.com. Retrieved from www.riaa.com/about-riaa/

About SoundExchange. (2019, January). SoundExchange. Retrieved from www.soundexchange.com/about/

Albiniak, P. (2002, February 25). Web radio rate set. *Broadcasting & Cable*, p. 16.

Annual Report. (2017). SiriusXM. Retrieved from http://s2.q4cdn.com/835250846/files/doc_financials/annual2017/feffeb79-c5ff-492a-ad94-5fe58fbe6734.pdf

Arbitron. (1999). Arbitron/Edison Media Research internet study III. Retrieved from www.arbitron.com/studies/internetIII.pdf

Arbitron. (2000). International webcaster, 'net-only sites top July webcast ratings. Retrieved from www.Arbitron.com/article1.htm

ASCAP Music Organization. (n.d.). *Encyclopaedia Britannica*. Retrieved from www.britannica.com/topic/ASCAP

Aswad, J. (2017, August 30). Traditional radio faces a grim future, new study says. *Variety*. Retrieved from https://variety.com/2017/music/news/traditional-radio-faces-a-grim-future-new-study-says-1202542681/

Audio today 2018: How America listens. (2018). Nielsen.com. Retrieved from www.nielsen.com/us/en/insights/reports/2018/state-of-the-media--audio-today-2018.html

Barrett, B. (2018, June 19). Google's new podcast app could turbocharge the industry. *Wired*. Retrieved from www.wired.com/story/google-podcasts-app-hands-on/

Berry, R. (2006). Will the iPod kill the radio star? Profiling podcasting as radio. *Convergence*, *12*(2), 143–162. doi:10.1177/1354856506066522

Biagi, S. (2017). *Media/Impact: An introduction to mass media*. Boston: Cengage.

BRS Media. (2000). BRS media's web-radio report strongest growth segment of webcasting in radio. Retrieved from www.brsmedia.com/press000920.html

Connolly, B. (2002, March 1). Copyright office panel proposes webcast performance royalties. *R&R*, p. 17.

Copyright Law of 1976, 17 U.S.C. §§ 106, 112, 114.

Dennison, C. (2004). Digital satellite radio. In C. H. Sterling (Ed.), *The Museum of Broadcast Communications encyclopedia of radio* (Vol. 1, pp. 466–469). New York: Fitzroy Dearborn.

Digital Performance Right in Sound Recordings Act of 1995, Pub. L. No. 104–39, 109 Stat. 339.

Edison Research. (2018). *The infinite dial 2018*. Somerville, NJ. Retrieved from www.slideshare.net/webby2001/infinite-dial-2018

Ely, G. (2018a, March 30). Radio's big challenge: Finding its way forward in this new digital world. *Forbes*. Retrieved from www.forbes.com/sites/geneely/2018/03/30/radios-big-challenge-finding-its-way-forward-in-this-new-digital-world/#4de7552e5a26

Ely, G. (2018b, May 18). For traditional radio, it's all about harnessing the power of digital. *Forbes*. Retrieved from www.forbes.com/sites/geneely/2018/05/18/for-traditional-radio-its-all-about-harnessing-the-power-of-digital/#4454d6b86438

Entercom to exit TuneIn, commits all stations to Radio.com for streaming. (2018, June 26). *RAIN News*. Retrieved from https://rainnews.com/entercom-to-exit-tunein-commits-all-stations-to-radio-com-for-streaming/

Goldthwaite, M. (2018, October 10). Why brands should look to audio. *Ad Age*. Retrieved from www.nielsen.com/us/en/insights/reports/2018/state-of-the-media--audio-today-2018.html

Hammersley, B. (2004, February 11). Audible revolution. *Guardian*. Retrieved from www.theguardian.com/media/2004/feb/12/broadcasting.digitalmedia

Harris, M. (2018, December 17). What is streaming music? *Lifewire*. Retrieved from www.lifewire.com/what-is-streaming-music-2438445

Head, S. W., & Sterling, C. H. (1990). *Broadcasting in America: A survey of electronic media*. 6th ed. Boston: Houghton Mifflin.

Highlights from Jacobs Media Techsurvey 2018. (2018, May 17). *Inside Radio*. Retrieved from www.insideradio.com/free/highlights-from-jacobs-media-techsurvey/article_9d4d253c-5998-11e8-9dbc-6b46c3ae9e3a.html

Is the radio broadcasting industry in the U.S. dying? An analysis. (2018, November 21). *Televisory*. Retrieved from www.televisory.com/blogs/-/blogs/is-radio-broadcasting-industry-in-the-u-s-dying-an-analysis

Johnston, C. (2002, March 27). CARP: What it means to radio. *Radio World*, pp. 77, 80–81.

Kiger, P. J. (2018, November 25). How Spotify and other streaming services broaden our musical horizons. *Fast Company*. Retrieved from www.fastcompany.com/90270574/how-spotify-and-other-streaming-services-broaden-our-musical-horizons

Komando, K. (1999, March 31). What online listeners really want. *Radio World*, p. 103.

Lind, R. A., & Medoff, N. J. (1999). Radio stations and the world wide web. *Journal of Radio Studies*, *6*(2), 203–221.

Liptak, A. (2018, February 4). Apple Music is set to surpass Spotify in paid US subscribers this summer: Apple now has 36 million paying subscribers. *The Verge*. Retrieved from www.theverge.com/2018/2/4/16971436/apple-music-surpass-spotify-us-subscribers

McClung, S., Mims, B., & Hong, C. (2003). College radio station managers express attitudes toward streaming in times of legal uncertainty. *Journal of Radio Studies*, *10*(2), 155–169.

McIntyre, H. (2018, May 25). The top 10 streaming music services by number of users. *Forbes*. Retrieved from www.forbes.com/sites/hughmcintyre/2018/05/25/the-top-10-streaming-music-services-by-number-of-users/#1981dc605178

Meyer, J. (2018). Letter to stockholders. SiriusXM. Retrieved from www.sec.gov/Archives/edgar/data/908937/000093041318001423/c90033_def14a.htm

Miller, L. S. (2017, August 30). *Paradigm shift: Why radio must adapt to the rise of digital*. Retrieved from http://musonomics.com/musonomics_report_paradigm_shift_why_radio_must_adapt_to_the_rise_of_digital_08.29.2017.pdf

Oxford Dictionary names "Podcast" 2005 word of the year. (2005, December 6). *Wired*. Retrieved from www.wired.com/2005/12/oxford-dictiona/

Pandora reports Q3 2018 financial results. (2018, November 5). Retrieved from http://investor.pandora.com/file/Index?KeyFile=395642778

Podcast playbook: A guide for marketers. (2017, August). Internet Advertising Bureau. Retrieved from www.iab.com/wp-content/uploads/2017/08/IAB_Podcast-Playbook_v8.pdf

Porter, J. (2018, September 24). SiriusXM buys Pandora for $3.5 billion. *The Verge*. Retrieved from www.theverge.com/2018/9/24/17895332/siriusxm-pandora-acquisition-music-streaming

Radio webcasts up 39% over last year. (2000, September 21). *R&R*. Retrieved from www.rronline.com

Raphael, J. (2000, September 4). Radio station leaves earth and enters cyberspace. *New York Times*, p. C.6.

Ryan, E. (2018, October 15). We want to make audio a first-class citizen. *Radio Ink*, *33*(12), 18–23.

Sirius completes acquisition of XM Satellite. (2008, July 9). Reuters. Retrieved from www.reuters.com/article/industry-satellite-dc/sirius-completes-acquisition-of-xm-satellite-idUSN2926292520080729?sp=true

The smart audio report, winter 2018. (2018). National Public Media. Retrieved from www.nationalpublicmedia.com/smart-audio-report/latest-report/

Smith, F. L. (1985). *Perspectives on radio and television: Telecommunication in the United States*. 2nd ed. New York: Harper & Row.

SoundExchange and "PurePlay" webcasters reach unprecedented experimental rate agreement. (2009, July 7). Sound Exchange. Retrieved from www.soundexchange.com/news/soundexchange-and-pureplay-webcasters-reach-unprecedented-experimental-rate-agreement/

Spotify: Quick facts. (2019). Spotify.com. Retrieved from https://investors.spotify.com/home/default.aspx

Sterling, C. H., & Kittross, J. M. (1990). *Stay tuned: A concise history of American broadcasting*. Belmont, CA: Wadsworth.

Taylor, M. R. (2018). *Radio: My life, my passion*. Herndon, VA: Mascot Books.

Tech terms: App. (2018). TechTerms.com. Retrieved from https://techterms.com/definition/app

United States Copyright Office, Library of Congress. (2002a). Appendix A: Summary of royalty rates for section 114(f)(2) and 112(e) statutory licenses. Retrieved from www.copyright.gov/carp/webcasting_rates_a.pdf

United States Copyright Office, Library of Congress. (2002b, February 20). Report of the Copyright Arbitration Royalty Panel (interim public version). Retrieved from www.copyright.gov/carp/webcasting_rates.pdf

Walsh, C. (2011, October 27). The podcast revolution: Two Berkman fellows helped to make it happen. *Harvard Gazette*. Retrieved from https://news.harvard.edu/gazette/story/2011/10/the-podcast-revolution/

Wilson, J. L. (2018, November 17). The best online music streaming services for 2019. *PCMag*. Retrieved from www.pcmag.com/article2/0,2817,2380776,00.asp

# 2

# Audience Research and Web Features of Radio Stations in a Time of Uncertainty

● ● ● ● ● ● ● ● ● ● ● ● ● ● ● ● ● ● ● ●

LU WU AND DANIEL RIFFE

Scholars suggest that news organizations tend to be more attentive to their audiences in times of uncertainty, shifting their emphasis from editorial judgment toward marketing (Beam, 1996). For example, newspaper editors might conduct readership research and then tailor future editorial content based on its results rather than on their own professional judgment (Beam, 1996). This audience orientation has been studied in print and TV news organizations (Beam, 2003; Daniels & Hollifield, 2002; Lowrey & Woo, 2010).

On the other hand, scholars have found that audience feedback exerts weak influence over newsroom decision making (Lowrey, 2012). News organizations typically resist making changes based on external conditions because established rules and routines have functioned effectively to make daily workloads manageable (Tuchman, 1973). A recent study of radio stations' Twitter use found that Twitter was mainly used as a tool to update news rather than to interact with audiences (Herrera-Damas & Hermida, 2014).

Still, factors such as threatened loss of revenue or unexpected growth of competition may force organizations to implement changes that alter routines (Lowrey & Woo, 2010). For example, competition level is associated with newsroom spending in intensely competitive markets; competition led to increased financial investment in the newsroom (Lacy & Blanchard, 2003).

It is widely acknowledged that contemporary news operations face "uncertainty" brought on by difficult economic times and the Internet. Presumably, radio news is no different. Radio still enjoys an important role for audiences, especially in medium and small markets, but the entire industry faces challenges from Internet radio stations, music streaming services, and podcasting.

Indeed, "terrestrial" radio is dealing with identifying and meeting the needs and wants of audiences whose listening habits are being radically transformed (Pluskota, 2015). Although news and news–talk radio still play an important role in conveying news to the public, the medium is losing market share to online radio streaming services. Online radio listenership reached unprecedented numbers in 2015 as over 50 percent of surveyed Americans reported listening to radio online in the past month (Vogt, 2015). Online audiences will likely continue to expand, and it is predicted that by 2019 the number of monthly online radio listeners in the United States will reach 191 million (Statista Dossier, 2015). Such growth projections highlight the importance of examining how environmental uncertainty affects radio news organizations.

Some radio stations are implementing changes to deal with the new reality. For example, iHeartMedia, a media company formerly known as Clear Channel Communications, now offers its own online radio streaming service called iHeartRadio. Similar to Pandora, it makes available any of iHeartMedia's 858 terrestrial radio stations for streaming online to audiences everywhere. It recently announced that it now serves eighty million registered users (Geddes, 2016).

But few individual radio stations, and even groups of stations, have the financial and research resources that iHeartMedia can draw on to deal with uncertainty. Nonetheless, many of them are being forced to adapt and deal with online delivery.

Unlike scholarship on newspapers or TV stations, the literature on radio station organizational behavior is rare and seldom updated. To our knowledge, no systematic analysis has yet been done to explore whether radio stations in today's financially uncertain environment react similarly to television and print news organizations—that is, by increasing the marketing orientation of online editorial content and features and monitoring audience involvement.

This study explores the broad question of how radio news operations have been responding to the increasing pressures for an expanded online presence. Are radio stations' website content and features developed with news audiences in mind? How do different factors such as competition, organizational goals, and resources relate to stations' online strategies and prioritization of features designed to attract and engage audience members? This study combines a national survey of news radio managers with data from a content analysis of radio station websites and secondary data from industry resources.

## Literature Review

### Audience Orientation

Journalism has long been a profession that values editorial independence over the prerogatives of publishers or advertisers, and that seeks to serve civic needs rather than meeting the preferences, wants, or desires of the audience (Beam, 1996). Audience-journalist relationship research suggested that news organizations traditionally took a producer-centric approach, meaning that journalists and editors predominantly relied on professional values for judgments, hardly bothering to understand their audiences. Flegel and Chaffee (1971) compared the different levels of influences on newspaper reporters and found that reporters were strongly directed by their own opinions, but the view from their readers was much less influential.

As a result, the published media content was miles apart from what audiences truly wanted (Lowrey, 2009). Their study of the aggregator Yahoo! News site found that users' most recommended stories did not correspond to the top stories picked by editors (Curtain, Dougall, & Mersey, 2007).

Not surprisingly, research found that there was a significant difference between what audiences desired and what websites actually offered (Potter, 2002). This "mismatch" of what audiences need and what's provided by new organizations remains unsolved as few radio stations invest in building or maintaining the interactive features of a site even a decade later ("Audio Graphics," 2013).

On the other hand, news organizations in general are dealing with pervasive financial difficulties brought on by fragmenting audiences, declining advertising revenues, and workforce shrinkages (Lowrey, 2012; Lowrey & Woo, 2010). Past research has found that the more uncertain a news organization's environment, the more likely its management will adopt a stronger audience orientation as well as increase audience monitoring (Beam, 1996; Lowrey & Woo, 2010).

Audience orientation research at newspapers has focused mainly on how audience information influences editorial decisions on content (Beam, 2003; Ferrucci, 2015). Among all the categories of news, readers consistently show they are most interested in *local* news and content (Beam, 1996). Beam (2003) found that strong market-oriented organizations (in this case newspapers) responded to the market by producing reduced amounts of news about government while increasing news concerning local arts and entertainment, lifestyle, and sports. In addition, they tended to publish more photos and infographics in general, spending more resources on creating a visually appealing product.

It has been more difficult to find academic literature that has looked at how radio stations' news operations respond to audience desires. Today, radio still holds a mainstream reach, especially for audiences in medium and small markets, but the industry is facing increasing challenges from Internet radio stations, music streaming services, and podcasting (Vogt, 2015). Specifically, the big challenge terrestrial radio faces today is how to meet the needs and wants of audiences whose listening habits are being quickly and constantly transformed (Pluskota, 2015).

That is, Internet radio is increasingly interactive and nonlinear (Neumark, 2006). Audiences no longer must listen "live" to their favorite programs or to topical news—audiences can access these broadcasts on demand from Internet archives. In addition, audiences can access personalized content, benefiting from the wide variety of formats and programs available online (Stark & Weichselbaum, 2013).

The Internet has also enabled audiences to provide timely feedback to news organizations (Napoli, 2011). In the past, the lack of a feedback channel has made it difficult for audiences to reach editors and reporters. The early feedback mechanism from audiences was limited to the letters to the editors or phone calls to the newsroom. Nowadays, in addition to listeners writing to the stations or calling the newsroom, the interaction between audiences and stations can also take place on the stations' websites and on their social media pages, which is an "engagement" strategy researchers have also documented on newspapers' websites and citizen journalists' news and blog sites (Lacy, Duffy, Riffe, Thorson, & Fleming, 2010; Lacy, Riffe, Thorson, & Duffy, 2009). News radio listeners can post comments on the stations' Facebook pages, providing feedback and expressing opinions toward a particular program or to the station as a whole (Bonini, 2014). Moreover, audiences expect to see evidence that radio stations are listening to them and responding to them (Garner, 2009).

Traditional radio stations have established their own online offerings, and some offer online streaming of their programs, including the revival of podcasting. Podcasting saw a breakthrough in 2014 in terms of numbers of listeners and new programs. The medium has been steadily growing its audience over the past several years, and online listenership has doubled since 2008. The investigative journalism podcast *Serial* became the most listened-to podcast ever, with five million streams by the end of 2014 (Gamerman, 2014).

Audience listening habits have indeed changed, particularly as more people are listening to regularly scheduled radio programs online ("State of the Media," 2014). The number of monthly online radio listeners has doubled since 2010, and SiriusXM, the only satellite radio platform in the United States, reported a 7 percent annual increase of subscribers in 2014 (Vogt, 2015). Radio audience behaviors and preferences are being reshaped by technology.

One form of audience research that's within the scope of this study is the research of audiences' interests and preferences online. Previous studies have identified two major methods of conducting audience research: through tracking quantitative audience metrics (e.g., Domingo et al., 2008; Kormelink & Meijer, 2018; MacGregor, 2007; Tandoc, Hellmueller, & Vos, 2013) or by collecting qualitative audience feedback data through websites and social media, as well as other digital and nondigital channels (e.g., Anderson, 2011; Borger, Van Hoof, &

Sanders, 2016; Chung & Nah, 2009; Davis Mersey, Malthouse, & Calder, 2010; Karlsson, Bergström, Clerwall, & Fast, 2015; Usher, 2016). This study focuses on the latter method of radio stations' audience research activities.

## Competition

While the transformation of audience tastes and behaviors might thus be expected to influence the news product—assuming someone is monitoring that transformation—the news organization is not responding in a vacuum: it faces competition for audience and advertising. A news radio station's major competitor may be another news radio station in the same market. A news radio station could also compete against a radio station of a different format, such as a country music station, for advertising. Even more broadly, radio stations also compete with TV stations and newspapers serving the same geographic area because of intermedia competition for advertising (McGregor, Driscoll, & McDowell, 2016).

Media economists have used the term "financial commitment" to explain the impact of competition on local news organizations' performance (Litman & Bridges, 1986). Lacy (1992) interpreted this model as a four-step process: first, as competition rises, more money will be spent on news production; second, as financial commitment to news increases, the quality of news content increases; third, a larger audience will consume the content; fourth, the news organization's circulation or ratings will improve.

Looking specifically at how competition impacted news radio stations more than two decades ago, Lacy and Riffe (1994) found that competition between local stations resulted in more staff-produced news stories in general and a higher proportion of broadcasting time devoted to news; but, interestingly, a lower percentage of the staff-prepared reports were devoted to the purely local news that would presumably appeal to a local audience.

## Organizational Characteristics

Competition and allocation of resources influences news content, so does staffing. But changes in strategy on how to allocate resources and staff reflect more than normative "civic" goals; they reflect organizational policy. Organizational level analysis emphasizes the influence of ownership, institutional goals, and management policy (Shoemaker & Reese, 2014). Because organizations differ in decision making and problem solving, an organizational level of analysis provides an insightful look at what makes each organization different from others, and how these differences influence media content.

## Ownership

Scholars have examined ownership across media platforms for its potential impact on news content and quality (Lacy & Fico, 1990). Media owners ultimately make decisions about what the news organization does over time. At privately owned organizations, publishers can operate as they see fit, but managers for publicly traded companies have a responsibility to maximize profit and can be replaced due to failure (Shoemaker & Reese, 2014).

The impact of ownership type on radio station content and diversity has received a great deal of scholarly attention, especially after the 1996 Telecommunications Act saw the commercial radio industry undergo unprecedented merger activity. Scholars stated that corporate business interests led to consolidation of ownership at stations across the country, leading to less local content in broadcasting and a spike in syndicated and outsourced programming (Crider, 2012; Herman & McChesney, 1997, p. 4; Saffran, 2011). However, a decrease in local programming has been critiqued as a failure of radio news journalism's duty to serve and inform the public.

## Organizational Goals and Resources

Organizational goals also influence how newsrooms perform. For most organizations, profit is the primary goal (Shoemaker & Reese, 2014). As an overarching influence, economic goals connect to other objectives such as producing quality content, achieving professional recognition, and serving the public. Surveys found that giving priority to making a profit has negative impacts on employees' job satisfaction, but the reaction differed between rank-and-file employees and management (Beam, 2006).

Industry consolidation inevitably resulted in shifts in organizational goals, personnel, and work processes (Pluskota, 2015). Newsrooms across the country are witnessing the shifting paradigm in radio station workforces and continuously shrinking news staff sizes (Weaver, Beam, Brownlee, Voakes, & Wilhoit, 2009).

# Research Questions

The guiding hypothesis for this study is that in current conditions of high environmental uncertainty, a strong audience orientation will emerge in radio stations, encouraging managers to strengthen audience monitoring, solicit audience feedback, and improve online features that engage the audience in order to keep up with local competitors and Internet radio.

As suggested in the literature review, a radio station website with a strong audience orientation would include website content that is interactive and nonlinear (Neumark, 2006) and features that are designed to collect audience feedback. Thus, this study catalogued radio stations' online features and efforts to engage listeners:

> RQ1a: To what degree is radio station website content interactive and nonlinear?

> RQ1b: To what degree are radio station website features designed to collect audience feedback?

Audience orientation is also influenced by organizational level factors because news organizations' response to environmental uncertainty varies by organizational characteristics (Lowrey & Woo, 2010). More specifically, the presence of competition is consistent with the financial commitment model, with high competition associated with more newsroom investment and therefore more success in gaining audiences (Lacy & Blanchard, 2003). In addition, ownership may largely determine the management policies and financial resources distribution in the sense that publicly owned and traded organizations are more likely to emphasize profits (Shoemaker & Reese, 2014). The following research question is suggested, using perceived marketing orientation as a criterion measure:

Organizational behaviors are undoubtedly affected by multiple factors operating simultaneously. Thus, our final research question also uses marketing orientation, but as a predictor variable:

RQ2: How do competition, ownership, and organizational goals and resources relate to website content and website features of radio stations?

## Method

The unit of analysis was a news-oriented radio station. Three levels of data were utilized: (1) data from a survey of station management at news-oriented radio stations, (2) data from a content analysis of websites from news-oriented stations, and (3) organizational (ownership and market) data about the stations.

The 2015 version of the *Complete Television, Radio &Cable Industry Directory* was used as a starting point to compile a list of news-oriented stations or using criteria adapted from Riffe and Shaw (1990): stations that broadcast programs formatted as either news, or news/talk; stations whose format also included selected special programming were also included as long as their main format was listed as news, news/talk, or both. This list was then cross-checked with Radio-locator.com, a search engine that allows users to find radio stations based on format. Because of market consolidation, multiple radio stations often share the same management. In such instances, only one of the listed stations was targeted for the survey.

Using the list of stations, a mail survey was then sent to 757 news radio managers across the United States, with 21.4 percent ($n=162$) completing and returning the survey. Nearly two-thirds (65 percent) of the respondents self-identified as radio presidents, owners, or general managers, and 35 percent were program directors, news directors, or other managers. The sample represented forty-two states. On average, respondents estimated that their stations broadcast fifty-three minutes of nonrepeating news during the morning drive cycle before starting to repeat segments and local news composed approximately 21 percent of that time.

Respondents estimated how much station content is available online. Over 85 percent of the respondents reported having "some" and "quite a bit" of the content online. More than three-fourths (78 percent) of respondents said their station offers some kind of live streaming of content on the station website.

At the end of the mail survey, respondents could choose or refuse to identify their station affiliation. A total of eighty-seven respondents voluntarily identified their stations. Those stations were further examined for their website content and features in the second stage of this study.

Researchers visited each website and scoured it thoroughly, searching for various features, including options for live streaming, podcasts, posting online comments and feedback, and social media activities. Among the eighty-seven stations, seven did not have a working website. One station's website denied access by showing malware messages and was dropped, leaving the number of stations at seventy-nine. In February 2016, two coders recorded the existence/absence of each feature on the website. One-fourth (twenty) of the seventy-nine sites were randomly selected for a coder reliability test. An initial reliability test yielded Scott's pi coefficient less than .80 for the multimedia variable. Coders were retrained and coded another ten cases to retest reliability on the variable. The reliability was improved to .83. Coder reliability is reported in Table 2.2.

## Measures

As noted, data were collected at the individual (survey respondent), station website (content analysis), and organizational (industry sources) levels.

As derived from the literature review, audience orientation was operationalized as two major concepts: (1) website content that meets audiences' needs and (2) website features that are for collecting audience feedback and comments. Each concept is operationalized as the following, and all data were collected through the content analysis.

### Website Content

Each of three types coded for presence (1) or absence (0) of *live streaming service:* if anywhere on the website (mostly on the home page) it offers live streaming options; *multimedia feature:* if the news content presented on the website also includes some type of multimedia feature such as a playback of the radio segment or a video clip; *podcast*: if the website podcasts are available online.

### Website Features

Website features that are designed for collecting audience feedback and comments include:

1. Contact info: Each of six types coded for presence (1) or absence (0): *contact tab* or "station information" tab (i.e., *station phone number*;

*staff phone numbers*; *station email* address; *staff email* addresses; *mailing address*).

2. Online feedback platforms: Each of four types coded for presence (1) or absence (0): *comments*: if the website contains features that allow audiences to provide comments or feedback; *comment box*: if the website has a dedicated area on the contact page for audience to provide feedback; *active solicitation of feedback*: if the website has statements such as "please tell us what you think, we value your opinion"; *social media activity*: if symbols anywhere on the website indicate that the website has social media profiles (e.g., Facebook, Twitter, etc.).

Secondary organizational and market data were collected for each station using annual industry sources:

## Competition

Competition was operationalized in three parts, including the number of radio stations in the market that also broadcast news, the number of radio stations that do not broadcast news, and the number of TV stations in the same market. The latter two measures indicate competition for advertising revenue. All data were collected from the *Complete Television, Radio & Cable Industry Directory*. Cronbach's alpha was .82 for the three measures. Cronbach's alpha is one of the most widely used reliability coefficients for an estimate of internal consistency among the items of the test (Serbetar & Sedlar, 2016). It is generally recommended that a Cronbach's alpha larger than .7 can indicate that the scales one may be using are internally consistent (Nunnally, 1978).

## Ownership

Ownership status data were collected from the *Complete Television, Radio & Cable Industry Directory* and have three categories: publicly traded ownership, private media group ownership, and independent ownership.

Survey data for the analysis included

Location of ownership: Respondents identified whether their station was locally owned or owned by a non-local entity or person.

Organizational goals: Survey respondents were asked to indicate agreement with three measures (Beam, 2006) tapping their perceptions of basic management objectives (1 = strongly disagree, 5 = strongly agree): earning above-average profits ($M = 3.94$, $SD = 1.40$); keeping the size of your audience as large as possible ($M = 4.62$, $SD = 0.69$); and producing high-quality journalism ($M = 4.45$, $SD = 0.84$).

Resources: Survey respondents reported the number of full-time news employees ($M = 5.46$, $SD = 6.96$) and whether there had been an increase in newsroom resources in the past five years ($M = 2.80$, $SD = 1.25$).

### Table 2.1
**Descriptive Statistics for All Survey Respondents and Stations**

| Variable | N | M | SD |
|---|---|---|---|
| Age, in years | 108 | 55.5 | 8.89 |
| Years in radio broadcasting | 141 | 32.21 | 11.58 |
| Years in current job | 150 | 18.03 | 11.96 |
| Full-time news and editorial employees | 135 | 4.31 | 5.62 |
| Level of competition (1–5 scale) | 125 | 2.94 | 0.98 |
| Level of news programing (as a %) | 91 | 0.60 | 0.35 |
| Morning drive cycle (in minutes) | 89 | 53.44 | 41.54 |
| Local news in morning drive (as a %) | 136 | 20.99 | 16.94 |
| Location and ownership (N = 162) | | % stations | |
| Market ranks: Large (1,000,000+) | | 24.2 | |
| Medium (400,000–1,000,000) | | 34.2 | |
| Small (<400,000) | | 41.6 | |
| Local ownership | | 58.1 | |
| Nonlocal ownership | | 40.3 | |
| Ownership status | | | |
| Independent | | 56.5 | |
| Owned by a private media group | | 22.7 | |
| Owned by a public company that is traded in the stock market | | 16.9 | |
| Total | | 96.1* | |

*3.9% answered Don't know.

## Results

### Preliminary Analysis

Table 2.1 reports descriptive data for the initial survey. As Table 2.1 shows, respondents in the initial survey averaged fifty-five years of age ($SD = 8.89$) and the average number of years working in radio broadcasting was thirty-two. Among the respondents' stations, 56.5 percent were independent and nearly 23 percent were owned by a private media group and 17 percent were owned by a public-traded company. About 40 percent of the stations were in small markets, about one-third served medium markets, and fewer than one-fourth were in large markets. Over half of the stations (58 percent) had a local ownership.

### Research Questions

RQ1a and RQ1b asked to what degree radio station website content is interactive and nonlinear and to what degree radio station website features are designed to collect audience feedback.

RQ1 was answered using content analysis data of seventy-nine stations' websites. As Table 2.2 shows, the website features varied from station to station, but over 90 percent of the seventy-nine stations provided "live streaming" service to

### Table 2.2
### Content Analysis of Website Features

| | | | Yes (%) | No (%) | Coding reliability |
|---|---|---|---|---|---|
| Website content | | Live streaming | 92.4 | 7.6 | .93 |
| | | Multimedia | 54.4 | 45.6 | .83 |
| | | Podcast | 46.8 | 53.2 | .87 |
| Total | | | $M = 1.94$ | $SD = 0.87$ | |
| Website features | Contact info | "Contact" tab | 94.9 | 5.1 | 1.00 |
| | | Station phone | 97.5 | 2.5 | .93 |
| | | Staff phone | 24.1 | 75.9 | .83 |
| | | Station email | 68.4 | 31.6 | .80 |
| | | Staff email | 69.6 | 30.4 | .83 |
| | | Mailing address | 93.7 | 6.3 | .93 |
| Total | | | $M = 4.48$ | $SD = 1.06$ | |
| | Online feedback platforms | Actively seeking feedback | 29.1 | 70.9 | .80 |
| | | Social media icons | 82.3 | 17.7 | 1.00 |
| | | Comments under content | 46.8 | 53.2 | .93 |
| | | Comment box | 25.3 | 74.7 | .93 |
| Total | | | $M = 1.84$ | $SD = 1.05$ | |
| Total audience features | | | $M = 8.25$ | $SD = 2.16$ | |

their users, more than half (54.6 percent) featured multimedia content, and just under half (46.8 percent) offered podcasts. An even larger percentage of stations (97.5 percent) provided direct contact information, including office phone numbers (97 percent) and email addresses (68–70 percent). In addition, 82.3 percent of stations invited contact through social media. However, only 29.1 percent of the websites made an explicit statement of policy that they welcome or value audience feedback, fewer than half of the stations had online commenting functions, and one in four offered a "comment box" on the site.

Each item was coded 1 for presence, 0 for absence. An index of "total audience features" was computed by summing the number of website content and website features coded as present for each site ($M = 8.25$, $SD = 2.16$).

RQ2 questions how station competition, ownership, and organizational-level characteristics predict website content and audience features. The dependent variable is the "total audience features" index. RQ2 was examined using regression analysis.

First, the seventy-nine stations included in the content analysis differed from the stations represented in the initial survey in Table 2.1: 63.3 percent of the content analysis stations were locally owned, compared to 58.1 percent of stations

### Table 2.3
### Competition Info for the Seventy-Nine Stations

| Competition levels in the market | M (SD) |
| --- | --- |
| Number of news radio stations | 3.23 (3.90) |
| Number of radio stations of other formats | 8.49 (7.18) |
| Number of TV stations | 3.51 (4.47) |
| Competition (total) | 15.23 (13.82) |

represented in the survey, and 16.9 percent of stations represented in the survey were publicly traded, compared to 25.7 percent of the content analysis stations. The literature suggests that publicly traded stations emphasize profit more than independent or privately owned stations because they have responsibility to stockholders (Shoemaker & Reese, 2014). For the purpose of the regression analysis, a dummy variable, *nonlocal-publicly traded*, was created as a predictor for the regression using the stations in the content analysis: seventeen stations (21 percent) qualified as "nonlocal-publicly traded" and were coded as 1, and the other sixty-two stations were coded as 0.

As Table 2.3 shows, Cronbach's alpha for the three items measuring competition (number of news radio stations, radio stations of other formats, and TV stations) was .82. While they differed in nature, the three items were summed to create a total "competition" variable ($M = 15.23$, $SD = 13.82$).

Similarly, the bivariate correlation (Pearson's $r$) between two key organizational goal variables ("earning above-average profits" and "keeping the size of audience" rating share) were significant and positive (.46, $p < .01$). To construct a parsimonious regression model, the two variables were averaged to create a new variable, "profit/rating" ($M = 4.13$, $SD = 0.94$), reflecting the yoked relationship of audience ratings and profit. Table 2.4 shows key bivariate correlations.

Table 2.5 shows the total audience features index regressed on competition, nonlocal-publicly traded, organizational goals, and finances and resources. The model significantly predicted the total audience features index ($F = 2.60$, $p = .02$) and explained 22 percent of variance in total audience features index. In the model, type of ownership ($\beta = 1.54$, $p < .05$) and "increase in newsroom resources" ($\beta = 0.44$, $p < .05$) were two significant predictors. However, competition, organizational goals, and number of full-time employees were not significantly associated with the total audience features index.

## Discussion and Conclusions

This study examined the relationships among competition, ownership, organizational characteristics, and the stations' website content and features. Descriptive results indicated that most radio stations included in this study have offered some type of live streaming service for audiences on their website, but

### Table 2.4
### Correlation among Key Variables

|  | Keeping the size of audience | Profit/rating | Producing high-quality journalism | Number of full-time employees |
|---|---|---|---|---|
| Keeping the size of audience | 1.00 | .69** | .18 | −.12 |
| Profit/rating |  | 1.00 | −.01 | −.23* |
| Producing high-quality journalism |  |  | 1.00 | .19 |
| Number of full-time employees |  |  |  | 1.00 |

$^*p<.05;\ ^{**}p<.01$

### Table 2.5
### Total Audience Features Index Regressed on Competition, Ownership, and Other Organizational Factors

| IVs | | Total audience features |
|---|---|---|
| Competition | | 0.01 |
| Ownership | | 1.54* |
| Organizational goals | Profit/rating | −0.34 |
| | Producing high-quality journalism | 0.26 |
| Finances and resources | Number of full-time employees | 0.04 |
| | Increase in newsroom resources | 0.44* |
| $R^2$ | | 0.22 |
| | | $F=2.60^*, p=.02$ |

$^*p<.05$

the availability of other types of online content varied greatly from station to station. Only about half of the stations offered multimedia content in addition to text-based and web stories. Fewer than half of the stations offered podcasts to their online audiences.

Nearly all radio stations in the sample had published contact information on their websites with at least a station phone number. Station websites also tended to include their mailing address but not phone numbers for individual staff.

On the other hand, the results suggest that radio stations' websites appear to be insufficient in actually providing tools and space for audience comments and feedback. Fewer than half of the websites allow audiences to leave comments below online articles. Only a quarter of the websites have a comment box for audiences to write comments directly to the station online. And fewer than one-third of the websites contain statements that encourage audiences to leave feedback and so on.

The sample in this study indicated that radio station websites had different levels of audience-oriented content and features. For stations that were weak in tracking audience feedback and comments, they may consider investing more resources into developing website features to build a site that encourages audience-station interaction. What's more, providing more podcast-like programs online can also meet modern-day listeners' needs of a flexible listening schedule and on-demand playing options.

As shown in the regression models, the level of audience-oriented content and features is significantly associated with two factors: (1) the type of station ownership and (2) increased newsroom resources. Although some previous literature suggested that increases in competition could result in more financial commitment and thus better quality news products (Lacy, 1992), the current study's finding did not confirm this. This may be partially explained by the traditional disconnect between editorial and business departments. Lowrey and Woo (2010) found evidence for a disconnection between business operations and editorial actions in both corporate-owned and privately owned newsrooms.

Public ownership did show a substantial impact on the degree to which stations provided audience-oriented website content and features including multimedia content and podcasts. This may be partly because corporate-owned stations often share the same website or content management templates, resulting in newer online standards and consistent features. On the other hand, privately owned stations had a range of website designs with the quality and features varying largely from site to site.

Newsroom finances and resources, especially "increase in newsroom resources," have a positive and significant relationship with the level of audience-oriented content and features. This makes intuitive sense, as a greater size of news staff would allow the stations to spare resources on other newsroom activities such as monitoring feedback and comments or other activities outside meeting the ends of daily news production.

On the other hand, the regression models demonstrated that organizational goals did not have a strong impact on the level of audience-oriented content and features. This may suggest that legacy media such as news radio stations are still seeing a disconnection between financial and editorial success and audience-oriented thinking.

To sum up, the findings suggest that, overall, what determined radio stations' website features largely resided in the ownership and resources allocation. The findings also indicate that environmental uncertainties didn't incentivize radio stations to actively collect audience data and conduct audience research.

This study is subject to some limitations. Foremost among them, of course, is the study's assumptions about industry-wide uncertainty, in general, and local market uncertainty, in particular. Beam's (1996) work suggests that greater market uncertainty *leads* to adoption of a stronger market orientation. While we looked at local market competition, and measured market orientation, we did not directly measure respondents' perception of market uncertainty.

Derived from a survey dataset, the number of cases available for the content analysis was limited. Inclusion of individual-respondent survey data, station content analysis data, and contextual (e.g., market and competition) data did not mitigate this limitation. The number of cases to independent variables ratio was low, despite variable reduction during the analysis. However, the analysis met the minimum requirement of having at least five times as many cases as the number of independent variables (Tabachnick, Fidell, & Osterlind 1983, p. 129), but possible skewness in dependent variables suggested that the effect size was anticipated to be small and resulting analysis was subject to higher possibility of a Type II error.

Despite these limitations, the study has offered a preliminary view into how news-oriented radio stations are developing content for online audiences and utilizing social media and other channels of contact with audience members, while illustrating the relationship among station ownership, station organizational resources, and the degree of audience-oriented content and features available online. Future research should address how audience research and engagement and organizational behaviors translate into ratings and market success.

## References

Anderson, C. (2011). Between creative and quantified audiences: Web metrics and changing patterns of news work in local US newsrooms. *Journalism, 12*(5), 550–566. doi:10.1177/1464884911402451

Audio Graphics. (2013, August 5). Retrieved from www.audiographics.com/agd/080513-1.htm

Beam, R. A. (1996). How perceived environmental uncertainty influences the marketing orientation of US daily newspapers. *Journalism and Mass Communication Quarterly, 73*(2), 285–303.

Beam, R. A. (2003). Content differences between daily newspapers with strong and weak market orientations. *Journalism and Mass Communication Quarterly, 80*(2), 368–390.

Beam, R. A. (2006). Organizational goals and priorities and the job satisfaction of US journalists. *Journalism and Mass Communication Quarterly, 83*(1), 169–185.

Bonini, T. (2014). Doing radio in the age of Facebook. *Radio Journal, 12*(1–2), 73–87.

Borger, M., Van Hoof, A., & Sanders, J. (2016). Expecting reciprocity: Towards a model of the participants' perspective on participatory journalism. *New Media & Society, 18*(5), 708–725.

Chung, D. S., & Nah, S. (2009). The effects of interactive news presentation on perceived user satisfaction of online community newspapers. *Journal of Computer-Mediated Communication, 14*(4), 855–874.

*Complete Television, Radio, & Cable Industry Directory.* (2015). Amenia, NY: Greyhouse Publishing.

Crider, D. (2012). A public sphere in decline: The state of localism in talk radio. *Journal of Broadcasting & Electronic Media, 56*(2), 225–244.

Curtain, P. A., Dougall, E., & Mersey, R. D. (2007). Study compares Yahoo! news story preferences. *Newspaper Research Journal, 28*(4), 22–35.

Daniels, G. L., & Hollifield, C. A. (2002). Times of turmoil: Short-and long-term effects of organizational change on newsroom employees. *Journalism and Mass Communication Quarterly, 79*(3), 661–680.

Davis Mersey, R., Malthouse, E. C., & Calder, B. J. (2010). Engagement with online media. *Journal of Media Business Studies, 7*(2), 39–56.

Domingo, D., Quandt, T., Heinonen, A., Paulussen, S., Singer, J., & Vujnovic, M. (2008). Participatory journalism practices in the media and beyond: An international comparative study of initiatives in online newspaper. *Journalism Practice, 2*(3), 326–342.

Ferrucci, P. (2015). Primary differences: How market orientation can influence content. *Journal of Media Practice, 16*(3), 195–210.

Flegel, R. C., & Chaffee, S. H. (1971). Influences of editors, readers, and personal opinions on reporters. *Journalism Quarterly, 48*(4), 645–651.

Gamerman, E. (2014, November 14). "Serial" podcast catches fire. *Wall Street Journal.* Retrieved from www.wsj.com/articles/serial-podcast-catches-fire-1415921853

Garner, K. (2009). Special issue of the Radio Journal: BBC listeners online. *Radio Journal, 7*(1), 5–8.

Geddes, J. (2016, January 23). iHeartRadio vs. Pandora: How the top U.S. online radio streaming services compare. *Tech Times.* Retrieved from www.techtimes.com/articles/126887/20160123/iheartradio-vs-pandora-how-the-top-u-s-online-radio-streaming-services-compare.htm

Herman, E., & McChesney, R. (1997). *Global Media: The new missionaries of global capitalism.* London: Cassell.

Herrera-Damas, S., & Hermida, A. (2014). Tweeting but not talking: The missing element in talk radio's institutional use of twitter. *Journal of Broadcasting & Electronic Media, 58*(4), 481–500.

Karlsson, M., Bergström, A., Clerwall, C., & Fast, K. (2015). Participatory journalism—The (r)evolution that wasn't. Content and user behavior in Sweden 2007–2013. *Journal of Computer-Mediated Communication, 20*(3), 295–311.

Kormelink, T. G., & Meijer, I. C. (2018). What clicks actually mean: Exploring digital news user practices. *Journalism, 19*(5), 668–683.

Lacy, S. (1992). The financial commitment approach to news media competition. *Journal of Media Economics, 5*(2), 5–21.

Lacy, S., & Blanchard, A. (2003). The impact of public ownership, profits, and competition on number of newsroom employees and starting salaries in mid-sized daily newspapers. *Journalism and Mass Communication Quarterly, 80*(4), 949–968.

Lacy, S., Duffy, M., Riffe, D., Thorson, E., & Fleming, K. (2010). Citizen journalism web sites complement newspapers. *Newspaper Research Journal, 31*(2), 34–46.

Lacy, S., & Fico, F. (1990). Newspaper quality & ownership: Rating the groups. *Newspaper Research Journal, 11*(2), 42–56.

Lacy, S., & Riffe, D. (1994). The impact of competition and group ownership on radio news. *Journalism Quarterly, 71*(3), 583–593.

Lacy, S., Riffe, D., Thorson, E., & Duffy, M. (2009). Examining the features, policies and resources of citizen journalism: Citizen news sites and blogs. *Web Journal of Mass Communication Research, 15*(1), 1–20.

Litman, B. R., & Bridges, J. (1986) An economic analysis of daily newspaper performance. *Newspaper Research Journal, 7*(3), 9–26.

Lowrey, W. (2009). Institutional roadblocks: Assessing journalism's response to changing audiences. In Z. Papacharissi (Ed.), *Journalism and citizenship* (pp. 62–86). New York: Routledge.

Lowrey, W. (2012). Journalism innovation and the ecology of news production institutional tendencies. *Journalism & Communication Monographs, 14*(4), 214–287.

Lowrey, W., and Woo, C. W. (2010). The news organization in uncertain times. Business or institution? *Journalism and Mass Communication Quarterly, 87*(1), 41–63.

MacGregor, P. (2007). Tracking the online audience: Metric data start a subtle revolution. *Journalism Studies, 8*(2), 280–298.

McGregor, M. A., Driscoll, P. D., & McDowell, W. (2016). *Head's broadcasting in America: A survey of electronic media*. New York: Routledge.

Napoli, P. M. (2011). *Audience evolution: New technologies and the transformation of media audiences*. New York: Columbia University Press.

Neumark, L. (2006). Different spaces, different times: Exploring possibilities for cross-platform "radio." *Convergence, 12*(2), 213–224.

Nunnally, J. C. (1978). *Psychometric theory* (2nd ed.). New York: McGraw-Hill.

Pluskota, J. P. (2015). The perfect technology: Radio and mobility. *Journal of Radio and Audio Media, 22*(2), 325–336.

Potter, R. F. (2002). Give the people what they want: A content analysis of FM radio station home pages. *Journal of Broadcasting & Electronic Media, 46*(3), 369–384.

Riffe, D., Lacy, S., & Fico, F. (2014). *Analyzing media messages: Using quantitative content analysis in research*. New York: Routledge.

Riffe, D., & Shaw, E. F. (1990). Ownership, operating, staffing and content characteristics of "news radio" stations. *Journalism and Mass Communication Quarterly, 67*(4), 684–691.

Saffran, M. J. (2011). Effects of local-market radio ownership concentration on radio localism, the public interest, and listener opinions and use of local radio. *Journal of Radio and Audio Media, 18*(2), 281–294.

Serbetar, I., & Sedlar, I. (2016). Assessing reliability of a multi-dimensional scale by coefficient alpha. *Revija za Elementarno Izobrazevanje, 9*(1/2), 189.

Shoemaker, P. J., & Reese, S. D. (2014). *Mediating the message in the 21st century: A media sociology perspective*. New York: Routledge.

Stark, B., & Weichselbaum, P. (2013). What attracts listeners to web radio? A case study from Germany. *Radio Journal, 11*(2), 185–202. doi:10.1386/rjao.11.2.185_1

State of the Media: Audio Today 2014. (2014, February). Retrieved from www.nielsen.com/content/dam/corporate/us/en/reports-downloads/2014%20Reports/state-of-the-media-audio-today-feb-2014.pdf

Statista Dossier. (2015). Radio in the U.S.-Facts and statistics on the radio market in the U.S. Retrieved from www.statista.com/study/13621/radio-in-the-us-statista-dossier/

Tabachnick, B. G., Fidell, L. S., & Osterlind, S. J. (1983). *Using multivariate statistics* (2nd ed.). New York: Harper & Row.

Tandoc, E. C., Jr., Hellmueller, L., & Vos, T. P. (2013). Mind the gap: Between journalistic role conception and role enactment. *Journalism Practice, 7*(5), 539–554.

Tuchman, G. (1973). Making news by doing work: Routinizing the unexpected. *American Journal of Sociology, 79*(1), 110–131.

Usher, N. (2016). *Interactive journalism: Hackers, data, and code*. Urbana: University of Illinois Press.

Vogt, N. (2015, April 29). Audio: Fact sheet. *State of the News Media 2015*. Retrieved from www.journalism.org/2015/04/29/audio-fact-sheet

Weaver, D. H., Beam, R. A., Brownlee, B. J., Voakes, P. S., & Wilhoit, G. C. (2009). *The American journalist in the 21st century: US news people at the dawn of a new millennium*. New York: Routledge.

# 3

# The Parasocial Nature of the Podcast

• • • • • • • • • • • • • • • • • • • •

LAITH ZURAIKAT

## The History of the Parasocial Interaction

Traditionally, when a person speaks about one of their friends or someone that they know, there is an assumption that the person in question is someone that the speaker has met in person and has interacted with in the physical world. However, what if the person in question has never actually met their "friend" or had any sort of actual communication or interaction with them? If a relationship is entirely one-sided, and one member of that relationship doesn't even know that the other person exists, what would make someone think that there is some sort of bond between the two parties? These types of "false" relationships and interactions have become increasingly prominent over the last century, specifically in regard to how people develop relationships with members of the media such as the character of a TV show or the host of a popular radio show. This increase is, in large part, due to the invention and rise in prominence of mass media:

> One of the striking characteristics of the new mass media-radio, television, and the movies is that they give the illusion of a face-to-face relationship with the performer. The conditions of response to the performer are analogous to those in a primary group. The most remote and illustrious men are met as if they

were in the circle of one's peers; the same is true of a character in a story who comes to life in these media in an especially vivid and arresting way. We propose to call this seeming face-to-face relationship between spectator and performer a para-social relationship. (Horton & Wohl, 1956, p. 216)

Parasocial theory and parasocial interaction are therefore most commonly associated with the work and writings of sociologists Donald Horton and Richard Wohl due to their focus on this communication between audience members and television actors. Horton and Wohl's decision to describe the communication between the viewer and the personae as parasocial was very intentional, as "the term *para* denotes a closeness of position: a correspondence of parts, a situation on the other side-but wrongness and irregularity" (Katz, Peters, Liebes, & Orloff, 2003, p. 138). Katz et al. argue this "wrongness" highlights there is a missing quality in the communication between the viewer and the personae, and as a result the corresponding interaction is less authentic than face-to-face interaction. The key component that seems to be missing in regard to parasocial interaction is the lack of actual response between the viewer and the personae. Viewers of TV shows and listeners of the radio are essentially engaged in a one-sided conversation as even though they may respond physically, verbally, or emotionally to the persona on TV or the radio, the persona cannot actually hear them. In this manner, parasocial interaction denotes the fabrication of an actual interaction and conversation. The creation of this false sense of relationship between the viewer and the persona is achieved in the following manner: "Para-social interaction imitates conversational give-and-take between the television persona and the unseen spectators. The persona accomplishes this by insinuating the absent viewer into his talk, thereby stimulating conversation between himself and them. The audience of unseen viewers is thought, in turn, to make the appropriate interactional response, thereby sustaining the fiction that the person is speaking with them and enabling him to continue his conversational routine" (Katz et al., 2003, pp. 138–139). While initial studies on this relationship focused on the television and radio consumer, thanks to the progression of time and the introduction of new mass media formats and devices, new interpretations of parasocial interactions and relationships have come to the fore, which has in turn affected the understanding and definition of this theory.

## The Evolution of Parasocial Theory

Further exploration of this theoretical concept has produced several developments and changes to the suggested characteristics of this relationship. One such development is a shift away from the viewing of the parasocial relationship as an illusionary one that occurs immediately and appears to be reciprocal, as Hartmann and Goldhoorn (2011) state, "In contrast to this initial understanding of parasocial interaction, many of the later studies in the field conceptualized Parasocial interaction as a kind of long-term identification or parasocial relationship with a media performer" (p. 1104). While Hartmann and Goldhoorn initially used the terms "parasocial interaction" and "relationship" interchangeably, Dibble, Hartmann, and Rosaen (2016) would later differentiate between these two terms arguing that a parasocial interaction is "characterized by a felt reciprocity with a TV performer that comprises a sense of mutual awareness, attention and adjustment" (p. 23). According to Dibble et al. a parasocial interaction occurs during a single exposure between the persona and the audience and may require the persona to "break the fourth wall" and acknowledge the audience. However, a parasocial relationship is defined as "the more enduring, long-term, and usually positive, one-sided intimacy at a distance that users develop toward media performers on repeated encounters" (Dibble et al., 2016, p. 24). Unlike a parasocial interaction, a parasocial relationship extends beyond a single exposure and can develop over time, even without an actor choosing to acknowledge the audience. This idea that the parasocial relationship can exist and grow over an extended period of time would serve as the basis for further research into the relationship that develops between regular viewers and listeners of television and radio programs and the host/actors.

## Measuring the Parasocial Relationship

This new understanding of the relationship as one that could endure and increase or decrease over time led to an interest in developing a system of measurement and ways to quantify these relationships. The most prominent scale that was developed from this desire was the Parasocial Interaction (PSI) scale, which "primarily captures users' friendship toward media performers, rather than users' feeling of being involved in an interaction with the performer during media exposure" (Hartmann & Goldhoorn, 2011, p. 1104). There are currently two versions of the PSI scale that researchers can choose to employ; one version contains twenty measurement items, while a shorter ten-item version of the scale also exists. This scale was "originally developed to measure parasocial interaction as viewers' social involvement to local TV newscasters. Since then it has been adapted to a multitude of other media characters to include online avatars, movie characters, and politicians" (Dibble et al., 2016, p. 26). While the PSI scale has been found to be internally consistent and unidimensional, Dibble et al. suggest that it is not without its flaws, including "that most parasocial interaction measures have not been put through adequate tests of construct validation. Moreover, parasocial interaction and parasocial relationships have undergone much theoretical and conceptual refinement since the first measures of these concepts emerged, and we suggest that extant measures have not been evaluated sufficiently for their correspondence with the latest theoretic and conceptual developments" (Dibble et al., 2016, p. 22).

Dibble et al. are not the only researchers who feel that the PSI scale is inadequate for quantifying parasocial interactions and relationships based upon the recent developments in the field. In 2011, Hartmann and Goldhoorn developed a new scale for measuring parasocial interaction known as the Experience of Parasocial Interaction (EPSI) scale. The EPSI scale is based upon an alternative six-item scale of measurement and "intends to measure users' experience of parasocial interaction, defined as an intuitive feeling of mutual awareness, attention, and adjustment with a media character in an exposure situation" (Dibble et al., 2016, p. 27). While this scale has not been fully studied and explored due to its newer nature, the limited studies of this scale that have been conducted have found it to be a potentially more accurate system of measurement than the traditional PSI scale. However, one of the main issues with both of these scales in regard to their applicability and accuracy of measuring the parasocial nature of the podcast is that they were developed in large part based upon the parasocial nature of television. As television is a visual medium, there are several aspects of the parasocial relationship that can develop between an actor and audience that are not replicable or applicable to the podcast host, which calls into question the potential usefulness of these scales in relation to this specific medium.

## Traditional Explorations of Parasocial Dynamics

Traditionally, when examining parasocial interaction research has focused on radio and television. Of the two mediums, the parasocial interaction that occurs between the listener of a podcast and the podcast host tends to have more similarities with the parasocial relationship of a radio listener and radio host, but there are several attributes of the parasocial relationship between the television persona and audience that are also applicable to the podcast. The parasocial interactions that occur between a television viewer and a television actor are defined to a great extent by the "illusion of being engaged in a social interaction with the TV performer. The audience responds with something more than mere running observation; it is, as it were, subtly insinuated into the programme's actions and transformed into a group which observes and participates in the show by turns" (Hartmann & Goldhoorn, 2011, p. 1105). As the parasocial relationship develops between the TV viewer and actor, a form of "mindreading" can potentially occur. Mindreading refers to the psychological phenomenon that suggests "that in any social encounter individuals engage in mindreading to infer the mental states of other people being present" (Hartmann & Goldhoorn, 2011, p. 1106). Mindreading occurs automatically and results in intuitive feelings, not elaborate or complex beliefs, being developed. Mindreading can occur when a person is viewing a TV program because it is an automatic activity that occurs in any social encounter. Therefore, it is plausible that TV viewers may engage in mindreading when they encounter TV performers. For example, when a TV performer looks directly into the camera, the TV viewer could automatically acquire the belief and feeling that said performer is looking at them personally (Hartmann & Goldhoorn, 2011).

Mindreading could also possibly occur between the listener of a podcast and the host of the podcast, as the conversational tone of the host can mimic a social interaction. While a podcast host cannot physically look at the listener, they can "speak" to the listener by addressing them, causing the audience to automatically engage in mindreading, resulting in the development of these intuitive feelings and assumptions about the current mental state of the podcast host. For example, if the host of a podcast were to loudly address his audience using vulgar language, the listener of the podcast might automatically assume that the host is currently angry, even though he or she doesn't actually know the mental state of the host at that time.

## The Parasocial Nature of Podcasts

While the initial focus of parasocial research focused on the parasocial dynamic that occurs in reference to television viewers and radio listeners, this relationship can now be extended to a variety of different new digital media. One such medium is the podcast. The podcast first came to prominence on the Internet in the mid-2000s and is best described as "audio files of varying types often featuring news and talk" (MacDougall, 2012, p. 168). The podcast serves as an evolution of the radio to some degree, as "podcasts move us beyond music listening to the consumption of talk, conversation, and other kinds of oral discourse as re-mediated through digital recording technology. These recordings of human voices consumed in a variety of contexts are, on the face of it, personal sound experiences. But they are often highly persuasive socio-political events as well" (MacDougall, 2012, p. 167). A podcast is usually a personal sound experience and can blur the lines between the traditional understanding of public and private thoughts as the podcast host is sharing "intimate" thoughts both to the individual, and the mass public, albeit not necessarily at the same time. The podcast potentially serves as the next step in the media consumption of audio content as "podcast consumption has similarities to both the traditional radio broadcast listener's experience and the tape-recorded radio show played back on a stationary tape player or mobile walkman" (MacDougall, 2012, p. 168). A key characteristic that is shared by the podcast and radio broadcast is the reliance that both mediums place on the power of the human voice. In the case of the podcast, this power dynamic is exploited via the host of the podcast. Podcasts allow the host to share personal experiences with a wider audience in their own words and with their own voice. MacDougall (2012) states, "Podcasting recasts the personal experience as well as the actual perspectives and preferences accessible to people on-the-fly via digital storage and playback of audio content" (p. 168).

Another key element of parasocial interactions is the lack of obligation, effort, and responsibility that they require of the spectator. Peters and Simonson (2004) assert, "He is free to withdraw at any moment. If he remains involved, these parasocial relations provide a framework within which much may be added by fantasy" (p. 374). This lack of obligation and responsibility is a key component of the parasocial nature of the podcast, as listeners of a podcast can choose to pause, stop, or even delete entirely the podcast that they are listening to, essentially ending the relationship with no repercussions. This ability to end a relationship and treat it as though it never occurred in the first place without any consequences is a major component of the illusionary nature of the parasocial relationship as "real" or tangible relationships with other members of society tend to be much harder to simply end abruptly.

One of the main appeals of a parasocial relationship is the potentially consistent and repetitive nature of the relationship. As mentioned previously in the research of Dibble et al. (2016), one of the major components of a parasocial relationship is that the interaction between the host and the listener persists over an extended period of time through numerous repeated interactions. In this manner, the host of the podcast, or the "persona," "offers above all, a continuing relationship. His appearance is a regular and dependable event, to be counted on, planned for, and integrated into the routines of daily life" (Peters & Simonson, 2004, p. 375). This constant false interaction can create an impression among the audience that they "know" the actor and help to develop this bond. When this bond is allowed to develop to the extreme, "the 'fan' comes to believe that he 'knows' the persona more intimately and profoundly than others do; that he understands his character and appreciates his values and motives" (Peters & Simonson, 2004, p. 9).

Podcasts are able to take advantage of this long-term bond through the consistent production of shows. Many podcasts operate on a weekly schedule and produce new content for episodes in a rather predictable manner. The consistency of a podcast and its release date allows the viewer to develop a parasocial relationship with the podcast host, as the consumption of a new podcast episode can become part of the listener's daily routine. Shows that produce new episodes on a consistent basis may be able to thus develop this relationship further, as podcast listeners start to believe that they "know" the host since they listen to them speak every week. The "interaction" with the podcast and its host thus becomes integrated into the listener's life to the extent that listening becomes almost a habit.

Another important component of the persona-listener relationship is the many emotional roles that the persona can provide for the listener: "The persona may be considered by his audience as a friend, a counselor, comforter, and model; but, unlike real associates, he has the peculiar virtue of being standardized according to the 'formula' for his character which he and his producers have worked out and embodied in an appropriate production format" (Peters & Simonson, 2004, p. 375). The diversity of podcasts and their hosts allows for listeners to determine to an extent what role the host will play for them, as depending upon what emotional release they may be seeking, they can simply pick a podcast whose host and content fit their current mood. If listeners desire to be entertained and to laugh, they pick a podcast hosted by a comedian; if they are looking for an educational experience, there exist a variety of informative news podcasts to choose from. The same can be said for political and sports talk, as the list of potential topics goes on and on. The specialized nature of the podcast means that there are a multitude of different types of podcasts and podcast hosts available for the listener to consume to an even greater extent and variety than is offered by the traditional TV persona.

### Differences between Radio Broadcasts and Podcasts

While the podcast shares many similarities with the traditional radio broadcast, there are several key aspects of this medium that separate it from its audio predecessor. Key among these differences is the component of listener choice and the need for active participation from the listener when it comes to choosing which podcast to consume. While it can be tempting to view a podcast in a sense as Internet radio, this is a misinformed belief, as nothing is being broadcast during a podcast: "To the contrary, and well beyond the casual tuning-in of a radio or television signal, podcast listeners must consciously point their browser to a particular web site that archives these compressed digital recordings and deliberately choose specific files to download" (MacDougall, 2012, p. 169).

Podcasts tend to differ from traditional radio broadcasts in regard to content as well as podcast shows that predominately feature narrative talk as opposed to music. However, the key distinguishing feature of the podcast is that it is an auditory experience, a trait that is shared by radio broadcasts. As a medium, the podcast is able to take advantage of one of the unique features of the human auditory sense in that "there is a tendency to incorporate or fold in what we see, taste, smell, and touch with what we hear. If the podcast originates in sound, it often ends up being a more total or whole sensory experience" (MacDougall, 2012, p. 170). This tendency to incorporate the additional sensory aspects of the area around us into our auditory experience in the manner that MacDougall describes can enhance the experience and the subsequent relationship with a host that the listener develops. Due to the portable nature of the podcast, listeners are able to have a much wider and diverse range of sensory experiences to incorporate into their relationship compared to the more stationary nature of the radio broadcast or even traditional television experience: "Podcasts and the appliances that enable their consumption, are among the latest instances of mobile digital technology that represent a further alteration of the phonological experience of everyday life.... The mobilization of such content has been shown to reorient the listener to the world and the world to the listener, prompting (internal) memory and (external) layout to function together as props and foils for the often detailed yet punctuate discourse that typifies the podcast" (MacDougall, 2012, p. 170). An ability to interact with a greater range of stimuli allows for the listeners of a podcast to have an enhanced listening experience, which can help to blur the line between the listener and content. When a listener interacts with multiple stimuli while listening to a podcast, the experience becomes more immersive, which in turn can cause the listener to feel as though he or she is having an actual real conversation and interaction with the podcast host. When interacting with another person in real life, very rarely does this interaction occur in a vacuum, and the ability to consume a podcast on the go, around other people and other stimuli, helps to create a more realistic simulation of an interaction. This mobile aspect of the podcast is an example of how the podcast constitutes an evolution of radio, as it serves as "a fundamentally new form of mediated interpersonal communication. Podcasts enhance the personal feel and all attendant psychodynamic effects of Fessenden's primordial radio show" (MacDougall, 2012, p. 171).

Differences also exist in the methods of measurement that are used to inform radio broadcasters about the demographics of their audience and those of the podcast creator. The main method employed by radio broadcast organizations is show ratings, "estimates of the number and statistic characteristics of persons listening to a media outlet in specified timeslots" (Wolfenden, 2014, p. 9). While there exist a wide range of potential methodologies that can be employed by modern broadcast companies to study their audience, ratings tend to be the dominant method employed by these companies to get to "know" their listeners. Radio broadcast companies use the data collected via these ratings to "develop listener profiles, match these profiles against 'target' audiences and seek to shape presenter's interaction in order to attract the desired audience" (Wolfenden, 2014, p. 9). Podcast creators, on the other hand, tend to rely less on the use of these types of ratings, as it can be harder to measure Internet-based listenership thanks to a multitude of podcast consumption options, both legal and otherwise. However, podcast hosts can use statistics of downloads, number of times streamed, qualitative online ratings, social media mentions, and "likes" to develop a better understanding of their audience.

The major issue that arises when seeking to measure podcast consumption lies in the manner of content delivery of the medium. Unlike a traditional radio broadcast, podcasts can be consumed in multiple manners, the most common of which is via downloading or streaming: "Podcast listeners acquire podcast files in one of two ways: either by downloading the file for later listening (downloaded), or by listening while the file is downloaded (online listening)" (Mulder & Shetty, 2017, p. 7). While these two methods of consumption are different in name and nature, they are technically the same in that both methods involve downloading the podcast, with the main difference between the two being where the file is stored during the download: "Online podcasts appear to be streamed, but the file is actually being downloaded while the listener is listening to the file.

The downloaded file is stored in a temporary location rather than to a library as with a downloaded podcast" (Mulder & Shetty, 2017, p. 7).

However, when it comes to actually measuring downloads and streams, both forms of consumption are recorded via digital server logs. These server logs are traditionally used to measure podcast consumption, as they "may include file requests for a combination of downloaded podcast files, dynamically inserted ads, and any content requested by the web page or application hosting the player. A number of factors are used to analyze log files" (Mulder & Shetty, 2017, p. 9). Once these logs have been measured, they can be filtered and analyzed via several unique factors, including IP address, unique downloads, and complete downloads, depending upon what specific information an individual may desire.

These filtering factors are especially important when attempting to examine how exposure to a podcast can influence the parasocial relationship, as a download of a podcast does not guarantee that an individual actually listened to the podcast. This differs from how a traditional radio broadcast is measured and analyzed, as due to the live nature of the radio broadcast, it is usually reasonable for researchers to assume that if an audience member is playing a radio broadcast they are also listening to that broadcast. In terms of the podcast, it would therefore be more accurate to equate the streaming numbers of a podcast to those of the live listenership of a radio broadcast. Even though the streaming of a podcast is not live per se, as the program has been prerecorded, streaming numbers help to measure active consumption of the program compared to downloads, which measure only that a program has been saved by a consumer for either immediate or future consumption.

## The Parasocial Nature of Podcasts Compared to Other Media

The ability of the podcast to engage and stimulate multiple senses of the viewer at once adds an element to the relationship of the podcast host and listener that is harder to be replicated in the relationship between the television viewer and actor. While actors on television must rely primarily upon the viewers' sense of sight to develop their particular parasocial dynamic, the relationship between the podcast host and listener can be aided by the listener's experiencing of multiple different senses at once. Television viewers to an extent have part of the parasocial relationship defined for them, they are placed in a world that is created for them by the television program. As noted earlier, a key component of the auditory experience of the podcast is that listeners incorporate elements of the world around them into their experience. This makes the relationship more tangible and immersive for consumers than the flatter, two-dimensional world of the television that they are placed into when they are interacting with the television persona. This is a weakness that is also shared to some extent by the radio, as it too is much less mobile a medium than the podcast. Even with the more portable nature of the modern radio experience thanks to the ability to listen to broadcasts in the car and on the move while in other modes of transportation, watching or listening to a program in the same space and location repeatedly makes it harder for the viewer to experience true escapism and dampens the parasocial relationship, as they are faced with constant subtle sensory reminders that they are still at home, at work, or in a vehicle, not with the host. Radio is thus limited to some extent in the experience that it can provide for the viewer in a manner that the podcast is not.

One of the key differences between television and the podcast is the manner in which the "bond of intimacy" is developed between the persona and the viewer. Creating an illusion of intimacy with their viewers is a critical method employed by TV actors to develop and strengthen the parasocial relationship with the viewer. For the television persona, creating this illusion is most often characterized by "the attempt of the persona to duplicate the gestures, conversational style, and milieu of an informal face-to-face gathering" (Peters & Simonson, 2004, p. 375). As the podcast is an audio medium, the podcast host must find a way to create this illusion of intimacy without reliance upon visually based measures such as hand gestures or facial expressions. In order to achieve this goal, the podcast host has much more in common with the traditional radio broadcast host. The uses of tone and patter to create a more conversational and less formal experience are some of the main methods employed by radio hosts as "the persona tries as far as possible to eradicate, or at least to blur, the line which divides him and his show, as formal performance, from the audience both in the studio and at home" (Peters & Simonson, 2004, p. 376). In this manner, podcasts already have an advantage over traditional radio broadcasts in that they tend to be recorded in a studio without a major audience and can be recorded pretty much anywhere the host desires, creating an already less formal ambiance for the show. Podcast hosts are also not as restricted by some of the more formal elements of radio broadcasts, including limitations of time, a consistent show format and structure, the use of advertisements, and restrictions on what can be talked about and the language used by the host. This lack of restriction helps podcast hosts to create a more informal atmosphere for their shows.

This is also an advantage that podcasts have over television programs, especially in regard to the restriction placed upon TV actors in terms of what they can and cannot say as well as the use of advertisements during television programs. It is this lack of reliance upon a formal structure that provides the podcast with a slight advantage over television broadcast when developing the parasocial relationship, as a traditional television program is limited to a thirty- or sixty-minute time slot and usually involves consistent interruptions for advertisements. Whenever a television program goes to an advertisement break, it creates a break in the relationship between the persona and the viewer and provides a repeated reminder to the viewer (whether consciously or not) that the relationship they have is not real. These advertisement breaks unintentionally rupture the "trance" of the parasocial relationship, which is not the case for many podcasts, as they are not as reliant on advertisements for funding and can choose to run any ads merely at the beginning or end of their broadcast, creating an uninterrupted relationship for the duration of their broadcast.

At the core of the difference in the development of the parasocial nature of the podcast and radio compared to that of television lies reliance upon two different senses. Television adds a visual component that the podcast and radio tend to lack due to their nature as solely audio-based forms of mass media. However, as an audio-based, portable form of media, the podcast tends to be consumed most often via headphones. As discussed earlier, a major aspect of the development of the parasocial relationship is the feeling that the listener or viewer gets of "being there" with the host. The illusion that the audience is sharing an experience with the persona helps to strengthen the bond between the two parties. The sense of being there with the host occurs in the context of television consumption as "watching someone on television often fosters a palpable sense of involvement, of being hailed or addressed personally" (MacDougall, 2012, p. 179). While the visual component of the relationship is one that the podcast and radio lack compared to other media, this does not mean that these audio-based mediums lack the ability to create parasocial interactions. One major benefit that the podcast has in creating this feeling of involvement with the viewer again returns to the predominant method of podcast consumption, that is, via headphones: "We all know how these viewing experiences are attended by a powerful sense of *being there*. It can be even more enveloping with words spoken to us through a pair of earphones" (MacDougall, 2012, p. 178). The addition of earphones for audio consumption creates a more intimate feeling for the listener, which in turn helps to bolster the illusion of a personal relationship, as the listener does not have to share her experience with others. In this manner, "podcasts take secondary orality, publicly, and the power of the parasocial relation to a new level. With headphones in place, we hear someone (or several people) speaking, quite literally, between our ears. And this, adds a certain reality to the phrase 'getting inside someone's head.' . . . Such a sentiment suggests that the experience generated by the mobile podcast listening is at least akin to having someone speaking to/with you while walking, sitting, or standing next to you" (MacDougall, 20102, p. 179). It is this ability to "get inside someone's head" is a critical distinguishing aspect between the podcast and radio. Since podcasts tend to provide listeners with prerecorded content, it is very easy for consumers to download and listen to these programs on personal music devices and thus use headphones. However, as radio is a medium that tends to rely more on live programming, it is less conducive to consumption via MP3 players and other personal music devices. While there are certainly ways to consume radio podcasts via an MP3 player or cell phone and then listen to that programming via headphones, traditionally radio broadcasts tend to be listened to "out loud," thus potentially negating (or at least lessening) the perception of having the host right there with the listener.

There are some aspects of visual nature of television that can affect the parasocial relationship that are harder to be replicated by podcasts. Previous research has found that factors such as perceived eye contact and body language of a performer can impact the parasocial relationship of the audience member on a nonverbal level (Hartmann & Goldhoorn, 2011). As podcasts are a nonvisual medium, the host cannot take advantage of this method of developing a relationship with the audience. Another key factor of the parasocial relationship can be the physical appearance of the actor, with perceived attractiveness having been found to play an important role in affecting the parasocial relationship with the viewer. This belief has been reinforced by the inclusion of the perceived attractiveness of the TV performer as a ratings criterion on the popular PSI scale. Furthermore, the meta-analytic studies of Schiappa, Allen, and Gregg (in press) found that the perceived attractiveness of a media character intensified the parasocial interaction between the character and viewer. According to Hartmann and Goldhoorn (2011), if TV viewers perceive a TV actor to be attractive, this can cause them to place more value on their relationship with the actor. Often the consumers of a podcast do not see the podcast host, so this aspect of the medium makes it harder for them to determine the physical attractiveness of the host.

While the podcast host may lack the amount of visual exposure that the television actor has with the audience, thanks to the web and computer-based aspects of the podcast, hosts can choose to inform the viewer of their appearance via images attached to their podcasts as well as to websites that host their podcast. While this may not impact the relationship to the same degree that seeing an actor on a consistent basis does, indeed it adds some visual element to the relationship. Additionally, podcast hosts can choose to host live shows that include an audience of their fans, which allows their fans to be exposed to their physical attributes, albeit possibly only to a small sampling of their total audience. The lack of a visual image of the podcast host for the consumer may not actually be a deterring factor to the strengthening of the parasocial relationship between the host and listener, as "leaving the visual picture to the imagination enhances the power, presence and, by extension, the very potent parasocial dynamic potentially created between the messenger and his message" (MacDougall, 2012, p. 180). In fact, it could be argued that leaving listeners to imagine what the host looks like could actually be beneficial to this relationship, as it allows them to create an idealized image of the host in their mind, as well as to ascribe potential physical characteristics to the host that while potentially not true are what consumers find to be personally attractive. This idealized version of the host, while illusionary, would most likely actually strengthen the bond between listener and host, as it allows the listener to essentially customize this aspect of the relationship. This is similar in manner to how readers create their own mental images of characters in books that they are reading based upon how they think the character "should" look. To an extent, this adds a greater component of individuality to the relationship for the listener that TV does not actually provide.

## Avenues for Further Exploration of the Parasocial Podcast Relationship

While the parasocial nature of the podcast shares many similarities with the relationships that develop between the audience and host of forms of media, there are several unique dynamics and aspects of the parasocial relationship that can exist between the podcast host and audience that require further examination. One critical area in which there currently exists a gap in knowledge is how to quantify and measure the parasocial interactions and relationships between podcast hosts and their listeners. To date, there exists no uniform scale or system of measurement for this relationship, with existing scales focusing on how these types of relationship develop via other media. Determining a way to measure the strength of the parasocial relationships that develops via listening to podcasts would potentially allow for researchers to compare and contrast the effects and strength of these interactions and relationships across different media. Being able to quantitatively measure and compare the parasocial relationships of podcasts with those of the radio would allow for greater understanding into how these two mediums are similar as well as how they differ in the ways that their audiences come to relate to the hosts of the mediums.

Furthermore, these types of scales could allow for a greater understanding as to what aspects of the podcast uniquely affect the parasocial dynamic of the host and consumer. Determining what factors can have the greatest effect upon the parasocial dynamic of a podcast not only could allow for the development of a more accurate and applicable scale of measurement, but also would serve to provide greater understanding for podcast hosts as to how their listeners are relating to them and how they can intentionally strengthen the bond between themselves and their subscribers. While the relationship between the listener and host is illusionary in nature, "in radio at least, the audience and the broadcaster cannot be thought of as independent from each other. While the focus has been on audience elements, both the audience and the broadcaster are active in constituting the relationship" (Wolfenden, 2014, p. 6). Wolfenden found that "broadcasters are active and reflexive in the way they constitute an audience, and that these processes involve high degrees of skill and experience on the part of presenters" (Wolfenden, 2014, p. 7). Knowing what factors can contribute to the dynamic between the host and audience would allow podcast hosts to be more intentional and active in how they "interact" with their audience and to create a potentially wider and more dedicated following for their show.

## Conclusion

The idea that consumers of mass media can come to believe that they "know" a character in the media that they are consuming and can develop an illusionary one-sided relationship with that character serves as the basis for the modern interpretation of parasocial theory. While the parasocial dynamic between media and the public has tended to be explored in regard to how these interactions and relationships develop between television and radio broadcast personae and their audience, this dynamic can extend to other newer forms of media as well. Particularly, the podcast serves as a potential next step in the evolution of this dynamic. Podcasts share several similarities and attributes of television and radio that can lead to the development of a parasocial dynamic between the podcast host or hosts and the listener of the podcast. However, as podcasts are a newer media, research into this relationship is still ongoing, and the differences between a podcast and traditional television or radio broadcast provide several avenues for new developments in this relationship. As such, new scales of parasocial measurement are most likely needed to better measure and understand the parasocial nature of the podcast.

## References

Dibble, J. L., Hartmann, T., & Rosaen, S. F. (2016). Parasocial interaction and parasocial relationship: Conceptual clarification and a critical assessment of measures. *Human Communication Research, 42*(1), 21–44. doi:10.1111/hcre.12063

Hartmann, T., & Goldhoorn, C. (2011). Horton and Wohl revisited: Exploring viewers' experience of parasocial interaction. *Journal of Communication, 6*, 1104–1121.

Horton, D., & Wohl, R. (1956). Mass communication and para-social interaction: Observations on intimacy at a distance. *Psychiatry, 19*, 215–229.

Katz, E., Peters, J. D., Liebes, T., & Orloff, A. (2003). *Canonic texts in media research: Are there any? Should there be? How about these?* Cambridge: Polity.

MacDougall, R. C. (2012). *Digination: Identity, organization, and public life in the age of small digital devices and big digital domains.* Madison, NJ: Fairleigh Dickinson University Press.

Mulder, S., & Shetty, A. (2017). *IAB Podcast Measurement Technical Guidelines Version 2.0* [Guide]. New York, NY: IAB Tech Lab Podcast Technical Working Group.

Peters, J. D., & Simonson, P. (2004). *Mass communication and American social thought: Key texts, 1919–1968.* Lanham, MD: Rowman & Littlefield.

Schiappa, E., Allen, M., & Gregg, P. B. (in press). Parasocial relationships and television: A metaanalysis of the effects. In R. Preiss, B. Gayle, N. Burrell, M. Allen, & J. Bryant (Eds.), *Mass media effects: Advances through meta-analysis.* Mahwah, NJ: Lawrence Erlbaum.

Wolfenden, H. (2014). I know exactly who they are: Radio presenters' conceptions of audience. *Radio Journal, 12*(1–2), 5–21. doi:10.1386/rjao.12.1-2.51

# 4

# Social Media Analytics, Radio Advertising, and Strategic Partnerships

• • • • • • • • • • • • • • • • • • • •

JOSEPH R. BLANEY

This chapter examines the current state of audience listenership and troubling revenue trends, the notion of digital and social media product as "new revenues," alternative ways of thinking about NTR (nontraditional revenue), the importance of a station cluster's social media analytics laboratory, and current industry practices across large and small markets. Those topics are discussed in that order.

## Listenership and Revenues: An Industry Snapshot

In terms of listenership, radio remains strong, albeit serious threats to long-term viability remain. Radio reaches more people than any other platform. While 93 percent of Americans listen to AM/FM radio, 89 percent watch television, 83 percent use smartphones, 50 percent use personal computers, and 37 percent use tablets such as iPads ("Audio Today," 2016). Country music formats remain the most popular listening choice, followed by news/talk and contemporary hit radio.

Moreover, concerns about generational listenership decline are unwarranted at this time. In all, 94 percent of Boomers (born between 1950 and 1964), 95 percent of Generation X (born between 1965 and 1979), and 92 percent of

Millennials (born between 1980 and 1996) listen every week ("Radio Facts," 2017). In other words, there is only a 2 percent decline in listening between the oldest demographic considered and the youngest, despite the technological means to do so (e.g., digital media players, Internet) being available to most Millennials early on in their lives.

So, what are the threats? They are twofold: (1) not adopting customizable digital streaming services and (2) potential disregard from historical allies in the automobile industry.

A full 51 percent of all music industry revenue can be attributed to digital streaming, as opposed to downloading music or buying physical recordings via CD or even vinyl (Ashworth, 2017). Failure of the radio industry to recognize the demand for highly customizable, niche-oriented programming could be perilous. While some companies (e.g., iHeart) have embraced the ability to aggregate available, unique terrestrial streams, others remain passive in their offerings. Local news/sports outlets provide another example of nichecasting that is augmenting business models and better serving local communities. One case in point might be WJBC-AM in Bloomington, Illinois, which on one recent Saturday provided high school football coverage of six different high school football playoff games featuring local teams. However, overreliance on only over-the-air programming and a single streamed simulcast will result in an inability to serve the existing audience as it gets used to highly idiosyncratic choices.

As far as the automobile and the listeners inside, three-fourths of all adults listen to radio in their cars (Ashworth, 2017). However, as the touch-screen automobile dashboard becomes more inundated with options for choosing connected phones and auto-to-web connectivity, AM/FM could find itself not only just one choice among many, but perhaps not even a prominent part of the mobile entertainment display. The National Association of Broadcasters is keenly aware of its need to keep the interest of car manufacturers.

Radio revenues exhibit a modest upward trend at the moment. Local spot, off-air, and digital revenues lead growth from $17.6 billion to $17.8 billion for the years 2017 and 2018 ("Kagan: Radio Revenues," 2018). Moreover, a predicted 1.0 percent growth in radio revenues (driven by modest over-the-air growth and healthy digital revenue expansion every year) stands to elevate radio to the fifth strongest local advertising sector by 2021 ("Radio's Digital Ad," 2017). This growth for an allegedly "old medium" would presumably be good news swimming against a tide of decline. However, consider that gross domestic product in the United States grew at a 3.1 percent rate in the second quarter of the year with anticipated continued growth ("Final Reading," 2017). To the extent that revenues have not kept pace with GDP, one could consider the industry as retracting.

There is no doubt that the methods for bringing in revenue and delivering a consuming audience are evolving. Traditional broadcasters need to be cognizant of their role on the margins of these new ways. A radical change in industry self-perception is necessary as advertising revenue is finite, and in many ways the radio industry is not experiencing any "new revenue" at all, but rather making claims on existing advertising dollars with expanded offerings of its brand. This recognition is taken up briefly in the next section.

## Rethinking NTR

The radio industry's notion of nontraditional revenue (NTR) has evolved over the years, but in many ways it is still in its infancy. For current purposes, NTR is defined as all station revenues not generated through sales of spot advertising. Through much of the seventies, eighties, and nineties, the preponderance of these revenues was brought about through sales of remote broadcasts and execution of events closely branded with the station. This would include the ubiquitous President's Day Sale broadcast at a local furniture store on the simple end and an enormous bridal show complete with a mass wedding for all the listeners interested in such a public method for nuptials. The bridal event might include many event sponsors, from vendors such as banquet halls to caterers, photographers, dress shops, florists, jewelers, travel agents, and apartment complexes.

In 2007, Entrepreneur.com noted that as radio station prices skyrocketed amid mergers and consolidations, a key portion of the radio business model included the aggressive scheduling of events such as these. As these events became more and more common and necessary, many companies created NTR departments tasked with the execution of these events and systematic inclusion in station rate cards ("Finding New Ways," 2007). Indeed, stations could charge only so much per spot due to rated audience size and there was only so much spot inventory available. As such, revenue limits were defined by those parameters. NTR departments were to tackle these challenges head-on.

By the mid-1990s, many stations began to develop a modest website presence. In some ways this was a programmatic response to Internet-only offerings such as Carl Malamud's Internet Talk Radio, which stood to peel off listenership as web access became rapidly adopted ("Video Killed," 2017). As web production and editing software became more affordable and easier to use, the level of sophistication for these station extensions improved. In terms of listener interaction, they provided places to enter station contests and otherwise communicate with station staffs. Many/most (a treatment of webstreaming fees/licensures is outside the scope of this project) began to offer a simulcast stream so that fans could listen online from their work computers. Eventually advertising banners became the norm and were available for sale as an NTR commodity. Programming staffs made concerted efforts to create audio, video, and textual content in addition to the main programming stream. These programming "extras" were sponsor-ready on station websites with the ability to add preroll commercials as well as preferred placements on the webpages. As social media came along, so did the opportunity for interaction between radio outlets, advertisers, and their listeners. A Pew Research Center study found that 71 percent of American adults had deployed Facebook accounts, opening up an avenue to stay in touch with listeners, reinforce station/personality brand, and publicize their clients. In short, the NTR model had expanded ("Social Media Update," 2015).

Therein lies the core of radio NTR today. However, the need to expand revenues in the face of competing and nimble platforms remains. In short, cluster managers are being asked for more revenues with finite sellable time/space opportunities. In this environment, what adaptation exists for "radio's next century"?

## The Social Media Analytics Lab: A Radio Imperative

Social media are ubiquitous. As cited above, 71 percent of American adults had Facebook accounts by 2014. LinkedIn and Pinterest have 28 percent of adults on board, while Instagram has 26 percent and Twitter 23 percent ("Social Media Update," 2015). Citizens/consumers use these platforms to augment their social and professional lives in various ways. One can easily surmise that the readers of this volume either use social media or have an elementary understanding of its gratifications. However, the existence of highly rich and informative data about user product preferences, lifestyle, and psychographics, which are publicly available, ought to give great encouragement to those with something to sell (Fan & Gordon, 2014). Moreover, stations with a fundamental understanding of their social media presence have an advantage in formulating proper audience interactivity (Al-Rawi, 2016).

Khan (2015) offered a typology of available social media data best understood as "seven layers." Namely, such data are (1) textual, (2) network-related, (3) actions, (4) hyperlinks, (5) mobile application data, (6) location-related, and (7) search engine data. These data can all be gathered from such diverse sources as the above-named social media platforms, but also blogs, video-sharing sites such as YouTube, website reviews, and news aggregate sites such as *Huffington Post* and *Breitbart*.

The value that such data could have for radio clients in search of customers ought to be somewhat obvious, but a short description is in order. *Textual data* from customers commenting on a large car dealer or car dealer chain could lend insight into customer satisfaction/dissatisfaction and afford a chance to change business practices (or even personnel). *Network data* can lend insight into the reach of influence of individual customers or aggregates of customers. *Actions* such as "re-tweeting" or sharing a Facebook post can lend insight into the nature of those messages that elicit strong (or weak) reactions from a relevant public. *Hyperlinks* lend insight into the people or organizations deemed relevant to given content. *Mobile application data* tell us why audiences use particular apps and what they were seeking to purchase or know by its use. *Location data* tell the analyst about the physical proximity of the media user to other locations, presumably those of most relevance to the analyst/client. Finally, *search engines data* are a treasure trove that can summarize everything from most sought-after content to desired purchases and massive psychosocial insights into those searching the web.

These data provide valuable insight in many contexts, but to a local establishment wanting to sell goods and services *they are absolutely essential.* It is a truism that the client understands his or her clientele better than the sales representative. However, every last client, no matter how observant of his or her clientele or potential clientele, could make use of generalizable information about customer sentiment, potential to reach existing customers and their contacts, and successful efforts to identify/connect with customers. These data unlock the mystery of customer tendencies in a sophisticated and predictable way.

Stations, sales representatives, promotions directors, and programmers all have a stake in such rich information. Programmers can use such analytics to understand which types of content its listeners find most compelling and adapt online data to inform the topicality offered by show hosts and digital content. This ought to be considered a form of immediate ratings feedback allowing for strategic planning and responses to the good news and bad news found in the analytics. However, it is the *service of analytics intelligence and analysis* that radio cluster management should see as a new and valuable commodity for sale. Sales representatives are already "boots on the ground," going into establishments and developing relationships of trust. With proper training, these representatives could offer advice using open-source and/or subscription-based software designed to provide intelligence necessary for brand/reputation management, message design, social network opportunities, and professional media buying advice (even on platforms not owned by the cluster). *Properly educated* sales representatives could add value to their portfolios with this skill set.

Consider the case of a major market radio/TV/digital cluster currently receiving social media analytics from a large Midwestern university. Using the social media analytics software NUVI and a number of open-source tools, the university is supplying analysis of publicly available information regarding (1) the number of all overall comments about the cluster, (2) "tone" (indicating negativity or positivity toward the cluster), (3) the most compelling topics as indicated by re-tweets and comments, and (4) identifiable trends of interest, which comes down to the judgment of the analyst when he or she "dives down deep" into the data where thematic prominence emerges. Notably, similar data were provided about the cluster's primary competitor. Obviously, the cluster will use these data in order to augment its own strengths and exploit its competitors' weaknesses. They provide rich descriptions for the state of the brand that a ratings company could not hope to provide whether in a timely or (more likely) greatly delayed manner.

Setting aside the possibilities for media company use of such data, consider strongly the potential for client relationship development if their sales department were able to deliver these data to clients across many sectors (automotive, furniture, electronics, restaurant, hotel, etc.). The benefit for a client would not only cement the amiability of the client-account representative relationship, but also make the representative's ongoing advice essential in a competitive local, regional, or even national economy.

While some stations have employed such analytics at a very basic level, the full potential for revenue and relationship enhancement is far from its utility. The state of such analytics is the subject of the next section.

## An Exploratory Inquiry into Radio Social Media Analytics Efforts

A survey was administered to cluster managers of commercial stations in a large Midwestern state asking for information about the station's approach to social media analytics. Eight clusters of seventy-one different commercial licensees answered the survey questions intended as quantitative measures. (The 11 percent response can be described only as disappointing. Although member surveys such as this have response rates varying between 5 percent-40 percent [Fowler, 2013], the survey in this study went directly to the heart of an issue with high salience for radio executives. No doubt, that $N = 8$ in this case limits generalizability. This limitation will be addressed frankly in the conclusion of the chapter. However, the results still bear scholarly attention.) Recognizing this problem, follow-up interviews were requested, and thankfully two organizations (one large market and one small market) agreed to provide in-depth feedback to the questions at hand. Some very tentative conclusions are drawn from the data collected, but they need to be approached skeptically. Still, discoveries here can be considered fodder for a more comprehensive study.

The cluster respondents were asked the following:

1. If you had to choose, how would you describe the market in which your station operates? Large or Small (forcing a choice and eliminating "Medium" as an option was intended to aid differentiation by size).
2. How many times per month do you run some form of social media analytics report in order to assess your social media? (Once, Twice, Weekly, Most Days, Never)
3. How many times per month do you run some form of social media analytics report to assess the tone of comments about your posting? (Once, Twice, Weekly, Most Days, Never)
4. How much do you agree with the statement, "My station receives much added value revenue from clients by providing social media support for their events and products?" (Agree Strongly, Agree, Neutral, Disagree, Disagree Strongly)
5. How much do you agree with the statement, "My station's sales representatives sell or include social media analytics Services to their clients

in addition to other things on the rate card?" (Agree Strongly, Agree, Neutral, Disagree, Disagree Strongly)
6. In the space below, please tell us what are the barriers to offering social media support (timely postings, etc.) to your advertisers.
7. In the space below, please tell us what are the barriers to your sales people offering social media analytics as additional client services.

Each question will receive its own summary paragraph.

*Market size.* The respondents were evenly divided at 50 percent large market and 50 percent small market.

*Reach analytics.* Of respondents, 25 percent said stations conducted analytics reports designed to measure reach once per month, while 37.5 percent reported doing so weekly and 37.5 percent reported doing so most days. In short, a little more than a third were monitoring daily.

*Tone analytics.* Of respondents, 25 percent said stations conducted analytics reports to assess tone (negative/positive/neutral) weekly, while 50 percent did so on most days and 25 percent reported never conducting such analysis.

*Added value revenue.* Of respondents, 12.5 percent agreed strongly that their stations received much added value revenue from clients by providing social media support for client events, while 50 percent agreed, 12.5 percent disagreed, and 25 percent disagreed strongly. In sum, 62.5 percent of respondents agreed or agreed strongly that social media support for client events added much to revenues.

*Analytics as part of the sale.* Of respondents, 12.5 percent agreed strongly that their sales staff sold analytics services as part of their packages, while 50 percent agreed, 12.5 percent disagreed, and 25 percent disagreed strongly. With percentages remarkably similar to the previous question, one should note that 62.5 percent of respondents agreed or agreed strongly that sales representatives sold analytics services to their clients.

*Barriers to social media support for client events.* While a majority of respondents agreed that social media support for client events was routine, some respondents provided insight into the barriers preventing such support. Among the barriers was a concern for programming purity: "Unless we're doing a major promotion with an advertiser, we keep our social media to promote the stations. If we didn't, our posts would be nothing but advertiser driven—something we believe listeners would get tired of." Another respondent opined that "the old school sales system isn't built for quick turnaround on social media." Still another respondent pointed to a lack of client interest or understanding of social media: "They often don't see how it could help grow their business or they say they don't have the staff to concentrate on social media." In short, lack of client enthusiasm explains some barriers, while concern for avoiding distractions from station messaging also emerged. Other responses addressed problems with sales representatives overpromising and a lack of client communication to make campaigns flow efficiently.

*Barriers to analytics as additional client service.* Again, 62.5 percent agreed that sales representatives routinely offered social media analytics as a client service, but barriers were identified by others. The most frequently cited problem was sales representative knowledge: "Some of our sales representatives don't quite comprehend the components of social media so it's hard for them to explain the importance of analytics and a thriving social media page." Similarly, the "old dogs" who are often the highest billers "don't know what they're talking about and don't care to learn." Still others pointed to motivation, saying that sales representatives "lack training and have greater interest in the immediate gain of a contract." These sentiments illustrate some of the problems in station sales representatives becoming social media analytics providers.

With an admittedly small sample hampering generalization, a more rich understanding of radio cluster social media efforts was sought. Two in-depth interviews were conducted: one with a director of digital media at a large market cluster and a second with a director of promotions in a small, yet rated, market. They'll be examined in that order.

*Large market.* The director of digital media dispelled any notions that the resources one might expect at a large corporate concern would necessarily lead to a sophisticated method for analytics. He spoke of a disciplined, weekly approach to their analytics that included examination of their Facebook, Twitter, and Instagram accounts. However, rather than using software capable of deep dives, they use the readily available features provided by the platforms themselves. For instance, they make regular use of Facebook's "7 Day Insight Tool" across all of the cluster stations. They are primarily interested in knowing about audience reach across the day parts in order to advise the personalities on the type of content that they ought to post. They do not assess tone systematically, but will note particulars if they observe a negative thread unfolding. In addition to the jocks, this cluster has three people on staff who do nothing but create additional video and textual content and analyze impact. So, while there does not appear to be a sophisticated level of analytics in this scenario, the approach to the information is methodical. The interviewee also pointed out that a recent high-profile, on-air hire was identified for his social media following and acumen rather than his on-air skills (which he described as mediocre at best).

In terms of this cluster's sales representatives providing analytics services, he noted that there are no front-end analytics sales. However, sales staff will use analytics in order to demonstrate the effectiveness of campaigns sold to the client. Their stations do sell added-value social media streams such as Facebook Live at a local air and water show. Additionally, sales representatives do sell online digital impressions.

*Small market.* The director of promotions at the small market cluster also described a scenario wherein only open-source tools were used for analytics purposes. In particular, she makes use of the Google Analytics settings for Facebook. This provides more information than simply tracking "likes," "shares," and "comments." A relatively simple setup results in data about who is visiting the station websites, who has clicked through to the landing page, and who wants to know more about the stations. In general, she looks for information about her cluster but does compare data with the other clusters in the market.

This cluster does not approach these analytics in any disciplined way. As one might imagine, the small market operation is somewhat dependent on part-time and student intern help. As such, the analytics take place when they have extra time or if a particular compelling question prompts collection of data. There are no systematic periods of time or search terms examined on a regular basis. Moreover, the part-time help is not given any systematic training on when and how to provide data. They are given open-source articles to read for advice on how and when to post to social media for maximum benefit. They will occasionally do "best practices for social media" searches for additional advice. It is fair to describe this approach to cluster social media efforts as a bit of an afterthought, easily attributable to a small, stretched staff.

Like the large market cluster, the small market group does not offer any upfront sale of analytics services. This is explained first by "the sales veterans being unmotivated and unknowledgeable about social media," most likely because they are more likely to tend to the larger, annual contracts and their renewal rather than the novelty of a social media analytics sale. Insofar as the sale of airtime is somewhat abstract to begin with, one might see how sales staff would be reluctant to sell the even more abstract value of "intelligence." Second, the cluster's management opines that a focus on sale of the analytics would detract from the value of its primary product, spot inventory.

However, social media analytics and digital media advice do come into play when servicing larger clients. When trying to offer premium service for an important account, representatives will receive the on-board analytics data from the part-time staff in order to demonstrate the success of a previous campaign or to identify potential vulnerabilities from competitors. Likewise, a larger client is apt to receive a complimentary website evaluation using an online platform called sitebeam.net. This tool will assess a client's website with an overall score plus measures of quality for accessibility, content, marketing, and technical strength (user interface, navigation, etc.). It offers additional advice for mobile optimization, traffic and awareness, and audience retargeting potential. In this sense, the analytics services have value but are not fodder for contract/sale.

The small market interviewee mentioned one additional concern of note. Multiple people creating content postings for a cluster can create problems. Air personalities should, of course, create their content and postings in accordance with their branding and programmatic expectations. However, having multiple part-time staff responsible for posting station-wide announcements and content can lead to problems of duplication and misinformation (e.g., different understandings of how a contest is being executed). The lesson here is that clusters without social-media-dedicated staff will need to be extra cautious in terms of assignment of social media responsibilities and intragroup communication.

## Conclusion

While the results should be considered most tentative, this chapter presented evidence that (1) stations do monitor social media for assessment of their reach; (2) they do monitor questions of tone in order to protect their image/reputation, albeit this monitoring is informal and without the value of a purposeful subscription service such as NUVI; (3) some stations are methodical, if unsophisticated, in their social media data collection; and (4) the selling of social media intelligence as a stand-alone product has not yet become part of radio's widespread business model, but sales representatives will use available analytics to please a larger existing client and to demonstrate the effectiveness of previous campaigns with the stations.

The implications from this chapter are primarily threefold: (1) need for systematic data collection, (2) need for professional development/education in social media analytics, and (3) a needed wake-up call to industry about its cooperation with educational institutions.

While it is understandable that some companies would not have the wherewithal to subscribe to sophisticated software offerings, they can take steps to make sure that their data collection is systematic. Just as staffs meet regularly to discuss the weekly calendar, problems/opportunities to be investigated, and overall station direction, personnel doing social media analytics should be required to perform their duties (part-time or otherwise) in a systematic fashion. Standing analytics time periods, search terms, and manual reading of commentary should be written down as station policy and procedure so that the data collected can be considered reliable.

As social media platforms proliferate and their use becomes more central for reception of station messaging/content and more relevant to station clients, social media analytics training needs to be more systematic and important in the skill set of the entry-level employee. Toward this end, stations should seek out from colleges and universities those students who have had course work and practical application experience with these analytic tools. Some universities (such as the one described in a scenario earlier) have dedicated social media laboratories where the next generation of communication professionals are being educated broadly to serve many industries. Broadcasters should identify these schools and become partners in job pipelines with them.

Finally, industry cooperation with education *must improve at the cluster level*. The National Association of Broadcasters has a strong partnership with the Broadcast Education Association at the national level, and many state broadcast associations (including the Illinois Broadcasters Association with its regular academics programming and benefits for educators) have strong relationships with America's colleges and universities. However, the primary limitation of this study (the low *cluster* response rate) speaks to not only an unwillingness at the management level to cooperate in creation of new knowledge that might aid the industry, but a lack of concern for its future talent development (understood broadly).

Lest the reader interpret the above paragraph as mere irritation on the author's part in response to a low response rate, consider a previous study. A graduate thesis (author not identified here in order to prevent identification of parties involved) examining the factors contributing to high radio sales representative attrition received scant response from sampled station cluster management in spite of direct mailings sent to named managers and follow-up emails. At long last, the investigator was forced to call stations to ask for their participation given the relevance of the topic to radio revenues. One follow-up call was met with consternation from a general manager with the dismissive statement, "You know, we don't really have a lot of time for surveys like this." Of course, this would beg the question of whether that GM had a lot of time for continually retraining new sales personnel.

In short, media scholars stand as a valuable resource engaged in questions of extreme relevance to local managers. Academe begs for their cooperation.

## References

Al-Rawi, A. (2016). Understanding the social media of radio stations. *Journal of Radio and Audio Media, 23,* 50–67.
Ashworth, S. (2017, August 31). Report: Digital threats demand that radio evolve. *Radioworld.com*. Retrieved from www.radioworld.com/news-and-business/report-digital-threats-demand-that-radio-evolve
Audio today: Radio 2016—Appealing far and wide. (2016, February 25). *Nielsen.com*. Retrieved from www.nielsen.com/us/en/insights/reports/2016/audio-today-radio-2016-appealing-far-and-wide.html
Fan, W., & Gordon, M. D. (2014). The power of social media analytics. *Communications of the ACM, 57*(6), 74–81.
Final reading on Q2 GDP up 3.1% v. 3% rise expected. (2017, September 28). *CNBC.com*. Retrieved from www.cnbc.com/2017/09/28/final-reading-on-q2-2017-gross-domestic-product.html
Finding new ways to generate revenue. (2007, January 2). *Entrepreneur.com*. www.entrepreneur.com/article/172496
Fowler, F. J. (2013). *Survey research methods.* Thousand Oaks, CA: Sage.
Internet talk radio. (n.d.). *Museum.media.org*. Retrieved from https://museum.media.org/radio/
Kagan: Radio revenues climb 1.1% to $17.8 billion in 2018. (2018, June 28). *Insideradio.com*. Retrieved from www.insideradio.com/kagan-radio-revenues-climb-to-billion-in/article_fa5faeee-7a94-11e8-b009-07a867dfdbc9.html
Khan, G. F. (2015). *Seven layers of social media analytics: Mining business insights from social media text, actions, networks, hyperlinks, apps, search engine, and location data.* Create Space Independent Publishing Platform.

Radio facts and figures. (2017). *Newsgeneration.com*. Retrieved from www.newsgeneration.com/broadcast-resources/radio-facts-and-figures/

Radio's digital ad revenue grew double digits in 2016. (2017, March 28). *Insideradio.com*. Retrieved from www.insideradio.com/radio-s-digital-ad-revenue-grew-double-digits-in/article_7986db56-137c-11e7-a4d1-875f50b7c499.html

Social media update 2014. (2015, January 9). *Pewinternet.org*. Retrieved from www.pewinternet.org/2015/01/09/social-media-update-2014/

Video killed the radio star. (2017, November 12). Retrieved from museum.media.org/radio/

# Part II
# Programming Matters
••••••••••••••••••••
Localism, Personalities, and Audiences

# 5

## The Shrinking Electronic Town Square

••••••••••••••••••••

Localism in American Talk Radio

DAVID CRIDER

The 2016 presidential election, one of the most bitterly fought campaigns in American history, symbolized a growing trend of nationalized political discourse. Presidential politics occupy a far greater share of Americans' attention than matters that directly affect their lives and families (Brooks & Collins, 2016). Local congressional races are seen as referenda on the national political picture (Kilgore, 2017), rather than a decision of who can best serve the needs of their district. The nationalizing of politics has been spurred in large part by the nationalizing of talk radio. In the wake of rampant ownership consolidation in the radio industry, nationally syndicated shows have replaced local voices and forums for discussing community issues. Although the reasons given are varied (e.g., less expensive to run satellite programming, company-wide layoffs, raising a station's profile by association with a popular national host), talk-formatted stations have shown an increasing preference for national programming over local.

This chapter advances the study of talk radio localism by converting previous research (Crider, 2012) into a longitudinal study. This study is informed by the sociological and political theories of Jürgen Habermas. Habermas's concepts of the public sphere and deliberative democracy serve as a proper theoretical foundation for studying localism in talk radio, aided by enhancements to the concepts from more recent scholars (Jacobson, 2006; Poindexter, 2016). Local radio is an important dissemination point for information to the community, and a lack of local content inhibits this flow of information. Public sphere theory indicates that a decrease in local programming produces clear and harmful effects on democracy at both the local and national levels, limiting both the opportunities for uninhibited discussion and the topics available to discuss. A comparison to the previous data will determine whether the presence of local talk radio continues to decline or is holding steady in the face of corporate downsizing. This analysis will not only help to recognize recent trends in radio localism, but also provide a basis for speculation about the future of local talk radio programming.

## Talk Radio and the Public Sphere

Habermas (2006) describes the public sphere as "an intermediary system between state and society" (p. 412) and as crucial to modern democracies as private autonomy and equality of citizenship. The public sphere is the centerpiece of Habermas's proposal of a deliberative form of democracy, one that privileges cooperation and a search for solutions rather than ideological purity or self-interest. Through the introduction of relevant topics and claims into the public sphere, people can evaluate and negotiate justifiable and reasonable outcomes to societal problems. The institutional design of such a democracy should guarantee not only free association and communication rights (consistent with the ideals of free press and speech), but also regulation that preserves an independent and diverse mass media.

The public sphere is not necessarily limited to discussions of hard news or political affairs, and Jacobson (2006) notes that the modern media also spread ideas through entertainment programs. Spoken-word radio has often straddled the line between information and entertainment; talk radio hosts seek to inform while using humor or exaggeration to make their points (Crider, 2016). Even on sports and lifestyle talk programs, political discussions may occasionally arise within the context of the show's primary subject area. Even on-air discussions about everyday matters can have political implications (Poindexter, 2016).

Habermas's concept of the public sphere is not without its critics. Although Habermas (2006) argues that the deliberative paradigm is designed to promote inclusivity and equal opportunity for participation, Poindexter (2016) notes that the emphasis on the public over the private and personal tends to exclude issues of importance to women or minorities. He adds that society has multiple public spheres, each reflecting the needs of culturally distinct groups, thus challenging Habermas's conception of one, homogeneous public sphere. Poindexter argues that talk radio can better align with a concept of the public sphere that emphasizes public voices and lets the public have their say in a less idealized manner.

Poindexter (2016) explains that radio stations and networks can create a viable and truly democratic public sphere when they accomplish three objectives. First, the target audience must bring together diverse segments of society, serving multiple demographics in such a way as to bridge differences among them. Second, the station or network must promote an atmosphere where listeners can feel free to express themselves at length or without interference from station personnel (hosts or producers). Finally, the station must be able to achieve financial sustainability so that it may continue providing such a forum in perpetuity.

## Localism in Decline

Talk radio has the capability to accomplish all of these things, but it is far more difficult to do so when programming caters to aggregated national audiences instead of a local community. The trend toward nationalized programming gathered steam in the flurry of consolidation that followed the Telecommunications Act of 1996, which severely deregulated radio. Corporate owners began to streamline program sourcing, preferring the economies of scale that allow one program to air in many markets (Conti, 2012). A handful of talk radio hosts had already achieved national prominence by the mid-1990s, but following the Telecommunications Act, consolidated owners such as Clear Channel and CBS began putting together full daily lineups of syndicated hosts to program their stations (Hilliard & Keith, 2005). Ironically, as programming sources were becoming more nationalized, talk radio was becoming more segmented, reorganizing audiences from a basis in location to a basis in political philosophy, and preventing substantive debate among different points of view (Poindexter, 2016).

These programming decisions reflect a growing preference for economic reasoning over proper discourse that Habermas calls "colonization of the lifeworld" (Jacobson, 2006, p. 29). As media industries become more concerned with financial priorities such as budgetary limits or debt concerns, the media will fail to represent the full range of cultural and political interests found in our society (Jacobson, 2006). Habermas (2006) admits that the commercial imperative of mass media to deliver an audience to advertisers has led to a commodification of programming, under which political journalism is being phased out, thus harming the public sphere and deliberative politics along with it. Jacobson (2006) argues that market priorities do not work well in all areas of the social world: "Producing representative and responsive public opinion is not like producing shoe laces" (p. 33).

The deregulation of radio ownership has clearly led to a shift in priorities from providing forums for local information and entertainment to financial concerns. Erickson (2017) laments that the sole imperative of the radio industry in the post-consolidation era is a constant slashing of expenses. The promised increases in advertising revenue from consolidation have failed to materialize. In fact, advertising rates are declining because the largest owners are so desperate to pay off their staggering debts that they have been forced to offer advertising time at bargain-basement prices. Lower revenues lead to even tighter budgets.

Since 1990, the number of broadcasting jobs has fallen by 27 percent; the industry lost nearly twenty thousand jobs between 2007 and 2010, as overleveraged radio companies buckled under the Great Recession ("Number of Broadcasting," 2016). Most of those jobs were in the areas of on-air talent and news. Meanwhile, radio mergers have continued: Alpha Media acquired Digity in 2015, nearly doubling the number of stations it owns ("Alpha Media Buys," 2015), and Entercom acquired CBS's radio division in 2017 ("CBS Radio Merges," 2017). Despite vows by leaders of Alpha and Entercom that they recognize the importance of local radio, the ultimate impact on local content at these larger companies remains to be seen. Local public radio stations are often lauded as the last bastion of local community reporting (Walker, 2017), but even those stations are often networked together, putting one regional news service over several local transmitters.

Taken together with the closure of many daily newspapers, these mergers and layoffs have turned many local communities into what *Columbia Journalism Review* terms "news deserts" (Bucay, Elliott, Kamin, & Park, 2017). Coverage of local and state governments has dramatically reduced, thereby leading to growing inattention to local issues (Brooks & Collins, 2016). By keeping listeners tuned to mostly national concerns on a daily basis, listeners begin to believe that only national issues matter. Simon (2016) notes that talk radio's obsession with presidential politics has caused many important local issues, such as ballot initiatives, to be ignored. *New York Times* columnist Arthur Brooks summarizes, "People are rooted in their hometowns—maybe even stuck—but not really engaged in them. The worst of all possible worlds. The result is that they stay in a terrible job market and keep their kids in failing schools, while complaining about the faraway federal government and the national election as if Donald Trump or Hillary Clinton were going to make their lives so much worse or better" (Brooks & Collins, 2016). The trend toward nationalized media and nationalized political discourse reflects a decline in localism. Localism in the media refers to a preference for both local control and local content (Croteau & Hoynes, 2001). Dunbar-Hester (2013) argues that localism is a fluid concept that covers such concerns as coverage of local affairs, public safety and disaster preparedness, and community autonomy. She finds the term usually defined in opposition to syndicated/automated programming or as a counterweight to corporate hegemony. Although radio has long promoted increased local content as a response to nationalized programming (Parmett, 2016), the issue of localism has especially gained traction as consolidated radio has eliminated local air talent and autonomy.

## Study of Declining Localism

A previous study of ninety-three local spoken-word radio stations found local programming to be less prevalent on small-market stations, which contributes to a shrinking public sphere in lesser populated parts of the country. Although corporate owner size did not impact these programming decisions, it was clear that the important local issues of these communities were being ignored. There were plenty of opportunities for small-market listeners to hear about and form opinions on national politics, but little chance to discuss local government in the unique forum that talk radio can provide (Crider, 2012).

Since this study was conducted, more scholarly evidence of declining localism in broadcasting has been gathered. Lacy et al. (2013) studied local government coverage by radio stations, finding that the downsized radio newsrooms had fewer and less diverse sources than their print competitors. They also produced fewer stories than print. If a station had competition in their local market, there was a weak but significant relationship with higher and more diverse sourcing. Public radio stations were singled out for having more and better sources in their local government stories, as opposed to commercial stations. Unfortunately, a limited number of markets had public stations that covered local news.

## Hypotheses and Research Questions

Consistent with the original study of talk radio localism (Crider, 2012), this updated study used the same two hypotheses:

> H1: There will be more local content on news/talk radio stations in larger markets.

> H2: There will be less local content on news/talk radio stations owned by larger corporations.

To address the longitudinal concerns of this study, three research questions were added:

> RQ1: How has the state of talk radio localism changed since the original study?

> RQ2: How has the state of localism changed in smaller markets since the original study?

> RQ3: Has ownership size made a difference in the state of localism since the original study?

## Methodology

This study was conducted through a content analysis of news/talk radio station websites because station websites provide the most readily available source of program schedules. Data collection and analysis took place in the spring of 2017, just over seven years after the initial analysis. The samples were chosen through cluster sampling. The 274 markets rated by Nielsen Audio were broken up into three categories based on population: large markets (population of one million+), medium-sized markets (population of 400,000 to one million), and small markets (population less than 400,000). The country was then divided into five regions (Northeast, Midwest, West, Southeast, and Southwest), and the markets were chosen through a random number generator, based on their Nielsen size ranking. Ten markets were chosen from each category (two from each region) for a total of thirty samples.

Every talk-formatted station in each market was considered, including sports talk stations. Most were found through Nielsen audio ratings data from Radio Online, an industry website ("Nielsen Audio Ratings," 2017); stations not subscribing to Nielsen were found through the radio locator website. Corporate owners were categorized as either "large" or "small." The "large" companies were those ranked in the most recent available listing of the top ten radio groups by revenue; these companies had annual revenues between $224 million and $2.6 billion ("iHeart Tops Industry," 2016). In addition, stations owned by Salem, Hearst, and Scripps were coded as large due to the overall size of these media conglomerates. All other owners were considered small. Because of the focus on corporate radio owners, noncommercial (e.g., National Public Radio) stations were excluded.

Of the 124 stations selected for analysis, 57 were in large markets, 39 were in medium-sized markets, and 28 were in small markets. Breaking the sample down by region, there were 21 stations in the Northeast, 24 in the Southeast, 23 in the Midwest, 29 in the Southwest, and 27 in the West. Overall, there were 55 news/talk stations, 11 talk stations, and 58 sports talk stations. Sixty-four stations were owned by what were considered large radio groups, and 60 had small corporate owners. Eight of the 124 stations did not list their broadcast schedules on their websites, and therefore were excluded from data analysis.

The on-air lineup provided on each station's website was coded for the presence or absence of local content. The hours for which a local personality was listed were coded as "local." When a syndicated personality was listed, or the time slot was not mentioned at all, those hours were coded as "syndicated." Radio stations lacking full program schedules tend to highlight only the local hosts and top syndicated hosts and leave out the network programming that fills their nighttime/overnight shifts. A "local" host was considered to be one whose program was carried in only one market. When a host was featured on stations in multiple markets, he or she was coded as "syndicated." In so doing, the two categories can be considered mutually exclusive (Frey, Botan, Friedman, & Kreps, 1992).

Talk shows are often carried on a tape-delay basis or are rebroadcast from earlier in the day; therefore, the live or prerecorded nature of the program was not considered as a separate category. Only the regular Monday to Friday programming lineup was considered as the weekday time period receives the most regular listening. Interruptions for live sports were disregarded, though mentioned in notes as an extension of local programming when warranted.

Two coders were used for this study: one was the researcher and the other was a student assistant. Intercoder reliability was determined by having each coder go through a separate reliability sample of ten station websites from three markets (one large, one medium, one small). Percentage agreement for the reliability sample was .70, and Krippendorff's alpha was .88 (Krippendorff's alpha was calculated by SPSS). The sample was then divided between the two coders; each coder had ninety-two station websites, allowing them to overlap on sixty. Disagreements during coding of the full sample were resolved by taking Coder 1's decision on the first disagreement, Coder 2's on the second, Coder 1's on the next, and so on. Percentage agreement for the full study sample was .54, and Krippendorff's alpha was .81; the latter number is considered an acceptable level of intercoder reliability (Lombard, Snyder-Duch, & Bracken, 2002).

## Results

To begin data analysis, cross tabulations were run for descriptive purposes, using the "local" and "syndicated" categories of programming and the three categories of market size. The numbers of hours coded for "local" and "syndicated" programming were collapsed into four categories: 0–5.9 hours, 6–11.9 hours, 12–17.9 hours, and 18–24 hours (see Tables 5.1 and 5.2 for full results). H1 was tested by means of a one-way ANOVA, using the numbers of local and syndicated hours of programming for each station and the three categories of market size. Because in some cases the hours of talk programming did not add up to twenty-four (e.g., day-timer stations that sign off at night, or stations that run other types of programming for part of the broadcast day), the local and syndicated hours were recoded into percentage variables. Another ANOVA was then run with the percentage data. An independent $t$-test was conducted to test H2, using the hours of programming and the "large" and "small" categories of corporate owner. As with the first hypothesis, the recoded percentage variables were then used for an additional test.

The results of the first ANOVA certainly found an inverse relationship between market size and amount of local versus syndicated programming. Only seven large-market stations programmed more than eighteen hours of local talk in a day, but there was a near-balance among the other three categories in terms of number of stations. Although there are many options for both local and

### Table 5.1
### Cross-tabulation of Amount of Local Talk Programming by Market Size and Size of Station Owner

| How many hours of local talk programming does this station run each weekday? | What size market is this station in? | | | What size corporation owns this station? | |
|---|---|---|---|---|---|
| | Large | Medium | Small | Large | Small |
| 0–5.9 hours | 17 | 25 | 18 | 28 | 32 |
| 6–11.9 hours | 14 | 9 | 6 | 16 | 13 |
| 12–17.9 hours | 15 | 4 | 1 | 13 | 7 |
| 18–24 hours | 7 | 0 | 0 | 5 | 2 |
| | (N=53) | (N=38) | (N=25) | (N=62) | (N=54) |
| | $p<.01$ | | | | |

### Table 5.2
### Cross-tabulation of Amount of Syndicated Talk Programming by Market Size and Size of Station Owner

| How many hours of syndicated talk programming does this station run each weekday? | What size market is this station in? | | | What size corporation owns this station? | |
|---|---|---|---|---|---|
| | Large | Medium | Small | Large | Small |
| 0–5.9 hours | 8 | 2 | 0 | 5 | 5 |
| 6–11.9 hours | 13 | 3 | 2 | 13 | 5 |
| 12–17.9 hours | 12 | 4 | 4 | 9 | 11 |
| 18–24 hours | 20 | 29 | 19 | 35 | 33 |
| | (N=53) | (N=38) | (N=25) | (N=62) | (N=54) |
| | $p<.01$ | | | | |

syndicated programming on large-market talk stations, medium and small markets are not so fortunate. No station outside of the large markets offers more than eighteen hours of local content per day, and only one small-market station offers more than twelve (KTTU-FM in Lubbock, Texas, which features daily play-by-play of Texas Tech University sporting events). Twenty-five of the thirty-eight medium-market stations offered less than six hours of local programming per day, as did eighteen of the twenty-five small-market stations. The results of this ANOVA were found to be statistically significant. The follow-up ANOVA that used the percentage data found similar results, though these results were not statistically significant (see Table 5.3).

The stations airing less than six hours of local content mostly relegated local shows to morning drive time (5–9 A.M.), afternoon drive time (2–6 or 3–7 P.M.), or portions of both. Many news/talk stations were local only during the morning drive, although others strategically scheduled their only local show opposite a national host on a rival station. KFAB-AM in Omaha breaks up its mostly local daytime schedule for Rush Limbaugh from 11 A.M. to 2 P.M. Competitor KOIL-AM has placed its one local talk show during that time period, giving

## Table 5.3
## One-Way Analyses of Variance for Amount of Local and Syndicated Talk Programming by Market Size

| | What size market is this station in? | | | | |
|---|---|---|---|---|---|
| Variable | Large Mean (SD) | Medium Mean (SD) | Small Mean (SD) | F | df |
| Hours of local programming per day* | 9.72 (7.08) | 4.74 (4.48) | 3.68 (3.14) | 13.51[a] | 115 |
| Hours of syndicated programming per day* | 13.76 (7.30) | 18.71 (5.57) | 19.72 (3.81) | 11.11[a] | 115 |
| Amount of talk programming that is local** | 0.42 (0.30) | 0.21 (0.21) | 0.16 (0.13) | 12.78 | 115 |
| Amount of talk programming that is syndicated** | 0.58 (0.30) | 0.79 (0.21) | 0.84 (0.13) | 12.78 | 115 |

*Results were coded 0 to 24 hours per day.
**Percentage expressed as a decimal.
[a] $p < .01$.

Omaha listeners the option of local programming from 5 A.M. to 6 P.M. Sports stations were heavily dependent on programming from one of the major syndicators (ESPN, CBS Sports, NBC Sports, or Fox Sports). Some of the medium and small markets (e.g., Fresno, Allentown-Bethlehem) had only one local show for the entire market, despite having multiple sports stations; other markets had no local sports talk shows at all.

In determining whether ownership size plays a role in these programming decisions, the *t*-test results actually favored larger owners. Stations owned by larger companies were found to air over two more hours of local programming per day than their smaller competitors (see Table 5.4). Two stations owned by smaller companies (KSL-AM in Salt Lake City and KEBC-AM in Oklahoma City) have more than eighteen hours of local content daily, as opposed to five stations owned by larger companies. A majority of the small-owner stations (32 of 54) aired less than six hours of local talk shows per day, while a majority of the large-owner stations (34 of 62) aired at least six local hours daily. Unlike in the previous study, the local programming *t*-test results were found to be statistically significant, though the results for syndicated programming were not.

To address the research questions dealing with changes over time since the original study, the original data from December 2009 were imported into the data set. An independent *t*-test was then conducted to see if the changes in local programming were statistically significant, breaking down the results by market size and ownership size. Overall, there was virtually no change in the amount of local programming from the first study to the second. Ownership size did not

### Table 5.4
### Independent $t$ Test for Amount of Local and Syndicated Talk Programming by Size of Station Owner

| | Station owner | | | |
| --- | --- | --- | --- | --- |
| | Large Mean (SD) | Small Mean (SD) | | |
| Variable | (N = 63) | (N = 53) | $t$ value | df |
| Hours of local talk programming per day | 7.85 (6.90) | 5.52 (5.07) | −2.03[a] | 114 |
| Hours of syndicated talk programming per day | 15.93 (7.03) | 17.55 (6.14) | 1.31 | 114 |
| Amount of talk programming that is local | 0.33 (0.29) | 0.25 (0.23) | −1.65 | 114 |
| Amount of talk programming that is syndicated | 0.67 (0.29) | 0.75 (0.23) | 1.65 | 114 |

*Results were coded 0 to 24 hours per day.
**Percentage expressed as a decimal.
[a] $p < .05$.

make much of a difference and changes were minimal for both large owners and small owners.

When broken down by market size, changes became more apparent. In smaller markets, local programming decreased by one hour per day from 2009 to 2017; local programming in medium-sized markets decreased by over half an hour per day. Local programming increased in larger markets by a small amount. Accordingly, the daily hours of syndicated programming increased in small and medium markets, while declining slightly in large markets (see Table 5.5). None of these results reached statistical significance; the increase in syndicated programming in small markets fell just shy of the $p < .05$ level. Similar results were found when using percentages of local and national programming (see Table 5.6), though, again, none of these results reached statistical significance.

Two markets (Louisville and Pittsburgh) were selected for both the original 2009 sample and the more recent sample; these two markets form a good case study to break out from the larger data set. All four Louisville stations from the original sample are under the same ownership and formats they had in 2009. Changes in the balance between local and national programming have been minor at the three stations owned by iHeartMedia: news/talk WHAS-AM went from thirteen local hours to twelve, sports-formatted WKRD-AM increased from eight and a half local hours to ten, and news/talk WKJK-AM remained at four local hours per day. Salem-owned WGTK-AM has maintained its completely syndicated schedule throughout. Overall, little has changed in this market.

Three Pittsburgh stations from the original sample still programmed spoken-word formats in 2017. CBS-owned KDKA-AM added an extra hour of local talk programming in the years between studies, going from seventeen to eighteen local hours per day. iHeartMedia-owned WBGG-AM held steady at

### Table 5.5
**Independent *t* Test for Hours of Local and Syndicated Talk Programming, 2009–2017**

| Variable | 2009 Mean (SD) | 2017 Mean (SD) | t value | df |
|---|---|---|---|---|
| Hours of local talk programming per day—overall | 6.83 (5.42) | 6.79 (6.22) | 0.06 | 207 |
| Hours of syndicated talk programming per day—overall | 16.29 (5.74) | 16.67 (6.66) | −0.43 | 203 |
| Hours of local talk programming per day—small markets | 4.67 (4.41) | 3.68 (3.14) | 0.90 | 46 |
| Hours of syndicated talk programming per day—small markets | 16.96 (6.05) | 19.72 (3.81) | −1.91 | 46 |
| Hours of local talk programming per day—medium markets | 5.36 (4.24) | 4.73 (4.48) | 0.59 | 68 |
| Hours of syndicated talk programming per day—medium markets | 17.78 (4.37) | 18.71 (5.57) | −0.75 | 66 |
| Hours of local talk programming per day—large markets | 9.38 (5.92) | 9.72 (7.08) | −0.24 | 89 |
| Hours of syndicated talk programming per day—large markets | 14.61 (6.23) | 13.76 (7.30) | 0.57 | 87 |
| Hours of local talk programming per day—small owner | 5.87 (4.71) | 5.52 (5.07) | 0.32 | 86 |
| Hours of syndicated talk programming per day—small owner | 17.19 (5.35) | 17.55 (6.14) | −0.27 | 82 |
| Hours of local talk programming per day—large owner | 7.41 (5.77) | 7.85 (6.90) | −0.38 | 119 |
| Hours of syndicated talk programming per day—large owner | 15.80 (5.92) | 15.93 (7.03) | −0.11 | 119 |

seven hours of local sports talk each day. The third station, sports-formatted WEAE-AM, changed owners. In 2009, ABC-owned WEAE aired eight hours of local shows each day. Now owned by Salem, the rebranded WPGP airs that company's syndicated lineup of conservative talk, although the station does include two local hours per day. However, this loss of local programming was more than offset by CBS's addition of sports-formatted KDKA-FM, which features over sixteen hours of local shows each day.

## Discussion

As in the original study, H1 was supported. Outside of large markets, local talk radio content can be difficult to find outside of morning and/or afternoon drive

## Table 5.6
**Independent *t* Test for Amount of Local and Syndicated Talk Programming, 2009–2017**

| Variable | 2009 Mean (SD) | 2017 Mean (SD) | t value | df |
|---|---|---|---|---|
| Amount of talk programming that is local—overall | 0.29 (0.24) | 0.30 (0.27) | −0.12 | 203 |
| Amount of talk programming that is syndicated—overall | 0.71 (0.24) | 0.70 (0.27) | 0.12 | 203 |
| Amount of talk programming that is local—small markets | 0.23 (0.24) | 0.16 (0.13) | 10.25 | 46 |
| Amount of talk programming that is syndicated—small markets | 0.77 (0.24) | 0.84 (0.13) | −10.25 | 46 |
| Amount of talk programming that is local—medium markets | 0.22 (0.17) | 0.21 (0.21) | −0.20 | 66 |
| Amount of talk programming that is syndicated—medium markets | 0.78 (0.17) | 0.79 (0.21) | 0.20 | 66 |
| Amount of talk programming that is local—large markets | 0.39 (0.26) | 0.42 (0.30) | −0.50 | 87 |
| Amount of talk programming that is syndicated—large markets | 0.61 (0.26) | 0.58 (0.30) | 0.50 | 87 |
| Amount of talk programming that is local—small owner | 0.24 (0.21) | 0.25 (0.23) | −0.23 | 82 |
| Amount of talk programming that is syndicated—small owner | 0.76 (0.21) | 0.75 (0.23) | 0.23 | 82 |
| Amount of talk programming that is local—large owner | 0.32 (0.25) | 0.33 (0.29) | −0.28 | 119 |
| Amount of talk programming that is syndicated—large owner | 0.68 (0.25) | 0.67 (0.29) | 0.28 | 119 |

time. In large markets, listeners can often find multiple talk stations and multiple sports talk stations, which gives them many options for hearing issues of local importance or national issues if they prefer. There are fewer options in smaller markets. Even if the market contains multiple talk and/or sports stations, these stations pit one mostly syndicated lineup against another. As a result, small and medium-sized markets continue to lack a vibrant broadcast public sphere for discussions of local issues.

Once again, H2 was not supported, and this time the results were significant. Larger companies were found to program more local content; however, larger companies possess a greater share of large-market stations, owning thirty-six of the fifty-three stations in the large-market sample. Of the sixty-three medium- and small-market stations, only twenty-six were owned by larger companies. This emphasis on larger-market stations may explain why consolidated radio owners were found to have programmed more local content overall. For example, iHeartMedia-owned stations in Houston, Cincinnati, and Los Angeles featured over sixteen hours of daily local talk, but medium-market stations owned by iHeartMedia had less than six hours of local content per day.

Of course, there are also markets that could serve as case studies for smaller companies looking to provide a proper local public sphere for their listeners. One such case is Akron, Ohio. iHeartMedia's WHLO-AM programmed only three hours of local talk per day—typical for this company in its smaller markets—but two rival news/talk stations owned by smaller companies featured much larger local presences. WNIR-FM, owned by Media-Com, boasted seventeen and a half hours of local programming each day, and Rubber City Radio's WAKR-AM had thirteen local hours on its weekday schedule. For a smaller market that lives in the shadow of large-market Cleveland, Akron has a very active broadcast public sphere, aided by a healthy presence of both local ownership and local content (Croteau & Hoynes, 2001).

In answer to the research questions, the overall state of talk radio localism continues to decline. Despite the lack of statistical significance, the data showing a decrease in local hours in small and medium-sized markets cannot be ignored. Such decreases are consistent with the moves of radio companies to downsize local content and expand national offerings in recent years. What's more, the modest decline in local programming provided by smaller companies suggests that they too face tightened programming budgets, no doubt caused by being forced to cut advertising rates to compete with their consolidated competitors (Erickson, 2017). When a station cannot achieve financial sustainability due to diminished advertising revenue, it sacrifices the opportunities to bring a community together through open discussion forums (Poindexter, 2016). Once again, financial concerns predominate over a need to foster discourse (Jacobson, 2006).

## Conclusion

Radio, especially talk radio, is capable of providing an active public sphere for listeners (Poindexter, 2016). When it comes to issues of local importance, it is imperative that listeners have the opportunity to hear and contribute to on-air discussions of things that affect their everyday lives. Emphasis on the national political discourse that comes with eliminating local programming causes further erosion of the mediated public sphere and an ill-informed public that does not know or understand what is happening in their own backyard (Brooks & Collins, 2016). Unfortunately, it is clear that outside of the nation's largest markets this damage to American political discourse continues to occur.

The quantitative content analysis format is helpful for a big-picture presentation of localism, but a closer, case-study analysis could also help shed some light on how talk radio localism has changed in recent years. A qualitative textual analysis of talk stations in one or a limited number of markets could specifically show how stations use local content. Are attempts made to "sound" local during mostly syndicated programming? Is a local morning show heavily reliant on regular syndicated segments for content? Another possible direction for future research could come from studying localism in entertainment-based radio formats. As noted above, talk radio is not the only radio format that allows for the dispensing of information into the public sphere (Jacobson, 2006; Poindexter, 2016). Music radio formats also spur listener engagement, and a large majority of listeners across a variety of music formats have shown a preference for live on-air personalities over prerecorded announcements (Jacobs, 2015).

Shining a light on the issue of localism, and the harm being done to radio as a public sphere, brings with it a call to action to prevent further damage. The FCC may further undermine localism by eliminating the Main Studio Rule, which requires radio stations to maintain a physical presence in the communities they serve ("FCC Sets Stage," 2017). Without the government requiring the ability to originate local programming from a physical studio, radio companies have license to continue prioritizing their bottom lines over the forums they provide for the public. Not only should the Main Studio Rule remain in place, there should be further action to protect local radio at all levels.

Although a shift to more localized talk radio may not reverse the trend toward nationalization of political discourse, it can at least provide a healthy local public sphere alongside the national one, allowing for balanced attention to each. Erickson (2017) suggests that consolidated owners be broken up through bankruptcy or government action. That scenario is unlikely to happen, but Erickson's thoughts on the matter certainly merit consideration: "It's time to admit this experiment— consolidation—has failed for everyone . . . listeners, employees, especially air talent, local communities . . . except an elite few at the very top of these companies."

## References

Alpha Media buys Digity. (2015, August 4). *All Access*. Retrieved from www.allaccess.com/net-news/archive/story/144178/alpha-media-buys-digity

Brooks, A. C., & Collins, G. (2016, November 8). It's better when all politics is local. *New York Times*. Retrieved from www.nytimes.com/2016/11/08/opinion/campaign-stops/its-better-when-all-politics-is-local.html

Bucay, Y., Elliott, V., Kamin, J., & Park, A. (2017, Spring). America's growing news deserts. *Columbia Journalism Review*. Retrieved from www.cjr.org/local_news/american-news-deserts-donuts-local.php

CBS Radio merges with Entercom, David Field to lead combined company. (2017, February 2). *All Access*. Retrieved from www.allaccess.com/net-news/archive/story/162276/cbs-corporation-and-entercom-announce-merger-of-cb

Conti, C. (2012). Accepting the mutability of broadcast localism: An analytic position. *CommLaw Conspectus, 21,* 106–150.

Crider, D. (2012). A public sphere in decline: The state of localism in talk radio. *Journal of Broadcasting and Electronic Media, 56*(2), 225–244.

Crider, D. (2016). *Performing personality: On-air radio identities in a changing media landscape.* Lanham, MD: Lexington.

Croteau, D., & Hoynes, W. (2001). *The business of media: Corporate media and the public interest.* Thousand Oaks, CA: Pine Forge Press.

Dunbar-Hester, C. (2013). What's local? Localism as a discursive boundary object in low-power radio policymaking. *Communication, Culture & Critique, 6,* 502–524.

Erickson, D. (2017, January 10). The talent pool: The failure of consolidation. *All Access.* Retrieved from www.allaccess.com/talent-pool/archive/25723/the-failure-of-consolidation

FCC sets stage for main studio & media rules redesign. (2017, April 28). *InsideRadio.* Retrieved from www.insideradio.com/free/fcc-sets-stage-for-main-studio-media-rules-redesign/article_d201da14-2be7-11e7-be42-cf82f1bef4a2.html

Frey, L. R., Botan, C. H., Friedman, P. G., & Kreps, G. L. (1992). *Interpreting communication research: A case study approach.* Englewood Cliffs, NJ: Prentice Hall.

Habermas, J. (2006). Political communication in media society: Does democracy still enjoy an epistemic dimension? The impact of normative theory on empirical research. *Communication Theory, 16,* 411–426.

Hilliard, R. L., & Keith, M. C. (2005). *The quieted voice: The rise and demise of localism in American radio.* Carbondale: Southern Illinois University Press.

iHeart tops industry revenue list with $2.6B—BIA/Kelsey. (2016, July 6). *Inside Radio.* Retrieved from www.insideradio.com/free/iheart-tops-industry-revenue-list-with-b-bia-kelsey/article_20a95652-4353-11e6-89ad-af8b4e743d24.html

Jacobs, L. (2015, November 2). Does live & local really matter? *NuVoodoo.* Retrieved from http://blog.nuvoodoo.com/2015/11/02/does-live-local-really-matter

Jacobson, T. (2006). Media development and speech in the public sphere. In Global Forum for Media Development, *Media matters: Perspectives on advancing governance & development from the Global Forum for Media Development* (pp. 27–33). London: Internews Europe.

Kilgore, E. (2017, June 21). Republicans win Georgia's special election, Democrats search for a moral victory. *New York.* Retrieved from http://nymag.com/daily/intelligencer/2017/06/handel-edges-ossoff-in-georgia-special-election-for-the-ages.html

Lacy, S., Wildman, S. S., Fico, F., Bergan, D., Baldwin, T., & Zube, P. (2013). How radio news uses sources to cover local government news and factors affecting source use. *Journalism and Mass Communication Quarterly, 90*(3), 457–477.

Lombard, M., Snyder-Duch, J., & Bracken, C. C. (2002). Content analysis in mass communication: Assessment and reporting of intercoder reliability. *Human Communication Research, 28*(4), 587–604.

Nielsen Audio ratings. (2017). *Radio Online.* Retrieved from http://ratings.radio-online.com/cgi-bin/rol.exe/arb_menu_date

Number of broadcasting jobs has fallen 27% since 1990. (2016, June 10). *All Access.* Retrieved from www.allaccess.com/net-news/archive/story/154483/number-of-broadcasting-jobs-has-fallen-27-since-19

Parmett, H. M. (2016). KVOS in the local, public interest: Early broadcasting and the constitution of the local. *Journal of Radio and Audio Media, 23*(1), 95–108.

Poindexter, M. (2016). Towards a democratic public sphere: A history of Radio FreeDom in Réunion. *Journal of Radio and Audio Media, 23*(1), 109–122.

Simon, P. M. (2016, December 2). The letter: From the island of misfit media. *All Access.* Retrieved from www.allaccess.com/the-letter/archive/25587/defining-ourselves

Walker, L. R. (2017, April 24). Local public radio: America's last public square. *Columbia Journalism Review.* Retrieved from www.cjr.org/opinion/local-public-radio-wnyc.php

# 6

# The Fandom of Howard Stern and Its Relationship to His Success

•••••••••••••••••••

The "King of All Media" and a Dynamic Audience

RACHEL SUSSMAN-WANDER KAPLAN

Howard Stern, the self-proclaimed "King of All Media," has cultivated a loyal audience over the course of a successful, lucrative, thirty-year radio career. Stern elicits emotional reactions ranging from love to hatred, and loyal fans pay money to listen to his radio show, which currently appears on SiriusXM satellite radio just three days a week—Mondays, Tuesdays, and Wednesdays. Before the advent of satellite radio, Stern battled with the Federal Communications Commission (FCC) over what the FCC deemed "indecent," lewd, and sexually explicit content. Because of his battle with the FCC, Stern chose to leave terrestrial radio in late 2004; in 2006, he launched his first show on satellite radio free from federal decency rules (Sisario, 2006, para. 8).

Stern and his staff gained creative freedom over content when "Mr. Stem has announced that he soon will leave over-the-air broadcasting and take his program to Sirius, a satellite digital audio provider (to which, like other subscription services such as cable and satellite TV, the FCC's indecency regime is legally much more problematic)" (Wiley & Secrest, 2004, p. 238). On satellite radio, Stern no longer had to contend with the FCC, and with the lack of regulation on SiriusXM Stern has maintained a large fandom dedicated to hearing him interview strippers, musicians, and famous people such as Jerry Seinfeld, Anderson Cooper, Snoop Dogg, Donald Trump, and Martha Stewart.

Brown (2015) measured the success of Stern's career objectively by naming him the highest-paid radio host, topping Rush Limbaugh, Glen Beck, and Ryan Seacrest. CNBC reporters noted, "Howard Stern has decided to continue working at Sirius Satellite Radio. He signed a new five-year deal that some reports suggest would pay him $90 million per year. That's up from the $80 million he earned in the previous contract" (Chemi & Fahey, 2015, para.1). Clearly, Stern's success has placed him in the upper echelon of earners in the United States. In addition, "According to data from the Social Security Administration, only 134 people in the United States earned at least $50 million in wages [in 2014]. That puts Stern not only in the top 1 percent, but the top .0001 percent of earners" (SSA, as cited in Chemi & Fahey, 2015, para. 6). Given these statistics, what makes *The Howard Stern Radio Show* so successful?

Howard Stern is known as a "shock jock" for his tendency to shock his audience with increasingly outrageous comments. His cult-like audience of millions has followed him from terrestrial radio to SiriusXM satellite radio. As a result, Stern, the self-proclaimed "King of All Media," enjoys a dynamic audience. A strong sense of fandom surrounds *The Howard Stern Radio Show*. Stern has attributed his success to his loyal audience. In fact, Stern has strongly influenced popular culture. As seen at Barnes and Noble in 1993 in Manhattan when he had a book signing for his first book, *Private Parts*, two hours before his scheduled appearance, two thousand people were in line to get Stern's autograph. The police later reported that there were approximately ten thousand fans waiting for an autograph, which was enough to stop traffic along Fifth Avenue in New York City (Hall, 1993, p. 1). His fans consistently show up and support him and his projects, adding to the sense of fandom.

This chapter explores Stern's life and early career, including the obstacles he experienced in his first few jobs, followed by a discussion of his strong partnership with cohost Robin Quivers. Their partnership rivals that of some marriages, and their dedication to one another in radio is arguably unparalleled. Last, the chapter analyzes Stern's radio market share and how Stern has cultivated connections to the audience.

The theoretical foundation for this chapter comes from the literature on the nature of fandom, identity and fandom, and fan relationships with stars. In 1956, Horton and Wohl discussed the fan-audience relationship as a form of "parasocial interaction" whereby the relationship serves as a surrogate relationship for a face-to-face relationship (p. 215). Grossberg (1992) studied fandom through the lens of cultural context and the psychological characterization of fans as "immature" or "passive," thus providing an elitist view of fandom; however, Grossberg later offered a more nuanced view of fans as active participants (pp. 50–58). In the chapter, Horton and Wohl's "para-social interaction" theory is applied to the type of relationship or kinship many listeners feel toward Howard Stern.

## Early Life and Career of Stern

Howard Stern started in radio in the "mid-70s, and by 1986 he had a nationally syndicated show, one that would eventually reach 20 million listeners" (Segal, 2016, para.11). Stern's rise to fandom and wealth was arduous; he contended with his childhood struggles, aired his marriage issues, and battled with the FCC, and for Stern, nothing was off limits. To his most "ardent fans, he loomed so large that he seemed like a lifestyle choice as much as an entertainer" (Segal, 2016, para. 11). His early life and early career is worthy of exploration to see how he has incorporated his life experiences into the show and used that to relate to his listeners.

Howard Stern was born on January 12, 1954, in Queens, New York, to Ben and Ray Stern (Andersen & Carlson, 1993, p. 60). In his autobiography *Private Parts*, Howard Stern (1993) wrote, "Ray my mom, raised me like 'veal.' . . . She was constantly attentive, totally overbearing, and would always put fear in me" (p. 24). His father Ben, a "no nonsense guy," often yelled at young Howard, referring to him as a moron (Andersen & Carlson, 1993, p. 60). Ben, a Manhattan radio engineer, instilled a strong interest in radio broadcasting in young Howard (Andersen & Carlson, 1993, p. 60). As a kid, Stern was described as "tall, gawky and somewhat of an outcast," though he had the desire to make people laugh (Mintzer, 2010, p. xv). Stern (1993) grew up in the predominantly African American community of Roosevelt on Long Island, New York, and has often reflected on this part of his childhood during his radio show. Stern holds back no details when describing being beat up by his classmates; for years, he was ostracized and bullied in Roosevelt. Stern has openly discussed "being the only White kid" and the physical and mental abuse he endured. Ray Stern believed that growing up in Roosevelt would help build his "character" (Stern, 1993, p. 64). On his show, Stern has frequently reflected on his experiences growing up, and Stern's parents have been frequent callers into the show.

Stern took his first radio job as a sophomore at Boston University, where he was eager to get on the air. Stern read the news and conducted interviews but longed for comedy. He worked with three seniors to produce a comedic talk show titled the "King Schmaltz Bagel Hour"; however, the racy talk show ended after just one show (Stern, 1993, p. 138). After Stern graduated from Boston College, he worked as a radio disc jockey, taking several jobs in the New York and Boston areas. Stern described himself as "nervous" and unhappy just playing music. In 1979, Stern took a radio job at WCCC, in Hartford, Connecticut, where things began to change for him. Stern began to conduct interviews in which he asked guests "bizarre," off-topic questions, such as questions about their dating life (Stern, 1993, p. 153). Stern's show, "which featured interviews with strippers, pornographers, prostitutes and second-tier celebrities," was considered different and highly unusual for the time (Flint, as cited in Soley, 2007, p. 77).

At WCCC, Stern met Fred Norris, who was attending college (Stern, 1993, p. 153). Norris is well known for his voice impersonations and sound effects and has since become an instrumental part of the current Stern show (Strauss, 2011, p. 40). In 1980, Stern left Hartford, Connecticut, and headed to Detroit, Michigan, to earn a salary of thirty thousand dollars (Stern, 1993, p. 159). Stern thought this was great money and was excited to connect to the audience. He regularly played games with the listeners, such as "Go Back to Bed Day" and "Dial-a-Date." The game of "Go Back to Bed Day" involved convincing bosses to allow contestants to go back to bed for the day with pay. The "Dial-a-Date" game involved Penthouse models as contestants. Another feature of the show called the Wack Pack was developed in Detroit. The current Wack Pack is a group of "superfans" who are a bit eccentric but devoted to the show. The Wack Pack began with Irene, "the Leather Weather Lady." Irene, a dominatrix, had been a consistent caller; Howard assigned her the daily weather report, and she often said outrageous things. Today, the Wack Pack is "an unpaid and rotating cast of eccentrics, who still have plenty of time to heckle one another and the staff, though some have been rechristened with less offensive names" (Segal, 2016, para. 38). This was the start of the audience becoming a part of the show and superfans becoming integrated into the fabric of the fandom surrounding Stern.

Howard once invited an entire motorcycle gang into the studio to interview them about their experiences. At the time, no one else was doing this type of comedy on the radio (Stern, 1993, p. 164). These antics won Stern the national spotlight—he won the Billboard award for the best album-oriented rock disc jockey and the Drake-Chenault Top Five Talent Search (Stern, 1993, p. 164). Stern received national attention and soon got offers from bigger markets; however, his main goal was New York City.

In 1981, Stern received a job offer from WWDC in Washington, D.C. This move influenced his entire format. The station paired him with Robin Quivers, a nurse who had broken into radio a year before. Quivers agreed to work with Stern after hearing a tape of him interviewing a prostitute (Stern, 1993, p. 166). She liked that he was not talking down to the prostitute, saying "you poor dear"; rather, Stern was interviewing the prostitute as he would anyone else (Stern, 1993, p. 168). At the time, the WWDC program director wanted Stern to follow a grid with the schedule of bits he planned to perform; however, Stern resisted adopting a formal format (Stern, 1993, p. 170). Stern wanted freedom to do what he wanted without the confines of a formal schedule—this too was a new approach. The audience found Stern's banter with Quivers engaging, and Stern felt she brought a more balanced approach to his talk show format (Stern, 1993, p. 167).

Stern's ratings quadrupled in Washington, and no topic was off limits (Stern, 1993, p. 187). Stern discussed his wife's miscarriage, shocking not only his wife but his audience as well (Stern, 1993, p. 185). Additionally, Stern pushed the boundaries of sexuality for the time. Stern insisted on opening Dial-a-Dates to the gay community; the station managers pushed back, and Stern pushed harder (Stern, 1993, p. 177). Stern's inclusion of the gay and lesbian community earned him a flattering article in the *Washington Blade*, Washington's leading gay newspaper (Stern, 1993, p. 177). This began Stern's advocacy for the gay community.

Washington is where Howard Stern's fandom began. Stern and Quivers were at a mall in a department store for a promotional visit, and "thousands and thousands" of people showed up (Stern, 1993, p. 187). So many people mobbed the store, the mall owners had to close the mall to control the crowds (Stern, 1993, p. 187).

Not long after that appearance, Stern was offered his dream job (or so he thought) at NBC in New York. Stern returned to his hometown of New York in 1982, after landing a show on NBC's flagship station, WNBC-AM. He was fired from there in 1985 for broadcasting a skit, "Bestiality Dial-A-Date," but was quickly picked up by Infinity's WXRK-FM (Soley, 2007, p. 79). However, the NBC executives attempted to make Stern more pliable by disbanding his team. In particular, the NBC executives refused to hire Robin Quivers, creating strife between Stern and Quivers. For this period, Quivers returned to an all-news station in Baltimore. Stern started his radio program at WNBC New York the Tuesday after Labor Day in 1982. In the summer of 1982, a TV program called *NBC Magazine* aired a segment on Howard Stern. The segment was not flattering, portraying Stern as a predator. The reporters on the NBC program stated,

> That is X-rated radio. And you could be hearing it next in your hometown. This is a story with a little twist to it. While we were in the process of producing this report, Howard Stern was lured away from his Washington radio station by a New York City station, which had offered him a big increase in salary. That station, you guessed it, is WNBC-AM, which is owned by NBC. Dom Fioravanti, the station's general manager, told us that WNBC-AM, and I quote, "is mindful of its responsibility to present programs in accordance with acceptable public taste." (Stern, 1993, p. 198)

This news report portrayed Stern in a negative light; consequently, he entered his new job with a sense of dread rather than with a sense of excitement. After that report, the station manager instituted rules and regulations that limited the things Stern could say on air. In addition, the radio manager forced him to listen to tapes of Imus; however, to Stern, Imus was boring and not innovative (Stern, 1993, p. 199). Stern felt Imus was not pushing new material and breaking through barriers as Stern wished to do.

Another hurdle for Howard Stern at WNBC involved being managed by Kevin Metheny, a person he referred to as Pig Virus. Stern felt Pig Virus was outrageously controlling. Stern was suspended at WNBC only a few months into his contract when he performed a bit about the Virgin Mary being chased by men in Jerusalem. Following his suspension, he explained to Pig Virus that he needed Robin to keep him in line—she let him know when these antics were inappropriate. Thus, Stern was able to bring Robin on board.

Robin soon witnessed Pig Virus's antics; for example, the manager threw objects at Stern's door while Stern was on the air (Stern, 1993, p. 191). The work environment was hostile, although Stern continued to push the boundaries. WNBC fired Stern in 1985 for "conceptual differences" (Stern, 1993, p. 232). Next, Stern signed a half-million-dollar contract with Infinity Broadcasting; his show aired on WXRK. Stern's show at WXRK lasted twenty years, and at the peak of his radio career he had over twenty million listeners (Sullivan, 2005). Stern's interview style kept listeners captivated (Strauss, 2011, pp. 40–42).

Stern asked stars provocative questions during interviews. For example, he asked Tori Spelling if she lived up to her airhead reputation (Stern, 1993, p. 249). He peppered her with questions such as "Who was Woody Allen?," "What was he being investigated for?," and "Who was Rodney King?" (Stern, 1993, p. 249). Spelling was able to answer those questions correctly. Finally, Stern asked Spelling if she knew the capital of New York State. She responded "New Jersey" (Stern, 1993, p. 249). He told her that her answer was incorrect, but as a consolation prize, she could get a kiss goodbye from him while he grabbed her buttocks (Stern, 1993, p. 250). These inappropriate and sexually demeaning comments put Howard at the center of controversy. Stern's antics outraged members of the FCC, who fined him frequently for inappropriate content. The inappropriate content did drive ratings high, and Howard impressed Mel Karmazin, then president of Infinity Broadcasting, with a large audience of men in the "prized 18–34 demographic group" and hired him (Colford, 1997, para. 21). Stern's show pushed a larger agenda at Infinity as "Infinity's strategy was to attract younger, "rock and roll" males with Stern on the rock station" (Soley, 2007, p. 76). Stern was able to deliver the ratings.

By happenstance, Donald Trump, the current leader of the Republican Party and president of the United States, was a frequent guest on *The Howard Stern Radio Show*. Donald Trump was quoted as saying, "I tune in to Howard to hear what you rarely get these days, straight talk and very close to the mark" (Trump as cited in Stern, 1993, p. 250). During one show, Stern and Trump rated several women, including Marla Maples, Stephanie Seymour, Kim Alley, Paulina Porizkova, Carolyn Sapp, and Ivanka Trump (Stern, 1993, p. 250). Additionally, Trump (as cited in Stern, 1993) said, "You have to be very selective. It's pretty dangerous out there. It's like Vietnam! Dating is my personal Vietnam!" (p. 251).

Stern's interview style allowed interpersonal questions to become the substance of the interview, not just the interviewees' professional lives. In fact, Stern's interviews were conversations, similar to sitting down with an intimate best friend to catch up—but broadcast live. However, Stern's questions about sexual content and references to "indecent" content garnered the attention of the FCC. In response, Stern and other broadcasters have complained the definition of indecent material is so vague they do not know what they can and cannot say on the radio without being fined (Rosenblat, 2006). The U.S. Supreme Court has allowed every FCC definition of indecency to remain unchallenged (Rosenblat, 2006, p. 176).

## Fines and the Federal Communications Commission

In 2006, Rosenblat explained the culture of the FCC and showed how the fining process worked. There was no FCC committee listening for infractions; rather, the FCC assigned fines based on complaints received (Rosenblat, 2006). "This means the FCC will not conduct an investigation of an allegedly indecent broadcast unless a listener or viewer takes the necessary steps to file a complaint" (Gurza, as cited in Rosenblat, 2006, p. 178). This has also meant that watchdogs, activist groups, and individuals can target specific broadcasters they deem indecent. Some broadcasters become targets. Jack Thompson, an indecency attorney, wrote a letter to Sumner Redstone, then head of Viacom, in November 2004 and threatened legal action for neglectfully supervising Stern and allowing indecent programming (Rosenblat, 2006). In the letter, Thompson promised to "go away" and not pursue any more complaints leading to fines if Redstone fired Stern (Rosenblat, 2006, p. 174). Stern responded to the FCC fines by calling them a "witch hunt" (Rosenblat, 2006, p. 188). The fines, external pressures from the FCC, and complaints from Thompson and other watchdog groups proved to be more of a problem than the media company wanted to deal with, as "Clear Channel removed Stern's radio show from several markets as a result of the FCC's crackdown" (Rosenblat, 2006, p. 189). However, the actions to remove Stern from the airwaves did not succeed (Rosenblat, 2006). Infinity Broadcasting picked up the show in four of the six markets Clear Channel had dropped, as well as adding it in five new markets (Rosenblat, 2006, p. 189). Even so, in 2004 Stern decided to avoid the FCC all together and move to satellite radio, where the FCC did not have the authority to regulate (Rosenblat, 2006).

## The Move to Satellite

In the early 1990s, David Margolese, the president of start-up Satellite CD Radio (later to become Sirius), petitioned the FCC to allocate frequency spectrum for a new digital audio radio service, commonly referred to as DARS (Navis & Glynn, 2010, p. 450). Margolese was a Canadian entrepreneur who collaborated with Rob Briskman, a NASA scientist, to develop the necessary technologies. Many groups expressed concerns over DARS; in particular, advertisers, radio station managers, and broadcasters were concerned DARS would pose a threat to the status quo. A battle lasting seven years ensued, led by the National Association of Broadcasters, whose members sought to protect the commercial interests of terrestrial radio (Navis & Glynn, 2010, p. 450).

In 1997, the FCC relented and auctioned the DARS licenses to two entrepreneurial firms: American Mobile Radio (later XM Satellite Radio), a wholly owned subsidiary of Motient Corporation, and Satellite CD Radio (later Sirius Satellite Radio), a de novo venture. Because XM lacked the typical resources of parent-company ventures, it faced obstacles similar to those Sirius faced (Helfat & Lieberman, 2002; Navis & Glynn, 2010, p. 450).

One of the obstacles XM leaders faced was the eighty million dollars needed to purchase the necessary licenses (Navis & Glynn, 2010, p. 450). Sirius had its first satellite in space in July 2000, five months earlier than XM, which had shown satellite radio was a "reality" and indeed possible (Navis & Glynn, 2010, p. 446). In the 1990s, the Yankee Group had concluded the listening public was concerned with "too many commercials," "lack of variety," and the need to switch the channel for lack of a clear signal; these concerns provided satellite a platform for growth (Warren, 2004, p. 167). Thus, satellite radio transformed the listener experience—listeners no longer needed to switch channels while driving through different geographic locations.

Early growth for Sirius satellite radio and XM was largely attributable to contracts with car manufacturers, especially for XM and their exclusive contracts with General Motors (Navis & Glynn, 2010, p. 451). In early 2004, Sirius focused on its competitive advantages and highlighted exclusive content as a means of becoming the market leader. Sirius secured contracts with Martha Stewart's Living Omnimedia brand and aimed to be the sports market leader by signing various athletic teams, from volleyball, skateboarding, and surfing. In a 2004 press release, Sirius leaders proudly announced they had signed Stern, praising Howard Stern as "an entertainment force of unprecedented recognition and popularity in the broadcast world, who is capable of changing the face of satellite radio and generating huge numbers of subscribers for Sirius" (Navis & Glynn, 2010, p. 456). In 2004, XM secured contracts with Major League Baseball to be the official satellite carrier of baseball games and secured shock jocks Opie and Anthony to try to compete with Sirius (Navis & Glynn, 2010, p. 455).

The high price of securing exclusive content meant neither XM nor Sirius was operating at a profit. In 2005, the *New York Post* reported speculation about a merger between the two companies: "The discussions never got to an advanced stage. But in the wake of Sirius' hiring of former Viacom President Mel Karmazin in November, the issue has gained renewed urgency, sources said" (Arango, 2005). In 2007, reporters at the *New York Times* explained how the merger would benefit both XM and Sirius. Later that year, both companies reported "close to 14 million subscribers [and] hoped to revolutionize the radio industry with a bevy of niche channels offering everything from fishing tips to salsa music, and media personalities like Howard Stern and Oprah Winfrey, with few commercials. But neither has yet turned an annual profit and both have had billions in losses" (Siklos & Sorken, 2007, para. 2).

The "Howard Stern effect" affected the urgency of the merger. Reporters for the *New York Times* wrote, "XM ended 2006 with nearly eight million customers but Sirius increased its subscriber base by 80 percent last year, to about six million, after it signed Mr. Stern in a $725 million cash and stock deal" (Siklos & Sorken, 2007, para. 12). CNN reported Stern's impact as well: "Shock jock Howard Stern has been widely credited for much of Sirius's success, helping the satellite radio operator finish 2006 with more than 6 million subscribers" (Ellis & La Monica, 2007, para. 2).

Talk of the merger between Sirius and XM prompted criticism. The National Association of Broadcasters issued a statement within hours of the XM-Sirius announcement, coming out strongly against the merger and Stern: "In coming weeks, policy makers will have to weigh whether an industry that makes Howard Stern its poster child should be rewarded with a monopoly" (Siklos & Sorken, 2007, para. 23). In addition, many on Wall Street were skeptical because the merger "would require antitrust approval from the Justice Department and would have to be considered in the public interest by the Federal Communications Commission" (Siklos & Sorken, 2007, para. 5). Officials from both companies made the argument that the merger would not form a monopoly and in fact faced competition from "other audio entertainment, like iPods, Internet radio, and HD radio" (Siklos & Sorken, 2007, para. 9). Ultimately, the merger was approved in March 2008. The Department of Justice ruled the XM-Sirius merger was not anticompetitive. The Justice Department "argued that other media companies such as Clear Channel, CBS, or even Apple with its iTunes software and iPod music player served as alternate options for music and media customer" (Goldman, 2008, para. 3).

As of 2017, Stern continues to attract customers to satellite radio. On his website, Stern wrote, "While on terrestrial radio, the Howard Stern Show became the #1 morning show in markets across the country—so in 2004 all eyes were on the King of All Media when he announced the decision to move to satellite radio with Sirius, which boasted only around 400,000 subscribers at the time. As the world has witnessed though, subscriptions skyrocketed with Howard at the mic since that very first day back in 2006" (Howard Stern Show, 2016, para. 5).

The growth of subscriptions has continued: "SiriusXM added 465,000 net new subscribers in the first quarter of 2016, resulting in a record-high of 30.1 million subscribers as of March 31, 2016" (Howard Stern Show, 2016, para. 4). Attracting 30 million subscribers was a goal for the company. Jim Meyer, the chief executive of SiriusXM, said, "I can tell you that having Howard here was certainly a major part of legitimizing this technology and getting this service the notoriety and the recognition that it needed in its early days" (Meyer, as cited in

Sisario, 2006). At the end of 2017 the SiriusXM "total subscriber count [was] approximately 32.7 million" (Stevens & Reilly, 2018, para. 5). Howard Stern was and is undoubtedly a part of satellite radio's success as, "Sirius executives noted that during Mr. Stern's long career in radio, he has shepherded thousands of people from his fan base of more than 12 million regular listeners to movie theaters, bookstores, cable shows, pay-per-view broadcasts and certain politicians" (Carter & Ives, 2004, para. 3). Thus, the value of Howard Stern resides in the people who have been willing to invest time and money in him and his products—in other words, his fans.

## Fandom

Howard Stern's fans have followed him in the millions, purchased his book in droves (keeping it on the *New York Times* best-seller list for nonfiction for five weeks), watched his movie, and supported his television appearances. In addition, Stern has the ability to jump-start careers. "Celebrities [can] get the amorphous, though palpable, sense that by appearing on the show they have climbed a few rungs on the fame ladder. This has something to do with the fervor of Mr. Stern's fans, and their ubiquity" (Segal, 2016, para. 7). For example, Judd Apatow sought out Amy Schumer to collaborate on the movie *Trainwreck* after her interview on Stern's show. Ike Barinholtz (as cited in Segal, 2016), an actor and comedian who has appeared on the show three times since 2014, said, "Aside from the fact that millions of people hear you, the cross section of who hears you is what blew me away." Fans tune into the show and watch the movies Stern recommends; there is little argument that the millions of fans actively listening to the show incorporate Stern's ideas in some way into their lived experiences.

Grossberg (1992) offered different views of fandom. One view is that fans of popular culture are thought to be easily manipulated and easily distracted from "serious" culture in order to make a profit (Grossberg, 1992). Some researchers have viewed fans as incapable of being discerning and realizing they are being exploited to make a profit (Grossberg, 1992). In addition, Grossberg presented the idea of a fan as immature and juvenile. On the other hand, a more nuanced view of fans as active participants exists; people are always struggling trying to make a text mean something in their lives, connecting it to their lived experiences (Grossberg, 1992). Stern connects what is occurring on the show with people's lives: "Today, if you go on a TV talk show and give a great six or seven minutes, people will link to it, if it's incredible. . . . But if you kill on Stern, it moves the needle" (Kay, as cited in Segal, 2016, para. 12). Stern's approach actively engages people with the show and its guests.

Fans' interpretations of a text is constantly changing—an omnipresent struggle exists regarding how a text is interpreted, how it functions, and how people can use the experiences to make the world a better place. Stern's listeners proudly admit to being "superfans" and part of Stern fandom culture. The fans have a jargon of their own, calling in using the phrase "hey now" and referring to the show's producer Gary Dell'Abate as "Baba Booey" (Stern, 1993). The frequent callers become part of the show, and musical parodies of the frequent callers entertain listeners.

Grossberg (1992) noted that audiences never deal with a singular cultural context; rather, ideas of economics, social relationships, gender, aesthetic conventions, and ideological commitments affect an audience member's relationship to fandom. Hence, a fan is not a cultural "dope" but an active participant choosing to partake in a community (Grossberg, 1992, pp. 52–54). Ideologies provide maps of meaning, which provide pictures of the world, and this is a product of social construction (Grossberg, 1992). People give the world meaning through language and assign meaning to experience through experience and affect (Grossberg, 1992). In the context of fandom, Grossberg defined *affect* as feelings and mood, often involving a sense of pleasure. Thus, fandom provides a sense of pleasure for those associating with the culture (Grossberg, 1992). Additionally, fans' investment in the fandom culture is akin to investing with dollars; how much stock fans choose to place in identifying themselves as fans is directly related to the amount of money, time, and effort they expend to shape their identities as a fan: "The fan gives authority to that which he or she invests in, letting the object of such investments speak for him or herself" (Grossberg, 1992, p. 59).

Fans let their investments in the fandom organize their emotional involvement and identities. The size of their investments—be it time or money—construct identity in the fan group. For example, superfan Maryann from Brooklyn calls into the show frequently and attends the majority of Stern's public appearances; she attended every taping of America's Got Talent to support Stern. Her strong investment in the fandom is a large source of her identity. Similarly, Bobo, a driving instructor from Florida, calls in to share his love of the show, even admitting to constructing a "shrine" of Howard Stern memorabilia. His daily routine involves listening intently to the show, and he invests a lot of himself to support the show.

Harrington and Bielby (1995) found "being a fan is not just a social but a personal phenomenon; by exploring both dimensions we have been able to consider fanship as a normal, everyday phenomenon" (p. 176). They explored the relationships fans had to different soap operas and concluded that pleasure was a main source of the investment in becoming a fan: "Fans and industry participants reciprocally construct the subculture" of the fandom of soap operas (Harrington & Bielby, 1995, p. 176). The *Howard Stern Show* has made listeners a part of the show—a Wack Pack of "superfans" call into the show with anecdotes, prank phone calls, and updates on their daily experiences. Akin to soap opera fans, Howard Stern fans and the staff of the show have co-constructed the subculture of fandom.

Stern's fans weave a fabric that is integral to the show. Listeners of the *Howard Stern Show* appear to form "para-social relationships" with other fans and with Stern. A parasocial relationship gives the illusion of friendship with television or radio personas: "The most remote and illustrious men are met *as if they* were in the circle of one's peers" (Horton & Wohl, 1956 p. 215). Horton and Wohl (1956) wrote about this phenomenon first, noting fans believe they know the personas on radio or television. Horton and Wohl found that listeners perceive an intimate connection with the personas and imagine a connection or bond with the media character. The personas become integrated into listeners' daily routines (Horton & Wohl, 1956, pp. 215–218). Stern has mastered the parasocial relationship. For example, one fan and longtime listener of the *Howard Stern Show* articulated,

> We end up learning a ton of the details about every member of the show, and as weird as it is to say it, you kind of get to feeling like you know them somewhat and think of them almost as "friends." The conversational style of the show can make you feel like you're just sitting amongst a circle of friends, listening to them chat (you just don't have much ability to provide *your* input). After a period of time, you get to know enough about the show and its players that you start to understand and even expect inside jokes, etc., which adds even more to the "bond" you feel with the show and its players. (Edmonds 2011, para. 4)

Similarly, a fan reported, "Howard Stern has been going for so long that it would be difficult for him to stop or for his fans to stop listening to him. They listen to Howard because Howard is on; and Howard is on because they listen to him" (Mixon, 2013, para. 5). In several fan interviews, the theme of talking like old friends recurred, and the words "truth" and "honesty" repeated. Thus, fans listen to Howard Stern because they feel a friendship, a "para-social" relationship.

In addition to feeling a kinship to Stern, fans said Stern discussed political and social concerns in a way that allowed listeners to be open to his ideas and consider his thoughts without becoming alienated or feeling negative. The relationship of fandom is one of empowerment, making it possible to move within and beyond "mattering maps," or what matters most to people (Grossberg, 1992). "The fans' relation to culture in fact opens up a range of political possibilities and it is often on the field of affective relations that political struggles intersect with popular concerns" (Grossberg, 1992, p. 590). Similarly, Hawkins (2012) wrote about Stern's political discussions, which are often areas of popular concern: "Howard has been outspoken about his support for marriage equality and is a staunch proponent of equal rights for LGBT people" (para. 1). Hawkins highlighted Stern's show the morning of Monday, February 6, 2012, when Stern and Quivers spent the morning discussing JCPenney leaders' decision to use Ellen DeGeneres as the store's spokesperson, and an antigay family group expressed outrage over the decision. Stern defended Ellen vigorously. Hawkins (2012) reported, "Howard insisted that everyone on the planet has a gay relative or friend, whether or not they are consciously aware of it, and that he will defend, to the end, DeGeneres' right to earn a living and not be treated like less of a person because of her sexuality" (p. 1). Thus, fandom is not for "cultural dopes" who blindly consume popular culture. Rather, after exploring and studying the fandom of Howard Stern, the conclusion that fans are active consumers is reasonable. In a mediated world in which people can tweet about the show directly to the hosts or call in, email, or write blog posts about the show, it is clear that passivity is not a part of the Stern fandom culture. Stern has the ability to connect with his listeners, and that connection is enough to inspire fans to dedicate a few hours of loyal listening to the radio show. In a 2015 CNBC report, Chemi and Fahey stated Howard Stern had signed a contract worth ninety million dollars a year for five years: "Stern's salary is so high that it dwarfs the compensation of the actual CEO of Sirius James Meyer . . . by a factor of 10" (Chemi & Fahey, 2015, p. 1). Clearly, Stern and his loyal following are powerful enough to warrant that type of compensation.

## References

Andersen, K., & Carlson, M. (1993). Big mouths. *Time, 142*(18), 60.
Arango, T. (2005, January 26). Satellite chat—Sirius, XM are exploring a possible merger. *New York Post*. Retrieved from http://nypost.com/2005/01/26/satellite-chat-sirius-xm-are-exploring-a-possible-merger/
Brown, A. (2015, 13 July). Meet America's highest-earning radio hosts: Howard Stern, Rush Limbaugh and more. *Forbes*. Retrieved from www.forbes.com/sites/abrambrown/2015/07/13/meet-americas-highest-earning-radio-hosts-howard-stern-rush-limbaugh-and-more/#785814bd4dd7
Carter, B., & Ives, N. (2004, October 11). Where some see just a shock jock, Sirius sees a top pitchman. *New York Times*. Retrieved from www.nytimes.com/2004/10/11/business/media/where-some-see-just-a-shock-jock-sirius-sees-a-top-pitchman.html
Chemi, M., & Fahey, M. (2015, December 16). Howard Stern would be the third-highest-paid CEO in America. *CNBC*. Retrieved from www.cnbc.com/2015/12/16/howard-stern-would-be-the-third-highest-paid-ceo-in-america.html
Colford, P. (1997). The Mel who would be king (CBS Station Group CEO Mel Karmazin). *Mediaweek, 7*(23), 32.
Edmonds, C. (2011, December 15). Why is Howard Stern so hugely popular? [Quora comment]. Retrieved from www.quora.com/Why-is-Howard-Stern-so-hugely-popular
Ellis, D., & La Monica, P. R. (2007). XM, Sirius announce merger. *CNN Money*. Retrieved from http://money.cnn.com/2007/02/19/news/companies/xm_sirius/index.htm
Goldman, D. (2008). XM-Sirius merger approved by DOJ. *CNNMoney*. Retrieved from http://money.cnn.com/2008/03/24/news/companies/xm_sirius/index.htm?postv
Grossberg, L. (1992). *Is there a fan in the house? The affective sensibility of fandom* (Vol. 59). London: Routledge.
Hall, J. (1993). Stern Causes Near-Riot at NYC Signing: Radio: The author of the best-selling "Private Parts" becomes caught in traffic himself as thousands of fans jam the bookstore. *Los Angeles Times*. Retrieved from http://articles.latimes.com/1993-10-15/entertainment/ca-45889_1_private-parts
Harrington, C. L., & Bielby, D. D. (1995). *Soap fans: Pursuing pleasure and making meaning in everyday life*. Philadelphia: Temple University Press.
Hawkins, W. (2012). Why I love Howard Stern and you should, too! *Huffington Post*. Retrieved from www.huffingtonpost.com/walt-hawkins/howard-stern_b_1264926.html

Helfat, C. E., & Lieberman, M. B. (2002). The birth of capabilities: Market entry and the importance of pre-history. *Industrial and Corporate Change, 11*(4), 725–760.

Horton, D., & Wohl, R. (1956). Mass communication and para-social interaction: Observations on intimacy at a distance. *Psychiatry, 19*(3), 215–229.

Howard Stern Show. (2016, April 11). Howard Stern leads the way as SiriusXM Radio hits 30 million subscribers. Retrieved from www.howardstern.com/show/2016/4/11/howard-stern-leads-way-siriusxm-radio-hits-30-million-subscribers

McBride, S. (2005, March 30). Battle stations: Two up starts vie for dominance in satellite radio. *Wall Street Journal*, A1.

Mintzer, R. (2010). *Howard Stern: A biography*. Westport, CT: ABC-CLIO/Greenwood.

Mixon, J. (2013, December 11). Why is Howard Stern so hugely popular? [Quora comment]. Retrieved from www.quora.com/Why-is-Howard-Stern-so-hugely-popular

Navis, C., & Glynn, M. A. (2010). How new market categories emerge: Temporal dynamics of legitimacy, identity, and entrepreneurship in satellite radio, 1990–2005. *Administrative Science Quarterly, 55*(3), 439–471.

Rosenblat, G. (2006). Stern penalties: How the Federal Communications Commission and Congress look to crackdown on indecent broadcasting. *Villanova Sports & Entertainment Law Journal, 13*(1), 167–205.

Segal, D. (2016). Confessor. Feminist. Adult. What the hell happened to Howard Stern? *New York Times*. Retrieved from www.nytimes.com/2016/07/31/arts/howard-stern-sirius.htm

Siklos, R., & Sorkin, A. R. (2007, February 20). Merger would end satellite radio's rivalry. *New York Times*. Retrieved from www.nytimes.com/2007/02/20/business/media/20radio.html

Sisario, B. (2006, January 10). Howard Stern embarks on world conquest via satellite. *New York Times*. Retrieved from www.nytimes.com/2006/01/10/arts/howard-stern-embarks-on-world-conquest-via-satellite.html

Sisario, B. (2015, December 15). Howard Stern and SiriusXM sign new deal for 5 years. *New York Times*. Retrieved from www.nytimes.com/2015/12/16/business/media/howard-stern-and-siriusxm-reach-new-deal.html?_r=0

Soley, L. (2007). Sex and shock jocks: An analysis of the Howard Stern and Bob & Tom shows. *Journal of Promotion Management, 13*(1–2), 75–93.

Stern, H. (1993). *Private parts*. New York: Simon & Schuster.

Stevens, H., & Reilly, P. (2018, January 31). SiriusXM reports fourth quarter and full-year 2017 results. Retrieved from http://investor.siriusxm.com/investor-overview/press-releases/press-release-details/2018/SiriusXM-Reports-Fourth-Quarter-and-Full-Year-2017-Results/default.aspx

Strauss, N. (2011). The happiest man alive. *Rolling Stone, 1127*, 40–76.

Sullivan, J. (2005, December 14). Love him or hate him, Stern is a true pioneer. *Today*. Retrieved from www.today.com/popculture/love-him-or-hate-him-stern-true-pioneer-wbna10454035

Warren, S. (2004). *Radio*. Abingdon, UK: Taylor & Francis.

Wiley, R. E., & Secrest, L. W. (2004). Recent developments in program content regulation. *Federal Communications Law Journal, 57*, 235–242.

# 7

## *The War of the Worlds* Broadcast

### Fake News or Engaging Storytelling?

JOHN F. BARBER

Since it was first broadcast, October 30, 1938, *The War of the Worlds* has been cited as "radio's most legendary hour" (Sconce, 2000, p. 110), the most famous American radio broadcast ever, the highpoint of radio drama, the first to extensively use fictional yet authentic-sounding news break-in reports as a narrative device, the source of a nationwide panic, a radio hoax, the origin of fake news (Schwartz, 2015).

Eight decades after its original broadcast, rather than fake news, this essay considers *The War of the Worlds* an experiment in radio storytelling, and specifically its use of news break-in announcements to move the narrative forward. When *The War of the Worlds*, directed by and starring Orson Welles, was first broadcast, American radio producers were exploring different content genres and storytelling *techne*, hoping to attract and retain listeners to the new radio medium.

One focus of this exploration was news, a familiar print-based information source. Would it remediate well for sound-based storytelling? *The March of Time* (1931–1945), an American radio news documentary and dramatization series, sought to find out. Created by Fred Smith and *Time* magazine executive

Roy Edward Larsen, *The March of Time* combined current news as reported in *Time* with authentic-sounding news reporting and sound effects to give listeners the impression of being virtually present at the event's reenactment. As will be seen, Welles had several uncredited appearances in *The March of Time* episodes.

The push for news came from other directions as well. Writing in his handbook, *Do's and Don'ts of Radio Writing*, Ralph Rogers (1937) said, "Don't overlook the fact that the radio audience responds heartily to news broadcasts. Capitalize on this desire for news whenever possible" (p. 14). The success of *The March of Time* and Rogers's advice encouraged further experimentation with first-person news reporting techniques in fictional stories (Geduld, 1995, pp. 262–265). For example, in *The Death Triangle*, the December 12, 1937, episode of *The Shadow*, starring Welles in the title role, writers used a fictional news break-in announcement to speed up the narrative action (Heyer, 2005, p. 28).

*The War of the Worlds* may well be a highpoint for this technique. The first half of this famous radio drama used primarily fictional news break-ins for both narrative content and delivery, and the results have been debated since. But, a highpoint implies previous examples, and *The War of the Worlds* was not the first to use break-in news reports or journalistic-style first-person reporting as narrative devices. Beyond *The March of Time* series and *The Death Triangle*, several other programs may have influenced Welles's production and performance of *The War of the Worlds*.

One of these programs was *Air Raid* (1938), written by Archibald MacLeish and broadcast just one week prior to *The War of the Worlds*. *The Crimson Wizard* series began broadcasting from Chicago just one month earlier, in September 1938. *The Fall of the City* (1937) also written by MacLeish, starred Welles as an on-the-scene reporter. *The Minister Is Murdered!* was broadcast on German radio in 1930. And in January 1926 *Broadcasting the Barricades*, written and voiced by a Catholic priest, was heard on BBC radio.

This essay suggests rehearing these radio dramatizations, and specifically *The War of the Worlds*, not as purposefully misleading or deceiving their audiences, but rather as creative practices exploring radio's potential as an artistic medium for engaging storytelling and inquiry (Barber, 2017), or, as Neil Verma suggested, educating and uplifting listeners (Verma, 2012). These radio productions sought to engage listeners in sound-based storytelling that, according to radio historian Susan Douglas, promoted "a confidence that your imaginings, your radio visions, were the best and truest ones of all" (Douglas, 1999, p. 39). These early experiments in radio storytelling, extended maximally by *The War of the Worlds*, illustrate, according to Hadley Cantril and Gordon Allport, the power of radio to engage with the imagination of its listeners as they visualize what they hear in their own minds (Cantril & Allport, 1935).

In following these approaches, this chapter suggests *The War of the Worlds* and its predecessors were not radio hoaxes—intentionally creating chaos—or fake news—intentionally misleading listening audiences—but rather deliberate utilizations of radio as a new medium for engaging storytelling.

## Call for Answers

On the morning of October 31, 1938, Orson Welles was surrounded by reporters, photographers, and newsreel cameras in the CBS building in New York. Welles, twenty-three years old, enjoyed widespread public recognition for his stage and radio performances. He had directed *The Cradle Will Rock*, a 1937 contemporary folk opera by Marc Blitzstein set against the backdrop of a steel strike. That same year, in November, Welles adapted, directed, and played the role of Marcus Brutus in Shakespeare's *Julius Caesar*.

In radio, Welles had made frequent appearances—uncredited—on *The March of Time* series since 1935. In 1937, he was cast in a seven-part radio adaptation of Victor Hugo's *Les Misérables*. In summer 1938, Welles completed his season-long, and character-defining, appearance as radio hero *The Shadow*. Based on this success, CBS asked Welles to produce his own weekly radio anthology show, *The Mercury Theatre on the Air*, to be broadcast from New York. The first episode was broadcast in July 1938.

The most recent episode, *The War of the Worlds*, directed by and starring Welles, broadcast the previous night, stunned radio listeners with authentic-sounding news reports about an invasion by beings from the planet Mars. This morning, newspapers across the country led with stories about confusion and panic caused by the radio drama. The press demanded explanations. One reporter asked Welles whether he might have taken unfair advantage of the public when using fictitious news reports, cast as authentic-sounding break-in announcements, as a narrative conveyance during his radio drama the previous night.

Break-in news announcements—"We interrupt this program for a special news report"—promising a quick report of something outside and in contrast to the regular, scheduled program are familiar today. But in 1938, two decades before television, and only one decade after the advent of radio broadcasting in America, interrupting the flow of regular programs with break-in announcements offering different and possibly unrelated information was uncommon. So, when on the night of October 30 Orson Welles and *The Mercury Theatre on the Air* used authentic-sounding break-in news announcements, some seemingly live on location, to advance the narrative of their radio dramatization of the H. G. Wells novel *The War of the Worlds*, the result was both nationwide confusion and enjoyable entertainment about an invasion of Earth by beings from the planet Mars.

Orson Welles, as recorded in photographs and newsreels, was seated in the CBS building, surrounded by reporters. Unshaven, Welles looked tired, having, he said, rehearsed most of the night for an upcoming stage performance. Sitting among the reporters, Welles was all but formally accused of causing panic and fear across the country with his realistic-sounding radio drama. He was concerned for his reputation. Following the media attention, Welles would be either a professional and social pariah, or internationally famous. Welles preferred the latter, and so his answers were meant to portray him as the shocked victim of unexpected outcomes from his radio dramatization.

With exaggerated sincerity, Welles replied to the reporter's question about the use of authentic-sounding but fictional news announcements, and whether he took unfair advantage of the listeners. "I don't believe that I have since it is not a method original with me. It is used by many radio programs. I am terribly shocked by the effect it has had. I don't believe the method is original with me or peculiar to the Mercury Theatre's presentation. Radio is new and we're learning about the effect it has on people" ("George Orson Welles Interviewed," 2012; "Orson Welles Apologizes," 2013).

In truth, several radio dramas had used journalistic reporting narrative styles and break-in news announcements prior to Welles's elevation of these techniques in his production the night before. How did these previous programs influence Welles's adaptation of *The War of the Worlds*, if at all? And did/do they represent radio hoaxes, fake news, or engaging storytelling? The answers are worthy and interesting and begin in London, in 1926.

## *Broadcasting the Barricades* (1926)

Just four years after the formation of the BBC, radio audiences throughout the United Kingdom tuned their receivers hoping for familiar entertainment, like music, literature, or drama. Instead, from 7:40 to 8:00 P.M., the snowy evening of Saturday, January 16, 1926, listeners heard *Broadcasting the Barricades*. Written and performed live by Father Ronald Arbuthnott Knox (1888–1957), an English theologian, Catholic priest, and author of detective fiction—his ten commandments for detective fiction remain a genre reference (Knox, 1929, pp. 12–16)—*Broadcasting the Barricades* originated from Station 2EH, the BBC's relay station in Edinburgh, Scotland, the twelfth radio station opened in the United Kingdom. The opening broadcast, on May 1, 1924, included the chimes of Big Ben, in London, striking 9:00 P.M. The first local program, a presentation for children, was broadcast the next day, at 5:00 P.M. (Walker, 2011, p. 38, 53). *Broadcasting the Barricades* was simultaneously rebroadcast by Station 2LO, in London, throughout the United Kingdom, according to the *Radio Times* program listing ("Saturday, Jan. 16," 1926, p. 100).

Knox's vocal presentation, or "talk" as it was described at the time, was arranged by George L. Marshall, Edinburgh station manager. According to David Walker, Marshall knew of Knox's reputation as both an author and humorist. He felt it necessary to warn the audience not to take Knox's talk too seriously (Walker, 2011, p. 54).

Evelyn Waugh, in his biography of Knox, said Marshall described the upcoming program as "a work of humor and imagination, enlivened by realistic 'sound effects' which were still a novelty. Read today, it seems barely credible that it could have caused a tremor of alarm in the most timid listener. [Knox] had no idea of imposing on anyone. The intention was broad parody" (Waugh, 1959, p. 190).

The talk began with a burst of static giving way to Knox imitating an elderly, lisping university don, William Donkinson, concluding a lecture on eighteenth-century literature. After a prolonged cough, followed by silence, Knox returned as the announcer and reported cricket scores and news of a young girl saved from drowning.

The British Broadcasting Company, the world's oldest and largest broadcaster, was founded by the British General Post Office, October 18, 1922. Broadcasts began November 14, 1922. The name was changed to British Broadcasting Corporation on January 1, 1927. Today, the BBC is the world's oldest and largest broadcaster.

In 1926, the BBC was regulated by the Post Office, which depended on the newspaper industry for much of its income. Newspapers, concerned about loss of income, used their leverage to prevent competition from the new radio medium. For example, broadcasters could read news bulletins, prepared by Reuters, only after 7:00 P.M. to prevent competition with the evening papers. Broadcasts of sporting results were similarly regulated. BBC programming consisted of such controlled news reports, classical music, talks, and drama. Comedy, popular music, and variety were also programmed, according to Ien Ang, "in a manner, context and style that revealed an upper-middle-class approach and orientation" (Ang, 1991, p. 108). Beginning September 28, 1923, programming information was published as a joint venture between the BBC and publisher George Newnes, Ltd. in *Radio Times* magazine, the world's first radio program listing.

Within this context, managing director John Reith—twenty-eight, a BBC engineer, appointed December 1922—pursued two approaches. On one hand, following the Government's Sykes Committee recommendation for more direct control by the BBC over its content subject and production, he insisted that only the best in thought and culture be broadcast, so to educate and elevate the tastes of the listening audience. This meant Christian, high-minded programming, infused with Victorian paternalism, delivered orally by predominately male presenters using a style of speaking called received pronunciation (RP), an accent associated with educated speakers and formal speech in Southern England.

On the other hand, Reith was concerned to grow the audience for BBC radio broadcasting and so constantly pushed the authorities to allow the BBC more latitude to produce and broadcast more mixed programming. So long as it met his guidelines, Reith was keen to try new genres and approaches to radio, hoping to attract more listeners. According to Paul Slade, Knox's talk, *Broadcasting the Barricades*, took full advantage (Slade, 2013).

Knox interrupted his news report of a young girl saved from drowning with a break-in report concerning an unruly crowd of unemployed demonstrators gathering in Trafalgar Square. Knox parodied the ponderous, deadpan RP announcing style, as he described the crowd following a suggestion by Mr. Popplebury, secretary of the National Movement for Abolishing Theatre Queues, to sack the National Gallery. He then announced listeners would be connected to the band at the Savoy Hotel.

Dance music played on the studio gramophone. Knox provided a weather report, and more news about the cricket match, before returning to the unemployed demonstration, then pouring through Admiralty Arch in a threatening manner and attacking waterfowl in St. James's Park with bottles.

Knox began an introduction of Sir Theophilius Gooch, K.B.E., of the Committee for the Inspection of Insanitary Dwellings, who would address the audience, but interrupted himself with another break-in announcing Gooch had been captured by demonstrators and was being roasted alive.

Knox continued with news bulletins, describing the destruction of the Big Ben clock tower with trench mortars. The Big Ben clock was the official national timepiece, striking the hours on its nine-ton bell. Knox announced that in its absence time would be given from Edinburgh on Uncle Leslie's repeating watch.

Uncle Leslie was a character in the daily program *Children's Hour*, broadcast originally from Station 5IT in Birmingham beginning in 1922 (Crisell, 2002, p. 20). Broadcast was moved to other BBC regional stations before the popular program began broadcasting from London in December 1923 (Dolan, 2003, p. 329). When broadcast from Station 2EH in Edinburgh, the character Uncle Leslie was voiced by George L. Marshall, station director and friend of Father Knox. The program ended in 1964.

Another break-in reported the hanging of the minister of traffic from a lamppost along the Vauxhall Bridge Road. Knox then, with great ceremony, announced a mistake in the reporting and provided a correction. The minister was hung not from a lamppost but from a tramway post. Listeners were once again connected with the Savoy Hotel Band.

Music was interrupted by the sound of an explosion, created by smashing a wooden produce case in the studio. *Broadcasting the Barricades* concluded with a series of break-ins announcing the destruction of the Savoy Hotel and the arrival of demonstrators at the BBC's London station. Knox reported Mr. Popplebury, secretary of the National Movement for Abolishing Theatre Queues, and several demonstrators in the waiting room where they were reading copies of *Radio Times*. Knox wished listeners a goodnight, and concluded his broadcast.

Within minutes, telephones rang at BBC stations. Later that evening, Station 2LO, in London, tried to reassure listeners by broadcasting apologies. "Some listeners, who apparently only heard part of Father Knox's talk at 7:40 this evening did not realise the humorous innuendo underlying the imaginary news items and have felt uneasy with the fate of London, Big Ben and other places mentioned in the talk. The preliminary announcement stated that the talk was a skit on broadcasting and the whole talk was, of course, a burlesque. We hope that any listeners who did not realise it will accept our sincere apologies for any uneasiness caused. London is safe, Big Ben is still chiming, and all is well" ("A Broadcast Scare," 1926, p. 7).

When it became apparent that confusion and concern were widespread, the BBC issued a more formal apology. "The B.B.C. regrets that any listeners should have been perturbed by this purely fantastic picture, but we would remind listeners that in this case, as in all similar cases, a preliminary warning was given that what followed was to be taken as an entertainment and not seriously. Incidents in the course of the skit itself also should have served to show its character, but it appears that the warning and such episodes were missed by listeners who came into the talk too late" ("A Broadcast Scare," 1926, p. 7).

In all, 249 complaints were received by the BBC. These were far outnumbered by positive comments (Lacey, 2013, p. 72). As a result of the broadcast, perhaps, applications for radio receiver licenses increased (Snoddy, 2005).

Part of the reaction to *Broadcasting the Barricades* may have been due to weather. A regional snowstorm on Sunday prevented wide delivery of newspapers ("Britain Is Alarmed," 1926, p. 3; "London Quite Safe," 1926, p. 2). Additionally, at the time of Knox's talk, radio, as a technology, as a cultural experience, and as a news source, was still quite novel throughout the United Kingdom. In 1926, there was no standardization for relaying urgent or breaking news bulletins. Interrupting the flow of an ongoing program with different and quite possibly unrelated information was uncommon. But the believability of Father Knox's reporting of the fictional news was unsettling, and left many listeners unsure of how to respond. And reference to revolution made listeners nervous. They were well aware of the Communist Revolution, November 7, 1917, in Russia, where civil unrest overturned the Provisional Government and forced the abdication of Nicholas II. The ruling and upper classes feared a similar revolt in the United Kingdom. Agitation and unrest between workers and police was already reported, so such fears were not entirely unfounded. Although not an immediate result of the radio broadcast, the General Strike happened soon enough, May 3–12, 1926.

Telephones also rang in newspaper offices around the United Kingdom. The next day's newspapers included reports of callers tuning in late and being confused or frightened ("A Broadcast Scare," 1926, p. 7), laments over the gullibility and inattention of audiences to the new medium of radio (Waugh, 2005, p. 290), and puffery about the best source for news ("Nervous and Knox," 1926, p. 7).

Much of this criticism of radio by newspapers might be seen as posturing. Newspapers, fearful of losing readers and advertisers, stood to benefit from any outcry against radio, and were happy to provide such. In the end, the BBC, stung by the experience, promised to maintain control over future talks, but continued to experiment, hoping to discover what listeners wanted to hear ("What Does the Public Want?," 1926, p. 2).

Criticism came from other directions as well. Father Knox's brother, Edmund George Valpy—known as E. V., editor of *Punch*, 1932–1949—commented, "I am inclined to think my brother over-estimated the people's sense of humour.... If my brother had discussed his intentions with me I should have advised him not to do it. But there is no limit to our credulity" ("Did the B.B.C. Blunder?," 1926, p. 3).

And Father Knox?

> The idea for this skit came to me while I was sitting at home listening to the results of the last election being broadcast. I endeavoured to visualise the breathlessness there would be throughout the country during a revolution, and I tried to imagine the news bulletins during such a time of popular excitement. I put my ideas on paper and then attempted to burlesque them.... I had no idea that listeners would take what I said seriously.... Even now, I cannot quite see how anyone could have misinterpreted my remarks. I am sure that my "news reports" were so far-fetched that no-one who thought them out could have been alarmed. ("Father Knox on B.B.C.," 1926, pp. 1–2).

According to George L. Marshall, Edinburgh station manager, "No one was more surprised than Father Knox that anyone should have taken his talk seriously. As for myself, when I heard of the alarm it had caused all over the country I was greatly surprised, because I duly announced before Father Knox began that it was not a serious lecture, but an entertainment in the nature of a skit on broadcasting.... The whole thing was an obvious farce, and could not possibly have deceived anyone who had listened carefully from the beginning" ("Radio Skit Causes Country-wide Scare," 1926, p. 3).

No recording was made of *Broadcasting the Barricades*. However, Father Knox's script was reproduced in several newspapers, including the *Manchester Guardian* ("Father Knox's Saturday Night," 1926, p. 5), the *Irish Times* ("Mr. Popplebury's Wireless Revolution," 1926, p. 5), and the *Daily News* ("What Father Knox Said," 1926, p. 8). Knox included the script as "A Forgotten Interlude" in his *Essays in Satire* (Knox, 1928, pp. 279–287). Using Father Knox's script, the broadcast was re-created as *The Riot That Never Was*. Produced by Paul Slade and Nick Baker, and featuring Ray Snoddy as the program presenter and Bob Sinfield as Father Knox, the program was broadcast on BBC 4 radio, 11:30–12:00 noon, Thursday, June 16, 2005 and repeated Monday, June 20, 2005, 12:15 A.M. ("The Riot That Never Was," 2005; Snoddy, 2005).

Within a few months, according to Waugh, the controversy had passed and Father Knox was heard again on BBC radio, parodying a scientific talk "illustrating the sounds, now made audible to the learned, of vegetables in pain" (Waugh, 2005, p. 290).

## The Minister Is Murdered! (September 1930)

During Welles's press conference, October 31, 1938, one reporter mentioned hearing a sensational radio drama while in Europe years earlier, one that apparently created quite some turmoil, and suggested Welles should have better anticipated the confusion his broadcast might produce.

That radio drama was *Der Minister ist ermordet!* (*The Minister Is Murdered!*), a two-hour radio play by Erich Ebermeyer, broadcast September 25, 1930, on Funkstunde, a Berlin station, almost exactly eight years prior to *The War of the Worlds* broadcast. During its broadcast, *The Minister Is Murdered!* was interrupted by a break-in news announcement: "Achtung! Achtung! [Attention! Attention!] This is an announcement by Radio Berlin and Königswusterhausen. Just moments ago, the Reich's Foreign Minister was murdered as he arrived at Friedrichstrasse station upon his return from the Geneva Conference. We will therefore stop this evening's entertainment immediately" ("Gross Nonsense," 1930, p. 3).

Ebermeyer enjoyed a reputation as a writer of expressionist novellas and dramas and was often heard on radio throughout Germany reading from them. His fictional radio drama, *The Minister Is Murdered!*, was based on the real-life murder of Foreign Minister Walter Rathenau in 1922 by right-wing extremists shortly after a treaty signing with the Soviet Union.

The years immediately following World War I brought Germany economic hyperinflation, political fragmentation, and burgeoning extremism on both the right and left. The country was characterized by instability, transience, and crisis. In November 1923, radio emerged as a closely regulated network of regional state-owned stations broadcasting preapproved programs funded in part by private investment but controlled by local and national governments aimed at licensed listeners (Lerg, 1970, p. 373).

Following the experimental film, theater, literature, music, cabaret, and criticism of the Weimar Republic at the time, visionary radio station directors wanted to develop "radiogenic" art forms (Lacey, 2013, p. 61). One was Hans Flesch (1896–1945), the first artistic director of the Frankfurt radio station, who, on October 24, 1924, produced *Zauberei auf dem Sender: Versuch einer Rundfunkgroteske* (*Wizardry on the Air: Attempt at a Radio Grotesque*), the first custom-produced radio drama broadcast in Germany (Lacey, 2013, p. 61). By 1929, Flesch was recruited to manage Berlin Funkstunde, Germany's largest and most important radio station. His mission was to rescue the station's waning artistic reputation (Leonhard, 1997, pp. 81–85; Weil, 1996).

In 1930, Ebermeyer hoped his drama would draw attention to the senselessness of political assassinations. Censors, however, recognized the political sensitivity of Ebermeyer's radio drama and rejected it on political and cultural grounds. Ebermeyer argued that *The Minister Is Murdered!* promoted literary education and demonstrated radiogenic merits supportive of the German state. His arguments were buffeted by bitter battles in the press and national politics about the increasing politicization of state radio (Lacey, 2013, p. 66).

When finally broadcast, *The Minister Is Murdered!* was presented as if its events were happening in real time, and listeners were scared. The fictional break-in news report sounded credible, especially since Adolph Hitler, testifying that same day before the Supreme Court in Leipzig, promised retribution for sanctions placed on Germany at the end of World War I, November 1918. Was a right-wing coup under way in Germany? The fictional reported murder of the foreign minister was conflated with the then foreign minister, Julius Curtius, who had just attended a conference in Geneva, and Rathenau's murder in 1922. Newspaper stories about *The Minister Is Murdered!* broadcast were printed throughout Germany. American newspapers, including the *Oakland Tribune* (California), the *Burlington Daily Times* (North Carolina), the *Hanover Evening Sun* (Pennsylvania), and the *New York Times*, all reprinted an Associated Press report about "several thousand radio listeners" recovering from what they thought was an actual news announcement of the assassination of Foreign Minister Curtius. According to the report, "The Minister of the Interior [Joseph Wirth] began an investigation to determine who was responsible for putting such a radio play on the air at a time of political tension in Germany" ("Murder Play," 1930, p. 22).

Responses to *The Minister Is Murdered!* included controversy over the responsibilities and censorship of radio, whether the radio drama was in good or bad taste, the artistic ambition of the performance and its realism, and what the performance said about the power of radio and the vulnerability of the listening audience (Jelavich, 2006, pp. 117–121; Lacey, 2013, pp. 66–71). Surely it was this alarm, eight years earlier, to which the reporter referred when questioning Welles the morning following his *The War of the Worlds* broadcast.

## The Fall of the City (1937)

*The Fall of the City*, a radio drama by Archibald MacLeish, was broadcast as an episode of *The Columbia Workshop* on April 11, 1937, using the format and language of a news broadcast, reminiscent of earlier episodes of *The March of Time*. Welles voiced the part of the announcer and delivered his lines as if reporting live from the scene of the events. There were no break-in news announcements.

Brad Schwartz said MacLeish wrote his verse allegory in news broadcast format thinking this would heighten listeners' sense of reality. Welles, according to Schwartz, later utilized MacLeish's technique to build his own radio series, *The Mercury Theatre on the Air*, and highlighted realistic-sounding but fictional break-in news announcements in *The War of the Worlds* (Schwartz, 2015, p. 37).

## *The Crimson Wizard* (1938)

Friday evening, September 30, 1938, one month before Welles's production of *The War of the Worlds*, listeners of WGN Radio in Chicago heard the first episode of *The Crimson Wizard*, a new radio drama series in which brilliant hunchback scientist Peter Quill used his scientific ingenuity to defend America against a communist spy ring, the Red Circle.

According to Karl Schadow, *The Crimson Wizard* was announced September 25, 1938, in the Graphic Section of the *Chicago Sunday Tribune*. Readers were encouraged to tune in to WGN radio the following Friday, September 30, for the first episode, and then read a permanent record in the paper the following Sunday compiled by "Special Agent" from secret reports and files (Schadow, 2004).

*The Crimson Wizard* radio series was created by Robert M. Lee, *Chicago Tribune* managing editor, and Blair Walliser, WGN program director. The *Chicago Tribune* owned WGN—World's Greatest Newspaper—so this collaborative effort was clearly designed to increase traffic for both media. The first episode was set in the WGN Washington, D.C., broadcasting studio where naval designer Eric Lambert delivered a talk about a new seventy-five-thousand-ton battleship he had designed. His report was interrupted by a police shortwave transmission by Secret Bureau Chief Allan Tyler, regarding a robbery and fire at the naval archives building. "All squads . . . all squads . . . calling all squads of the secret service . . . all squads . . . the naval vaults . . . robbers." Following the break-in, Maida Travers, female vocalist, love interest for Lambert, and inspiration for Quill, began to sing. She was quickly cut off, however, by further police break-ins, including a request for more fire engines. In between the secret service squad reporting about blocking roads and questioning motorists, a hollow voice was heard repeating, "Peter Quill . . . Peter Quill . . . Peter Quill." The voice was that of Ivan Molokoff, Red Circle spy, who worked undercover as the radio station's assistant engineer. Molokoff intended to rob Peter Quill of his invention, invisible lightning, and carry it to Red Circle headquarters. He used the radio to create fear in Chicago (Special Agent, 1938, pp. 1, 2, 3, 9).

Apparently, his efforts were successful. The *Chicago Tribune* reported the next day that hundreds of people contacted their offices, and those of city, county, and state police, asking whether the radio reports were true. "They started out last night to be just another radio mystery thriller. But before W-G-N and the Mutual Broadcasting System had half completed the first episode of the spy drama public attention had been swerved from war and baseball to the theft of naval secrets and the mysteries of espionage. . . . The presentation had been so real that the listeners demanded more information and verification of the story" ("Hundreds Call Police," 1938, p. 1). Interestingly, the *Chicago Tribune* barely covered *The War of the Worlds* radio drama broadcast, perhaps to avoid comparisons to *The Crimson Wizard*.

*The Crimson Wizard* ran for three seasons. No scripts or recordings have been found (Schadow, 2004).

## *Air Raid* (1938)

Another potential inspiration for Welles was *Air Raid*, written by Archibald MacLeish, produced by *The Columbia Workshop*, and broadcast on October 27, 1938, just three days before Welles's performance of *The War of the Worlds*. Inspired by the bombing of Guernica during the Spanish Civil War, *Air Raid* told of the bombing of a fictional small European town from the perspective of a news announcer. Frank Brady wrote, in his biography of Welles, *Citizen Welles*, that MacLeish began writing his script about seven months prior to its debut (Brady, 1989, p. 166). This was MacLeish's second radio drama produced by *The Columbia Workshop*. As he had in *The Fall of the City*, MacLeish used a journalistic reporting style as the basis for his narrative.

Welles never acknowledged being influenced by either *The Fall of the City* or *Air Raid*. But he certainly knew of both productions. He had, after all, a major role in *The Fall of the City*. And even though he had no speaking part in *Air Raid*, according to radio historian Irving Settel, a CBS photographer documented him during rehearsal talking with Ray Collins, lead voice actor, William N. Robson, director, and MacLeish as if he were a member of the cast (Settel, 1967, p. 102). Additionally, biographer Frank Brady said Welles listened to the broadcast of *Air Raid* and was deeply impressed (Brady, 1989, p. 166).

Despite this lack of acknowledgment, it is clear Welles used the techniques of news reporting narrative style and break-in news announcements he learned from his connection to both *The Fall of the City* and *Air Raid* to turn *The War of the Worlds*, a radio drama, into (fictional) news (Geduld, 1995, p. 263). As Brad Schwartz said, "Knowing what MacLeish had prepared for *The Columbia Workshop* very likely encouraged Welles to do something similar with 'War of the Worlds,' though his approach would be less poetic than MacLeish's" (Schwartz, 2015, p. 52).

## *The War of the Worlds* (1938)

Readers are no doubt familiar with *The War of the Worlds* radio broadcast. Considered the most (in)famous radio broadcast of all time, *The War of the Worlds* used fictional but authentic-sounding news break-in announcements to move the narrative forward with a sense of immediacy. Other results included confusion and, allegedly, panic.

The radio drama was adapted from *The War of the Worlds*, a science fiction novel written by H. G. Wells (1866–1946). First published in nine serialized parts in 1897, the entire novel was published in 1898 and has remained in print ever since. The novel describes the invasion of Southern England by beings from the planet Mars through the observations of an unnamed narrator and his brother, also unnamed. After devastating the countryside and London, the Martians are themselves conquered by common Earth bacteria to which they have no immunity.

The radio adaptation of Wells's novel was written by Howard E. Koch, a lawyer turned playwright. According to Frank Brady, Welles told Koch to "modernize the language and dialogue, to localize the action, and to dramatize the story in the form of radio news bulletins" (Brady, 1989, p. 164). After producing the first drafts of *The War of the Worlds* script, Koch continued as a scriptwriter, writing some of the most influential radio and film productions of the mid-twentieth century, including coauthoring the screenplay for *Casablanca*, for which he won an Academy Award in 1944.

*The War of the Worlds* was produced and performed by the cast and crew of *The Mercury Theatre on the Air*, an offshoot of the Mercury Theatre, a New York drama company founded by Welles and John Houseman in 1937. Actors like Martin Gabel, Alice Frost, Ray Collins, Virginia Welles (Mrs. Orson Welles), Agnes Moorehead, Everett Sloane, and George Coulouris appeared in numerous productions.

Dramatic stories were chosen for their adaptability to the radio medium. *Dracula* opened the new radio series, broadcast on July 11, 1938. Other shows included *Treasure Island*, *A Tale of Two Cities*, *The 39 Steps*, *Abraham Lincoln*, *The Count of Monte Cristo*, *The Man Who Was Thursday*, *The Immortal Sherlock Holmes*, and *Around the World in Eighty Days*, among others. With its innovative use of sound effects and music, and Welles's performances, *The Mercury Theatre on the Air* quickly became known for inventive and high-quality radio drama. *The Mercury Theatre on the Air* is often acknowledged as producing the finest radio drama of the 1930s, even though most of its work is, today, relatively unknown, save for *The War of the Worlds* (Scarborough, n.d.).

*The War of the Worlds* radio dramatization was interrupted very soon after its start by a news break-in reporting explosions occurring at regular intervals on the planet Mars. Programming returned to a New York City hotel where dance music was being offered. The music was soon interrupted by another break-in reporting a government request that several large observatories around the country watch for further disturbances on the planet Mars.

An interview by reporter Carl Phillips with noted astronomer Professor Pierson was arranged. Pierson (Welles) assured Phillips that the chances of intelligent life on Mars were not likely and the distance between Mars and Earth—forty million miles—provided safety.

Another break-in announced the crash of a meteorite at a New Jersey farm. As Phillips described the scene, a large metal cylinder lay half buried in an impact pit, surrounded by spectators and police. A creature emerged from the cylinder, rose up from the pit, and incinerated with a heat ray many of the cars and people gathered around. Phillips described the ray approaching his position, then silence.

From this point, multiple break-ins from government and military officials, several seemingly live on location, each sounding authentic, described the Martian fighting machines ravaging the countryside, wading across the Hudson River, and conquering New York. The first half of *The War of the Worlds* ended with silence punctuated by boat whistles and the voice of a radio operator calling for response, for survivors. In the second half of the performance, Professor Pierson recounted the destruction wrought by the Martians as they advanced toward New York. He found them there, in Central Park, dead, victims of common Earth bacteria to which they had no immunity.

## Not So Innocent

The next morning, October 31, 1938, Welles met with reporters in the CBS building in New York to talk about the previous evening's broadcast of *The War of the Worlds*. Reporters and photographers crowded around Welles. Concern and outrage, along with threats of lawsuits and possible regulations were building in the national press and government. Everyone wanted answers.

Welles began by reading a prepared statement. "Despite my deep regret over any misapprehension which our broadcast last night created among some listeners, I am even more bewildered over this misunderstanding in the light of an analysis of the broadcast itself." Welles then outlined four factors "which should have in any event maintained the illusion of fiction in the broadcast." The first was that the radio drama was performed as if occurring in the future. The second was the broadcast occurred during the regular *Mercury Theatre* program time, and was announced in newspapers. The third was that listeners were informed at the beginning, at the middle, and at the end of the broadcast that the program was an adaptation of the H. G. Wells's novel. The fourth, "seems to me to have been the most pertinent of all. That is the familiarity of the fable, within the American idiom, of Mars and the Martians" ("The Aftermath: Orson Welles," 2008; Brady, 1989, p. 173). Following his statement, Welles answered questions.

> REPORTER  Were you aware of the terror going on throughout the nation while you were giving the broadcast?
> 
> WELLES  Oh no, of course not. I was frankly terribly shocked to learn it did. You must realize that when I left the broadcast last night I went into a dress rehearsal for a play that's opening in two days [*Danton's Death*] and I've had almost no sleep. So I know less about this than you do. I haven't read the papers. I'm terribly shocked by the effect it's had. The technique I used was not original with me, or peculiar to the Mercury Theater's presentation. It was not even new. I anticipated nothing unusual. ("Panic!," 1938)

Although he did his best to appear the victim, others suggested Welles was not as innocent as he looked. For example, in 1940, just two years after *The War of the Worlds* radio broadcast, Hadley Cantril, Hazel Gaudet, and Herta Herzog, in their study of the psychological effects associated with the Welles's dramatization, cited *Broadcasting the Barricades* as a previous example of a panic broadcast (Cantril, Gaudet, & Herzog, 1940, p. xxvii). In his biography of Father Knox, Evelyn Waugh suggested that Orson Welles knew of *Broadcasting the Barricades* and set out to imitate the effect with his own production of *The War of the Worlds* (Waugh 2005). In his essay, "Holy Terror: The First Great Radio Hoax," Paul Slade considers whether *Broadcasting the Barricades* provided direct influence on *The War of the Worlds* broadcast in 1938 (Slade, 2013).

But there is nothing like hearing admission of guilt from the accused. And, years after *The War of the Worlds* broadcast, according to biographer Frank Brady, in a television interview, Welles said, "Radio in those days, before the tube and the transistor, wasn't just a noise in somebody's pocket—it was a voice of authority. Too much so. At least, I thought so.... It was time for someone to take the starch... out of some of that authority: hence my broadcast" (Brady, 1989, p. 164).

More specifically, on June 19, 1955, during the fifth episode of *Orson Welles' Sketch Book*, titled *The War of the Worlds*, Welles reflected on "our little experiment with radio." He admitted, "I suppose we had it coming to us because in fact we were not as innocent as we meant to be. When we did the Martian broadcast we were fed up with the way in which everything that came over this new magic box, the radio, became swallowed... believed.... So in a way our broadcast was an assault on the credibility of that machine. We wanted people to understand that they shouldn't take an opinion predigested and they shouldn't swallow everything that came through the tap, whether it was radio or not" ("Orson Welles on War of the Worlds," 2010; "Orson Welles Sketchbook," 2013).

In 1969, Welles and film director Peter Bogdanovich began recording a series of conversations, a practice they continued for several years. Transcriptions were published as *This Is Orson Welles* in both print and audiobook versions in 1992. In both, Welles acknowledged that *Broadcasting the Barricades* gave him the idea for and influenced his production of *The War of the Worlds*. As Welles said, "I got the idea from a BBC show that had gone on the year before [*sic*], when a Catholic priest told how some Communists had seized London and a lot of people in London believed it. And I thought that'd be fun to do on a big scale, let's have it from outer space—that's how I got the idea" (Welles & Bogdanovich, 1992).

In an interview, May 1, 1975, with Thomas James "Tom" Snyder, host of *The Tomorrow Show*, a late night television talk show on the NBC television network, Welles said, "There are pictures of me made about three hours after the broadcast looking as much as I could like an early Christian saint. As if I didn't know what I was doing... but I'm afraid it was about as hypocritical as anyone could possibly get!" ("Welles Interview," 1975). In an October 30, 1978 interview on the *Today* television show, on the fortieth anniversary of the original broadcast, Welles was asked, "Did you get a laugh out of it, Orson?" According to Brady,

Welles replied, "Huge, huge, yes, a huge laugh. I never thought it was anything but funny" (Brady, 1989, p. 175).

Welles elaborately feigned innocence in 1938 because he was afraid of losing his job and career. Welles told Bogdanovich he faced $12 million in lawsuits (Welles & Bogdanovich, 1992, p. 19). John Houseman, cofounder, with Welles, of *The Mercury Theatre on the Air*, estimated the total to be around $750,000 (Houseman, 1972, p. 405). Barbara Leaming, a Welles biographer, put the total at $200,000 (Leaming, 1985, p. 162).

However, within days following the broadcast, it was clear that public response was favorable. There would be no government regulation. Welles was famous throughout the world. Plus, a rider to his contract with CBS, added by his lawyer Arnold Weissberger, shielded him from responsibility for any lawsuits brought against the network so long as he had not plagiarized anything or libeled anyone (Brady, 1989, p. 176; Houseman, 1972, p. 405; Leaming 1985, pp. 162–163). Welles, although never as innocent as he pretended, played the role until he was clearly out of trouble.

## So What?

What does all this mean? And why is it important? This essay makes two points. The first is that *The War of the Worlds* was not fake news. Rather, it was an experiment with the relatively new radio medium to determine what kinds of content and what forms of delivery might promote engaging storytelling for listening audiences. The second point concerns the power of radio to spark listeners' imaginations. Radio dramas like *The War of the Worlds*, and radio itself as a new medium seeking to discover its own affordances and abilities to engage listeners, leveraged this power into an art form.

Brad Schwartz has forever tied *The War of the Worlds*, and the emerging radio art form, with fake news. Schwartz uses the term "fake news" multiple times in his book, *Broadcast Hysteria: Orson Welles's War of the Worlds and the Art of Fake News*, but does not provide a clear definition. In this absence, one might define fake news as intentionally misleading listening audiences by providing incomplete, inaccurate, or incorrect information. A radio hoax, also not defined by Schwartz, might be considered an intentional effort to create and maintain confusion.

Based on these definitions, and the examination by this essay, *The War of the Worlds* was neither a radio hoax nor fake news. If Welles is to be believed, it was transformative radio drama, cleverly created and exquisitely delivered so to elevate the critical listening skills of its audience, even while providing entertainment.

Despite Welles and the cast and producers of *The Mercury Theatre on the Air* stretching the confidence of their audience, as well as the traditions and expectations of content subjects and their presentation, *The War of the Worlds* radio drama continues to be, now eight decades after its original broadcast, a touchstone against which to consider the potential for purposeful hoaxes or fake news. When Welles told reporters that the use of fictional break-in news reports was not original or particular to his dramatization he was being truthful, if not sly, with his answer.

## In the Balance

Another point of this inquiry is to better understand the ability of radio drama to create believable reality, and to attract and maintain engagement with listeners' imaginations. Richard J. Hand and Mary Traynor argue this reality results from combining words (narration/dialogue/speech), sounds (sound effects, including use of previously recorded sound history, or previously recorded dialogue), music, and silence. When combined and interpreted through the listener's imagination, these "constituent parts" communicate specific ideas and contribute to the radio drama form (Hand & Traynor, 2011, p. 40).

As an example, Hand and Trayner point to what they call the first "specific radio play" in Great Britain, *A Comedy of Danger*, written by twenty-three-year-old Richard Hughes. Broadcast on BBC, January 15, 1924, this radio play introduced the potential to inspire audience imagination when, in the second spoken line, the character Jack says, "The lights have gone out!" The play was commissioned by the BBC as a "listening play," and consciously utilized "the potential of the radio form" (Hand & Traynor, 2011, p. 16).

There are reports of earlier broadcasts of radio drama. For example, *The Truth about Father Christmas* is said to have been broadcast on December 24, 1922. Asa Briggs said scenes from Shakespeare's *Julius Caesar, Henry VIII*, and *Much Ado about Nothing* were broadcast February 16, 1923, from the BBC's Marconi House on the Strand in central London (Briggs, 1995). And a complete version of *Twelfth Night* was reportedly broadcast on May 28, 1923. But according to John Drakakis, "Setting aside the broadcast of *The Truth about Father Christmas*, [*A Comedy of Danger*] is generally acknowledged [as] the first play to be produced especially for radio" (Drakakis, 1981, p. 4).

In the years between World War I and World War II, radio was a new social, cultural, and technological phenomena, something strange, even electrifying. According to Susan Douglas, never before had people experienced disembodied voices arriving, as if by magic through the air, creating an imaginative space wherein the gap between machinery and spirituality was reconciled (Douglas, 1999, p. 41). Affordable and readily available, radio sets were common in American homes during the 1930s. Following *The War of the Worlds* broadcast, questions were asked: How might radio be used? How should it be managed? What content could be produced? What content would most attract listeners? What content and delivery style would promote engaging storytelling?

A focus of early radio programming was familiar entertainment, like music, literature, or drama. But should radio broadcasts of dramatic performances provide the familiarity of the traditional stage, or explore new features and affordances, even the constraints, of radio? Should radio drama performances be considered separate from world events, or should they draw upon current social, political, and/or cultural trends? Should radio drama promote entertainment, or thought-provoking experiences, for the listening audience?

In response to such questions, American radio producers and broadcasters experimented with different content forms and presentation modes. They constantly tested the radio medium, seeking to learn its affordances for narrative and storytelling, even while trying to monetize the results (Schwartz, 2015, p. 221). Commercialization and creativity, as different visions of radio, produced tensions. To address these tensions, the Communications Act of 1934 empowered the Federal Communications Commission (FCC) to establish regulations regarding radio broadcasting.

A central understanding was that the atmosphere between broadcasters and listeners through which radio waves traveled were publicly owned. In order to broadcast radio programs, one had to, said Minna F. Kassner, apply to the FCC for a radio station operating/broadcasting license. Licenses should be awarded only to those stations operating in the "public interest, convenience, or necessity." No guidelines were provided for what this meant, said Kassner, because the FCC "repeatedly stated that it does not have the power under the [communications] act to make regulations covering the contents of radio programs or even various types of advertising, because of the prohibition against censorship contained [in another section of the Communications Act]" (Kassner, 1939, p. 82). If a station failed the public interest test, its license could be revoked. To avoid trouble with the FCC over public interest, radio stations offered an array of programming, hoping to attract the interest of as many different listeners as possible. Programs during the 1930s were often defined by their inventiveness and creativity. Often, programs were supported by the radio networks rather than a corporate sponsor.

So, for a brief period during the 1930s, American radio hung in the balance between commerce and control on one side, and creativity on the other. By the following decade, commerce had won. Sponsors controlled the programming, and they allowed only programs with broad appeal and thus income potential from advertising. The network supported shows were gone, as was radio as a free, experimental medium (Schwartz, 2015, pp. 222–223).

## Legacy of Experimentation with Engaging Storytelling

British radio historian Paddy Scannell argued that early British radio talk shows taught producers how to create radio and listeners how to listen (Scannell, 2013).

How might early radio producers in Great Britain and America have learned the power of radio to spark listeners' imaginations? The answer: experimentation.

This essay considers the radio dramas *Broadcasting the Barricades, The Minister Is Murdered!, The Fall of the City, The Crimson Wizard, Air Raid*, and *The War of the Worlds* as legacy experiments with a medium new to both its producers and consumers.

Even early in the history of American radio, the mid-1930s, the power of radio was known to reside in the imagination of its listeners who would visualize what they heard in their own minds. As Hadley Cantril and Gordon Allport note, "Given the slightest encouragement, the listener can build his own imaginative scene.... Listeners can jump through time and space with alacrity that defies even the advanced techniques of the stage or screen" (Cantril & Allport, 1935, p. 232).

Said another way, a radio listener is in the world imagined by the radio program, immersed in her private listening experience, yet connected with others through the shared act of listening. According to radio historian Susan Douglas, "The magic was—and is—in the act of listening itself, in relying on and trusting your ears alone to produce ideas and emotions. The magic comes from entering a world of sound, and from using that sound to make your own vision, your own dream, your own world" (Douglas, 1999, p. 28). "Listening to it [radio drama]," said Tom Pear, "one has, or is, only ears. *Only?* Let us remember that we hear not with our ears but with our minds. The simple sounds are interpreted by perception and imagination" (Pear, 1931, p. 90, emphasis original).

When *Broadcasting the Barricades, The Minister Is Murdered!, The Fall of the City, The Crimson Wizard, Air Raid*, and *The War of the Worlds* were broadcast, listeners had significant experience reading about world news events in newspapers, but less experience hearing news spoken to them. Radio was a new experience, and according to Barbara Leaming, radio listeners did not appreciate blurring the "reassuring distinctions between fiction and fact that serve as signposts, orienting us whenever we are exposed to made-up stories, whether in novels, the theater, radio, or the movies" (Leaming, 1985, p. 161).

Still, these radio dramas seemed real because the reporting narrative styles and break-in news reports they employed sounded real, official, and, more importantly, believable. Those listeners who understood the parodic nature of the fictional news break-in, and the use of reporting style to build narrative, enjoyed the result. Those who did not understand, or did not listen carefully, missed the point and were, perhaps, confused or panicked.

By providing sounds and voices, perhaps previously unheard, even unimagined, radio dramas like *The War of the Worlds* enlarged frontiers of personal experience while connecting listeners with others across the country. And, according to Neil Verma, radio of the 1930s often focused on "social effects," how radio might be used to educate and uplift listeners, to empower them through "their newfound connection to world events" (Verma, 2012, pp. 121–123). Such power, said Douglas, comes from radio's ability to carry people "back into the realms of pre literacy, into orality, to a mode of communication reliant on storytelling, listening, and group memory" (Douglas, 1999, p. 29). *Broadcasting the Barricades, The Minister Is Murdered!, The Fall of the City, The Crimson Wizard, Air Raid,* and *The War of the Worlds* were all built on modes of listening that were centuries old, even while simultaneously promoting new thoughts about technology and community and questioning whether the former destroyed the latter or reconfigured traditions (Douglas, 1999, p. 39).

This is not to say these radio dramatizations sought to deceive their audiences. Instead, they sought to engage listeners in sound-based storytelling that, according to Douglas, "reactivated, extended, and intensified particular cognitive modes that encouraged, simultaneously, a sense of belonging to a community, an audience, and a confidence that your imaginings, your radio visions, were the best and truest ones of all" (Douglas, 1999, p. 39).

As noted earlier, radio listeners are immersed in private listening experiences, guided by their imaginations, prompted by what they hear. As a result, there is opportunity for experimentation with engaging forms of storytelling. Through experimentation with the affordances, constraints, infrastructure, and technologies of the radio medium, radio dramas like *The War of the Worlds* became radio art in their efforts to produce and broadcast creative sound-based artifacts.

## Conclusion

As noted in this essay, by providing sounds and voices, perhaps previously unheard, even unimagined, radio enlarges our frontiers of personal experience, reminding us always of human endeavors in other places. This was—and is—the core of radio's power as an art medium, and a storyteller. Radio sends a sound-based story throughout the country, or the world, inviting itself into a silent home, or waiting at a noisy pub, ready and able to entertain us. Radio extends the traditional and powerful art of storytelling by engaging audiences, forging connections, and arousing their imaginations in new but very familiar ways.

Rather than fake news, *Broadcasting the Barricades, The Minister Is Murdered!, Air Raid, The Crimson Wizard,* and *The War of the Worlds* are some of radio's experiments with engaging storytelling. They move radio culture, practice, and listening beyond traditional roles of commerce and/or control to engage the listening audience with radio storytelling (Barber, 2017). How effective is this ability? As this essay has argued, quite strong, and quite compelling.

## References

The aftermath: Orson Welles "The War of the Worlds" Halloween press conference, 1938. (2008, October 31). *Wellesnet: The Orson Welles Web Resource.* Retrieved from www.wellesnet.com/the-aftermath-orson-welles-the-war-of-the-worlds-halloween-press-conference-1938/

Ang, J. (1991). *Desperately seeking the audience*. Florence, KY: Routledge.
Barber, J. (2017). Radio art: A (mass) medium becomes an (artistic) medium. *Hyperrhiz: New Media Cultures, 17*. Retrieved from https://doi.org/10.20415/hyp/017
Brady, F. (1989). *Citizen Welles: A biography of Orson Welles*. New York: Scribner.
Briggs, A. (1995). *The history of broadcasting in the United Kingdom*. Oxford: Oxford University Press.
Britain is alarmed by burlesque radio news of revolt in London and bombing of Commons. (1926, January 18). *New York Times*, p. 3.
A broadcast scare. News parody taken seriously. London rising. B.B.C. apology for the alarm caused. (1926, January 18). *Daily News*, p. 7.
Cantril, H., & Allport, G. W. (1935). *The psychology of radio*. New York: Harper and Brothers.
Cantril, H., Gaudet, H., & Herzog, H. (1940). *The invasion from Mars: A study in the psychology of panic*. New York: Harper & Row.
Crisell, A. (2002). *Understanding radio*. Milton Park, UK: Taylor & Francis.
Did the B.B.C. blunder? Theory that nation lacks a sense of humour. A credulous people. Opinion divided on broadcast skit scare. (1926, January 19). *Daily Sketch*, p. 3.
Dolan, J. (2003). Aunties and uncles: The BBC's Children's Hour and liminal concerns in the 1920s. *Historical Journal of Film, Radio & Television, 23*(4), 329–340.
Douglas, S. (1999). *Listening in: Radio and the American imagination*. New York: Random House.
Drakakis, J. (Ed.). (1981). *British radio drama*. Cambridge: Cambridge University Press.
Father Knox on B.B.C. scare. Very sorry but cannot understand it. (1926, January 19). *Evening Standard*, pp. 1, 2.
Father Knox's Saturday night. The revolution of 1926. Had listeners-in excuse for alarm? The skit reproduced. (1926, January 19). *Manchester Guardian*, p. 5.
Geduld, H. M. (1995). Welles or Wells?—A matter of adaptation. In M. Beja (Ed.), *Perspectives on Orson Welles* (pp. 260–272). Boston: G.K. Hall.
George Orson Welles interviewed by journalists after "The War of The Worlds" broadcast [Video file]. (2012). Retrieved from www.youtube.com/watch?v=rsFtgc2WswM
Gross nonsense: Berlin Funkstunde's grotesque tastelessness. (1930, September 26). Astrid Ensslin (Trans.). *Berliner Börsen-Zeitung*, p. 3. Retrieved from http://zefys.staatsbibliothek-berlin.de/index.php?id=dfg-viewer&set%5Bimage%5D=3&set%5Bzoom%5D=default&set%5Bdebug%5D=0&set%5Bdouble%5D=0&set%5Bmets%5D=http%3A%2F%2Fcontent.staatsbibliothek-berlin.de%2Fzefys%2FSNP2436020X-19300926-0-0-0-0.xml
Hand, R. J., & Traynor, M. (2011). *The radio drama handbook: Audio drama in context and practice*. London: Continuum.
Heyer, P. (2005). *The medium and magician: Orson Welles, the radio years, 1934–1952*. Lanham, MD: Rowman & Littlefield.
Houseman, J. (1972). *Run-through: A memoir*. New York: Simon & Schuster.
Hundreds call police to ask of Peter Quill. (1938, October 1). *Chicago Daily Tribune*, p. 1.
Jelavich, P. (2006). *Berlin alexanderplatz: Radio, film, and the death of the Weimar culture*. Berkeley: University of California Press.
Kassner, M. F. (1939). Radio censorship. In S. B. Harrison (Ed.), *Radio censorship* (pp. 80–82, 183–190). New York: H.W. Wilson.
Knox, R. (1928). A forgotten interlude. In *Essays in satire* (pp. 279–287). London: Sheed and Ward.
Knox, R. A. (1929). Introduction. In R. Knox & K. Harrington (Eds.), *The best English detective stories of 1928* (pp. 9–26). New York: Horace Liveright.

Lacey, K. (2013). Assassination, insurrection and alien invasion: Interwar wireless scares in cross-national comparison. In J. Hayes & K. Battles (Eds.), *War of the Worlds to social media: Mediated communication in times of crisis* (pp. 57–82). Bern: Peter Lang.

Leaming, B. (1985). *Orson Welles: A biography*. New York: Viking.

Leonhard, J. F. (1997). *Programmgeschichte des höfunks in der Weimarer Republik*. Munich: Deutscher Taschenbuch Verlag.

Lerg, W. B. (1970). *Die entstehung des rundfuks in Deutchland: Herkunft und entwicklung eines publizistischen mittels*. Frankfurt am Main: Knect Verlag.

London quite safe: B.B.C.'s news skit that led to a scare. Big Ben blown up! (1926, January 18). *Daily Mirror*, p. 2.

Marshall, E. (1926, January 24). Hoaxes and politics fail to win Britain: Father Knox's radio revolution and Lloyd George's shifts fall flat with public. *New York Times*, p. E1

Mr. Popplebury's wireless revolution. Father Knox's burlesque. (1926, January 19). *Irish Times*, p. 5.

Murder play on Berlin radio starts assassination rumors. (1930, September 27). *New York Times*, p. 22.

Nervous and Knox. (1926, January 18). *Daily Sketch*, p. 7.

Orson Welles apologizes for *The War of the Worlds* mass panic [Video file]. (2013). Retrieved from www.youtube.com/watch?v=8vbYyDh-BRI)

Orson Welles on War of the Worlds [Video file]. (2010). Retrieved from www.youtube.com/watch?v=gfNsCcOHsNI

Orson Welles Sketchbook—Episode 5: The War of the Worlds [Video file]. (2013). Retrieved from www.youtube.com/watch?v=7VMbFnconTA

Panic! (1938, November 19). *Radio Guide, 8*(5), 2–5.

Pear, T. H. (1931). *Voice and personality as applied to radio broadcasting*. Hoboken, NJ: John Wiley.

Radio skit causes country-wide scare. Obvious joke taken seriously. Father Ronald Knox surprised by mild panic caused by his humorous broadcast of an imaginary mob's activities in London. (1926, January 18). *Daily Sketch*, p. 3.

The riot that never was. (2005, June 16). *Radio Times, 4237*, 131. Retrieved from https://genome.ch.bbc.co.uk/fb6b4764395744758862159631d1ac3f

Rogers, R. (1937). *Do's and don'ts of radio writing*. Boston: Associated Radio Writers.

Saturday, Jan. 16th. (1926, January 8). *Radio Times, 120*, 100. Retrieved from http://genome.ch.bbc.co.uk/schedules/2lo/1926-01-16

Scannell, P. (2013, April 25). *Live on air: The ontology of voice*. Opening plenary presentation at What Is Radio? Exploring the Past, Present, and Future of Radio conference, University of Oregon, Portland.

Scarborough, K. (n.d.). The Mercury Theatre on the air. Retrieved from www.mercurytheatre.info/

Schadow, K. H. (2004, October). Peter Quill, the Crimson Wizard. Metropolitan Washington Old Time Radio Club. Retrieved from www.mwotrc.com/rr2004_10/quill.htm

Schwartz, A. B. (2015). *Broadcast hysteria: Orson Welles's War of the Worlds and the art of fake news*. New York: Hill & Wang.

Sconce, J. (2000). *Haunted media: Electronic presence from telegraphy to television*. Durham, NC: Duke University Press.

Settel, I. (1967). *A pictorial history of radio*. New York: Grosset & Dunlap.

Slade, P. (2013). Holy terror: The first great radio hoax. *PlanetSlade*. Retrieved from www.planetslade.com/ronald-knox.html

Snoddy, R. (2005, June 13). Show that sparked a riot. *NewsWatch*. Retrieved from http://news.bbc.co.uk/newswatch/ukfs/hi/newsid_4080000/newsid_4081000/4081060.stm

Special Agent. (1938, October 2). The Crimson Wizard. *Chicago Tribune*, Color Graphic sec., pp. 1, 2, 3, 9. Retrieved from https://chicagotribune.newspapers.com/#

Verma, N. (2012). *Theater of the mind: Imagination, aesthetics, and American radio drama*. Chicago, IL: University of Chicago Press.

Walker, D. P. (2011). *The BBC in Scotland: The first 50 years*. Edinburgh: Luath Press.

Waugh, E. (1959). *Life of the Right Reverend Ronald Knox: Fellow of Trinity College, Oxford and Protonotary Apostolic to his Holiness Pope Pius XII compiled from the original sources*. London: Chapman & Hall.

Waugh, E. (2005). *Two lives: Edmund Campion and Ronald Knox*. London: Continuum.

Weil, M. (1996). Hans Flesch: Rundfunkintendant in Berlin. *Rundfunk und Geschichte*, *22*(4), 223–243.

Welles, O., & Bogdanovich, P. (1992). *This is Orson Welles*. New York: HarperCollins.

Welles Interview. Tomorrow. Tom Snyder interviewer. NBC News Archives. (1975, May 1). Retrieved from B. Holmsten & A. Lubertozzi (Eds.), *The War of the Worlds: Mars' invasion of Earth, inciting panic and inspiring terror from H.G. Wells to Orson Welles and beyond* [Audio file] (2001). Sourcebooks.

What does the public want? B.B.C. puzzled at its taste in humour. Scare's effect. (1926, January 19). *Daily Graphic*, p. 2.

What Father Knox said. Spoof news bulletin. The great scare. (1926, January 19). *Daily News*, p. 8.

# 8

## Unpredictable Programming

••••••••••••••••••••

### A Freeform Approach to Building Audiences

EMILY W. EASTON

Most American music radio is predictable on purpose. Formats organize radio programming into carefully planned patterns of genre, styles, and even songs. Formats describe the style of music the station plays so audiences can choose a station that plays to their tastes (e.g., hard rock fans tune into hard rock radio because hard rock radio plays the hits they want to hear). To ensure the content sounds similar (if not identical) across stations in the same format, mass-market stations employ centralized programming strategies (e.g., whether those hard rock fans are in Omaha or Chicago, they can find their same favorites on the hard rock station). Formatted stations use predictable programming to build audiences.

But freeform radio offers no such predictable programming patterns. By delegating the decision of what to play to the DJs, freeform radio stations frequently feature a variety of genres and tend to focus on playing lesser heard, unfamiliar music. Hard rock fans might hear an underground heavy metal favorite here or there, but they are just as likely to be surprised with a set of Albanian folk music or psychedelic soul; it's up to the DJ. This presents an interesting challenge for freeform stations, which must build an audience for the station while balancing their DJ's autonomy to choose what the station will sound like at any given moment. Freeform radio stations must build an audience for programming that is predictably unpredictable.

This chapter explains how freeform's approach to building audiences evolved in the longer history of American radio and how one freeform station approached the challenge of building their audience, drawing on participant observation research at WLPN in Chicago, Illinois. Freeform radio can claim roots in music radio's earliest incarnations, taking shape from mass-market and niche programming strategies developed in response to political, economic, and cultural contexts. With the advent of Top 40, stations aiming at niche audiences established funding structures that could survive on small audiences, laying the groundwork for college and community stations, which most commonly feature freeform now. Modern freeform radio stations must develop a station identity that attracts a niche audience by relying on individual DJs' personal programming philosophies to fulfill the audience's expectations. WLPN, a new freeform radio station in Chicago, began building an audience before they went on air at 105.5 FM. To establish their station's interpretation of the freeform audience, the station management recruited DJs with professional experience alongside volunteers and explicitly communicated their station's expectations for music that was both "weird and accessible." DJs used a range of programming philosophies to choose music for their audiences, which made for programming that defied any prediction.

## The Evolution of Niche Programming and Freeform Radio

Freeform radio is distinctive among other types of stations because individual DJs choose the music for broadcast, often with a priority on lesser heard music that does not explicitly conform to its audience's tastes. Freeform "underground rock" FM stations of the 1960s have been cited as the beginnings of freeform (Barnard, 2000; Barnouw, 1968). This marks the first notable uses of the term and certainly laid the groundwork for its antiestablishment tendencies, but freeform radio draws on a longer history of niche radio and even mainstream radio programming that attempted to expand audiences tastes with something new.

In 1921, Chicago's KYW became the first dedicated music station when Westinghouse gave transmission control to Mary Garden, the general director of the Chicago Civic Opera. Broadcasts with the best ratings had thus far been election results and sporting events, but music audiences surpassed all predictions: "At the beginning of the season there were thought to be 1,300 receivers.... By the end of the opera season 20,000 sets were reporting in operation in Chicago" (Barnouw, 1966, p. 88). Mary Garden's experiment, which defied the existing data on what audiences wanted to hear, proved profitable.

As music radio became popular, niche radio stations popped up to introduce audiences to smaller scale music that did not receive airplay on the mass-market stations, though this happened out of necessity in the 1940s, when the American Society of Composers, Authors, and Publishers (ASCAP) attempted to raise royalty rates on the most popular songs. The unaffiliated, niche stations partnered with smaller labels and record promoters to form a "grass-roots music industry" that opened the audience's ears to new genres like bebop, blues, and bluegrass (Fisher, 2007, pp. 12–13). But the unaffiliated stations in the grassroots networks also provide an early example of the financial challenges of appealing to niche audiences. For example, some smaller stations played (the unfortunately termed) "race music," which refers to music made by black musicians. Race music attracted white audiences, but only in small numbers. Major networks could not be bothered for such narrow, disparate tastes and sponsors dropped out when there was too much black-made music on the air (Chapman, 1992, p. 13). Because they drew smaller audiences and took risks on music that defied the racist social conventions, unaffiliated niche stations struggled to remain financially viable.

Todd Storz bought one of these unaffiliated stations, KOWH in Omaha, in 1949. Storz used his new acquisition to experiment with Top 40, which became standard nationwide and marked a triumphant turn in predicting popular culture tastes. Storz developed Top 40 based on a University of Omaha industrial testing project that revealed his audience wanted to hear their favorites multiple times, contrary to his own story of inventing Top 40 in a diner. The idea of repeating the same songs drew snickers from other station owners at first, but the audiences came in droves, along with the advertisers. Within a year, almost 50 percent of Omaha were regular KOWH listeners, up from just 4 percent when Storz had bought the station (Fisher, 2007). Top 40 went nationwide on Storz's networks, which quickly multiplied, and his competitors' stations followed suit. Top 40 stations used audience data from their own station, as well as jukebox plays, record sales, sheet sales, and bandleader requests, to condense everything into a single program of the most popular music. By the 1950s, using data to determine the music for broadcast became more widely known as "format" radio (Chapman, 1992, p. 14). The definition of format radio here makes an important inclusion: format radio refers to the categorical organization by genre or style, but also to how those categories are determined by audience demand as understood by data that attempt to anticipate their tastes. Top 40 also transferred programming decisions from the on-air talent to the program director (Barnouw, 1966, p. 84; Simpson, 2011, p. 12). The first use of the term "disc jockey" also comes from the Top 40 programming strategy: the disc jockey rides the carefully determined pattern of music, musical genre, commercials, and news, keeping audiences tuned in (Chapman, 1992, p. 14). In Top 40 and eventually most of formatted radio, the DJ has nothing to do with choosing the music, even though the audience might hear it that way.

As Top 40 radio became the dominant style on AM radio, niche programming moved to the newly available FM frequencies to reach the audiences who were interested in an alternative. Most major networks had no financial incentive to explore the possibilities of FM, even though interest had increased through the 1950s. Advertisers, however, remained disinterested because of the lack of concrete data on FM audiences; they had come to rely on predictable results from predetermined programming that delivered audiences with reliable marketing potential (Sterling & Keith, 2008, p. 123). Major networks could not afford to experiment on new programming without an audience demand in place, but smaller stations took a shot. By the early 1960s, FM programming strategy fit into two categories: a rebroadcast of the same content from the older sister station on the AM dial or a new, more ambitious type of programming that attempted to reach the niche adult audience who had lost interest in hearing only the hits.

Only 20 percent of FM stations existed without an affiliation to a larger network with an AM presence, but the minority established audiences with more sophisticated tastes drawn in by the hits of yesterday. KABL in San Francisco pioneered this formatting strategy, which came to be known as "beautiful music." The format featured the sweeping sounds of artists like Henry Mancini, now known as "easy listening," which was the alternative programming of its time. Beautiful music also shifted the syntax of Top 40 programming by building in room for sweeping sets of music that would later become a hallmark of the FM dial. WFMT in Chicago took advantage of the FM opportunity to broadcast classical music, along with presidential press conferences and a talk show hosted by a young Studs Terkel. The WFMT station owner invested $50,000 (approximately $315,000 today) in his record collection and began sharing international music festivals and operas in their entirety (Sterling & Keith, 2008, pp. 114–115). Unaffiliated FM stations, like their AM predecessors, used their broadcast power to reach a new kind of audience by experimenting with what would hold their attention before freeform rock stations came along.

Unaffiliated FM stations also developed alternative funding models that relied on their audiences instead of advertisers, setting precedent for public and nonprofit radio. Beautiful music stations sold on subscriptions and program guides, tapping into the interest of their listeners. That same station owner at WFMT took an even more direct approach: he went on air twice in the station's first year to ask the audience for money. And they responded with donations. Unlike the stations that needed to rely on the reliable audiences they had created, the smaller audiences of the independently owned stations could take risks because their audiences wanted—and personally supported—something different. Listeners over the age of twenty-five stopped tuning in for the predictable pop on the AM dial (Sterling & Keith, 2008). By the mid-1960s, FM radio stations had quadrupled in just a few years and attracted a newer, broader group of listeners, expanding the FM audience well beyond its previously small boundaries.

The FCC's 1967 programming duplication restriction created the conditions for the rise of freeform "underground rock" by creating a vacuum on the FM dial. Stations in cities with more than a hundred thousand people were required to reduce their duplicate programming to 50 percent of their broadcast week (Federal Communications Commission, 1965, p. 119). Even though the ruling was not fully implemented until 1967, it left Top 40 stations (among others) with hours to fill (Sterling & Keith, 2008, p. 133). The new FM stations sought to bring in audiences with a different approach to programming; instead of playing the popular, the stations would draw from a wider catalog to introduce audiences to artists and albums. The rise of underground rock radio coincided with the rise of the LP; 45s, featuring single songs, had been the dominant musical object for popular music listeners until the 1960s. Albums meant a wider range of tracks from the artist, offering the DJ more options to share. At New York's WOR-FM, the first underground rock music station to serve a major market, the freeform format supposedly came from a DJ's flip decision to play the Association's "Requiem for the Masses" (perhaps a coincidentally pointed choice for an underground station), which generated a flood of excited calls. The station earned a local reputation for playing innovative, new music (Simpson, 2011). Stations that did not categorize their shows by genre or any other category came to be known as "freeform" radio.

Rock radio stations of the 1960s defined freeform. The underground rock stations' approach has been described as "progressive, alternative, freeform, psychedelic, and even the 'anti-format' format" (Sterling & Keith, 2008, p. 129), and a few DJs have attempted to claim credit. San Francisco freeform DJ Tom Donahue used freeform to describe his own style of playing a three—to four-song set without talking between the tracks in 1967 (Elborough, 2009, p. 285). DJ Bob Fass at WBAI in New York explained that his show, Radio Unnamable, "set out to show that all music ... relates to each other and that none of it has to be categorized. ... The show was completely free, and there you had freeform" (Sterling & Keith, 2008, p. 131). The unifying principle was that DJs had more autonomy to choose the content for their shows. Freeform DJs also rejected the established role of the disc jockey down to the term: they preferred to be called "announcers," whose role was to announce the songs of a larger set (Sterling & Keith, 2008, p. 133). Freeform radio developed an identity that purposefully went against the tendencies of Top 40 programming by avoiding the hits, playing a variety of music across genres, and putting individual DJs in control of their airwaves.

The social and political climate of the 1960s also favored an antiestablishment aesthetic. Broadcasting typically taboo content drew in more new audience. Underground radio of the mid-sixties took on an anticapitalist agenda: DJs would often downplay on-air advertising or take on sponsorships from alternative vendors and products, such as headshops (Sterling & Keith, 2008). Underground radio gave American men growing up in the 1960s an alternate site to negotiate manhood, in sharp contrast to the more dominant images of militarized men during the Vietnam War (Simpson, 2011, p. 106). The radio programming reflected and contributed to the decade's legendary cultural experimentation and the (majority) male DJs could use their airtime to oppose political and aesthetic oppression.

Freeform rock radio evolved as an innovative, alternative approach to some social mores, but the atypical approach did not extend very far into gender. Women were, not surprisingly, underrepresented in the early days of freeform radio, though not entirely absent. KMPX had a show hosted by five women DJs that lasted through the early 1970s. Other types of FM stations featured more women on air, especially as journalists on National Public Radio and female music DJs with dedicated audiences (Sterling & Keith, 2008, pp. 133–134). However, while there may have been more female DJs, many gender norms remained in most of the music industry. Chauvinism pervaded the station management at many stations (Simpson, 2011, p. 104; Sterling & Keith, 2008). Simpson (2011) identifies the subtler sexism that appeared in the stations' directives to DJs that they should not play any manufactured or "bubblegum" music, which was primarily aimed at younger, female audiences. Simpson also cites a 1968 *Rock World* record list for any "self-respecting" freeform station, featuring 123 artists, only 8 of which included female vocals (Simpson, 2011, p. 8). Even in an environment that encouraged musical experimentation, playing music for or made by women carried some stigma.

The freeform rock stations of the 1960s did not remain underground, or freeform, for long. As audience sizes increased, corporate ownership took notice and FM stations began to shift toward a more profit-oriented, album-oriented rock (AOR) format (Sterling & Keith, 2008, p. 133). The name explains the approach of playing albums as an alternative to Top 40. DJs lost more and more of their control over the broadcast as the seventies set in. An example of the shift can be seen in a memo from the program director at New York's WPLJ-FM, an ABC-owned affiliate:

> We currently have three record lists. There is an A list of hit singles. There is a B list of currently popular albums.... There is a C list of standard progressive rock oldies. This list at this time is in your heads and includes familiar tracks of Dylan, Beatles, Stones, etc. In the next few days, we should have a C list available to you.... The key time zones—:00, :15, and :45 (indicated by the dot) should be filled with A, B, C track.... In the daytime there should be a minimum total of four B tracks.... In a four day period, you should have played every item on the A list at least one. We will be having weekly music meetings on Tuesday to discuss new records, recommended tracks, and the A, B, and C lists. (Memo from WPLJ-FM 1971 New York in Keith, 1997, p. 60)

As of the writing of the memo, DJs could still use their own discretion on what constituted a "familiar track," but the content describes an increasingly standardized selection process, communicated in writing and through weekly meetings.

WPLI management now played a significant role in deciding what records would be played and when to feature new music.

When FM stations became profitable, programming innovation stalled. Before the end of the 1970s, around two thousand FM stations nationwide would not even require a DJ, having shifted to automated music programming. The DJ's only role was to speak in the scheduled spaces between the preselected tracks (Sterling & Keith, 2008, p. 137). AOR morphed into "classic rock" and "classic hits" by the 1980s, drawing on the same rock canon of the 1960s and 1970s. Rothenbuhler (1985) described the centralized staffing structures in AOR programming strategies, where music and program directors at the station worked with consultants to build playlists based on trade and industry publications. Successful programmers relied on their knowledge of the radio industry, not the community or the music (Rothenbuhler, 1985). Radio programming returned to its commercially successful patterns of playing to their audiences' existing tastes. Freeform radio moved to college and community stations.

College stations gained a reputation in the music industry during the 1980s, when they played a central role in establishing audiences for then smaller acts like R.E.M. and U2 (Azerrad, 2001; Kruse, 2003). Commercial FM freeform stations had established an audience taste for more diverse, DJ-driven programming, which some college stations picked up by playing the rock, punk, and new wave that more mainstream rock stations did not feature. Not all college stations embraced the alternative format; many operated as commercial stations to prepare students for careers at formatted radio stations (Kruse, 2003). And stations that focused on alternative music did not always take a freeform approach. Many college stations, even those focused on underground content, still employ some sort of formatting structure, most often to create data that support their relationships with record labels. Noncommercial college stations make fewer demands on their DJs, often requesting that DJs play a certain number of tracks from albums on one or more predetermined lists during their shows. Stations reported the albums played on air to the *CMJ New Music Report*. CMJ published individual and compiled charts on who played what, offering data to record labels on which stations should continue to receive promotional copies. Alternative college radio DJs might have more freedom to choose music than their peers in commercial or commercial college radio, but most college stations are not completely freeform.

Unlike alternative college radio, community radio stations also did not attract the same attention from record labels (Kruse, 2003, p. 78). Individual DJs might build relationships with certain labels, but there is no version of CMJ for community radio, so labels do not have easy access to what receives airplay. Also, because community radio defines its audiences at the local station level, the data on what people tune in for (assuming the station even bothers) have very limited use outside that station; data on what works at one community station are unlikely to be much good at forecasting what will work at another. Community radio stations may adopt formats to communicate with their audiences what to tune in for but can also be more open to the freeform programming that puts DJ autonomy at the center of the individual show's programming strategy.

Formatted commercial radio became even more centralized as the century ended. The Telecommunications Act of 1996 removed the upper-limit nationwide station owner, meaning a single company could now buy hundreds of stations nationwide. Limits on ownership within a market slackened as well. The FCC increased the number of stations that could be owned by one entity in proportion to how many stations existed in that market. In smaller communities, with fourteen or fewer stations, one company could own as many as a 36 percent of the radio stations (Rodman, 2016, p. 242; Sterling & Keith, 2008, pp. 179–180). Centralized ownership, of course, meant more standardized programming. Clear Channel was perhaps the most notable beneficiary of the turn: within three years of the Telecommunications Act, they owned nearly a thousand stations, many of which featured the same, centrally developed content (Sterling & Keith, 2008, p. 183). Formatted radio audiences can tune into multiple stations that play similar rotations of the same artists, albums, and songs. Since 2000, formats have multiplied but remained reliant on the existing tastes of their audiences by promoting nostalgic programming that draws from a wider range of previously successful hits (Rodman, 2016, p. 246). There may be more options, but these options tend to play the same songs they played a few decades before, when those songs were new.

But even within these centralized decision structures, radio programmers also employ programming philosophies that shape the content. Ahlkvist (2001) noted that some programmers took a musicologist philosophy to programs, drawing on their more informed tastes to educate audiences on music they might not otherwise hear. For the musicologist, the challenge was "balancing their personally high standards (music they are proud of) with what the market will bear (music they can justify, but do not personally like)" (Ahlkvist, 2001, p. 347). Musicologist programmers still need to play music that attracts their defined audiences but could also incorporate their professional judgment on the quality of the music to use.

In the twenty-first century, satellite networks like SiriusXM and Internet streaming services like Pandora and Spotify have attempted to serve audience needs even more specifically. Satellite radio stations do not need to rely on the limited number of broadcast frequencies; SiriusXM, for example, offers 994 stations for their subscribers to choose from, ranging from team-specific sports stations to music stations curated by well-known artists such as Pearl Jam, Willie Nelson, and Bob Dylan, as well as lesser known authorities such as Handsome Dick Manitoba from the Dictators and Aquarium Drunkard, a music blog site that highlights lesser heard artists, old and new. Audiences pay in advance for more options. Pandora, by contrast, takes immediate direction from the listener's feedback; the music streaming service can approve or skip songs based on listener preference, which informs the algorithm that chooses what song will play next. It might appear to be the opposite of formatted radio, which draws in large audiences with organized blocks of predictably popular music, but both use the same strategy of appealing to the audience's preexisting tastes. The listener might be able to customize the programming, but the listener is still choosing from a set of songs that the organization has decided on through data analysis (Pandora, for example, uses the Music Genome Project). Attempting to zero in on specific, crowd-sourced patterns of approval, or "hyper affiliation," does not necessarily expand audience tastes (Rodman, 2016, p. 250). In both instances, audiences have more choices to affiliate with, but they still choose stations with some individual taste or expectation of what genre or style of music will be played.

More recently, community radio stations have experienced their largest period of growth. In January 2011, the Local Community Radio Act reopened several spots on the FM frequency for smaller, lower wattage stations. The FCC invited applications for low power FM (LPFM) stations in 2013, creating opportunities for nonprofit organizations to claim a small stake on the broadcast airwaves (Local Community Radio Act, n.d.). The study in this chapter comes from participant observation research at one of the stations that secured a license: WLPN in Chicago.

New community stations must compete with ever-expanding options for audiences. Radio stations attracting niche audiences competed with more mass-market radio for most of the twentieth century, but mass-market satellite and Internet radio services currently offer niche programming alongside their more popular options. Freeform community stations have a renewed opportunity to connect with the terrestrial radio audience, but must establish an identity as an alternative, among many. Because DJs choose the music, every show is an experiment with the audience's tastes that relies on different information on what they might stay tuned for.

## Building an Audience at WLPN

Freeform radio stations must attract audiences without relying on a clearly recognized style (e.g., Top 40) or assuming a consistent definition of the freeform sound. Within the broad parameters of DJ autonomy, freeform radio stations develop individual interpretations of their specific station identity. WLPN presented a description of their station on their website: "A non-commercial radical radio station from Chicago (on 105.5 FM) that showcases innovative ideas, plays highly curated music, and broadcasts commentary on the issues of our day . . . for the people that live and work in the city, people everywhere that love Chicago's underground cultures, and people who love the idea of freeform radio wherever they are" ("About Us," 2017, para. 1). The description does not reference any specific type of music but includes other language that helps listeners understand what they might be tuning in for. WLPN calls their content "radical" and "innovative," as well as highlighting care that goes into the musical decision making by noting their music is "curated." WLPN also specifically speaks to their intended audiences as local, already interested in less mainstream culture and fans of freeform. WLPN directly defines itself not as a freeform station, but as a station programmed for that audience, borrowing a familiar logic from formatted radio: fans of freeform should listen to WLPN because the station plays freeform radio that freeform radio fans want to hear.

Other stations present their approach differently. For example, WFMU, the longest running freeform station in the United States, describes their programming and emphasizes the role of DJ. The description starts with a mix of increasingly obscure genres that cleverly outlines the atypical variety: "WFMU's programming ranges from flat-out uncategorizable strangeness to rock and roll, experimental music, 78 RPM Records, jazz, psychedelia, hip-hop, electronica, hand-cranked wax cylinders, punk rock, gospel, exotica, R&B, radio improvisation, cooking instructions, classic radio airchecks, found sound, dopey call-in shows, interviews with obscure radio personalities and notable science-world luminaries, spoken-word collages, Andrew Lloyd Webber soundtracks in languages other than English as well as Country and western music" ("About WFMU," 2018, para. 5). Next, the station description explains WFMU's priority on DJ autonomy: "All of the station's programming is controlled by individual DJs and is not beholden to any type of station-wide playlist or rotation schedule. Experimentation, spontaneity and humor are among the station's most frequently noted distinguishing traits. WFMU does not belong to any existing public radio network, and close to 100% of its programming originates at the station" ("About WFMU," 2018, para. 6). The second section establishes WFMU's perspective on programming in contrast to the centralized approach found at other, more commercial stations. The "experimentation, spontaneity, and humor" they are known for is presented as an outcome of that approach, not a station policy or even intention. WFMU centers their approach to freeform on their DJs' autonomy without providing a clear definition of the audience, unlike WLPN, which specifically describes the audiences for whom they are programming.

To understand how WLPN established their audiences, this chapter draws on participant observation research. Participant observation is its own method (Wolcott, 2008), but can also be considered a substrategy of ethnography that emphasizes the researcher's role in shaping her research context as an active participant which, in this project, included listening to the music and talking with the DJs as they played live on air. The research here reflects three months of participant observation with six volunteer DJs at WLPN in 2015 and 2016.

WLPN explained their expectations to DJs at station meetings and even with individual DJs as necessary. Because they would be competing with mainstream stations on the FM frequency, WLPN emphasized to DJs that they should not play music audiences could hear on other stations. The station director noted he would be addressing this with some of the less experienced DJs who had volunteered. It was not a quality but a station identity issue: the station manager explained that while he enjoyed artists like Erykah Badu and D'Angelo, other radio stations play those artists, which ran counter to the station's identity, and the DJs needed to dig deeper to choose their music. WLPN's approach highlights another way that freeform differs dramatically from mainstream stations, where individual stations purposefully standardize their offerings to stay consistent with their peers (Rothenbuhler, 1985). At WLPN, DJs needed to do the opposite to attract audience attention.

But WLPN also established expectations for DJs to make their music listenable. At the first WLPN station meeting, the station director and the owner emphasized the difficult but important balance between playing music that challenged listeners, but did not drive them away. The station director summarized the expectation: "I do want our weirdness to be accessible." Earlier in the same meeting, the director, Ed, had also noted that DJs could play all sorts of sounds, including "squirrels chattering or me farting," but that it should also be "listenable." The station manager noted this was especially important for drive time, when commuters might be scanning the dial. Merzbow, a noise artist who specializes in especially aggressive soundscapes, came up as an example of something that would also not fit with WLPN's expectations of programming. DJs could decide how to interpret "weird" and "accessible" for themselves, but the station management offered ongoing feedback to ensure their programs matched their intended audience.

WLPN recruited DJs with professional experience in striking this balance with live audiences, alongside volunteers who responded to the wider call. The DJs who participated in this research all had experience playing music at bars and clubs that served the aforementioned underground music cultures; many had DJ experience at the affiliated Maria's Community Bar. One DJ served as the music director for Maria's and expressed similar frustration at less experienced DJs playing music that did not fit their intended audience. He described having to follow up with a new DJ who had played Madonna's megahit "Holiday" and expressed a staccato confusion over the incident, asking, "Why play Madonna at Maria's?" Other bars might play popular hits, but Maria's, like WLPN, aimed to play lesser heard music, which was part of their identity as a venue. By choosing DJs familiar with that type of audience in person, WLPN established a roster of reliable curators who had professional experience playing lesser heard music.

The experienced DJs also understood how to keep things listenable from their experiences with live audiences. Another WLPN DJ compared her role as a live DJ to a sculptor, explaining that she feels sound builds the space in the same way physical objects do. When she DJs, she brings a wide variety of music so she can read and react to the crowd. She tries to pick up clues on what they might like by observing how old they are and how they move. She often (though not always) tries to keep the mood of the room steady at first before pushing their boundaries with tracks that have "a little bit of grab" to shift the response even they might expect; she offered the example of the time she got her friend's metal band, Cyanide, to dance to a J. Geils Band song at a party. They may not have been classic rock fans or even dancers, but the right track and the right time brought them to the floor. To get the crowd's attention occasionally, she uses the Chipmunk Punk cover of Tom Petty's "Refugee." The odd and often initially unfamiliar cover version of a megahit that even the most casual of rock fans can usually sing by memory usually gets a few people to raise their heads. Live audiences offer immediate feedback to the DJ by dancing, nodding, and (hopefully) buying more drinks. DJs who play music that disrupts the audience risk not being invited back to a paid gig. But the same DJ who managed Maria's clarified that playing for an audience was not the same as playing to their tastes. He first joked "I don't give a shit what the crowd wants," but quickly explained that part of his job was not to play the songs everyone knew and already loved, and he did sometimes prioritize more accessible music during busy, weekend nights when it competed with conversations and activity. He might play music that is more experimental early on a Friday, but by 10 P.M. or so the music needed to be understood alongside the talking. Music, he continued, has a rhythm and the DJ had to find the right rhythm.

But radio audiences are invisible. DJs needed to construct an idea of their specific audience that aligned with the station's expectations and their programming philosophies. A few DJs took an approach similar to the musicologist programmers at commercial stations by balancing their own tastes with what would sound right for WLPN. Without a strict structure to guide those decisions, DJs took different approaches to sharing something unpredictable with audiences.

Shows focused on a genre aimed to stretch their audience's expectations of what that might sound like. One DJ tried to expand his audience's definition of country, titling the show "Country My Way" and featuring primarily 45s to showcase artists that were too small scale to afford a full record. Another show featured "vintage Latin sounds" that the DJs organized by topic, explicitly not focusing on music by country to highlight the diversity of Latin musical styles for their audience; one February show, for example, focused on representations of African heritage in music from more than a dozen Central and South American nations in honor of U.S. Black History Month. Other DJs highlighted lesser heard tracks by more well-known artists, like freeform rock DJs in the 1960s playing deep cuts from albums or playing popular hits at a different speed to change the sound. Even when DJs played a familiar artist or even track, they experimented with their audience's tastes to introduce something new.

Other DJs used the flexibility of freeform to build shows that spanned genres. Two DJs explicitly planned for their shows to cross musical categories. One of them chose music with an imagined audience in mind: she played up-tempo music for an audience member she imagined was stuck working late during her 4 to 6 P.M. time slot. The other chose music according to the sensory experience of the evening, picking minimalist and minor key songs on a cold winter night that she noted she would not play in the summer. She selected music for her local audience with clear ideas of how the music fit with the weather and the time of day. One DJ changed his show theme almost every week. His first show, Thrift Score, focused on tracks from older records commonly found in bargain bins, but next week he played an intentionally different mix of psychedelic soul, blues, and free jazz. He eventually shifted to a show with an even looser definition, "Eclectic Ladyland," where he warned listeners to "expect the unexpected." Eclectic Ladyland could be anything he wanted audiences to hear that day. By not limiting themselves to genres, these DJs could build shows on more personal programming philosophies.

The variety within and between shows came from the DJ's individual interpretations of WLPN's station identity. The broad parameters left plenty of room to play for and play with audiences, experimenting with tracks that might not fit in a live set or songs that would not be played on other stations. DJs expressed enthusiasm for the opportunity. One DJ described her show at WLPN as "an honor." Another explained that DJing live and DJing at WLPN were "two versions of the best thing ever," but that he was a "pig in shit" at WLPN, where he could share his deep love of music with new audiences. The DJs approached their shows with their passion as music fans, as well as experienced musical curators who knew how to introduce audiences to the unfamiliar.

WLPN's specific approach highlights a key paradox of freeform radio programming: DJs are "free" to choose anything, but within the station's expectations of what that might mean. The balance can be difficult. With so much music to draw from, and a mandate to be appropriately strange, it is easy to misstep—or, rather, miscue. Freeform stations must decide who their intended audience is and shape their programs without telling the DJs exactly what to play. Not all freeform stations establish the same parameters. A quick search of WFMU's historical playlists indicates that DJs have played songs by Madonna 124 times, including 6 plays of "Holiday" and 4 from her early punk band, the Breakfast Club, as well as 222 tracks by Merzbow. WLPN expected DJs to avoid megahits and mega-artists, as well as keeping things listenable, but experienced DJs did not interpret this as a limitation: DJs saw it as an opportunity to support a station that would encourage their listeners to experiment with their tastes.

## Conclusion

Freeform radio is unpredictable by design. Freeform radio draws on the expertise of the DJ to find music that audiences will tune in for, while formatted radio predicts its audiences' tastes based on industry data. It is important to resist "the temptation to assume that formatting and programming according to the charts [or even audience data] is bad" (Kruse, 2003, p. 74). By using data on what people like, formatted radio helps guide more people to products they enjoy, even if those products are restricted to a small sample of the music that is available (Hesmondhalgh, 2008). Freeform radio DJs and their stations use different data. Stations shape the programming by selecting experienced DJs and communicating station expectations online and in person, drawing on interpretations of what their niche audiences will tune in for at that time. Individual DJs used their experience, their musical expertise, and their individual interpretations of the station's audience. Freeform radio stations also aim to guide audiences to something they will enjoy, just not something they will expect.

Niche audiences have more options than ever, but the freeform approach raises important, but familiar, questions for how these expanded options serve their audiences' tastes. Streaming services like Pandora and Spotify offer listeners the opportunity to hear music programs based on their existing tastes, using data on similar listeners to present music that's likely to land. By drawing individual listening data, streaming services present a new, highly specific iteration of formats. But other online platforms also present an opportunity for the freeform approach. SoundCloud and other sites allow individuals to upload curated mixes and playlists to share their tastes with those audiences, and some freeform stations, such as oWOW Radio, exist entirely online alongside terrestrial freeform stations with Internet streaming. The challenge for these new iterations of niche programming remains how to attract audiences interested in expanding their tastes, when audiences themselves can't predict those tastes.

## References

About us. (2017). Retrieved from www.lumpenradio.com/about.html
About WFMU. (2018). Retrieved from https://wfmu.org/about/
Ahlkvist, J. (2001). Programming philosophies and the rationalization of music radio. *Media, Culture & Society, 23*, 339–358. doi:10.1177/016344301023003004
Azerrad, M. (2001). *Our band could be your life: Scenes from the American indie underground, 1981–1991.* Boston: Little, Brown.
Barnard, S. (2000). *Studying radio.* London: Arnold.
Barnouw, E. (1966). *A tower in Babel: To 1933.* New York: Oxford University Press.
Barnouw, E. (1968). *The golden web: 1933–1953.* New York: Oxford University Press.
Chapman, R. (1992). *Selling the sixties: The pirates and pop music radio.* London: Routledge.
Elborough, T. (2009). *The vinyl countdown: The album from vinyl to iPod and back again.* Berkeley, CA: Soft Skull Press.
Federal Communications Commission. (1965). *31st annual report: For the fiscal year 1965.* Washington, DC: U.S. Government Printing Office.
Fisher, M. (2007). *Something in the air: Radio, rock, and the revolution that shaped a generation.* New York: Random House.
Hesmondhalgh, D. (2008). Cultural and creative industries. In T. Bennett & J. Frow (Eds.), *The SAGE handbook of cultural analysis* (pp. 552–569). London: Sage.
Keith, M. C. (1997). *Voices in the purple haze: Underground radio and the sixties.* Westport, CT: Praeger.

Kruse, H. (2003). *Site and sound: Understanding independent music scenes*. New York: Peter Lang.

Local Community Radio Act. (n.d.). Retrieved from www.prometheusradio.org

Rodman, R. (2016). Radio formats in the United States: A hyper fragmentation of the imagination. In C. Baade & J. Deaville (Eds.), *Music and the broadcast experience: Performance, production, and audiences* (pp. 235–257). New York: Oxford University Press.

Rothenbuhler, E. W. (1985). Programming decision making in popular music radio. *Communication Research, 12*(2), 209–232.

Simpson, K. (2011). *Early '70s radio: The American format revolution*. New York: Continuum.

Sterling, C. H., & Keith, M. C. (2008). *Sounds of change: A history of FM broadcasting in America*. Chapel Hill: University of North Carolina Press.

Wolcott, H. F. (2008). *Ethnography: A way of seeing*. Lanham, MD: Altamira.

# Part III
# Social Issues
## Contemporary Overtones

# 9

# Air to the Kingdom

• • • • • • • • • • • • • • • • • • • •

Religion and the Soul of Radio

MARK WARD SR.

The sheer presence of religion on the dial affirms that radio's "theater of the mind" can be a numinous experience. In the United States, the Religious format is the third largest by station count, behind only News/Talk and Country. When religious music and Spanish-language religious formats are added—Contemporary Christian, Contemporary Inspirational, Christian Adult Contemporary, Gospel, Southern Gospel, Spanish Religious, Spanish Contemporary Christian—the count of AM and FM religious radio outlets tops the News/Talk format by 50 percent and Country by 70 percent. These nearly three thousand stations account for one in five of the nation's full-power outlets and attract a combined national audience share that would rank fifth among rated formats (Rodrigues, Green, & Virshup, 2013). They serve the one in four adults who identify as evangelical Christians (Pew Research Center, 2015) and the one in five who consume religious media on a daily basis. More adults access these media each month than attend church, and religious radio attracts a larger percentage of these consumers than religious television, periodicals, or websites (Barna Group, 2005).

As radio looks back on its first century and ahead to its second, several observations about religious radio stand out. First, religious radio may preach a heavenly message, but the genre has been a bellwether for worldly changes in radio economics, technology, and regulation (Ward, 2013, 2017)—a mirror to the soul of radio. Second, ownership concentration in religious radio since the 1990s (Ward, 2009, 2012) has killed localism, homogenized the genre's voice, and entrenched white male dominance on the air and in the boardroom (Ward, 2018a). Third, consolidation has created religious media conglomerates whose control of devotional and educational resources replicates the functions of the historic Protestant denominations (Ward, 2019). Fourth, the large conglomerates and syndicators have exploited every conceivable form of new digital media technology (Ward, 2018b). Fifth, the same proliferation of media platforms that has fragmented national audiences (Ward, 2016a) has divided the evangelical movement into a Pentecostal-Charismatic community drawn to religious television and a non-Pentecostal community drawn to religious radio (Ward, 2016b).

This chapter chronicles religious radio's past and present and, with these as prologue, projects the genre's future. As will be seen, religious radio is fruitfully analyzed not only in terms of economic, technical, and regulatory change but also for the sociohistorical continuities of evangelical mass culture (Ward, 2014)—a claim built here on the theoretical foundations of Holmes's (2005) concept of *broadcast integration* and Lindlof's (1988, 2002) concept of *interpretive community*. Holmes demonstrated how a media genre audience can be socially integrated without direct interaction as audience members share media rituals associated with the genre and vicariously monitor what people with shared interests are watching and hearing. Lindlof posited that a media genre audience can build a community as members' shared interpretation of media content becomes communally validated over time and guides members' actions within the community. Since the 1980s, analyses of the media-religion interface have hewed either to technological determinism (the values of technology necessarily colonize the values of religious media; e.g., Christians, 1990; Postman, 1985) or cultural studies (religious media are only symptomatic of larger structural trends within society; e.g., Hoover, 1988; Schultze, 1991). Yet, these approaches seem insufficiently nuanced for the complexities of today's digital media environment. Thus, the present study ultimately takes its cue from the recent "pragmatic turn" in media and religion research where the key question is how genre audiences make shared sense of media content to build communities (Stout, 2016). For while the history recounted below is replete with change, religious radio remains integral today to a vast evangelical subculture, with which one in four Americans identifies, suggesting the genre has a secure place in radio's second century.

## Religious Radio—Past

The first century of religious radio may be divided into five eras (Ward, 2013) starting with the unregulated "wildcat" days of the 1920s and "golden" network era of the 1930s and 1940s, then the wilderness time of the 1950s and 1960s after the ascendance of television and the genre's subsequent revival as a niche format in the 1970s and 1980s, and finally the present era of radio deregulation and industry consolidation as evangelical media conglomerates now distribute syndicated radio content across multiple vertically integrated media platforms including terrestrial and satellite radio, personal computers, tablets, smartphones, gaming consoles, streaming TV, and social media.

Though Reginald Fessenden's first wireless voice transmission on Christmas eve 1906 included scripture readings, the first true religious broadcast was a Sunday vespers service aired January 2, 1921, by KDKA from Pittsburgh's Calvary Episcopal Church (Armstrong, 1979; Siedell, 1971; Ward, 1994). Some evangelicals decried radio as a tool of the devil since the Bible describes Satan as "the prince of the power of the air" (Ephesians 2:2). Yet by 1927, 10 percent of the nation's more than six hundred stations were owned by religious organizations (Sterling & Kitross, 2002). Many belonged to local churches that broadcast only on Sunday, but some stations were sponsored by national ministries such as KFSG/Los Angeles, operated by Aimee Semple McPherson's Church of the Foursquare Gospel, and WMBI/Chicago, operated by the Moody Bible Institute. However, great citywide crusades had for fifty years been the proven means for mass evangelism. Could a voice over a radio convert the lost? As one preacher put it, "Can unction be transmitted?" (Ward, 1994, p. 31).

Most influential in answering that question was evangelist Paul Rader, who launched WJBT/Chicago in 1927 with made-for-radio religious programming, and who spoke not as a pulpiteer but in a conversational tone, featuring well-produced music in a contemporary style and employing radio to build a broader organization with enterprises ranging from food pantries to summer camps. Because the airwaves were relatively uncluttered, Rader and other early radio preachers elicited, to their amazement and delight, responses from listeners across the country. Radio precipitated the decline of crusade evangelism as the new medium competed for people's leisure time and accustomed them to higher standards of entertainment (Kerr, 1939). Famed crusade evangelist Billy Sunday, for example, was never invited to a major city after 1921 (Dorsett, 1990). By contrast, R. R. Brown became known as the "Billy Sunday of the Air" when his weekly *Radio Chapel Service*, originating since 1923 from Omaha, attracted half a million listeners, many of whom wrote in for membership cards in his "Worldwide Radio Congregation" (Armstrong, 1978; Ward, 1994).

Yet the popularity of radio was nearly its undoing. People who purchased expensive radio sets complained they could not receive clear signals because unregulated broadcasters were free to change signal strength and direction, broadcast hours, even frequencies at will. Congress in 1927 created a Federal Radio Commission that required stations to use professional equipment and operators, and adhere to assigned frequencies, signals, and hours. Within months, 150 of the nation's 732 stations surrendered their licenses (Hilliard & Keith, 2001). Many church-owned stations could not afford to comply; between 1927 and 1933, the number of stations licensed to religious groups declined from about sixty to fewer than thirty (Ward, 1994). Yet, as the faithful might claim, God closed one door but opened another. "Chain broadcasting," or simulcasting over multiple radio stations, had been demonstrated as early as 1921. During the 1920s, millions tuned in to chain broadcasts of major news and sporting events. The 1927 debuts of the NBC and CBS networks offered radio evangelists a new possibility: purchase time on a network and instantly gain a national audience without the effort and expense of operating a station. Philadelphia's Donald Grey Barnhouse was the first preacher in 1928 to purchase time on a national network for his *Bible Study Hour*. Two years later, when evangelist Walter Maier bought time on CBS, his *Lutheran Hour* attracted five million weekly listeners, drew more fan mail than *Amos 'n Andy,* and averaged contributions of two thousand dollars per week (Ward, 2017).

But because fund-raising on the air was controversial, by 1931 both NBC and CBS stopped selling airtime for religious programs and instead donated time for Protestant broadcasts to the theologically liberal Federal Council of Churches (Hangen, 2002). Evangelicals were shut out until 1934 when the Mutual Broadcasting System debuted and, needing revenues to compete with its two larger rivals, accepted paid religious programs. Radio evangelism entered its own golden age with coast-to-coast Mutual broadcasts of the *Young People's Church of the Air, The Lutheran Hour, Radio Bible Class, Back to the Bible, The Light and Life Hour, The Word of Life Hour,* and others. The *Old Fashioned Revival Hour* with Charles Fuller set the pace, drawing twenty million weekly listeners by 1943 and spending a million and a half dollars—more than any other broadcaster, religious or secular—that year on Mutual airtime (Fuller, 1972). As the fan cultures of these broadcasts spread—through citywide rallies, summer conferences, magazines, books, music recordings, and songbooks—evangelicals developed a cohesive mass subculture as they listened for the first time, across denominational lines, to the same popular preachers and music.

By 1944 Mutual was more established, feared being typecast as a religious network, and sensitive to advertiser complaints that programs adjacent to religious broadcasts suffered from audience turnover. That year the network joined NBC and CBS in prohibiting on-air fund-raising. Two years earlier, in 1942, news that Mutual was wavering prompted formation of the National Association of Evangelicals, an unprecedented move among groups that historically prized their independence. They made headway in 1949 when an upstart network, ABC, reversed its policy and accepted paid religious programs. Within a few years, the other networks followed suit. But by then the ascendance of network television had brought an end to network radio.

Nevertheless, religious radio was buoyed by another development when the Federal Communications Commission (FCC) in 1946 ended its wartime licensing freeze and began permitting hundreds of new radio stations. In the 1950s the number of religious stations grew about ten per year, while a few evangelical organizations began assembling small networks. Radio preachers discovered they could avoid the uncertain access of mainstream stations and enjoy reliably supportive listeners, while religious stations that sold airtime to preachers gained reliable income that insulated them from ratings competition with mainstream radio. From fewer than a dozen religious stations in 1950, more than three hundred were on the air by 1970 (Ward, 1994). The future of religious radio had shifted back to local station ownership, the business model that network radio had once eclipsed. Yet the network era had a lasting effect on the evangelical movement. Having tasted the mainstream via their network radio exposure, evangelical leaders increasingly found cultural separatism unsatisfying and moved toward engagement with the surrounding American society. The issue was joined in 1947, when Fuller founded a progressive new seminary (Marsden, 1995), and effectively decided in 1957, when famed evangelist Billy Graham—who first went on radio in 1943 and whose *Hour of Decision* was heard nationally over the ABC radio network—accepted the sponsorship of mainline churches for his New York City Crusade (Carpenter, 1997). Though arguments between separatistic "fundamentalists" and engaged "evangelicals" continue to this day, the latter have dominated the movement since the postwar years.

When the Supreme Court, in its *Red Lion* decision of 1969, applied the FCC's Fairness Doctrine to religious radio stations, evangelical broadcasters feared they must either mute their message or invite financial ruin by giving free airtime to anyone who disagreed with any radio sermon. Yet, the new business model for religious radio, where preachers gained reliable access to supportive listeners and stations reaped reliable income from the sale of airtime, proved resilient. During the 1970s the number of religious stations tripled to more than a thousand (Ward, 1995). As radio preachers and religious stations grew together, enough evangelical programming became available (and willing to pay) for stations to broadcast a religious format full-time. New celebrities emerged: James Dobson of *Focus on the Family*, Chuck Swindoll of *Insight for Living*, Charles Stanley of *In Touch*, D. James Kennedy of *Truths That Transform*, John MacArthur of *Grace to You*. While televangelism garnered public attention, "Christian radio" gave the evangelical subculture everyday sustenance. For one, the growing number of stations made contemporary Christian and southern gospel music charting possible, forging a link between radio and retail. For another, preachers discovered that evangelical media could both proclaim the gospel and mobilize the faithful. The National Religious Broadcasters association became a key organization in the Religious Right, and its conventions in Washington were addressed by presidents Ford, Carter, Reagan, and Bush. Jerry Falwell, whose *Old Time Gospel Hour* (an homage to Fuller's *Old Fashioned Revival Hour*) aired weekly on television but daily on religious radio, founded the Moral Majority in 1979. The group registered legions of evangelical voters who helped put Ronald Reagan over the top in the watershed 1980 presidential election. Seven years later, evangelical broadcasters got their fondest wish when the FCC rescinded the Fairness Doctrine as part of the agency's move to ditch the traditional trusteeship model of broadcasting and declare that market forces could best determine the public interest. That same year, a series of financial and sexual scandals involving celebrity televangelists Oral Roberts, Jim Bakker, and Jimmy Swaggart rocked the electronic church. Ultimately, however, the market forces unleashed by the Reagan-era FCC proved the more decisive development, ushering in "a new era dominated less by faces and more by corporations" (Ward, 2013, p. 111).

## Religious Radio—Present

The new era began in the 1990s as pressure mounted to deregulate the radio industry, culminating in the Telecommunications Act of 1996, which eliminated the national cap on how many stations any one broadcaster could own. That year alone, some 2,157 stations changed hands (Fratrik, 2002). Whereas 82 percent of the top fifty markets were unconcentrated in 1992, 86 percent were heavily or moderately concentrated five years later (Drushel, 1998). By 2002, more than 40 percent of U.S. radio stations were under new ownership (Sterling, 2004), and the total number of station owners fell by a third (Williams & Roberts, 2002). The twenty-one largest radio groups, including four religious broadcasters, owned one-fifth of U.S. radio stations (DiCola & Thomson, 2002). The impact of consolidation in religious radio was soon felt as the number of group-owned stations rose in the nation's top fifty media markets (Ward, 2009). Lesser known radio preachers were pushed out of these markets by the rising prices and higher production values demanded by the networks and a switch from quarter-hour to half-hour daily broadcasts as the industry standard (Ward, 2012).

In today's consolidated industry, large syndicators have prospered—Dobson, Swindoll, Stanley, Kennedy, and MacArthur, along with David Jeremiah's *Turning Point*, Adrian Rogers's *Love Worth Finding*, and Tony Evans's *The Alternative*—while a new generation of successful daily half-hour preaching programs have found audiences with Greg Laurie's *A New Beginning*, Michael Youssef's *Leading the Way*, Alistair Begg's *Truth for Life*, and Ravi Zacharias's *Let My People Think*. But where religious radio listeners in the 1970s and 1980s heard an eclectic "dollar for a holler" mix of quarter-hour programs over locally owned stations with comparatively weak AM signals, today's listeners hear a largely homogenized menu of celebrity preachers who can afford national syndication on up to two thousand radio outlets, whose voices and production values fit the networks' sound, and who reach the major media markets through network-owned stations with strong FM and AM signals. Localism, which in "Christian radio" means access for local churches to the airwaves, is effectively confined to the remaining independent stations, with weak signals and low airtime rates, and to smaller and unranked media markets.

Today, religious radio is dominated by a handful of large networks including Salem Media Group (118 owned and operated stations, most in top fifty media markets, plus 2,700 news/talk and music programming affiliates in 300 markets),

American Family Radio (200 stations in thirty states, plus 1,200 news/talk affiliates), USA Radio (500 news/talk affiliates), Moody Radio (80 stations and translators in twenty-five states, plus 900 teaching/talk affiliates in forty-nine states), Christian Satellite Network (430 stations and translators in all fifty states), K-LOVE (450 stations and translators in forty-seven states), and Air1 (200 stations and translators in forty-one states). Commercially licensed (and publicly traded) Salem, plus noncommercial American Family and Moody, set the pace for teaching and talk programs, while Salem, American Family, and USA dominate top-of-the-hour news. These networks' teaching and news/talk, delivered "from a Christian perspective" (Ward, in press) that has been homogenized by consolidation, serve crucial agenda-setting functions for the evangelical movement (Wrench, 2016). Meanwhile, noncommercial Christian Satellite, K-LOVE, and Air1—the latter two both owned by the Educational Media Foundation—set the standards for Contemporary Christian music programming. These national Christian music radio networks, driven by the economics of the music and radio industries, share relatively narrow playlists of catchy "praise" songs that test well. In turn, the networks heavily influence what is sung in churches and have become the virtual "hymnal" of contemporary evangelicalism (Smith & Seignious, 2016).

While supporters of industry consolidation can claim that today's religious radio enjoys increased reach, better sound, and greater financial health, opponents can cite a diminished diversity of voices. Lesser-known syndicators and local churches have, as explained earlier, less access to the airwaves. Further, conglomeration has locked in white male dominance of network boardrooms. One study (Ward, 2018a) discovered that in 2016 the founders, directors, senior executives, division heads, and talk show hosts at Salem Media Group were all white men. Though American Family Radio retained a black man as its general counsel, the network was led by five white men and its eight daily talk shows were hosted or cohosted by eight white men and three white women. The founder and eight directors of the Educational Media Foundation were all white men, supported by an executive committee of five white men and two white women, while deejays at the K-LOVE and Air1 networks were seven white men and seven white women. Similarly, the officers of the Christian Satellite Network were all white men. Moody Radio's four top managers were white men, and its fourteen teaching and talk programs were hosted or cohosted by fourteen white men, five white women, and two black men. The ninety-member volunteer board of the National Religious Broadcasters association included only three black persons. Its ten-member executive committee was composed of eight white men, one white woman, and one black woman, and its seven standing committees were chaired by five white men, one white woman, and one Asian man.

Recently, a media ethnographer spent a year listening to a Salem station in a top ten media market and reported that on-air discourses "frequently objectify those presumed to be needy," "there are often conversations about pursuing wealth," "commercials [indicate] listeners are mostly well-educated, well-to-do or middle class," and "spots that urged listeners to help send missionaries to 'remote places' and 'jungles' carried an odor of racism" (Vance, 2016, pp. 27–28, 44). As to the genre's gender ideology, she found,

> The Bible is used to support the notion of essentialist gender roles and argue that the respective behaviors of women and men are driven by their biology.... Male speakers and callers routinely described their struggles with "headship" or wisely fulfilling their role as head of the family. Husbands were told that, because women are emotional and "want men who are strong and tender," wise headship requires listening to their wives and considering their needs. Women speakers and callers agreed they are called to respect male headship ... [and] testified how they came to see God's wisdom in creating women and men to find satisfaction in their "different but equal" roles. (pp. 39–40)

Unleashed by the media deregulation of the 1990s, the religious media conglomerates arguably constitute a new form of church organization that, with their interlocking control of electronic and print resources for religious devotion and education, serve for American evangelicals the functions provided to other Protestants by their denominations (Ward, 2019). Salem Media Group, for example, dominates commercial evangelical radio through station ownership in the nation's top media markets, and distributes network-produced news/talk and music programming carried by thousands of affiliates in virtually every other media market. Its Salem Web Network aggregates nationally syndicated evangelical radio and television programs through its own web portal and, along with other Salem faith-based sites, generates a reported 107 million monthly mobile app sessions, 31 million monthly computer sessions, 42 million Facebook fans, and 13 million email subscribers (Salem Web Network, 2017). The company also operates three radio music programming services and acquired the top fan magazines for the contemporary Christian and southern gospel music genres. In print media, Salem publishes professional magazines for pastors and youth workers, plus popular magazines for evangelical book fans, and provides self-publishing services for faith-based authors. Pastors can download sermon preparation materials from Salem, plus graphics and videos to supplement their messages, while worship leaders can download song tracks and worship visuals, and youth workers can access video lessons for children. Salem search engines help users find local evangelical churches, schools, and bookstores and to apply for church and missionary jobs. The faithful can also improve their lives through Salem's line of wellness products and its monthly financial investment newsletters and weekly trading services. The company has moved into politics by producing seven general-market conservative radio talk shows and acquiring the leading conservative book publisher, along with major conservative websites, news services, and blogs.

As the example of Salem Media Group suggests, religious radio has become not only consolidated but also convergent with new digital media platforms. To name just one example, Salem teamed with a leading evangelical publisher to create a daily radio feature, aired during Salem's *Mike Gallagher Show* that is syndicated on 130 stations nationwide and carried on Salem's SiriusXM satellite radio channel, based on the best-selling daily devotional book *Jesus Calling* (Young, 2004). The volume sold three hundred thousand units in 2012, was repurposed that year as an iPad and iPhone app that by 2014 garnered two hundred thousand downloads at $9.99 each (HarperCollins, 2014), and today may be followed via its own website that offers an email newsletter, blog community, streaming video series, and podcast series. The podcasts boast half a million subscribers and have featured interviews with country and gospel music artists Reba McEntire, Charlie Daniels, Dolly Parton, Kathie Lee Gifford, Josh Turner, and Amy Grant (HarperCollins, 2017). Together with its presence on Facebook, Twitter, Pinterest, and Instagram, *Jesus Calling* has been "experienced" via print, radio, and the web by an estimated twenty million people (Jesus Calling, 2017). All the major evangelical radio networks and syndicators now stream their programming for computer, tablet, and mobile app users (Ward, 2018b). One leading syndicator, Focus on the Family, reaches evangelical audiences through eleven radio and two TV programs, six radio program podcasts, four original podcasts, four websites, four blogs, eight email newsletters, Facebook and Twitter accounts, a YouTube channel, small-group DVD curricula, and four print magazines (Mesaros-Winckles & Winckles, 2016). Meanwhile, some sixteen hundred local religious radio stations stream their teaching, talk, or music over the internet (Rodrigues et al., 2013).

Yet despite the unprecedented outreach of religious media, its public profile is lower than it was a generation ago. In the 1980s when consumers had comparatively few media choices, leading TV and radio preachers reached broad national audiences and became public figures who spoke on national political issues. Today's proliferation of media choices, however, has fragmented national audiences, relegating religious broadcasting to a niche medium so that TV and radio preachers are now celebrities only within an insular subculture (Ward, 2016a). Thirty years ago a sex scandal involving televangelist Jim Bakker was intensively covered by the mainstream news media; in 2010 a sex scandal involving televangelist Marcus Lamb, whose Daystar Television Network in 2014 reported $233 million in assets and reaps viewer contributions averaging $35 million per year (Burnett, 2014), passed unnoticed.

A peak behind the veil of today's electronic church was provided in a 2017 *Washington Post* investigation of Christian lawyer and religious radio syndicator Jay Sekulow, whose daily *Jay Sekulow Live* talk show airs on 850 stations and made him well known among evangelicals as a leading defender of "religious liberty." The report discovered that Sekulow's "charity empire" of interlocking organizations took in donations of nearly $230 million between 2011 and 2015, of which $5.5 million was paid in salaries or other compensation to six Sekulow family members, with additional payments totaling $23.5 million made to three private businesses owned wholly or in part by a Sekulow family member (Davis & Boburg, 2017). Yet, Sekulow drew attention only when he emerged as a spokesman for President Donald Trump's legal team. Otherwise, religious broadcasters and conglomerates operate with little public scrutiny or accountability. Stephen Winzenburg (2005), whose periodic financial "scorecards" of religious broadcasters drew international headlines in the 1980s and 1990s, lamented in 2005 that interest "has dropped to the point that even Christian publications are no longer interested in reporting the results" (p. 9).

A further irony in the proliferation of media choices and resultant fragmentation of audiences is a bifurcation of the evangelical movement itself. In the 1970s and 1980s, religious broadcasters united the movement by promoting an ambiguous "Christian worldview" with which to combat "secular humanism" (Ward, in press; Worthen, 2013). The rhetoric glossed over historic differences between Pentecostal-Charismatic believers who view faith as an experience, and non-Pentecostals who view the gospel as a set of propositional truths. Thirty years later, the rhetorical gloss has worn thin. Religious television is now largely the province of Pentecostal-Charismatic syndicators who prize the performative possibilities of the visual medium to preach a "prosperity gospel" (Bowler, 2013) of material and emotional blessing through faith. The Religious radio format, however, is the domain of non-Pentecostal syndicators who privilege the conversational properties of the aural medium for expositing and deliberating biblical truths (Ward, 2016b).

## Religious Radio—Future

The key to projecting the future of religious radio lies in the sociohistorical continuities of evangelical mass culture (Steiner, 2016). In the most widely accepted definition, known as Bebbington's (1989) quadrilateral, evangelicalism is characterized by conversionism, activism, biblicism, and crucicentrism. This author (Ward, 2014) has elsewhere outlined a history of American evangelicalism that demonstrates, through the theoretical frameworks of Holmes's (2005) *broadcast integration* and Lindlof's (1988, 2002) *interpretive communities*, how nineteenth-century mass periodicals, and then twentieth-century radio, created and sustained a subcultural media ecology in which conversionism, activism, biblicism, and crucicentrism have remained remarkably stable as communal values and reference points for social action.

In contrast to the *social interaction* approach to media theory that sees all media as tools to convey messages and compares all media to face-to-face communication, Holmes's and Lindlof's theories follow a *social integration* approach that sees all media as environments in which users share rituals and build communities. Social integration occurs because, as Holmes (2005) observed, media audiences are not merely "an indefinite range of recipients" but are "specific to definite genres and times, and constitute a remarkably high degree of solidarity" (p. 147).

In turn, "This solidarity is channeled totemically and ritually through 'media agents'—the characters, the presenters, the hosts and the media workers... It is through these agents that individual members of a given audience 'interact' with each other. Instead of having a directly horizontal communicative relationship with others, a detour is taken via media agents" (p. 147). Such broadcast integration "brings about a high level of recognition between audiences and media producers" as "audiences come to identify strongly with media presenters" (Holmes, 2005, p. 148). The latter "are bestowed with charisma as a reflex of the concentration of consciousness in their person." Yet, presenters "are merely the conduit by which solidarity is achieved with other viewers, listeners and readers" as the broadcast medium enables each "to 'reflexively monitor' what it is that other audience members are consuming" (p. 148). As such, "broadcast media enable a form of reciprocity... able to facilitate a sense of belonging, security and community, even if individuals are not directly interacting" (p. 148).

Lindlof (1988) also noted that the meanings given to media content are not purely idiosyncratic and individual constructions, since audience members are situated in communities that share rules of interpretation. In turn, these interpretations become concretized through communal validation. Thus, interpretive communities are formed not around traditional social referents such as kinship or class, but "come into being with the typically ritualistic or rule-governed enactment of communicative events whose sense for interlocutors is the sharing of media technologies, content... and occasions" (p. 92). Once a community arises through members' interpretation of a media genre, the interpretation gains "historical" validity that stabilizes the community and furnishes rules for members' social actions. Over time, the interpretation generates a unity of interests and purposes, produces a shared code of moral obligations, symbols, and narratives that direct core communal values, and establishes communicative occasions that govern membership.

Using the theoretical frameworks just described, the sociohistorical continuities of evangelical conversionism, activism, biblicism, and crucicentrism become evident in the movement's media ecology since the late nineteenth century. Evangelical Protestantism dominated the religious and civic life of the early American republic (Noll, 2002), but the impacts of the American Civil War and the rise of higher biblical criticism and Darwinian science threw evangelicals on the defensive. By the 1870s they mobilized to reclaim the old verities, led by Dwight Lyman Moody. The Chicago-based evangelist readily cooperated with the "penny press," a new cultural phenomenon brought about by a technological "revolution in cheap print" (Starr, 2004) that made possible mass-circulation newspapers and periodicals. Moody realized that press coverage would fill the pews at his citywide crusades, while editors discovered that puffing the evangelist and his events would build circulation (Evensen, 2003). Cheap print not only secured international celebrity for the evangelist, but ensured that a vast corpus of writings by Moody, about Moody, and inspired by Moody would circulate widely among evangelicals and give rise to an interpretive community built around conversionism, activism, biblicism, and crucicentrism. By the time he died in 1899, "Moody was a progenitor of fundamentalism—it could even be argued that he was its principal progenitor" (Marsden, 1980, p. 33). Through the medium of cheap mass-circulation print, Moody and his ideas enjoyed a "pervasive resonance and cultural reception" so that "as a cultural icon, Moody may serve as a window through to which to view the historical backdrop of the emergence of the [evangelical] movement" (Metzger, 2007, p. 17).

Yet, print is consumed privately and asynchronously: "Missing was a means to socially integrate these masses into a broadly coherent culture—missing, that is, until radio" (Ward, 2014, p. 122). The popular network preachers of radio's golden age "literally transferred the format of the old Moody revival meetings—music, testimony, message—and adapted it to the airwaves" (p. 115), thus integrating the evangelical interpretive community. The twenty million weekly listeners who tuned in the *Old Fashioned Revival Hour*, for example, shared a communicative occasion each Sunday evening as they engaged in media rituals from the opening theme ("Give the winds a mighty voice! Jesus saves! Jesus saves!") to the weekly musical program, listener letters read by Mrs. Grace Fuller, and a short and folksy sermon from Charles Fuller. "Suddenly, evangelicals were—even across traditional denominational boundaries—referencing the same celebrities, listening to the same music, purchasing the same books, using the same catchphrases, and sharing the same rules for interpreting one another's talk" (p. 124). Even the names of the era's popular broadcasts—*Old Fashioned Revival Hour, Radio Revival Hour, Revivaltime, Hour of Decision, Radio Chapel Service, Chapel of the Air, Young People's Church of the Air, Bible Fellowship Hour, Back to the Bible, Radio Bible Study, Radio Bible Class, Word of Truth, Word of Life Hour, Light and Life Hour*, and many others—reflect themes of conversionism, activism, and biblicism as shared discursive strategies and communally validated social actions.

In response to the Sexual Revolution of the 1960s, the old "religious-sounding" radio program titles that directly emphasized conversionism, activism, biblicism, and crucicentrism began giving way by the late 1970s to a new tactical reading. Three new programs set the pace: *Focus on the Family* with host James Dobson, *Insight for Living* with speaker Chuck Swindoll, and *In Touch* with speaker Charles Stanley. Following these three innovators, "the new programs of evangelicalism's third wave rewrote the text; revival was now interpreted through such 'feminine' screens as relating, living, touching" (Ward, 2014, p. 125). Thus,

> In addition to *Focus on the Family, Insight for Living* and *In Touch,* major syndicated programs launched in the 1970s thru 1990s included *Grace To You, Turning Point, Love Worth Finding, Somebody Loves You, A New Beginning, Matters of the Heart, FamilyLife Today, The Living Way, Leading the Way, Winning Walk, Truth for Life, Truths That Transform, Renewing Your Mind,*

and *Let My People Think*. Conversionism ("turning," "finding," "beginning," "transform"), activism ("you," "life," "love," "renewing"), biblicism ("truth") ... were still apparent, but ... tactically reread through "feminine" values of nurture, care, and personal development. (pp. 125–126)

Given that the aural medium shaped and reflected American evangelicalism throughout radio's first century, religious programming is poised to thrive in radio's second century as the genre maintains its integral role in the evangelical community. Further confidence comes from understanding the role of the electronic church in the evangelical social system. At the macro level of the system are evangelical institutions and their mass-mediated representations that transmit normative values and interpretations, at the meso level are Sunday sermons and other organizational discourses that structure joint deliberation and action at the congregational level, and at the micro level are spontaneous natural talk and private role enactments (Ward, 2010).

The interlocking dynamics of this system were illustrated in recent fieldwork (Ward, 2018c). In September 2016, the Billy Graham Evangelistic Association published a special online edition of its monthly *Decision* magazine. The "2016 Presidential Election Guide" featured articles, commentaries, interviews, and quotations from popular religious radio syndicators Adrian Rogers (*Love Worth Finding*; aired on 2,700 stations), David Jeremiah (*Turning Point*; 2,000 stations), Eric Metaxas (*Breakpoint*; 1,400 stations), James Dobson (*Family Talk*; 900 stations), Tony Perkins (*Washington Watch*; 280 stations), and Mat Staver (*Freedom's Call*; 170 stations). This macro-level media representation of communal norms and interpretations was picked up at the meso level in an October sermon by a local church pastor that, in this author's hearing, reprised the magazine's comparison of the Republican and Democratic Party platforms and repeated a litany of culture-laden evangelical speech codes such as *biblical, worldview, marriage, life*. That these interpretations functioned, in turn, as reference points for church members' micro-level social actions is affirmed by the fact that 81 percent of white evangelical Protestants voted for Trump (Smith & Martinez, 2016).

Religious radio is so interwoven into the fabric of American evangelicalism that it has survived the ascendance of television and end of network radio, the emergence of radio as a niche medium of specialized formats, the advent of streaming media, and the proliferation of digital platforms. Evangelicals and their media conglomerates are too heavily invested in radio and aural media, and in the channels to distribute spoken-word and music content, to forsake the infrastructure they have developed over decades. If anything, the "old" broadcast medium of religious radio uniquely lends itself to the mobility of the "new" digital platforms. Content is still the driver of today's digital media universe, and in radio the conglomerates and syndicators have content aplenty that can be repackaged for digital platforms at attractive economies of scale and low distribution costs.

More broadly, the experience of religious radio is a cautionary tale that speaks to the soul of radio broadcasting. For the tale illuminates a question at the heart of the "people's medium," the medium that historically has afforded diverse voices the greatest opportunities for media access. The highest-rated radio formats will survive. But how does industry consolidation impact the lesser-rated niche formats, from classical to educational, that give voice to important sectors of American life? The story of religious radio suggests that, while consolidation can bring gains in reach, sound, and profitability, it may also require broadcasters to sell their souls.

## References

Armstrong, B. (1978). *Religious broadcasting sourcebook*. Morristown, NJ: National Religious Broadcasters.

———. (1979). *The electric church*. Nashville, TN: Thomas Nelson.

Barna Group. (2005). *More people use Christian media than attend church*. Retrieved from www.barna.com/research/more-people-use-christian-media-than-attend-church/

Bebbington, D. W. (1989). *Evangelicalism in modern Britain: A history from the 1730s to the 1980s*. London: Routledge.

Bowler, K. (2013). *Blessed: A history of the American prosperity gospel*. New York: Oxford University Press.

Burnett, J. (2014). *Can a television network be a church? The IRS says yes*. National Public Radio, April 1. Retrieved from www.npr.org/2014/04/01/282496855/can-a-television-network-be-a-church-the-irs-says-yes

Carpenter, J. A. (1997). *Revive us again: The reawakening of American fundamentalism*. New York: Oxford University Press.

Christians, C. G. (1990). Redemptive media as the evangelical's cultural task. In Q. J. Schultze (Ed.), *American evangelicals and the mass media* (pp. 331–356). Grand Rapids, MI: Zondervan.

Davis, A. C., & Boburg, S. (2017). Trump attorney Jay Sekulow's family has been paid millions from charities they control. *Washington Post*, June 27. Retrieved from www.washingtonpost.com/investigations/trump-attorney-jay-sekulows-family-has-been-paid-millions-from-charities-they-control/2017/06/27/6428d988-5852-11e7-ba90-f5875b7d1876_story.html

DiCola, P., & Thomson, K. (2002). *Radio deregulation: Has it served citizens and musicians? A report on the effects of radio ownership consolidation following the 1996 Telecommunications Act*. Washington, DC: Future of Music Coalition.

Dorsett, L. W. (1990). *Billy Sunday and the redemption of urban America*. Grand Rapids, MI: Eerdmans.

Drushel, B. E. (1998). The Telecommunications Act of 1996 and radio market structure. *Journal of Media Economics, 11*(3), 3–20.

Evensen, B. J. (2003). *God's man for the Gilded Age: D. L. Moody and the rise of modern evangelism*. New York: Oxford University Press.

Fratrik, M. (2002). *Radio transactions 2001: Where did all the deals go?* Chantilly, VA: BIA Financial Networks.

Fuller, D. P. (1972). *Give the winds a mighty voice: The story of Charles E. Fuller*. Waco, TX: Word.

Hangen, T. J. (2002). *Redeeming the dial: Radio, religion, and popular culture in America.* Chapel Hill: University of North Carolina Press.

HarperCollins Christian Publishing. (2014). *Bestselling Jesus Calling brand celebrates 10 years and 10 million sold.* Retrieved from www.harpercollinschristian.com/?s=jesus+calling

———. (2017). *Superstar Dolly Parton appears on the Jesus Calling podcast.* Retrieved from www.harpercollinschristian.com/?s=jesus+calling

Hilliard, R. L., & Keith, M. C. (2001). *The broadcast century and beyond: A biography of American broadcasting* (3rd ed.). Boston: Focal Press.

Holmes, D. (2005). *Communication theory: Media, technology and society.* Thousand Oaks, CA: Sage.

Hoover, S. M. (1988). *Mass media religion: The social sources of the electronic church.* Newbury Park, CA: Sage.

Jesus Calling. (2017). *Over 20 million have experienced Jesus Calling.* Retrieved from www.jesuscalling.com

Kerr, P. (1939). *Music in evangelism.* Glendale, GA: Gospel Music Publishers.

Lindlof, T. R. (1988). Media audiences as interpretive communities. In J. A. Anderson (Ed.), *Communication yearbook 11* (pp. 81–107). Newbury Park, CA: Sage.

———. (2002). Interpretive community: An approach to media and religion. *Journal of Media and Religion, 1,* 61–74.

Marsden, G. M. (1980). *Fundamentalism and American culture: The shaping of twentieth-century evangelicalism, 1870–1925.* New York: Oxford University Press.

———. (1995). *Reforming fundamentalism: Fuller Seminary and the new evangelicalism.* Grand Rapids, MI: Eerdmans.

Mesaros-Winckles, C., & Winckles, A. O. (2016). Focus on the (changing) family: A hot message encounters a cool medium. In M. Ward, Sr. (Ed.), *The electronic church in the digital age: Cultural impacts of evangelical mass media* (Vol. 2, pp. 31–55). Santa Barbara, CA: Praeger.

Metzger, P. L. (2007). *Consuming Jesus: Beyond race and class divisions in a consumer church.* Grand Rapids, MI: Eerdmans.

Noll, M. A. (2002). *America's God: From Jonathan Edwards to Abraham Lincoln.* New York: Oxford University Press.

Pew Research Center. (2015). *America's changing religious landscape.* Washington, DC: Pew Research Center. Retrieved from http://assets.pewresearch.org/wp-content/uploads/sites/11/2015/05/RLS-08-26-full-report.pdf

Postman, N. (1985). *Amusing ourselves to death: Public discourse in the age of television.* New York: Viking.

Rodrigues, R., Green, J., & Virshup, L. (2013). *Radio today: How Americans listen to radio.* Columbia, MD: Arbitron.

Salem Web Network. (2017). *Further your reach.* Retrieved from www.salemwebnetwork.com/

Schultze, Q. J. (1991). *Televangelism and American culture: The business of popular religion.* Grand Rapids, MI: Baker.

Siedell, B. (1971). *Gospel radio.* Lincoln, NE: Good News Broadcasting Association.

Smith, G. A., & Martinez, J. (2016). How the faithful voted: A preliminary 2016 analysis. Pew Research Center. Retrieved from www.pewresearch.org/fact-tank/2016/11/09/how-the-faithful-voted-a-preliminary-2016-analysis

Smith, L. R., & Seignious, M. H. (2016). Medium, message, and ministry: How music radio shapes evangelical culture. In M. Ward, Sr. (Ed.), *The electronic church in the digital age: Cultural impacts of evangelical mass media* (Vol. 1, pp. 101–125). Santa Barbara, CA: Praeger.

Starr, P. (2004). *The creation of the media: Political origins of modern communications.* New York: Basic Books.

Steiner, M. A. (2016). A research agenda for the electronic church in the digital age. In M. Ward, Sr. (Ed.), *The electronic church in the digital age: Cultural impacts of evangelical mass media* (Vol. 1, pp. 1–23). Santa Barbara, CA: Praeger.

Sterling, C. H. (2004). The Telecommunications Act of 1996. In C. H. Sterling (Ed.), *Museum of broadcast communications encyclopedia of radio* (Vol. 3, pp. 1382–1384). Chicago: Fitzroy Dearborn.

Sterling, C. H., & Kitross, J. M. (2002). *Stay tuned: A history of American broadcasting.* Mahwah, NJ: Lawrence Erlbaum.

Stout, D. A. (2016). Foreword. In M. Ward, Sr. (Ed.), *The electronic church in the digital age: Cultural impacts of evangelical mass media* (Vol. 1, pp. ix–xiv). Santa Barbara, CA: Praeger.

Vance, D. C. (2016). The flesh and the spirit: Communicating evangelical identity via "Christian radio." In M. Ward, Sr. (Ed.), *The electronic church in the digital age: Cultural impacts of evangelical mass media* (pp. 27–51). Santa Barbara, CA: Praeger.

Ward, M., Sr. (1994). *Air of salvation: The story of Christian broadcasting.* Grand Rapids, MI: Baker.

———. (1995). Radio and retail: What's in the mix? *Christian Retailing, 41*(7), 54–56.

———. (2009). Dark preachers: The impact of radio consolidation on independent religious syndicators. *Journal of Media and Religion, 8,* 79–96.

———. (2010). "I was saved at an early age": An ethnography of fundamentalist speech and cultural performance. *Journal of Communication and Religion, 33,* 108–144.

———. (2012). Consolidating the gospel: The impact of the 1996 Telecommunications Act on religious radio ownership. *Journal of Media and Religion, 11,* 11–30.

———. (2013). Air of the King: Evangelicals and radio. In R. H. Woods, Jr. (Ed.), *Evangelicals and popular culture: Pop goes the gospel* (Vol. 1, pp. 101–118). Santa Barbara, CA: Praeger.

———. (2014). Give the winds a mighty voice: Evangelical culture as radio ecology. *Journal of Radio and Audio Media, 21,* 115–133.

———. (2016a). Televangelism, audience fragmentation, and the changing coverage of scandal. In H. Mandell & G. M. Chen (Eds.), *Scandal in a digital age* (pp. 53–68). New York: Palgrave Macmillan.

———. (2016b). In spirit *or* in truth? The great evangelical divide, from analog to digital. In M. Ward, Sr. (Ed.), *The electronic church in the digital age: Cultural impacts of evangelical mass media* (Vol. 1, pp. 193–218). Santa Barbara, CA: Praeger.

———. (2017). *The Lord's radio: Gospel music broadcasting and the making of evangelical culture, 1920–1960.* Jefferson, NC: McFarland.

———. (2018a). Segregating the dial: Institutional racism in evangelical radio. In O. O. Banjo & K. M. Williams (Eds.), *Contemporary Christian culture: Messages, missions, and dilemmas* (pp. 45–56). Lanham, MD: Lexington.

———. (2018b). Digital religion and media economics: Concentration and convergence in the electronic church. *Journal of Religion, Media, and Digital Culture, 7*(1), 90–120.

———. (2018c). The dangers of getting what you wished for: What do you say to evangelicals? In S.-L. S. Chen, N. Allaire & Z. J. Chen (Eds.), *Constructing narratives in response to Trump's election: How various populations make sense of an unexpected victory* (pp. 61–81). Lanham, MD: Lexington.

———. (2019). A new kind of church: The religious media conglomerate as a "denomination." *Journal of Media and Religion, 17*(3/4), 117–133.

———. (in press). "From a Christian perspective": News/talk in evangelical mass media.

In A. M. Nadler & A. J. Bauer (Eds.), *News on the right: Studying conservative news cultures*. New York: Oxford University Press.

Williams, G., & Roberts, S. (2002). *Radio industry review 2002: Trends in ownership, format, and finance*. Media ownership working group paper 11. Washington, DC: Federal Communications Commission.

Winzenburg, S. (2005). *TV ministries' use of airtime, Fall 2004*. Retrieved from http://faculty.grandview.edu/swinzenburg/tv_ministries_study.pdf

Worthen, M. (2013). *Apostles of reason: The crisis of authority in American evangelicalism*. New York: Oxford University Press.

Wrench, J. S. (2016). Setting the evangelical agenda: The role of "Christian radio." In M. Ward, Sr. (Ed.), *The electronic church in the digital age: Cultural impacts of evangelical mass media* (Vol. 1, pp. 173–192). Santa Barbara, CA: Praeger.

Young, S. (2004). *Jesus calling: Enjoying peace in his presence*. Nashville, TN: Thomas Nelson.

## 10

## "A More Inclusive Public Service"
• • • • • • • • • • • • • • • • • • • •
Can NPR Serve All of America?

JOHN MARK DEMPSEY

National Public Radio proclaimed a ratings increase in the fall of 2016. Ratings of NPR's *Morning Edition* were up 26 percent, with 13.5 million weekly listeners. Ratings of the afternoon program *All Things Considered* were up 43 percent, with 13.3 million listeners in the twenty-five to fifty-four demographic. Even allowing for the fact that this was in the midst of the fierce and bitter presidential election campaign pitting Donald Trump against Hillary Clinton, this was an exceptional performance. The morning ratings for commercial all-news radio in fall 2016 increased 15 percent, while the morning ratings on NPR stations increased 26 percent; the afternoon ratings on commercial all-news stations increased 19 percent, but increased 43 percent for NPR stations ("NPR Sees Large," 2016).

But does National Public Radio truly serve the entire nation with its programming? The Public Broadcasting Act of 1967 created the Corporation for Public Broadcasting, which provides federal funding for NPR and the Public Broadcasting Service, the public television network. The act states that its purpose is to address "the needs of unserved and underserved audiences, particularly children and minorities" (Public Broadcasting Act, 1967, para. a6).

For much of its history, NPR was accused of elitism. A young Latino user quoted in a study on that image problem said, "NPR, I feel, is mostly for educated adults from middle class and up. That is my impression" (Everhart, 2010, para. 5). Political columnist and commentator Juan Williams of the *Washington Post* and Fox News, fired from NPR in 2010 after making controversial comments about Muslims, said, "It is a very elitist, and in this case, white institution that I think is struggling with the changing demographics of American society" (Hagey, 2011, para. 4). NPR's ratings remained high into early 2018. Nielsen Audio reported that the network had its highest broadcast ratings ever—37.7 million listeners—in the fall of 2017 ("NPR maintains," 2018).

As of 2015, about 87 percent of NPR's listeners were white, 10 percent greater than the national figure. While African Americans make up 12 percent of the adult population, they are 5 percent of NPR listeners (Hushock, 2016; Powell, 2015; Schumacher-Matos, 2012). NPR's own promotional materials proclaim: "Across platforms, NPR reaches the nation's best and brightest. On air and online, the NPR audience is influential, affluent and curious.... NPR listeners are 133% more likely to be top management and 148% more likely to be C-suite executives.... NPR listeners are 380% more likely to have a doctorate degree. ("Audience: Cultural," 2018, p. 1, p. 3) An NPR demographic report notes that the average annual household income of NPR listeners is $85,675 ("NPR Audience Profile," 2018, p. 1). A 2012 Pew Research Center study found that 43 percent of NPR listeners earn above $75,000 per year, second only to readers of the *Economist*, the upscale British news magazine ("In Changing," 2012). Further, it may be questioned if NPR truly serves a *national* audience. Of NPR's ten highest-rated stations, only one is a southern station, WUNC of Raleigh, North Carolina (Hushock, 2016).

This chapter examines the history and content of NPR programming, reviews the existing proposals to broaden the audience for the network, and makes original suggestions for reaching a wider, more inclusive listening audience.

## "Strengthening the Diversity of Voices and Views"

NPR boasts a loyal and passionate audience, but because it primarily appeals to listeners who are much more affluent and well educated than average U.S. radio listeners, the size of the audience, and therefore support for NPR, is less than it might be if it appealed to a broader swath of the U.S. population.

A 2010 Corporation for Public Broadcasting report advanced the same objective advocated in this study: "Commit to a more inclusive public service: Deepen the value of public radio for all its audiences by strengthening the diversity of voices and views in public radio's mainstream news and music programming, by encouraging multiple, differentiated services that reach a wider range of listeners" ("Grow the Audience," 2010, p. 2). Nielsen Audio research in 2015 indicated that the news-talk format—which includes most NPR stations—does not make the top five favorite formats among African Americans and Hispanics in any age group, including older listeners, who are most inclined to listen to radio news and talk. Media reporter Justin Fox (2015) commented, "That seems to be the biggest issue of all for NPR, and other news broadcasters. The segment of the radio audience that's growing isn't interested in listening to the news—or at least not to the news that's currently on offer" (para. 10).

A chronicler of NPR's history, Michael McCauley (2005) noted the success of the network in providing "service to college-educated Americans.... As NPR helps current listeners to become even better informed, it will naturally face the question of whether it also should do more to attract people who have generally not listened in the past" (p. 124).

## Beginnings of Public Radio

Public (or "educational") radio broadcasting long predates National Public Radio. Professors of physics and engineers were experimenting with audio transmissions at U.S. universities throughout the first two decades of the twentieth century. During the 1920s, after the beginning of radio broadcasting, the federal government granted educational broadcasting licenses to more than two hundred college-owned radio stations. Despite the organization in 1925 of the Association of College and University Radio Stations (later the National Association of Education Broadcasters), the stations operated on an entirely local basis, featuring professors' lectures, public-affairs programs, music and entertainment, farm reports, and the like. Gradually, commercial radio began to eclipse educational radio broadcasting on the U.S. airwaves.

By the 1950s, as television and FM radio began to emerge, the powerful Rockefeller and Ford foundations became interested in public broadcasting, bringing a revival of interest in educational broadcasting. A couple of small educational broadcasting networks were created, and then, in the mid-1960s, the fateful moment for public radio and television came when as part of President Lyndon Johnson's "Great Society" the Carnegie Commission was appointed and recommended the establishment of the Corporation for Public Broadcasting (McCauley, 2005).

The Public Broadcasting Act of 1967 created the Corporation for Public Broadcasting to promote the development of noncommercial television and radio. Later came the Public Broadcasting System and National Public Radio. Radio was very much an afterthought. The words "and radio" were actually "Scotch-taped" into the text after every reference to "television." Historian Jack Mitchell (2005) wrote, "Radio was inserted by cellophane tape into the final draft, which was photocopied. So, via some midnight oil and Scotch tape, radio got into the President's draft of what was still the Public Television Bill creating the Corporation for Public Television" (p. 36).

The language of the act is broad in describing the type of programming it encourages—programs of "high quality, diversity, creativity, excellence and innovation . . . both in particular localities and throughout the United States" (Public Broadcasting Act, 1967, pp. 1, 4).

NPR was created in 1970 with a local public radio station manager from Minnesota, Bill Siemering, tagged as its first program director. "[He] wanted something that was not, and is not, available in very many places on the radio dial. He wanted quietness. He wanted calm conversation, analysis, and explication," wrote longtime NPR reporter Linda Wertheimer (1995, p. xix).

NPR took the air on April 20, 1971, providing coverage of U.S. Senate hearings on the Vietnam War, and its iconic afternoon/evening news program *All Things Considered* aired for the first time on May 3, 1971, with coverage of massive protests against the war on the streets of Washington, D.C. When a protestor was reportedly hit by a police motorcycle, NPR reporter Jeff Kamen asked an officer, "Excuse me, Sergeant. Is that a technique? Where the men actually try to drive the motorcycles right into the demonstrators?" The nonplussed officer replied, "No, it's no technique. We're trying to go down the road, and the people get in front of you. What are you going to do?" (Stamberg, 2010, p. 13).

## Growing the Audience

While the demographics of NPR listeners are impressive, they also reveal large segments of the population that, for whatever reason, are not regular listeners. It could be argued that those with less than a college education and earning closer to the average annual household income are not being served by NPR.

Scholars have studied the question of how public radio can serve a broader audience while still being true to its value of providing the highest quality public service programming. David Giovannoni and George Bailey (1988) observed: "Public radio must reconsider its music programming if it is to significantly increase its audience" (p. 1). Later, Giovannoni (1994) commented on the idea that public radio must compromise its values to attract larger audiences: "It incorrectly assumes that audience size and values are inversely correlated; (that) one gets bigger only when the other gets smaller" (p. 5). McCauley (2002), in a study of how NPR's programming has evolved as a result of economic realities, suggested that, with the development of the Internet and satellite radio, NPR might develop multiple program services.

A 2012 article emphasized the challenge NPR and other public radio stations have in "growing the audience." An article by music professor Kurt Ellenberger (2012) specifically addressed the audience for jazz, but the article might also apply to other genres, musical and otherwise, favored by public radio. Ellenberger said jazz is "cognitively demanding," making it a challenge to market, package, and program in the "dominant popular culture. . . . That's a tall order that seems insurmountable. Frankly speaking, it can't be done, at least not as part of a prefabricated 'strategy' to build an audience" (paras. 6, 7).

Besides NPR news offerings, a staple of public radio is classical music. British journalist Simon Winchester (1981) argued that public radio "is not really 'public' at all . . . [it] appeals only to the tiniest and most privileged subgroups in the community" (p. 25). Responding to a loss of listeners a few years ago, NPR's response was to launch an advertising campaign targeted at "quirky" listeners—"a sky-diving algebra teacher . . . a Sudoku-playing barista" (Jensen, 2012, para. 1).

NPR's emphasis on news is at once a strength and a weakness. A 2012 Pew Center study shows that news/talk/information was the second most popular format with 12.1 percent of audience share; however, that means the vast majority of the radio audience is listening for one music format or another. Also, the study found that 57 percent of the audience for news/talk/information is fifty-five or older ("The State of the News Media," 2012).

The vast majority of U.S. radio listening is devoted to music formats. While news/talk is the overall top format in terms of total listeners, eight of the top ten formats are music based. The top four formats for listeners twenty-five to fifty-four are music formats, and the top nine formats for listeners eighteen to thirty-four are music based ("Tops of 2015," 2015).

NPR's limited popular music programming tends to emphasize music on the margins of the public's awareness. *World Café* and *All Songs Considered* are worthy programs that feature music in the style of AAA (adult album alternative) commercial stations. However, the AAA format does not appear among the top ten formats in any demographic ("Tops of 2015," 2015). Four of the top ten radio markets do not have an AAA station, and three of the AAA stations in the top ten markets are NPR-affiliated stations, WXPN in Philadelphia, KKXT in Dallas, and WFUV in New York ("Nielsen Audio Ratings," 2017).

Over the years, music programming has lost airtime to news on NPR stations, but innovators have developed other vehicles for music. Bob Boilen created the web-only program *All Songs Considered* in 2000. A new era was dawning, the digital era. *All Songs Considered* and other programs in the NPR Music division are primarily created to be heard in a streaming format, rather than broadcast over the air. In recent years, this has been a familiar programming strategy for NPR (Roberts et al., 2010).

## Recent Programming Efforts

NPR's recent growth in listenership has coincided with an effort to reach younger listeners, mainly through its digital offerings such as podcasts and smartphone apps like NPR One, rather than an attempt to reach a broader racial, income, or geographic demography. This has met with considerable success but of course does not necessarily promote the local stations that pay fees for NPR programming to younger listeners. Further, digital, on-demand audio and video content does not use the free, public airwaves as specifically addressed by the Public Broadcasting Act of 1967, and the funding generated by the Corporation for Public Broadcasting presumably is still provided for actual broadcasting (Public Broadcasting Act, 1967).

While the ratings for NPR stations saw an upswing in 2016, that was not the case a few years ago. Listening to NPR programming was down about 1 percent in 2011 from 2010, at about 26.8 million listeners compared to 27.2 million the year before, although the numbers do not include online listeners (Phelps, 2012; "The State of the News Media," 2012). Listenership to NPR's *Morning Edition* declined 5 percent from spring 2011 to spring 2012, from 13 million to 12.3 million, and the audience for *All Things Considered* dropped 4 percent, from 12.3 million to 11.8 million (Jensen, 2013).

In 2015, the longtime head of NPR programming, Eric Nuzum, spoke to a group of NPR trustees and board members. He showed them a photo of a young woman and said, "This is Lara. Lara is the future of NPR. NPR's mission must be to serve that woman the way we served her parents. Nothing else matters." The average age of the NPR listener had increased from forty-five years old in the mid-1990s to fifty-four in 2015 (Neyfakh, 2016, paras. 1–2).

Ironically, even as he spoke, Nuzum had decided to leave NPR to take a position with the audiobook company Audible. Reportedly, Nuzum and other NPR programmers were frustrated that NPR was hesitant to aggressively promote the new on-demand features on the airwaves, lest the promotion undercut the interests of the local stations. "Let's talk about the ideas that you always wanted to do but could never do," Audible CEO Donald Katz persuaded Nuzum (Ragusea, 2015, para. 1). Nuzum, who had been with NPR for about a decade, apparently decided that he could not achieve his vision at NPR. Moreover, as the online magazine *Slate* put it, he may have wondered about the long-term viability of *Morning Edition* and *All Things Considered*, NPR's flagship programs, "in an age when its terrestrial audience is growing older and younger listeners seem to prefer addictive, irreverent, and entertaining podcasts over the news?" (Neyfakh, 2016, para. 9).

Even before Nuzum's departure, NPR had launched the highly popular program *Invisibilia*, exploring "the invisible forces that shape human behavior—things like ideas, beliefs, assumptions and emotions" (para. 1). The show launched in January 2015 and reaches as many as 900,000 podcast listeners per week, in addition to airing on about 350 NPR stations ("About 'Invisibilia,'" 2014; "NPR's 'Invisibilia' Returns," 2017).

Anya Grundmann, the longtime director of NPR Music, succeeded Nuzum as NPR's lead programmer. She had been instrumental in developing new, primarily online audio and video programs such as *Jazz Night in America*, featuring live jazz concerts; the *Tiny Desk Concerts*, featuring live indie rock performances literally from the desk of *All Songs Considered* host Bob Boilen; and a hip-hop interview program, *Microphone Check* ("Anya Grundmann Named," 2016).

With Grundmann at the programming helm, NPR continued to expand its on-demand programming. For example, in mid-2017, NPR announced plans to create a new podcast for comedian Paula Poundstone, a popular panelist on *Wait, Wait Don't Tell Me* (a weekend quiz show). In *Live from the Poundstone Institute*, she contemplates such discoveries as what music cats like and what we can learn about coffee spills from fluid dynamics ("Introducing a New Comedy," 2017). Another new podcast, *What's Good with Stretch & Bobbito*, veteran New York hip-hop DJs Adrian Bartos and Robert Garcia started in July 2017. "We've grown up quite a bit," said Bartos. "If you were to only know us from the '90s, I would think that maybe you'd think twice about putting Stretch and Bob in anything NPR related" ("Hip-Hop Radio DJs," 2017, para. 20).

If attracting a young audience equates with podcasting, NPR has made strides. As of mid-2016, the network claimed 7.5 million monthly podcast listeners, making it the most popular source of podcasts in the United States. "We're seeing some very encouraging signs that younger people are coming into NPR that previously haven't listened," NPR president Jarl Mohn said (Battaglio, 2016, p. E8).

The statistics on podcasts and other on-demand listening are certainly notable. NPR is the top source of podcasts in the United States, according to Podtrac.com, with a unique monthly audience of nearly seventeen million listeners in the United States and four of the top ten podcasts: *Up First*, *TED Radio Hour*, *Fresh Air*, and *Planet Money*, as of mid-2018 ("Podcast Industry," 2018). However, the impression that listening to web-based streaming audio has eclipsed traditional radio is inaccurate. This will be addressed in the discussion.

## The "E" Word

*New York Times* media critic David Carr once characterized NPR as "the prissy, embattled bastion of the quiet left," and that was in a column extolling the network's coverage of Hurricane Katrina (Roberts et al., 2010, p. 267).

It is one thing for NPR to improve its appeal to young listeners, but appealing to listeners outside of NPR's upscale, highly educated, predominantly white audience is another question. Despite such recent pop-culture-friendly podcasting endeavors as *Microphone Check* and *What's Good with Stretch and Bobbito*, NPR critics often hurl the "elitist" epithet at the network.

Onetime NPR chief executive Vivian Schiller was asked if NPR is elitist. "No, we're not, but I think the reason some non-listeners might think of us as elitist has to do with the nature of our sound.... We have to be very mindful of the way that we sound," Schiller said. She continued that the voices and tone of certain NPR hosts may sound "occasionally stuffy, and we're moving away from that—and quite successfully" (Friedman, 2010, paras. 4–5). This followed a study commissioned by NPR that found the audience for public radio would be larger if NPR and other public broadcasters would make an effort to eliminate perceptions that their programs are "elitist and stuffy.... Producers would have to make shows that are more lively and conversational and promoters would have to take greater care when describing public radio as 'intelligent' and 'serious,'" the Los Angeles–based consulting firm SmithGeiger found ("Audience Opportunity Study," 2010, para. 1). The study stated that listeners outside of NPR's main demographic feel excluded. NPR vice president of programming Margaret Low Smith said, "It is really important that people hear themselves in the programming. We're talking about a private party, versus a party where everyone's included" (Everhart, 2010, paras. 2–4).

An atypical NPR program has been *Car Talk*, hosted by brothers Tom and Ray Magliozzi, which originated on Boston's WBUR in 1987, and which was heard in new episodes on NPR from 1987 to 2012. The popularity of *Car Talk* was such that it continued in reruns after the brothers retired, and even after Tom died in 2014. Known as "Click and Clack, the Tappet Brothers," the Magliozzis were known as much for their good-humored, blue-collar Boston banter as their automotive advice. "They never learned how to do 'stuffy public radio announcer,'" their executive producer Doug Berman (2010, p. 172) said.

Demographics that NPR cites in supporting its appeal to potential underwriters tend to contribute to the impression that the network mainly appeals to the upper economic and educational echelons of society. Besides the previous examples cited, NPR says its listeners are 19 percent more likely to be owners or partners in their own businesses, 22 percent more likely to be chief executive officers, and 88 percent more likely to be "B2B" (business to business) decision makers involved in purchase decisions valued at more than a thousand dollars ("National Public Media: Audience," 2017).

All of this makes NPR an inviting target for critics who allege that a media organization with such a well-educated, well-heeled audience can be successful without the government funding provided for in the Public Broadcasting Act of 1967. Conservative political commentator George Will has often made the argument that public broadcasting's successful appeal to an affluent audience and the advent of digital, on-demand media have made public funding of NPR and PBS superfluous. But Will (2017) further suggests that, from the beginning, the notion that public radio and television were needed to serve the interests of the American people was seriously misguided: "Public broadcasting began as a response to what progressives nowadays call 'market failure.' This usually means the market's failure to supply what the public has not demanded but surely would demand if it understood its real 'interest'" (para. 7).

Whether, as CEO Vivian Schiller said in 2010, NPR has successfully changed audience perceptions that its programs are "stuffy sounding" (Friedman, 2010, paras. 1–3), the network has made conscious efforts to do so, especially with its podcast programs. The very popular *Invisibilia* program—which is heard on some NPR stations but has achieved most of its notoriety as a podcast—is an example. Media reporter Sara Larson (2015) commented in the *New Yorker*, "Another hallmark of the style of *Invisibilia*, and of its forebears, is light-hearted fun—little asides and moments of whimsy, which can either be enjoyable or a bit cute" (para. 14). When NPR announced the development of the new podcast featuring Paula Poundstone, she wryly commented, "Every week we'll keep looking for knowledge, because we know we left it somewhere" ("Introducing a New Comedy," 2017, para. 2). As described previously, the development of other music programming and podcasts has been designed with a young audience in mind. However, as the NPR local station managers have often pointed out, podcasting is not broadcasting (Jensen, 2016). Public radio is free and serves the public interest under the requirements of the Federal Communications Commission and the Public Broadcasting Act of 1967, whereas podcasts are not free and do not have a public interest mandate.

Any effort to sound less "intelligent" and "serious" in order to appeal to a wider segment of U.S. citizens will be met with fierce resistance from a sizable segment of NPR listeners. *Slate* writer Farhad Najoo (2011) said he is an everyday NPR listener, but he was unsparing in his comments on the network's audience: "For proof that NPR letter-writers are the stodgiest, whiniest, most self-importantly insufferable snobs of all time, just search through the network's archives.... Among the many, many topics that listeners have deemed off-limits for NPR, you'll find blogging ('another example of the slow decline of our once-educated society')... Twitter ('the CB radio of our era—just as much hype, just as much lasting impact')... and, perennially, sports" (para. 4). For example, NPR sports correspondent Mike Pesca noted, "You can't mention sports without someone saying, 'Why are you covering sports—it's just a bunch of Neanderthals, it's just a bunch of fascists!'" (para. 4).

Writer Paul Resnikoff (2017), who describes himself as a daily NPR listener, sometimes tuning in for hours at a time, and someone who has donated more than ten thousand dollars to public radio over the previous decade, commented, "Even a die-hard liberal can't deny the stuffy liberalism that infuses almost every second of NPR's reporting. The pompous accents, the ridiculous pronunciations, the topic selection, it's all baked in" (para. 8).

## Local Public Radio

The original model for NPR, and in particular *All Things Considered*, was one that would take advantage of frequent contributions from local stations (McCauley, 2005; McCourt, 1999). Historian Ralph Engelman (1996) said NPR's original program director Bill Siemering "envisaged a decentralized system reflecting the diversity of the nation: A system of local audio laboratories to train radio producers, submissions of programs to the network by affiliates, and reciprocal trade of material among stations" (p. 91). Public radio's roots were in the experimental, noncommercial radio stations that operated at land-grant universities from the 1920s into the 1950s, and Siemering "sought a return to the folksiness of the land grant radio of his youth" (McCourt, 1999, p. 45). As early NPR producer Art Silverman put it, "As much as people need to hear two more reports about Eastern Europe or the Third World, they also need to hear about how to pick rhubarb for a pie" (McCourt, 1999, p. 45). CPB reports that public radio stations (many of them NPR affiliates) produce about 40 percent of their programming locally ("About Public Media," 2018).

In the early 1980s, British journalist Simon Winchester observed that NPR's listeners tended to compose a highly educated, economically upscale audience and saw a contradiction between that and its original mission. Winchester saw that a greater emphasis on local, grassroots programming, both on NPR itself and its member stations, was one answer. He conducted a case study of KAXE-FM in Grand Rapids, Michigan. Winchester (1981) wrote, "Jazz, intelligent information, discussion and humor, farming news and sweet music—the odds and ends that, in other words, do not in themselves provide commercial programmers with giant markets for which to seek lucrative advertising rates—come only from KAXE" (p. 26). Winchester commented that while small community stations and major-market NPR stations might not seem to have a lot in common, they each devote 40 percent of their broadcast hours to the Washington, D.C.-based network. He advocated that *Morning Edition*, *All Things Considered*, and other NPR news programs should, as originally planned, air a significant amount of material produced and submitted by the local member stations. Winchester (1981) wrote that NPR and its stations should move in the direction of "either a more populist, more public approach to radio, or toward a more elitist pursuit of radio excellence" (p. 29). Winchester described a close relationship between KAXE and its listeners. When technical problems caused the station to be off the air for a day, listeners were dismayed. He wrote, "What on earth had been wrong, people would ask me. It was like losing an ear for the day, they said" (p. 29). Winchester (1981) observed that life in the Grand Rapids area would be "immeasurably diminished" without KAXE-FM (p. 26).

Over the years, KAXE has remained staunchly local in its programming and generally self-sufficient, relying on NPR for a relatively small part of its daily schedule. Much of the station's daily programming is locally produced. KAXE and its affiliate KBXE (licensed to Bemidji, Minnesota) broadcast their own morning program, composed of local features including "arts, nature, sports, weather and more," including Americana music selections. A regular segment is *Have You Had Your Breakfast Yet?*, a friendly telephone chat with a listener. *On the River*, a midday program, is a "mix of folk, rock, blues, jazz and world music." The station does carry *All Things Considered* and a Canadian Broadcasting Corporation news program, *As It Happens*, but otherwise its programming is local and music driven, with the exception of the NPR music program *World Café* ("KAXE Weekly," 2018). The station's highly active Twitter page has more than nineteen hundred followers ("KAXE-KBXE Radio," 2018).

Together, the two stations refer to themselves as Northern Community Radio. Their website states, "When you tune in to NCR you hear northern Minnesota . . . its people, communities and attitude. . . . A first-of-its-kind rural public radio station, NCR is a national model for regional rural public radio of its type" ("About us," 2017, paras. 4–5).

## Alternative Programming Opportunities

In this segment of the chapter, there is a reimagining of some alternate realities for NPR. If some seem fanciful, the reader is reminded that NPR itself was fanciful at one time. This chapter has described NPR's efforts to reach a broader and younger audience. It may be that NPR could learn from its British public radio cousin, the BBC.

In many respects, to compare NPR to the BBC is to compare apples and oranges. Most notably, NPR, via its member stations, receives a modest amount of federal funding via the Corporation for Public Broadcasting, while the BBC is completely funded by license fees levied on all televisions and radios in Great Britain. NPR is a network providing particular programs to independent local stations, while the BBC operates numerous full-time national and regional radio stations. And yet, they are both noncommercial broadcasting organizations functioning in very similar cultures. Are there lessons NPR could learn from its venerable cousin? And are the programming differences between NPR and the public radio media of Great Britain and Canada owing more to differences in funding or philosophy?

The admittedly imperfect comparisons of the programming philosophies of NPR and the BBC have been made since the early years of NPR. The article titled "Ersatz BBC" by Simon Winchester (1981) stated, "The public needs to be served: not just the Volvo-driving public of Chevy Chase, Shaker Heights and Grosse Pointe, but the rural public, the intelligent center-city public, the minorities and the disadvantaged, too" (p. 29).

Author Jack Mitchell (2001), commenting on the demand that NPR serve a wider audience, also compared the network to the BBC: "The BBC eventually had to succumb to the public's demands to hear what it wanted, not what [BBC founder John] Reith wanted them to hear. . . . In the United States, public radio never attracted an audience near as diverse as NPR's founding purposes hoped. Public radio sincerely welcomed all, but those who chose to listen represented such a narrow type that 'NPR listener' became a meaningful term" (p. 419). In other words, the BBC came to realize that it must appeal as nearly as possible to all Britons, not a narrow segment of the population.

The most popular radio station in Great Britain for many years has been BBC Radio 2 (Cridland, 2016). It has achieved its popularity in competition against a robust commercial radio market as well as against other BBC stations and, in recent years, despite the advent of "new" media. It is targeted to a mainstream adult audience, in the twenty-five to fifty-four demographic. Still, Radio 2 operates according to the BBC's stated mission: "To enrich people's lives with programmes and services that inform, educate and entertain" ("Inside the BBC: Values," 2018, para. 2). One writer describes Radio 2, combining a daily format of adult contemporary and oldies music—Adele, Gnarls Barkley, James Taylor—with news, interview segments, special topic shows, and personality-driven programming, as a "reassuring blend of easy listening and chatter" (Bell, 2010, p. 86).

A daily BBC Radio 2 program that exemplifies the mix of popular music and topics of interest to a broad audience is *The Jeremy Vine Show* in which the erudite but relatable host—who while in college played drums in "the most unfashionable punk band in the country" (Sleigh, 2012, para. 2)—tackles issues of the day with experts and callers, while also playing Radio 2's wide-ranging mix of popular music. Subjects have included coping with loneliness after losing a partner, the fiftieth anniversary of the cash (automatic teller) machine; how we explain terrorism to children; and "Songs My Son Loved," which includes conversations with mothers who have lost military sons and the songs that were meaningful to the young men (*The Jeremy Vine Show*, 2018, p. 1).

*The Jeremy Vine Show* is a daily program on a twenty-four-hour-a-day, fully funded national station. Whether or not NPR decided to create a similar program, the network might consider adopting Radio 2's affable, unassuming tone and its broad subject matter—which is informational but not necessarily hard news or politics oriented—in its own programs, NPR's efforts at sounding less "serious" notwithstanding. However, there is an example in the history of U.S. broadcasting of a weekend radio program that might serve as a model for NPR in an effort to expand its audience.

*Monitor* was a legendary NBC radio program that aired Saturdays and Sundays from 1955 to 1975. Created by the visionary programming executive Sylvester L. "Pat" Weaver (who conceived NBC-TV's *Today* and *Tonight* shows), *Monitor* represented a new direction for network radio following the rapid emergence of television. The author of *Monitor, the Last Great Radio Show*, Dennis Hart (2002), wrote, "It had everything—news, sports, comedy, interviews, remote pick-ups from around the world, music—a true magazine of the air. Each weekend, *Monitor* promised listeners they'd be 'going places and doing things,' and then made it happen. During any *Monitor* weekend, listeners could be transported to the world's biggest cities or smallest towns to meet some of the most important people around—or some of the quirkiest" (pp. xiv–xv). *Monitor* originally aired for forty consecutive hours, from 8 A.M. Saturday to midnight Sunday, and then occupied more limited hours in later years.

A longtime writer for *Monitor*, Charles Garment, compared *Monitor* to NPR's longest-running, perhaps best-known program: "They call it *All Things Considered*. They don't have all the things that we considered 'all things.' We had music, we had everything" (Hart, 2002, p. 205).

Hart believes a program like *Monitor* could again be successful on public radio. "It almost surprises me to say this, but *Monitor*—though off the air for 40 years—would sound fresh and new right now, if it came back in exactly the same form as it was in the '60s and early '70s," he commented. "Back in its heyday, *Monitor* was the Internet of radio—going anywhere instantaneously to cover anything in the weekend world that was interesting. Or entertaining. Or informative. Or 'happening'" (D. Hart, personal communication, July 27, 2017).

"It could do the same thing now," he continued, "with hosts interacting with and reacting to emails or Facebook as they took us all along on a ride that included everything you've mentioned that *Monitor* covered—news, sports, comedy, variety, live remotes from around the nation and the world, weather—you name it" (D. Hart, personal communication, July 27, 2017).

The "big-name hosts" Hart refers to included television personalities of the era, including Dave Garroway, Hugh Downs, Monty Hall, and Ed McMahon. For this reason, he says a modern-day *Monitor* would be expensive to produce. Whether it would be necessary for a latter-day *Monitor* to have celebrity hosts is debatable. Nor would a marathon broadcast similar to *Monitor* be essential. A two- to three-hour program would be a reasonable start. NPR could repurpose much of its existing content in providing feature material for the program.

NBC canceled *Monitor* after twenty years because of the decline in the AM radio audience and the long-standing trend of local stations moving from network programming to locally originated music programming, for which the stations could claim all of the advertising revenue. Still, Pat Weaver believed NBC made a mistake: "Pity that NBC management was, in this case, as in most, without some basic knowledge of advertising . . . programming . . . and even station realities. 'Monitor' could have been reshaped" (Hart, 2002, p. 204).

In any case, NPR stations are accustomed to carrying a heavy schedule of network programming, and in most cases a *Monitor*-styled program would not detract from the local schedule. By scheduling such a program on the weekend it would not be disruptive of the regular schedule of daily NPR programs, and might promote NPR to a broader audience. In fact, NPR stations have long attempted to bolster what is characterized as "a soft spot in the public radio schedule" on weekend afternoons (McCauley, 2005, p. 106).

Another public radio organization from which NPR might draw inspiration is RTE (Radio Telefís Éireann; Radio Television Ireland) Radio 1, which maintains a block format of programs including news, talk, live sports, drama, documentaries, and music (popular, rock, Irish traditional), and broadcasts in both English and the Irish language. RTE says its "vision is to enrich Irish life: to inform, *entertain* and challenge; to connect with the lives of *all the people*." Its mission statement says partially, "Provide the *broadest range* of value-for-money, quality content and services for *all ages, interests and communities*" ("RTE: Today," 2012, paras. 2, 4, emphasis added).

Like the BBC (and unlike NPR), RTE maintains several national stations covering several formats, and receives public funding from radio and television receiver license fees ("Inside the BBC: License Fees," 2018). Like BBC Radio 2, it is the highest rated station in the country, with more than a million listeners each week, in competition with commercial stations in Ireland as well as the other RTE stations. Unlike either the BBC or NPR, RTE also draws revenue from limited advertising ("RTE About," 2017; "RTE's Weekly Reach," 2017). NPR, of course, is forbidden from accepting advertising.

## Discussion

NPR has always had a trickier challenge than most media organizations. Referring to public broadcasting in general, author Tom McCourt (1999) commented, "The system has been riven from the outset by a contradictory mission: to create a single national identity while giving a voice to those excluded from the marketplace" (p. 1). And so, given that it receives limited funding from the federal government and must otherwise fend for itself without advertising, it is understandable why the network has chosen the direction it has—to provide an alternative to the conventional approach of commercial broadcasting that appeals to an upscale, highly educated, cosmopolitan audience that is willing and able to contribute financially, either as individuals or via corporate support.

NPR historian Michael McCauley (2005) observed that after about ten years of broadcasting, NPR's management reached a fuller understanding of its audience. He wrote, "Audience research helped public radio fuse its programs more snugly to the values, beliefs and attitudes of the people who tuned in (and pledged their financial support) most often" (p. 6).

McCourt (1999) noted, "Charged by the Carnegie Commission to 'provide a voice for groups in the community that may otherwise be unheard,' public broadcasting increasingly has embraced the marketplace through programming, sponsorship, and entrepreneurial activities that undermine its very *raison d'etre*" (p. 4).

The question is, should NPR be expected to better cater to "the needs of unserved and underserved audiences, particularly children and minorities" as stated in the Public Broadcasting Act of 1967? Or is it enough to use tax dollars—however limited—to provide programs for "the nation's best and brightest . . . [the] influential, affluent," to quote NPR's own marketing pitch? The language of the Public Broadcasting Act of 1967 suggests that the masters of noncommercial television and radio should always be open to new approaches: "The [CPB] board of directors shall . . . review on a regular basis, national public broadcasting programming for quality, diversity, creativity, excellence, innovation, objectivity and balance, as well as for any needs not met by such programming" (Public Broadcasting Act, 1967, p. 23).

NPR's promotional language ("the best and brightest") reinforces the "elitist" image it has tried to escape. McCauley (2005) is not a spokesman for NPR, but a statement such as "a college education—and the mature set of values that comes with it—is the primary variable that predicts whether a person will listen to public radio" begs the question (p. 127).

NPR deserves credit for attempting to reach a larger number of young listeners, mainly by increasing its roster of podcasts, some of which are broadcast over NPR stations. But podcasting, while it may have a brilliant future, is not broadcasting. While the impression is often given that broadcast radio is on its last legs, 93 percent of the U.S. population still listens to radio each week ("Tops of 2016," 2016), so it is too early to abandon ship. By comparison, as of 2016, about 21 percent of the U.S. population listened to podcasts in a typical month ("The Podcast Consumer," 2016). In addition—crucially—broadcast radio remains free to anyone with an AM-FM receiver whether in the car or at home, which is not true of online, digital content such as podcasts.

BBC's Radio 2 remains the most listened to radio station in Great Britain (Cridland, 2016). Again, acknowledging the very significant differences between NPR and the BBC, it remains that a publicly supported, noncommercial radio station has targeted and successfully won a vast mainstream audience, rather than appealing to a small niche of listeners. It may be possible that this is owing not only to funding, but also to the philosophy and approach of the broadcasters. It is notable that the BBC mission statement includes the word "entertain" while the NPR mission does not ("Inside the BBC: Values," 2018; "Our Mission," 2017).

Referring to the "full-service" approach to radio programming, McCauley (2005) commented that critics of NPR may be "waxing nostalgic" for a radio format that has been gone for many years (p. 5). Yet, it seems more than nostalgia is behind the current success of BBC Radio 2. If the changing realities of commercial radio ultimately caused the demise of the broad, all-encompassing approach to radio broadcasting represented by *Monitor*, perhaps that provides an opportunity for public radio—even decades later—to fulfill its stated purpose.

The issue of appealing more broadly to minority listeners might be partially aided by a weekend popular-music-oriented program aimed at a general adult audience, but that alone would not adequately address the issue. McCauley (2005) commented, "To maximize its chances for success, NPR would first need to create an alternative network with programs that appeal primarily to African American and, perhaps, Hispanic audiences" (p. 126). This would be a costly proposition.

Of course the third rail for public broadcasting is the issue of advertising. While NPR and PBS (and their stations) accept "underwriting," advertising as such is banned. However, as Ireland's RTE Radio explains, "The majority of RTÉ's activities are of a public service nature. The cost of providing these services, however, exceeds the amount of license fee revenue that RTÉ receives. As a result, RTÉ engages in commercial activities to bridge the funding gap" ("How RTE," 2017, p. 4).

Concerning the role of local radio, an article in the *Columbia Journalism Review* (Walker, 2017) praised public radio programs such as *The Takeaway* and

*Indivisible America* for taking a more "local" view of the news, but of course they are nationally produced and distributed programs that cannot be expected to regularly address the interests of local audiences in cities and towns across America. Ironically, the article itself, "Local Public Radio: America's Last Public Square," seemed to misunderstand the nature of "local" radio, making reference only to the national shows, as if local issues could be addressed only by network programs. Also, while *The Takeaway* and *Indivisible America* are heard on many stations that carry NPR programs, they are not produced by NPR.

NPR chronicler Michael P. McCauley (2005), certainly not a detractor of the network, effectively summarized the views of those who argue that NPR should offer "more inclusive public service" in the words of the Public Broadcasting Act of 1967: "Over the years, many people have criticized the network for targeting its programs almost exclusively to an audience of upscale baby boomers. Those who take this position seem to long, instead, for a national broadcaster that could offer meaningful programs for people from all socioeconomic and cultural groups—including those that are not well-served by the dominant commercial broadcasting system" (p. 5).

## References

About "Invisibilia." (2014, December 18). Retrieved from www.npr.org/templates/story/story.php?storyId=5064

About public media. (2018). Retrieved from www.cpb.org/aboutpb/what-public-media

About us. (2017). Retrieved from http://kaxe.org/about-us

Anya Grundmann named NPR VP of programming & audience development. (2016, January 6). NPR Press Room. Retrieved from www.npr.org/about-npr/462129514/anya-grundmann-named-npr-vp-of-programming-audience-development

Audience: Cultural, connected, intellectual and influential. (2018). National Public Radio. Retrieved from http://nationalpublicmedia.com/npr/audience/

Audience opportunity study. (2010). Retrieved from https://current.org/wp-content/uploads/2013/01/NPR-Aud-Oppty-Study-Smith-Geiger-2010.pdf

Battaglio, S. (2016, July). Podcasts bring younger audience to National Public Radio. *Press of Atlantic City*, E8. Retrieved from www.pressofatlanticcity.com/life/podcasts-bring-younger-audience-to-national-public-radio/article_81576a66-aad3-5530-a5e2-36459263df60.html

Bell, M. (2010, October 3). Forget radio 2: In five years' time, we'll all be going Smooth. *Independent on Sunday*, pp. 86–87. Retrieved from www.independent.co.uk/news/media/tv-radio/forget-radio-2-in-five-years-time-well-all-be-going-smoooth-2096078.html

Berman, D. (2010). The Origins of Car Talk. In C. Roberts, S. Stamberg, N. Adams, J. Ydstie, R. Montagne, A. Shapiro, & D. Folkenflik (Eds.), *This is NPR* (p. 172). San Francisco: Chronicle Books.

Cridland, J. (2016, October 26). The most popular radio stations in the UK. Retrieved from https://media.info/radio/data/the-most-popular-radio-stations-in-the-uk

Ellenberger, K. (2012, May 23). "It can't be done": The difficulty of growing a jazz audience. Retrieved from www.npr.org/blogs/ablogsupreme/2012/05/23/153461410/it-cant-be-done-the-difficulty-of-growing-a-jazz-audience

Engelman, R. (1996). *Public Radio and television in America: A political history*. Thousand Oaks, CA: Sage.

Everhart, K. (2010, September 20). Study sees growth if NPR loosens up, sounds less elite. Retrieved from https://current.org/2010/09/study-sees-growth-if-npr-loosens-up-sounds-less-elite/

Fox, J. (2015, November 23). Here's who isn't listening to public radio. *Chicago Tribune*. Retrieved from www.chicagotribune.com/news/opinion/commentary/ct-npr-public-radio-listeners-old-20151123-story.html

Friedman, J. (2010, October 20). NPR: Don't give us the "elitist" label. Retrieved from www.marketwatch.com/story/you-can-call-npr-stuffy-but-not-elitist-2010-10-20

Giovannoni, D. (1994, August). Public Service, values and ratings. Washington, DC: Corporation for Public Broadcasting. Retrieved from www.dgio.net/pubs/doc-0058.pdf

Giovannoni, D., & Bailey, G. (1988). Appeal and public radio's music. Washington, DC: Corporation for Public Broadcasting. Retrieved from http://justiceandpeace.net/WFCRdemocracy/news/music.pdf

Grow the audience for public radio: Public radio in the new network age. (2010). Station Resource Group, Walrus Research, Corporation for Public Broadcasting. Retrieved from www.srg.org/GTA/Public_Radio_in_the_New_Network_Age.pdf

Hagey, K. (2011, July 21). Williams on NPR: Elitist and White. *Politico*. Retrieved from www.politico.com/story/2011/07/williams-on-npr-elitist-and-white-059549

Hart, D. (2002). *"Monitor": The Last Great Radio Show*. Lincoln, NE: Writer's Club Press (iUniverse).

Hip-Hop radio DJs Stretch and Bobbito return to the airwaves with NPR podcast. (2017, July 19). *All Things Considered*. Retrieved from www.npr.org/2017/07/19/538148881/hip-hop-radio-djs-stretch-and-bobbito-return-to-the-airwaves-with-npr-podcast

How RTE is run. (2017). *About RTE*. Retrieved from www.rte.ie/about/en/how-rte-is-run/2012/0221/291618-the-license-fee/

Hushock, H. (2016, November 1). To combat the rigging charge, National Public Radio should be more . . . national. *National Review*. Retrieved from www.manhattan-institute.org/html/combat-rigging-charge-npr-should-be-more-national-9438.html

In changing news landscape, even television is vulnerable: Trends in news consumption: 1991–2012. Section 4: Demographics and political views of news audiences. (2012, September 27). Pew Research Center. Retrieved from www.people-press.org/2012/09/27/section-4-demographics-and-political-views-of-news-audiences/

Inside the BBC: License fees. (2018). Retrieved from www.bbc.co.uk/aboutthebbc/insidethebbc/whoweare/licencefee/

Inside the BBC: Values. (2018). Retrieved from www.bbc.co.uk/aboutthebbc/insidethebbc/whoweare/mission_and_values

Introducing a new comedy podcast from Paula Poundstone. (2017, July 6). NPR Press Room. Retrieved from www.npr.org/2017/07/06/535660117/introducing-a-new-comedy-podcast-from-paula-poundstone

Jensen, E. (2012, June 18). New hits needed; Apply to NPR. *New York Times*. Retrieved from www.nytimes.com/2012/06/19/arts/npr-looks-to-new-shows-like-ask-me-another.html

———. (2013, February 10). NPR campaign seeks the quirky listener. *New York Times*. Retrieved from http://mediadecoder.blogs.nytimes.com/2013/02/10/npr-campaign-seeks-the-quirky-listener/

———. (2016, March 18). Why NPR changed how it talks about podcasts. *NPR Ombudsmen*. Retrieved from www.npr.org/sections/ombudsman/2016/03/18/470876553/why-npr-changed-how-it-talks-about-podcasts

*The Jeremy Vine Show*. (2018). BBC Radio 2. Retrieved from www.bbc.co.uk/programmes/b006wr3p

KAXE-KBXE radio. (2018). Retrieved from https://twitter.com/KAXE

KAXE Weekly Schedule. (2018). Retrieved from www.kaxe.org/schedule/week#stream/0

Larson, S. (2015, January 21). "Invisibilia" and the evolving art of radio. *New Yorker.* Retrieved from www.newyorker.com/culture/sarah-larson/invisibilia-evolving-art-radio

McCauley, M. P. (2002, June). Leveraging the NPR brand: Serving the public while boosting the bottom line. *Journal of Radio Studies, 9*(1), 65–91.

———. (2005). *NPR: The trials and triumphs of National Public Radio.* New York: Columbia University Press.

McCourt, T. (1999). *Conflicting communication interests in America: The case of National Public Radio.* Westport, CT: Praeger.

Mitchell, J. (2001). Lead us not into temptation: American public radio in a world of infinite possibilities. In M. Hilmes & J. Loviglio (Eds.), *Radio reader: Essays in the cultural history of radio* (pp. 405–422). New York: Routledge.

———. (2005). *Listener supported: The culture and history of public radio.* Westport, CT: Praeger.

Najoo, F. (2011, March 2). "We listen to NPR precisely to avoid this sort of stupidity": The tedious, annoying complaints of public radio listeners. *Slate.* Retrieved from www.slate.com/articles/life/a_fine_whine/2011/03/we_listen_to_npr_precisely_to_avoid_this_sort_of_stupidity.html

National Public Media: Audience. (2017). Retrieved from http://nationalpublicmedia.com/npr/audience/

Neyfakh, L. (2016, April 11). The fight for the future of NPR—A slow-moving bureaucracy. And antiquated business model. *Slate.* Retrieved from www.slate.com/articles/news_and_politics/cover_story/2016/04/the_fight_for_the_future_of_npr_can_public_radio_survive_the_podcast_revolution.html?src=longreads

Nielsen audio ratings. (2017). *Radio-online.* Retrieved from http://ratings.radio-online.com/cgi-bin/rol.exe/arb_menu_001

NPR audience profile. (2018). Retrieved from https://cache.trustedpartner.com/docs/library/000316/NPR%20Jazz%20Demographics.pdf

NPR maintains highest ratings ever. (2018, March 28). NPR Press Room. Retrieved from www.npr.org/about-npr/597590072/npr-maintains-highest-ratings-ever

NPR sees large ratings increase. (2016, October 20). NPR Press Room. Retrieved from www.npr.org/2016/10/18/498390457/npr-sees-large-ratings-increase

NPR's "Invisibilia" returns for its third season. (2017, May 18). NPR Press Room. Retrieved from www.npr.org/about-npr/528824118/nprs-invisibilia-returns-for-its-third-season

Our mission and vision. (2017). Retrieved from www.npr.org/about-npr/178659563/our-mission-and-vision

Phelps, A. (2012, March 19). NPR's audience shrank a hair in 2011, pushing public radio further toward a digital future. *Nieman Journalism Lab.* Retrieved from www.niemanlab.org/2012/03/nprs-audience-shrunk-a-hair-in-2011-pushing-public-radio-further-toward-a-digital-future/

The podcast consumer. (2016). Edison Research. Retrieved from www.edisonresearch.com/wp-content/uploads/2016/05/The-Podcast-Consumer-2016.pdf

Podcast Industry Audience Rankings. (2018). Retrieved from https://analytics.podtrac.com/industry-rankings/

Powell, T. (2015, May 22). Are podcasts the new path to diversifying public radio? *Columbia Journalism Review.* Retrieved from www.cjr.org/analysis/are_podcasts_the_new_path_to_diversifying_public_radio.php

Public Broadcasting Act of 1967. (1967). Retrieved from www.cpb.org/aboutpb/act

Ragusea, A. (2015, May 28). The pub, #20: What Eric Nuzum will do at Audible that he couldn't do at NPR. Retrieved from https://current.org/2015/05/the-pub-20-what-eric-nuzum-will-do-at-audible-that-he-couldnt-do-at-npr/

Resnikoff, P. (2017, March 16). Does the world really need NPR? *Digital Music News*. Retrieved from www.digitalmusicnews.com/2017/03/16/world-need-national-public-radio-npr/

Roberts, C., Stamberg, S., Adams, N., Ydstie, J., Montagne, R., Shapiro, A., & Folkenflik, D. (Eds.). (2010). *This is NPR: The first forty years*. San Francisco: Chronicle Books.

RTE: Today, Tomorrow, Together. (2012). Retrieved from https://static.rasset.ie/documents/about/18259-rte-statement-performancecommitment-v2.pdf

RTE About. (2017). Retrieved from www.rte.ie/about/en/information-and-feedback/contact-rte/

RTE's weekly reach on radio is almost 2 million. (2017). Retrieved from www.rte.ie/about/en/press-office/press-releases/2017/0727/893344-rtes-weekly-reach-on-radio-is-almost-2-million/

Schumacher-Matos, E. (2012, April 10). Black, Latino and White: Diversity at NPR. Retrieved from www.npr.org/sections/ombudsman/2012/04/10/150367888/black-latino-asian-and-white-diversity-at-npr

Sleigh, S. (2012, July 5). Jeremy and Tim Vines pop-punk past revealed. *Guardian*. Retrieved from www.yourlocalguardian.co.uk/news/suttonnews/9798472.display/

Stamberg, S. (2010). Introduction: In the beginning there was sound but no chairs. In Roberts et al. (Eds.), *This is NPR* (pp. 13–15). San Francisco: Chronicle Books.

The State of the news media 2012: An annual report on American journalism. (2012). Pew Research Center. Retrieved from http://stateofthemedia.org/2012/audio-how-far-will-digital-go/audio-by-the-numbers/

Tops of 2015: Audio. (2015). *Nielsen Audio*. Retrieved from www.nielsen.com/us/en/insights/news/2015/tops-of-2015-audio.html

Tops of 2016: Audio. (2016). *Nielsen Audio*. Retrieved from www.nielsen.com/us/en/insights/news/2016/tops-of-2016-audio.html

Walker, L. R. (2017, April 24). Local public radio: America's last public square. *Columbia Journalism Review*. Retrieved from www.cjr.org/opinion/local-public-radio-wnyc.php

Wertheimer, L. (Ed.). (1995). *Listening to America*. Boston: Houghton Mifflin.

Will, G. (2017, June 2). Public broadcasting's immortality defies reason. *Washington Post*. Retrieved from www.washingtonpost.com/opinions/public-broadcastings-immortality-defies-reason/2017/06/02/f5de02be-46fe-11e7-a196-a1bb629f64cb_story.html?utm_term=.a7bb7355838b

Winchester, S. (1981, March). Ersatz BBC. *Harper's Magazine*, pp. 24–29.

# 11

## The Sound of Yellow Rain

• • • • • • • • • • • • • • • • • • • •

Resisting Podcasting's Sonic
Whiteness

ANJULI JOSHI BREKKE

When podcasting, as a relatively inexpensive medium in terms of creating and broadcasting content, first began to boom around 2005, media scholars hoped it would open the soundscape to new voices and modes of listening (Berry, 2006; Madsen & Potts, 2010). Despite early claims of podcasting as a "disruptive technology" (Berry, 2006, p. 144), Sterne, Morris, Baker, and Moscote Freire (2008) note that "major media companies have adjusted to the introduction of podcasts with ease" (Podcasting vs. Broadcasting sec., para. 1). Listenership within the United States continues to be concentrated around a relatively small number of programs that are outgrowths of traditional media organizations with the resources for high production quality and rapid productivity and whose hosts and producers are predominantly white and male (Locke, 2015; PodTrac, 2017). Narrative sound design norms within podcasting perpetuate the aural preferences of their chiefly white male creators. In order to challenge practices that center a "sonic whiteness" within audio storytelling, scholars need to understand how these practices came to be and how they operate within larger discursive structures surrounding race. Stoever (2016) argues that although sound studies has grown in recent years, work that engages with the intersections of sound and race has been limited in a field that has traditionally been dominated by white male voices. Accordingly, this essay develops a framework to analyze the relationship between racialized production and listening practices and emergent modes of audio storytelling in the digital age.

On September 24, 2012, the podcast *Radiolab*, produced by WNYC, broadcast an episode titled "The Fact of the Matter." "Yellow Rain," the second story in the episode, created controversy by questioning the claims of Hmong genocide survivors alleging chemical warfare against their communities during the Cold War. "Yellow Rain" provides a useful case study to analyze the interplay between racial ideologies and narrative sound design techniques in audio storytelling. It centers a "sonic whiteness" that pits scientific rationality against Hmong testimony. The problem of privileging whiteness within narrative sound design is not unique to "Yellow Rain," but rather points to a larger issue within the greater audio ecosystem. Expanding current research on race and sonic culture, this study uses the term "sonic whiteness" to encompass crafted soundscapes that unreflexively frame whiteness as synonymous with rationality. Sonic whiteness is reinforced through its juxtaposition with "sonic orientalism," the term used to describe the practice of constructing racialized sonic bodies as aberrant, excessive, hysterical, and/or exotic. While the sonic centering of whiteness has a long history in radio, this study argues that the mobility of podcast listening and the ease with which podcasts are shared online impact how sonic whiteness is experienced and taken up by listeners.

In the case of "Yellow Rain," podcast producers made full use of the affordances of the medium to establish a narrative of the past in which *Radiolab* had the last word and the Hmong genocide survivors had limited capacity to dissent on the original platform. While the constructed soundscape of "Yellow Rain" is grounded in a sonic whiteness, different listening communities interpreted the segment and reacted on social media in distinct ways. Although listening publics have always been active participants in coproducing meaning from audio stories, digital technologies have enabled counterhegemonic listening practices to be amplified to a wider public. This analysis identifies the opportunities afforded by online, networked culture to provide a space where marginalized communities can connect and collectively interrupt the hegemony of sonic whiteness. Although the digital age has not led to a utopian democratization of the media landscape, it has offered new pathways for resistance.

In the following pages, this study begins by defining sonic whiteness and tracing its historical development in radio and podcasting. Next, after a brief overview of the "Yellow Rain" segment and ensuing controversy, this study examines how *Radiolab* employs strategic sound design to center a sonic whiteness that places the "facts" at odds with the Hmong narrative. Finally, the study concludes with a discussion of how social media makes visible the divergent listening practices among different racialized and gendered communities and provides a space for these communities to call out *Radiolab*'s sonic whiteness.

## Sonic Whiteness

In conceptualizing sonic whiteness, this study draws from Kheshti's (2012) theorization of the "aural imaginary" and Thompson's (2017) notion of "white aurality." Listening is not universal, but rather happens at the intersections of the material and the social; its processes occur within space and time, and within gendered and raced bodies. In her ethnographic fieldwork of the world music industry, Kheshti (2012) found that fans of the genre often engage in a kind of "aural imaginary," a sonic fantasy in which "sound, the listener's body, escape, and affect double in on one another to construct an imaginary site of contact with other bodies" (p. 268). Consuming music, radio, and podcasts often conjures affective fantasies between the listener and the imagined other. Just as Kheshti found that race and gender played an important role in the aural imaginaries constructed through the world music industry, this study argues podcast sound design can be racialized and gendered in ways that encourage exoticized consumption of the other.

In contrast to racialized soundscapes that are often marketed as exotic and enticing, sonic whiteness is marked by its absence. Thompson (2017) critiques researchers within sound studies who fail to attend to the ways in which material practices of interpreting sound are situated within bodies who exist within discourse. Understanding affect and materiality in relation to sound, she argues, is important but cannot be divorced from processes of signification and representation. Too often studies of the material nature of sound presume an unnamed white listening ear. Thompson (2017) emphasizes that white aurality "is not an ahistorical, unchanging perceptual schema" and must be understood "as co-constitutive with, amongst other things, Eurological histories, practices, ontologies, epistemologies and technologies of sound, music and audition" (p. 274). Much of sonic whiteness in the realm of radio and podcasting goes unnamed.

Current literature on narrative sound design and racial ideologies in the United States focuses on a white/black divide. The case of "Yellow Rain" adds to this body of work by illustrating how the relationship between sonic whiteness and sonic orientalism is deployed in audio storytelling in the United States. Composer-performer Ayyaz Bhunnoo (2011) theorizes sonic orientalism as the process by which sound is employed "indexically and unreflexively to denote an exotic alterity" (p. 221). *Radiolab*'s sound design of "Yellow Rain" constructs a sonic orientalism by unreflexively positioning Hmong testimony as exotic and enticing, but ultimately unreliable. This sonic orientalism reifies sonic whiteness, which in turn structures authority and rationality in the work of white scientists and science journalists. To understand how, this study first looks at the history of sonic whiteness.

## Radio, Podcasting, and a History of Sonic Whiteness

Throughout its history, radio in the United States has reflected and reproduced dominant racial ideologies. In her book *The Sonic Color Line: Race and the Cultural Politics of Listening*, Stoever (2016) writes that despite optimistic hopes in the 1940s that radio was "a medium of truth, freedom and color blindness," in actuality it worked to institutionalize white middle-class sonic norms and create a hierarchy of sonic racial difference (p. 234). Consequently, Stoever traces a history of normative listening practices within the United States that have configured the aural tastes of white elites as "universal, objective truth" and the "keynote of American identity" (pp. 10–12). Similarly, Shulman (2016) notes that in the United States "radio enforced and carefully regulated the distinction between racial auralities" (p. 465). The constructed sound of the "white voice" broadcast through radio became generalizable; it instituted "the normative way of speaking in the nation" (p. 464). This aural whiteness was shaped in contradistinction to the "black voice." These culturally constructed auralities were policed to "reinforce the sonic color-line," such as white directors in the 1940s instructing African American radio performers on how to sound properly "black" (Shulman, 2016, p. 464). Stoever (2016) documents several African American performers who pushed their colleagues to resist both pressures to conform to a "white-authored negro dialect" while also refusing to assimilate their speech into the constructed patterns of the "white voice" (p. 244).

Currently, people of color working in public radio in the United States are pressured to speak in ways that remove audible markers of difference (Kumanyika, 2015). While this practice may resist stereotypical constructions of the "black voice," it perpetuates the privileging of whiteness as the voice of the nation. Kumanyika (2015) notes that people of color are underrepresented on public radio, and when their voices are featured they are often edited in a way that diminishes the power and texture of voices that deviate from the constructed standard. Despite hopes that podcasting would provide marginalized communities the tools to create grassroots content outside of the constraints of traditional media organizations, new podcasters of color often realize that podcasting, "for all its openness, still presents barriers to hosts of color and their relevant subject matter" (Friess, 2017, para. 4). Even as the overall percentage of podcast listeners who identify as nonwhite grows, the iTunes Top 100 chart is dominated by white hosts (Friess, 2017; Locke, 2015).

While mainstream radio and podcasts have centered and continue to center sonic whiteness, minoritized groups have long created community radio stations and, more recently, podcasting networks that have flourished "under the radar" of white U.S. audiences (Casillas, 2014; Di Leonardo, 2012, p. 663). Florini (2015), for example, has documented the emergence of black podcasting networks. She notes that while these shows do not accrue the same volume of downloads as those on the iTunes Top 100 chart, the listenership is loyal and overlapping throughout the network of shows. This creates a listening community, Florini (2015) argues, that allows the podcasters to create sonic black social spaces safe from the intrusion of the "mainstream gaze" (p. 214). Listening then becomes an act of resistance, an aural imaginary turned on its head that conjures up spaces of black sociality, providing a sonic "cocoon" for listeners to retreat from hegemonic white spaces. Although sonic whiteness pervades the airwaves, communities of color have developed various strategies for subverting this soundscape. In the case of "Yellow Rain," as will be discussed later in this essay, social media provided a space for listeners of color to call out *Radiolab*'s sonic whiteness.

## "Yellow Rain" and Its Controversy

In the "Yellow Rain" segment, *Radiolab* hosts Jad Abumrad and Robert Krulwich attempt to solve a Cold War mystery regarding a substance known as yellow rain that descended upon areas of Southeast Asia after the Vietnam War. During the war, the Central Intelligence Agency recruited and trained Hmong men to fight against the North Vietnamese. When the U.S. military left Southeast Asia, a communist group known as the Pathet Lao took control of Laos. The Pathet Lao targeted those they believed had helped the Americans, including civilians.

This is when the first accounts of yellow rain surfaced, as the *Radiolab* introduction states: "And that's when they started seeing it—yellow droplets that fell from the sky and splattered the landscape, followed by dying plants, animals, and eventually friends and family doubled over with stomach problems" (Abumrad & Krulwich, 2012, para. 2). The Reagan administration was quick to weaponize these allegations against the Soviet Union, which had been supporting the communist governments in Southeast Asia. This gives the story immense political implications. As *Radiolab* host Robert Krulwich states, "The fact that the most powerful man in the world, Ronald Reagan, used this story to order the manufacture of chemical weapons for the first time in twenty years, I mean, that is not unimportant, that's hugely important" (Abumrad & Krulwich, 2012, 21:47–22:10).

The segment presents a pair of controversial scientific findings; initial research that supports the claim that yellow rain is the result of chemical warfare, with later research claiming it to be nothing more than bee feces falling from the sky. The narrative becomes complicated, however, by *Radiolab*'s decision to interview a member of the Hmong community, Eng Yang. The Thai government had enlisted Yang to observe atrocities against the Hmong. In the segment, Yang recounts his personal experience of the horrors of yellow rain as a chemical weapon, a perspective that runs counter to the scientific findings presented in the segment.

Yang is interviewed with his niece and author, Kao Kalia Yang, translating. In an article posted after the podcast aired, K. Yang says that she and her uncle had been led to believe the interview would give them a chance to finally tell the Hmong story, to give public voice to the neglected Hmong experience of trauma (Yang, 2012). What started as an interview, however, turns into an interrogation of the veracity of the Yangs' claims, devolving into tears and angry words as two conflicting narratives of the past collide. The segment ends in a discussion between the two hosts and their producer, Pat Walters, with Krulwich defending the way *Radiolab* had constructed the segment; and Walters and Abumrad questioning whether, perhaps, *Radiolab* had missed something important. After the episode aired, K. Yang (2012) wrote a response in *Hyphen Magazine* accusing *Radiolab* of discounting the Hmong experience and denouncing the episode for "the privileging of Western education over indigenous knowledge" (para. 18).

Both the official Reagan administration account and the *Radiolab* counternarrative remembered yellow rain primarily because of its role in escalating political tensions between world powers. *Radiolab* positioned the Yangs' testimony in terms of unverified evidentiary support for the Reagan administration narrative, thus making it hard to disentangle the Hmong experience from the actions of the Reagan administration to restart the chemical weapons program. The segment positions the accusations of yellow rain as chemical warfare as *the* deciding factor in the Reagan administration's decision to renew the chemical weapons program. According to Devine (1990), the Yellow Rain incident was but one piece of the accumulating fears the government harbored regarding Soviet chemical weapons capabilities. Although *Radiolab* admits the Hmong were under real attack, by overstating the sole significance of Hmong testimony in restarting the U.S. chemical weapons program, the Hmong experience of genocide is pushed to the margins.

After initial listener outrage, *Radiolab* went back into the editing room and made small but crucial changes to the original "Yellow Rain" piece. Eckstein (2014) argues that *Radiolab* exploits "the podcast's 'on demand' broadcast model to tweak 'Yellow Rain' and strategically maneuver around audience expectation" (p. 50). He traces *Radiolab*'s decision to revise the original podcast to address pushback from their audience and stem similar criticism from subsequent audiences. Although insightful in understanding the ethics of post-broadcast revisions, his analysis misses how music and editing were used throughout the original broadcast to construct a sonic whiteness. This use of tactical sound design to discredit the Yangs remains in the final edited broadcast. In contrast to Eckstein's assessment, this study argues that even after the podcast was reworked to account for audience pushback, the rhetorical undercutting of the Hmong testimony remains. Additionally, Eckstein does not account for the polysemous interpretations of the podcast among different listening communities.

## Analysis of "Yellow Rain"

"Yellow Rain" presents an opportunity to trace how one instantiation of sonic whiteness is constructed and contested within the medium of podcasting. To do so, this section discusses how podcast producers employ the materiality of the medium to construct a sense of intimacy between host and listener and unpacks how *Radiolab* employs editing of sound and voice to position their narrative of yellow rain's legacy as authoritative.

### Constructing an Intimate Space

Radio and podcast producers take advantage of sound technologies to construct a feeling of intimacy and affective connection between host and listener. Madsen and Potts (2010) note that like radio, podcasts exploit "the intrinsic qualities of the human voice, building relationships between host and audience on the desirable aspects of voice" (p. 45). In an interview with the podcast *On the Media*, *Radiolab* host Jad Abumrad explains the proximity effect generated when a host leans into the microphone. This creates a heavier bass, as if the host whispers privileged knowledge directly into the ears of each listener. Brooke Gladstone (2018), host of *On the Media*, states, "There is a sort of, I'm *really* in your head," to which Abumrad replies, "That's what I want from podcasts, that's what I want from radio, I want someone to be speaking from inside me, in a way" (15:26–15:48). The host is not just someone speaking to the listener, but someone speaking from *within* the listener. The line between host and audience blurs. In the "Yellow Rain" segment, *Radiolab* producers play off of this intimacy between host and listener to position the "truth" with their constructed sound of rationality and against the Hmong survivors.

The texture of the host's voice paired with expertly crafted sound design is a hallmark of *Radiolab*'s style. Kheshti (2012) argues that listening is "a corporeal rather than merely aural process" (p. 269). Soundscapes work on and through the body, creating a unique sense of place and embodiment. The mode and mobility of podcast listening alters the experience. The sound design and texture of the recorded voices mix with the comfort of the headphones, the seeping in of nearby conversations, and the feel of the body moving through space. Because for many listeners phones have become an extension of themselves, listening through podcasts and apps blurs "the distinction between medium and content, source and channel, and sender and receiver," and thus, MacDougall (2011) asserts, "the listener is a cyborg—part medium, part message" (p. 731). While the deep voices of the *Radiolab* hosts as they lean into the mic signal to the listener a sense of intimacy and trust, the producers use the sound design to cast suspicion on other voices encountered on the journey, such as those of the Hmong survivors.

### Narrative Sound Design and the Use of Leitmotifs

During the first half of the piece, *Radiolab* employs music and editing to strategically position the official Reagan administration account, and by extension the

Hmong narrative, as conspiracy theory that is exposed by the facts of scientific research. A building sense of intrigue around the conspiracy functions rhetorically as a bait and switch; the escalation is later revealed to be a clever misdirection. In an interview with Ejnes (2013) from designingsound.org, Abumrad elaborates on his process of sound design for *Radiolab*: "You want the sounds to be sort of familiar and inviting but also slightly disturbing, and you're seducing people so that you can kind of disturb them in a way. That's sort of the process that you go through, you want that 'Come here, come here, come here . . . BOO! Come here, come here, come here . . . OOF!' That's kind of what you do as a storyteller" (para. 6). Abumrad emphasizes how crucial sound design is in navigating listeners through the events being described, taking the audience on a dramatic journey with an epic twist. The first half of the "Yellow Rain" segment follows this pattern; it leads the audience through an increasingly complex and disturbing plot, punctuated through music and editing, to suspect they know the culprit. Their fears, however, are ultimately shown to be misguided: yellow rain is shown to be nothing more than bee poop. The audience is meant to realize the absurdity of the seductive Reagan administration narrative buttressed only by untrustworthy Hmong testimony.

The narrative journey of "Yellow Rain" is, in part, constituted through the use of leitmotifs in sound design. A leitmotif is a short, repeated melody that acts as a narrative device signaling to the audience the main characters in the unfolding drama. In an interview with SoundWorks Collection (2016), Dylan Keefe, director of sound design at *Radiolab*, emphasized the importance of music in guiding the audience through the cast of characters: "There's a real art to being able to tell a storyline and have music sort of bubble underneath the surface, and always propping up the story, always propping up the characters that are in it" (2:03–2:11). Musical themes used to prop up the characters also give the audience a sense of who to trust. *Radiolab* uses three main leitmotifs in the sound design of "Yellow Rain" that guide the affective experience of listening. This study refers to them as "boogieman chimes," "sound of reason," and "drums of war."

As the segment opens, producer Pat Walters introduces retired CIA officer Merle Prebbenow, who was stationed in Laos in 1981. Prebbenow refers to his assignment in "the sticks" and "the boonies" (Abumrad & Krulwich, 2012, 0:52–0:53). Walters adds that "it turned out that this little backwater was ground zero for what was about to become one of the strangest stories of the Cold War" (1:25–1:27). The "boogieman chimes" leitmotif first appears as Walters says these words. The melody mimics the mysterious substance falling from the sky and descends through a C# minor pentatonic scale. Each note reverberates, creating competition among the cascading overtones resulting in a murky half resolution. This cadence creates an affect of unresolved tension, which is emphasized by an acute crescendo. The reverberation is followed by a brief silence creating a sense of disquiet. As the Yangs discuss how the Hmong had become targets of the Pathet Lao after the war, quiet, but perceptible music plays beneath their voices. The music shifts from D major to B minor as the Yangs discuss how their people were murdered, building a sense of suspense. When Prebbenow is reintroduced and begins talking there is no music. It is only on his last line, the first mention of yellow rain, that the "boogieman chimes" appear again. Their overall contour rises slightly only to get lost beneath the podcast voices. As Eng Yang tells his story with K. Yang interpreting, a G tone holds for a half minute under their voices. This barely perceptible pitch, the same pitch of a storm alarm, creates a sense of unease. The production uses this held G tone as a subliminal backdrop upon which they build sounds of scratchy glissandos and other extended techniques to punctuate sentences. The G tone ties the "boogieman chimes" to the voices of the Yangs, giving the listener a sense that danger is near.

This music halts or diminishes, however, when the team speaks with experts, separating their testimony from the suspense of the building conspiracy. For example, the music stops as Prebbenow recounts that "in those kind of situations and in Southeast Asia generally there are tons of rumors, you have to be careful of what you believe and what you don't believe" (Abumrad & Krulwich, 2012, 5:50–5:57). The absence of music separates his account from the disturbing and mysterious account presented by the Yangs. This separation signals to the audience that perhaps they should not be taken in by these enticing appeals of intrigue and conspiracy, that perhaps they should be careful of what they take as truth.

Another leitmotif, the "sound of reason," makes its debut as Walters discusses the initial scientific evidence regarding the samples of yellow rain. This motif is marked by a major scale, tonality, and regular rhythm. It signifies a shift away from the firsthand accounts of the Hmong survivors toward veracity assessment by white scientists. The music stops momentarily as chemical weapons expert Matt Meselson says the first findings suggested that this was indeed chemical warfare. His words are followed immediately by a third leitmotif—the "drums of war." This intense, sustained percussion plays underneath an audio montage of old media coverage and sound bites of government officials warning of the new evidence of Soviet-backed chemical warfare. A simple bass line appears on top of the percussion but does not line up with it. Other musical "voices" overlap with the sound of news media, creating a restless, runaway cacophony. As one media account exclaims, "The Soviet Union may be engaging in biological warfare," the "boogieman chimes" layers into the frantic soundscape (Abumrad & Krulwich, 2012, 8:04–8:06). Ronald Reagan states in the next clip, "There is conclusive evidence that the Soviet government has been providing toxins for use in Laos and Kampuchea" (8:27–8:33). Walters then explains that after this news breaks, the United States begins producing chemical weapons for the first time in twenty years. As Walters concludes, "All of this, in effect, because of the yellow rain"; the soundscape trails off through a reverberating decrescendo (9:03–9:06). The whole scene creates a sense of movement and excitement as well as confusion and fear.

Walters then cuts back to Meselson (speaking without music), who explains an additional layer of supposed intrigue. Walters states, "And this is when things really start to get weird" (Abumrad & Krulwich, 2012, 9:19–9:21). The samples contained high levels of pollen, meaning that the Soviets must have found a way to engineer the chemicals to use flower pollen as a vector. The "boogieman chimes" play briefly as Meselson discusses this theory but stop abruptly when he proclaims that this theory is "completely bonkers" (10:17). The big reveal, in which the samples are shown to be nothing more than bee feces, is punctuated by a loud, sharp blurt of a horn, as if to say Ha! As the surprising finding of "bee shit" (edited for broadcast) is repeated, the horn punctuates each repetition, overemphasizing the findings for comedic effect (10:59). The listeners, who have been seduced through pounding percussion, eerie chimes, and repeated references to mystery in a far-off land, are presented with the equally odd "fact" of the matter. The odious Soviet plot turned out to be nothing more than bee droppings.

A bleak sonic conspiracy gives way to a brisk and upbeat arpeggiation on a B major chord, as scientists begin their debunking of yellow rain. As they describe the cleansing flight of the bees, a rendition of the "boogieman chimes" plays. The "drums of war" motif beats under Walters's narration as he lays out the U.S. government's attempts to squash the scientific evidence for the bee poop theory. As the scientists fight against government objections and reassert the importance of evidence, the "sound of reason" plays underneath the narration. The "boogieman chimes" sound for a final time as the scientists describe being covered in bee feces on their scientific mission in the Laotian rainforest. The earlier sense of fear and suspense associated with the chimes turns to comedy as the cascading notes are punctuated with the giddy laugh of biologist Tom Seeley.

Through the rhetorical use of leitmotifs and the music and editing described above, *Radiolab* warns against being swept away by the conspiracy arguments of the official account regarding yellow rain, which are supported by what they present as a single, poorly conducted lab test and unproven and unreliable Hmong testimony.

## Sonic Rationality

In his discussion of Euro-American fetishization of "Eastern" music, Ayyaz Bhunnoo (2011) paints sonic orientalism as a type of "sonic tourism" that "captures the 'ethnic' and colonises the ear" (p. 255). *Radiolab* isolates the Yangs' voices and pairs their stories with tones signaling alarm and adventure in the far East. This signals to the listener that although the voices of the Yangs present an exciting narrative, their words are ultimately unreliable.

Whereas Walters and former CIA agent Prebbenow chat back and forth in an affirming dialogue, the Yangs' voices are isolated, there is no voice reaffirming their experience. Whereas the Yangs' voices are embellished with eerie music and the sound of a far-off alarm, Prebbenow's voice is free from background music. Prebbenow's portrayal of Southeast Asia as an uncivilized "backwater" where untrustworthy rumors fly among uneducated locals is therefore presented as the authoritative one (Abumrad & Krulwich, 2012, 1:08–1:09). The undercutting of Hmong testimony using music and editing for rhetorical effect is implicitly justified as what is needed in order for the scientific facts to debunk the official Reagan account and thereby assert a type of sonic rationality. This rationality inadvertently acts as a sonic orientalism, centering the white male scientists and their standpoints while constructing the Hmong voices as the uneducated but enticing exotic other.

The development of scientific institutions and conventions is intertwined with legacies of colonialism and racism (Smith, 2012). Haraway (1988) critiques the positivist epistemological privileging of disembodied objectivity and stresses the importance of situated knowledge. Rather than give way to relativism that similarly decenters embodiment, Haraway proposes a grounded, multifaceted knowledge "of elaborate specificity and difference" and stresses the potential embedded in "the loving care people might take to learn how to see faithfully from another's point of view" (p. 583). Although all ways of seeing and listening are open to critical examination, the standpoints of the subjugated are more likely to interrogate the "god trick" of disembodied objectivity and make visible "modes of denial through repression, forgetting, and disappearing acts" (Haraway, 1998, p. 584). *Radiolab*'s editing and sound design help to structure the scientific facts against the Hmong experience and thereby work to push their voices, their situated knowledge, to the margins of memory. The sound design gives authoritative weight to the voices of the scientists and science journalists, all of whom are white men, while isolating the voices of the Yangs.

## Dialogue and the Rupture of Rationality

Although Krulwich (2012) proclaims in a follow-up to the episode on the *Radiolab* website that he had interviewed Eng Yang in order to "understand if the scientists had considered all the evidence," his skeptical tone throughout the interview seems to imply that no description of their experience would have proven sufficient evidence to make him seriously reconsider the perspective of the scientists featured earlier in the segment (para. 8). When K. Yang translates her uncle's words with a voice strained by pain, "I speak to what I've seen, and there is no inkling in my mind that those deaths were not caused by starvation, dysentery—there were chemicals that were killing my people" (15:56–16:01), Krulwich's voice responds, in a skeptical, almost interrogating tone:

KRULWICH  Was there always a plane and then rain? A plane and then rain? Or did sometimes the rain happen without a plane?
YANGS  [conceding] We never saw what it was. They said that it was always just being dropped on them. And it was always being dropped where there were heavy concentrations of Hmong people. That's what we knew.
KRULWICH  [dismissive] You don't know whether there was a plane causing it, or did you just see the dust?

E. YANG   ... [translated by K. Yang] Everybody runs when you hear the planes, so Hmong people didn't watch bombs coming down. You came out, you sneak your head out, and you watch what happened in the aftermath. You saw broken trees, you saw yellow in the aftermath of what had been bombed. [K. Yang continues, voice breaking] With my own eyes I saw pollen that could kill grass, could kill leaves, could kill trees.

KRULWICH  [almost annoyed] But he himself is not clear whether it's the bee stuff or the other stuff, because there was so much stuff coming down from the sky? (Abumrad & Krulwich, 2012, 16:11–17:30)

From Krulwich's standpoint, accepting the Hmong experience of the past would risk pushing aside the scientific facts and thus allow the Reagan administration's official narrative to retain its hegemony over public memory. Krulwich treats Eng Yang as a hostile witness, seemingly unwilling or unable to hear the pain in the voices of his interviewees. His interview turns into an interrogation, an attempt to gather evidence, and thus their account is dismissed with Krulwich's assessment that "all of this is hearsay" (18:14–18:15).

*Radiolab*'s carefully constructed sonic rationality is destabilized by the intensifying heat and searing pain present in K. Yang's voice as she and her uncle attempt to resist Krulwich's interrogation and reassert the intimate horrors of living through a genocide. The pitch of her voice rises, and the flow of her words jumbles as she gasps for breath. Through sobs she proclaims,

> That's why he agreed to the interview, that the Hmong heart is broken and our leaders have been silenced, and what we know has been questioned again and again. . . . I agreed to the interview for the same reason, that *Radiolab* was interested in the Hmong story, that they were interested in documenting the deaths that happened. There was so much that was not told. Everybody knows that chemical warfare was being used. How do you create bombs if not with chemicals? We can play the semantics game, we can, but I'm not interested, my uncle is not interested. We have lost too much heart, and too many people in the process. I, I think the interview is done. (Abumrad & Krulwich, 2012, 18:53–19:37)

This brief but powerful rupture pulls the audience out of the normal *Radiolab* listening experience, standing in stark contrast to the highly edited soundscape. After K. Yang's broken voice slices through the story, fifteen seconds of silence ensues emphasizing the depth of this rupture. To *Radiolab*'s credit, they did not edit out this emotional plea to recognition. Had they, the bulk of the listening audience may never have been jarred out of their comfortable listening experience; they may have never questioned *Radiolab*'s narrative framing and made these misgivings public by flooding the comments sections. Although *Radiolab* did not edit out their clash with the Yangs entirely, they also, however, did not allow the Yangs the space to respond, to contextualize the significance of this rupture.

Although barred from further debate on the original platform, K. Yang was able to reach a portion of the original audience through writing her side of the experience in her response for *Hyphen Magazine*. As Eckstein (2014) notes, "Digital arguments refuse to be contained on one particular site" (p. 52). The *Radiolab* webpage for the "Yellow Rain" segment offers several links to stories associated with yellow rain but does not link to K. Yang's response. In the listener comments, however, several posters refer to the response and provide links to the *Hyphen Magazine* article. Listeners also provide links to the article on the *Radiolab* Facebook page, and through Twitter and other social media pages. K. Yang's response shifts the narrative from voices of science pushing back against a politically entrenched myth to the crushed heart of the Hmong survivors. In her response, K. Yang (2012) admonishes Krulwich, whom she describes as a "a white man in power calling from the safety of time, his class, and popular position" who she states brands "the Hmong experience of chemical warfare [as] one founded on ignorance" (para. 18). As K. Yang explains, for her community the war is not a distant event in political history, but a traumatic memory that blurs the boundaries of past and present.

## After Airing: Reception

Eckstein (2014) states that after the edited podcast aired, "the tide of the comments on the website changed from anger to praise" (p. 52). This formulation, however, assumes a singular homogenous audience that interprets and responds to content and medium in the same way. When reading through the roughly 120 comments regarding "Yellow Rain" posted on *Radiolab*'s Facebook page, it becomes clear that the listenership was responding not in unison, but as different listening communities.

Listeners are active agents in the meaning-making process. Kheshti (2012) notes, "Listening functions performatively to enact into incorporeal materialism what it imagines aurally" (p. 282). *Radiolab* producers construct sonic templates that are reconstructed in the aural imaginary of each listener. Although one's positionality shapes how one listens, no one aspect of identity determines how a listener will finish the painting. Identities are complex and changing articulations of differences.

In the case of "Yellow Rain," trends in listener responses can be identified based on race and gender, with three important caveats: these trends represent correlation, not causation; comments are anonymized to protect posters in accordance with ethical digital research practices; and screen identity does not always correspond to wallet identity. On this last point, this section defers to how individuals present themselves (or self-identify) in terms of race and gender.

Users posted fifty-six comments on Facebook after the original episode aired on September 24, 2012. Another sixty-one comments were posted after Robert Krulwich added his response on the *Radiolab* Facebook page apologizing for his tone while defending the content of the segment as a whole. There are three broad trends in how listeners reacted to the segment, each associated with a different identity group: white men, white women, and people of color of all genders.

The majority of comments came from responders who appear to be white men. Their responses appear to remain constant between the comments on the original broadcast post and comments made after the apology/rebroadcast. The majority of white men commended *Radiolab* for placing a commitment to scientific truth above emotional appeals. After Krulwich posted his apology, the response from this segment of the listenership largely questioned why the apology was needed at all. One comment made on the original broadcast states: "Pay no attention to those that complain about the Laos segment. What happened to those people was horrible indeed, but this episode was about TRUTH, not compassion and you did the right thing" (Radiolab Podcast, 2012a). Another comment left on Robert Krulwich's apology post states: "There is zero reason for you to apologize to either your viewers nor to the Yang family. You were patient and reasonable. The atrocities that happened to their family and thousands of other families in Southeast Asia are unfathomable, but when lies can potentially lead to global thermonuclear war, it's preferable to get to the bottom of things, even at the expense of a few tears. Anyone who thinks otherwise is simply being unreasonable" (Radiolab Podcast, 2012b). These commenters applaud *Radiolab*'s willingness to embrace logos and resist their detractors' appeals to pathos. For these commenters, K. Yang's cry at the end of the segment seems to be heard as hysterical, irrational, and an assault on truth, like a scream that engenders feminized and racialized connotations (Thompson, 2013, p. 151). They do not seem to hear, nor question the segment's constructed sonic whiteness.

The second trend in listener responses was from listeners who appear to be predominantly white women who followed the pattern of response put forth by Eckstein (2014), namely a turn from "anger to praise" (p. 52). Whereas 83 percent of responses from these listeners expressed some form of outrage with the original broadcast, those who disapproved dropped to only 17 percent after Krulwich posted his apology. While the posts under the original broadcast mostly expressed anger or discomfort when listening to the segment, the posts under Krulwich's apology are largely positive, reframing the initial discomfort as a productive moment in assessing the various perspectives. One responder posts, "I found it interesting and thought-provoking that it was the seasoned reporter who did not want to back down, and who kept pushing for the truth (or all the truths). It was hard to hear the interview with the family, but I thought the subsequent discussion between Robert, Jad, and Pat was fascinating. I don't always feel like reporters are pushing as hard these days, and it's a service to the public to do so" (Radiolab Podcast, 2012b). The destabilizing emotion of K. Yang's voice momentarily pulled these listeners out of the otherwise tightly crafted sonic whiteness of the segment. Such comments show, however, that although listening to K. Yang's broken voice was "hard to hear" and may have created a brief rupture for some listeners, this break was largely bridged by *Radiolab*'s post-broadcast edits and Krulwich's apology.

Last, for responders who appear to be people of color regardless of gender, disapproval with the podcast was nearly unanimous after the original broadcast—and remained so after the edited rebroadcast and Krulwich's apology. Some described the episode as capitalizing on Hmong trauma. Several called out the editing and sound design as being manipulative. One poster writes, "The Yellow Rain segment is the most infuriating radio piece I've heard in a long time. Not only was your treatment of your interviewees callous, but the arrogance and deception is first rate. Good job in the editing process because obviously many have believed that your manipulative cut is 'honest' and 'obsessed with truth.' The blog afterwards is total blah and shows no sense of remorse. I used to be a fan" (Radiolab Podcast, 2012b). While some of these responses provide lengthy rebukes to the episode, many simply link to K. Yang's response in *Hyphen Magazine*.

Through the power of sound design and editing, and through the intimacy imbedded in podcasting as a medium, *Radiolab* sought to center the sound of scientific "rationality." While this sound seemed to resonate with the majority of white listeners who responded to the piece on social media, *Radiolab*'s curated sonic whiteness did not seem to have the same effect for listeners of color. These listeners were more likely to decode the podcast, rather than an objective and rational investigation into truth, as one listener response puts it, as "nothing short of imperialist bullying" (Radiolab Podcast, 2012b). Although *Radiolab* producers have sway over their large listenership through sound design and editing, within the greater online ecology, dissenting voices like those of the Yangs cannot be fully edited out. This analysis of the "Yellow Rain" segment shows that although power over audiences remains concentrated among elites in the digital age, marginalized communities are finding new pathways to amplify their voices and disrupt sonic whiteness.

## Conclusion

The "Yellow Rain" segment presents a case in which scientific researchers and science journalists unreflexively undermine the voices of genocide survivors in an attempt to speak truth to the perceived myths propagated by powerful political interests. The narrative sound design functions rhetorically to seduce the audience into believing the Soviet conspiracy presented by the Reagan administration, experiencing it as Americans in the 1980s might have, with musical frenzy replicating Cold War frenzy. That conspiracy is eventually undercut by the trusted voices of white scientists. This affective roller coaster is grounded in a sonic whiteness and sonic orientalism constructed to give the audience the excitement of engaging with the exotic other while ultimately rejecting these voices in favor of what is positioned as scientific "truth."

Despite early promises of podcasting's participatory potential, gendered and raced inequities persist in terms of who is producing top-rated shows. While greater access to the means of production is important, it is just as important to consider who is listening and how. The bulk of audiences continue to be concentrated around mainstream media organizations whose programs perpetuate a sonic whiteness. This does not mean, however, that listeners are passively consuming this content. The resistance to "Yellow Rain" illustrates how networked culture may be leveraged to disrupt the hegemony of sonic whiteness.

## References

Abumrad, J., & Krulwich, R. (Hosts). (2012, September 26). *Yellow Rain* [Audio podcast]. Retrieved from www.radiolab.org/story/239549-yellow-rain/

Ayyaz Bhunnoo, S. (2011). Reconfiguring the Islamic sonic-social in the Bird Ghost at the Zaouia by Seth Ayyaz. *Organised Sound, 16*(3), 220–229.

Berry, R. (2006). Will the iPod kill the radio star? Profiling podcasting as radio. *Convergence, 12*(2), 143–162.

Casillas, D. (2014). *Sounds of belonging: U.S. Spanish-language radio and public advocacy* (Critical cultural communication). New York: New York University Press.

Devine, T. (1990). The U.S. decision to produce chemical weapons. *Fletcher Forum of World Affairs, 14*(2), 372–393.

Di Leonardo, M. (2012). Grown folks radio: U.S. election politics and a "hidden" black counterpublic. *American Ethnologist, 39*(4), 661–672.

Eckstein, J. (2014). Yellow Rain: Radiolab and the acoustics of strategic maneuvering. *Journal of Argumentation in Context, 3*(1), 35–56.

Ejnes, S. (2013, August 15). Noise, storytelling with sound, and visuals on the radio with Radiolab's Jad Abumrad. *Designing Sound*. Retrieved from http://designingsound.org/2013/08/noise-storytelling-with-sound-and-visuals-on-the-radio-with-radiolabs-jad-abumrad/

Florini, S. (2015). The podcast "Chitlin' Circuit": Black podcasters, alternative media, and audio enclaves. *Journal of Radio and Audio Media, 22*(2), 209–219.

Friess, S. (2017, March 21). Why are #PodcastsSoWhite? *Columbia Journalism Review*. Retrieved from www.cjr.org/the_feature/podcasts-diversity.php

Gladstone, B. (2018, January 18). Joe Frank: The known-unknown. In *On the Media Podcast* [Audio podcast]. Retrieved from www.wnyc.org/story/joe-frank-known-unknown/

Haraway, D. (1988). Situated knowledges: The science question in feminism and the privilege of partial perspective. *Feminist Studies, 14*(3), 575–599.

Kheshti, R. (2012). Touching listening: The aural imaginary in the world music culture industry. In K. Keeling & J. Kun (Eds.), *Sound clash: Listening to American studies* (pp. 267–285). Baltimore: Johns Hopkins University Press.

Krulwich, R. (2012, September 30). From Robert Krulwich on yellow rain. *Radiolab Blogland*. Retrieved from www.radiolab.org/story/240899-robert-krulwich-yellowrain/?utm_source=sharedUrl&utm_medium=metatag&utm_campaign=sharedUrl

Kumanyika, C. (2015, January 22). Vocal color in public radio. *Transom*. Available at https://transom.org/2015/chenjerai-kumanyika/

Locke, C. (2015, August 31). Podcasts' biggest problem isn't discovery, it's diversity. *Wired*. Retrieved from www.wired.com/2015/08/podcast-discovery-vs-diversity/

MacDougall, R. (2011). Podcasting and political life. *American Behavioral Scientist, 55*(6), 714–732.

Madsen, V., & Potts, J. (2010). Voice-cast: The distribution of the voice via podcasting. In N. Neumark, R. Gibson, & T. Van Leeuwen (Eds.), *Voice: Vocal aesthetics in digital arts and media* (pp. 33–61). Cambridge, MA: MIT Press.

PodTrac. (2017). *Podcast industry ranking highlights top 10 podcast publishers*. Retrieved from http://analytics.podtrac.com/industry-rankings/

Radiolab Podcast. (2012a, September 25). Brand-new hour! The fact of the matter [Facebook post]. Available at www.facebook.com/Radiolab/

———. (2012b, October 1). From Robert Krulwich on Yellow Rain [Facebook post]. Available at www.facebook.com/Radiolab/

Shulman, M. (2016). Tuning the black voice: Colour-deafness and the American Negro Theatre's radio dramas. *Modern Drama, 59*(4), 456–477.

Smith, L. (2012). *Decolonizing methodologies: Research and indigenous peoples* (2nd ed.). London: Zed Books.

SoundWorks Collection. (2016, December 5). Jad Abumrad: The sound of radiolab [Video file]. *SoundWorks Collection*. Retrieved from http://soundworkscollection.com/news/jad-abumrad-the-sound-of-radiolab

Sterne, J., Morris, J. W., Baker, M. B., & Moscote Freire, A. (2008). The politics of podcasting. *Fibreculture Journal, 13*. Retrieved from http://thirteen.fibreculturejournal.org/fcj-087-the-politics-of-podcasting/

Stoever, J. (2016). *The sonic color line: Race and the cultural politics of listening* (Postmillennial pop). New York: New York University Press.

Thompson, M. (2013). Three screams. In M. Thompson & I. Biddle (Eds.), *Sound, music, affect: Theorizing sonic experience* (pp. 147–162). New York: Bloomsbury Academic.

———. (2017). Whiteness and the ontological turn in sound studies. *Parallax, 23*(3), 266–282.

Yang, K. K. (2012, October 22). The science of racism: Radiolab's treatment of Hmong experience. *Hyphen Magazine*. Retrieved from www.hyphenmagazine.com/blog/archive/2012/10/science-racism-radiolabs-treatment-hmong-experience

# Part IV

# International Perspectives

Modern Paradigms

# 12

## Canadian Community/ Campus Radio
• • • • • • • • • • • • • • • • • • • •

Struggling and Coping on the Cusp of Change

ANNE F. MacLENNAN

For the last century, Canadian radio stations have been scattered across the country with a significant portion of small, independent broadcasters. The enduring challenges for small Canadian radio stations have been producing original programming, federal regulation, finances, and volunteers in the case of community/campus radio. These shared trials and tribulations of early commercial broadcasters and contemporary community/campus radio stations demonstrate the importance of radio to their communities. Their survival despite the poor odds for success is a testament to the passion of the broadcasters and their audiences.

Historically the Canadian broadcasting environment, described as a "mixed or hybrid" framework, grew in stages to encompass a national, public network, commercial broadcasting, and community/campus radio (MacLennan, 2001, Raboy, 1990; Skinner, 2005, Vipond, 1994). The three separate radio broadcasting systems did not emerge intentionally or simultaneously. In the 1920s radio stations operated independently without a national network linking public or commercial broadcasters, which helped to establish an expectation of local programming (MacLennan, 2013). After a decade of private broadcasting, a national public broadcasting network was established, first as the Canadian Radio Broadcasting Commission in 1932, then as the Canadian Broadcasting Corporation in 1936, but only after the American commercial broadcasting networks, NBC, CBS, and Mutual, established their own affiliates inside Canada (MacLennan, 2001, 2016, 2018).

In the 1920s and 1930s, radio broadcasters shared many of the challenges of contemporary community/campus radio. According to *Wireless and Aviation News*, the first radio license holders, in 1922, were newspapers, radio manufacturers, or sales concerns, and one telephone company purchased the first Canadian radio broadcasting licenses in 1922; in the next decade, this group expanded to include broadcasters, religious interests, educational interests, broadcasting associations, broadcasting companies, railways, and other groups (as cited in Vipond, 1992, p. 21). The prohibitive cost of operating a radio station kept many small groups, such as religious groups, off the air (Johnston, 1994). The reallocation of North American radio frequencies, following the American Radio Act of 1927 and the General Order 40 in 1928, resulted in dominant American commercial networks, when CBS and NBC were assigned the majority of the clear channels (McChesney, 1993). Four Canadian stations that almost immediately after the reallocation of frequencies became CBS and NBS American affiliates within Canada received places on the six clear channels (MacLennan, 2018). The reallocation of frequencies did not have the same impact in Canada as in the United States. The higher technical standards and greater pressure to broadcast live favored commercially successful stations in the United States. In Canada, however, the lack of early networks, national or commercial, permitted local and community programs to continue, if not flourish.

Some of the early stations were operating with very basic equipment, such as ship-to-shore transmitters removed from ships. Most cities shared one frequency, effectively limiting some stations to a few hours daily. Dennis Duffy describes the egregious case of CFCT that moved without approval to Victoria, British Columbia, for an Easter Sunday broadcast, but its struggles were exacerbated by the failure of equipment and routine recalled by CFCT technician Dick Batey: "In 1939, it was a thoroughly run-down, utterly haywire operation . . . we didn't have a 33 1/3 r. p. m. turntable that worked. . . . You got comparatively [adept] at turning the thing at the right speed with your finger" (Duffy, 1983, p. 25). This lack of regulation of technical standards for the smaller stations allowed them to persist. Thus, Canada's early radio history was characterized by small, independent stations serving large and small communities across the country with limited resources and no access to the programming and connections provided by the networks. The larger cities and communities clustered closer to the southern border of Canada created a natural framework for a national network and most radio stations.

Many underserved regions with smaller populations had to wait longer for the expansion of radio and still have fewer radio stations. Early northern telegraph links were established by the Royal Canadian Corps of Signals in 1923, to be replaced when CBC began to provide a northern service in 1958. The introduction of FM stations added to the number of stations, opening the possibility for a greater number of stations in the 1960s and in the 1970s; particularly with the launch of the Anik satellite in 1972 even more stations were available, especially in the North (Fauteux, 2015; MacLennan, 2011). Soon after the formation of the Canadian Radio and Television Commission (CRTC; later the Canadian Radio-Television and Telecommunications Commission) as regulator in 1968, community radio broadcasting grew. Community stations were first licensed in the early 1970s experimentally, then regulated with limited advertising in 1975 and reexamined in 1984 when commercial stations questioned the stations as competitors (Fauteux, 2015). This slow evolution of the current Canadian broadcasting environment makes it distinct, and the CRTC charges the community/campus stations with the provision of cultural diversity, thereby filling in the gaps left by the national and commercial broadcasters.

Lewis and Booth (1990), in their international study of community radio, reported that community radio expanded to 139 "Native radio" stations serving the North, 15 "student radio" stations on university campuses, and 23 more broadly defined community radio stations, all but two in Quebec. These stations amounted to 9 percent of the 1,363 Canadian radio stations in 1990 (Lewis & Booth, 1990). Quebec proved a particularly fertile ground for the growth of community radio; the quiet revolution punctuated by the violence of the Front de Libération du Québec (FLQ) promoted an alternate vision of society and nation necessitating new media outlets (Fauteux, 2008, 2015; Raboy, 1990). Less political, community, campus, and native radio spread across the country to serve various smaller, local regions.

The growing impact of digital and global media on radio, as well as other media, has provoked research on Canadian community radio, but remained focused primarily on significant and traditionally important areas of Canadian policy or rights (Armstrong, 2016; O'Neill, 2007, 2008; Raboy, 1990; Raboy & Shtern, 2010). More recently Brian Fauteux argued, "In an increasingly global and digital society, the campus radio sector poses a significant challenge to the increasingly centralized and homogenous cultural offering of the commercial radio sector" (Fauteux, 2015, p. 193). Kozolanka, Mazepa, and Skinner (2012) bring to light the importance of an alternate media to stand in opposition to commercial media. In the recent research literature, global and digital commercial media are major foci, however there has been a rise in the research on radio in the areas of ethnicity, indigeneity, and Quebec as part of the research on Canada's alternative media (Bredin, 2012; Karim, 2012; Light, 2012). Light (2012), Fauteux (2015), and Mastrocola (2016) provide some of the limited empirical research on the operations of the stations. More of this recent research departs from the historical focus in the research literature on policy to interrogate the quotidian challenges of community, campus, and cultural groups working with volunteers and limited budgets to represent their communities.

Canadian community and campus radio is outlined by the CRTC in Section 3(1)(d)(iii) of the Broadcasting Act (Government of Canada, 1991):

> The Canadian broadcasting system should reflect the linguistic duality and multicultural and multiracial nature of Canadian society and the special place of Aboriginal peoples. The cultural diversity present in many Canadian communities places [their] campus and community stations ... in a position to make a strong contribution to the reflection of that cultural diversity ... providing exposure to new and emerging artists from underserved cultural groups, namely ethnocultural minorities, Aboriginal peoples and persons with disabilities. [They] ... provide spoken word programming that reflects the perspectives and concerns of diverse cultural groups, including official language minority communities. The Commission expects [them] to maintain and strengthen their efforts in these areas in their programming, volunteer involvement and employment practices. (CRTC, 2010, p. 5)

Sweeping changes that are potentially envisioned by the CRTC's *Three-Year Plan 2016–2019* have not been undertaken since the changes precipitated by the installation of the Anik satellite in the early 1970s. The needs of communities were being served by small local stations, and the introduction of the sweeping changes of satellite communication meant that northern voices, among others, feared being overwhelmed by the CBC and the culture of the South, in this case the CBC (MacLennan, 2011). Radio remains crucial in communities where it serves publics that are not a part of the CBC's mandate as well as those that have distinctive needs, such as Indigenous communities, small cultural, local communities, or other groups, such as the elderly, who do not have easy access to broadband (MacLennan & Knezevic, 2012). Although the CRTC's investigation could have a positive impact on Canada's community/campus radio, the communities serve a variety of types of communities, so their regulation and a united vision is complex. The grassroots and socially engaged nature of a great deal of the programming is essential.

Regular review of broadcasting regulatory policy through hearings has resulted in forward thinking regarding content production, funding, technology, volunteers, and other concerns at the core of community, campus, and native broadcasting. At the January 2010 broadcasting policy hearings, "some parties suggested [Canadian content development] funding directed to campus and community stations could ... fund the development of technical briefs and ... in kind technical support ... old equipment, expertise and tower rental fees. [Additionally, it] could be used to: increase online presence; enhance programming; train volunteers" (CRTC, 2010). Training, technology, program development, volunteers, and online considerations continue to be considered by CRTC.

Canadian community/campus radio is on the cusp of change as the CRTC implements its *Three-Year Plan 2016–2019*. Canadian community/campus radio is often charged with the grassroots socially engaged action and information for communities. Community/campus radio in Canada is faced with providing original programming for local or regional audiences, cultural diversity, Indigenous radio, official languages programming, multicultural radio, and other programming outside of the scope of the Canadian Broadcasting Corporation and the commercial broadcasters. This analysis is based on data collected from the reports that accompany the renewal applications. Normally, every seven years broadcasters must apply to renew their licenses, and these reports provide detailed narratives of the challenges and the strain of working within communities with limited funds and lofty goals. The final impact is upon the communities themselves that serve publics that are not a part of the CBC's mandate as well as communities that have distinctive needs such as Indigenous communities and small cultural and local communities or groups, such as the elderly who do not have easy access to broadband (MacLennan & Knezevic, 2012).

The CRTC *Three-Year Plan 2016–2019* "is intended to provide Canadians, industry and other interested stakeholders and groups with important information to prepare for and participate in the CRTC's public processes. The communications environment evolves constantly." The CRTC plan "is intended to provide Canadians, industry and other interested stakeholders and groups with important information to prepare for and participate in the CRTC's public processes. The communications environment evolves constantly" (CRTC, 2016d, p. 1). This plan follows the pattern of the successful, multiyear evaluation of Canadian television that resulted in the report *Let's Talk TV: A Conversation with Canadians* (CRTC 2018). The CRTC *Three-Year Plan 2016–2019* is an investigation of programming, production, regulation, and audience. The larger focus of the plan is television, music, official languages, and cultural diversity, but it also focuses specifically on Indigenous radio policy and multicultural radio licensing. Significantly radio is included in this plan at a time when the place of technological changes, such as streaming services that compete with digital and terrestrial radio, need consideration with respect to policy and planning.

Although the early aspirations for community/campus radio included the coverage of underserved communities and regions, Figure 12.1 demonstrates that the distribution is similar to that of commercial radio stations and clearly the Canadian population. The stations are located largely in the more populous areas of the country where the commercial and network stations are also located (CRTC, 2016d, p. 1).

As a sample, the 239 license applications and renewals from 2007 to 2017 submitted to the CRTC provide a rich resource of information about the daily operations of Canadian community/campus radio. The stations focus on their

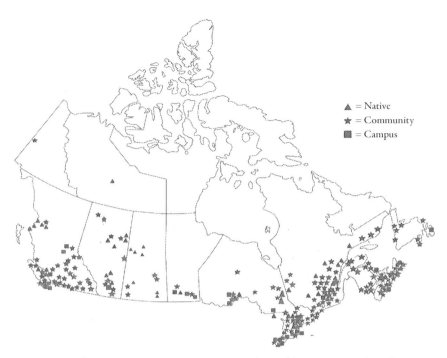

FIG. 12.1 Canadian community, campus, and Native (A & B) licenses, 2017. The radio stations were plotted as part of this research.

local communities as well as cultural or ethnic diversity, multilingual broadcasting, religious programming, and other programming that meets the mandate of locally produced and original programming. The applications and renewals are an example of "putting your best foot forward," but offer details about required topics that include finances, programming, and volunteers.

Volunteers play a key role in the community/campus radio sector. The commission considers that campus and community radio distinguishes itself by virtue of its place in the communities served, reflection of the communities' needs and values, and the requirement for volunteers in programming and other aspects of station operations (CRTC, 2010). Finances and the connection to the community make them essential to their operation. The CRTC "considers that CCD [Canadian content development] given to campus and community radio stations should be directed primarily to enhancing programming and volunteer training" (CRTC, 2010, p. 21). Programming in the sector is primarily developed and produced by volunteers and at some stations almost exclusively, so the two are codependent.

In 2011, the CRTC's brief survey of community and campus radio stations revealed that there was an average of 73 volunteers per station with an average of 52 volunteers involved on average with 52 hours of programs (CRTC, 2011). Significantly, campus stations averaged more than double the volunteers, at 125 volunteers per station while the community station average was 61 (CRTC, 2011). The report attributed the difference to the available pool of volunteers on university and college campuses. The report also demonstrated that volunteers were very active beyond the programming of radio stations and participated in governance, fund-raising, training, outreach and community presence, station administration, programming support, maintenance, public service announcements, and other activities. The survey also determined that the average number of volunteers at English-language stations was 118, 75 at French-language stations, and 30 at official language minority community stations that represent English or French in areas where they are minorities (CRTC, 2011). The crucial and extensive role of volunteers makes these differences significant to the daily operations of the stations.

Most stations make mention of their plans to train and recruit volunteers in their applications or renewal forms. The Organism Communautaire CHIL FM in Saint-Laurent, Quebec, Voice of the Shuswap Broadcast Society in Salmon Arm, British Columbia, Bonne Bay Cottage Hospital Heritage Corporation in Norris Point, Newfoundland and Labrador, and the Prince George Community Radio Society are among the many that make this standard promise (CRTC, 2009a, 2012, 2013a, 2016a). Bay of Island Radio Inc. in Newfoundland and Labrador went further to say that it would be solely operated by volunteers (CRTC, 2016b). Radio Communautaire Cornwall-Alexandria Inc. actively recruited students, particularly high school students, required to complete volunteer hours to graduate (Conseil de la Radiodiffusion et des Télécommunications Canadiennes, 2006).

Consistent with the findings of the CRTC survey in 2011, university and college applications provided detailed accounts of their volunteer recruitment. In the case of the 2014 Radio Ryerson Inc. application for an AM station, the plan "to attract at least 150 volunteers for its first year of licensed operations [included] a compulsory orientation session followed by specific training, as well as mandatory attendance at least one of two annual volunteer Meetings" (CRTC, 2014e). CRTC Broadcasting Decision 2011–56 revoked the license of CKLN-FM due to noncompliance. The impact of this decision is evident in Ryerson's application for an AM license; governance and compliance were carefully incorporated into the submission. While volunteers are more readily available on university and college campuses, a framework for governance and regulation is more important due to among other factors the shorter-term commitment of volunteers. Similarly, CKUT in Montreal, CFRC in Kingston, and CHRY in Toronto all provide detailed and extensive descriptions of the role, training, recruitment, experience, regulation, and contribution of volunteers (CRTC, 2013b). CHRY begins its description of its efforts to facilitate access and participation of volunteers by saying,

> CHRY 105.5FM is a volunteer driven organization which makes our volunteers the heart and centre of media creation. Each month we facilitate intake

orientations to invite new folks to participate in our organization. To be accessible to people of different skill sets and abilities we have created three tiers of volunteer involvement based on the following criteria: time commitment, difficulty of task, execution, and skill set. This allows us to fairly recognize and reward the efforts of all the volunteers in our space. Because we offer so many diverse volunteer experiences from long term to events-based experiences it is of utmost importance that all the efforts of volunteers are recognized. (CRTC, 2013c, p. 3)

Daniela Mastrocola, former staff member, argues that the access for volunteers at CHRY changed drastically when "volunteer contributors—some of whom had been programmers since the station's inception—were told that none of their programming contracts would be renewed as of the start of the new fiscal year. On May 1, 2015 a new programming cycle began under the banner of 'VIBE105' (VIBE, henceforth), the new broadcast division of CHRY Community Radio Inc." (Mastrocola, 2016, p. 2). Mastrocola explains that the station moved away from its identification as a campus/community station to a "new urban alternative format." CHRY's renewal application reflects concerns about compliance and quality as well as a connection with York University and its students. The decision of May 1, 2015, to end all volunteer commitments and selectively allow volunteers to return reflects the reality of working in the station's volunteer environment. The campus stations submit greater detail about volunteer training and recruitment because it is a constant process. Brock University student radio describes similar challenges: "Student involvement is difficult to expect when students are too busy to consume—let alone produce media—on a volunteer basis. Some real barriers students face to becoming engaged in general are obvious ones; lack of time, finances, motivation, perceived skill, and their transient nature. If student media is lacking student involvement, it should seek to remove these barriers while the student union should recognize these realities and also help to address them" ("Defund Brock University," 2013, paras. 58–59). The limited stay of a student will mean that there are always new volunteers to be trained, which may stand in contrast to a community or native station that has a limited pool from which to recruit but may be able to retain their volunteers for a longer period.

While native, community, and campus radio are all mandated to produce local and original content, some of the real differences emerge in the resources supporting these efforts. At the CRTC Campus and Community Radio Sector-Informal Stakeholder Meetings from March to April 2009, "Commission staff was reminded that before broadcasters they are each producers of local content, serving also as focal points for local communities" (CRTC, 2009a, para. 12). The meetings also noted that "volunteer participation far outstrips the implication of paid staff and ... that any economic activities are undertaken in order to better serve their mandate rather than having a mandate for economic gain (as with commercial radio)" (CRTC, 2009a, para. 12). Some varied initiatives to support campus and community radio have included the National Campus and Community Radio Association, supported by a Trillium Foundation grant, and the Community Radio Fund of Canada, started with a $1.4 million contribution from Astral Media (Skinner, 2012).

While grants and funding from various sources such as the National Campus and Community Radio Association, the Community Radio Fund of Canada, and the Trillium Foundation can provide some much-needed support, ongoing support is most likely to come from a few regular sources. In the case of campus radio, student levies usually provide the "lion's share" of the budget but can be supplemented by national advertisers, local advertising, fund-raising, and grants. For Indigenous stations, Band Councils sometimes provide needed support for "native" stations. Community stations with a religious component often have the ongoing support of their religious group, continuing a tradition of some of the early radio stations, but they usually need to supplement their funds with advertising, fund-raising, and grants, as do other community stations.

Native, community, and campus radio programming and operations are inextricably bound by the limits of each station's budget and ability to stretch its limits with volunteer support. Set costs of equipment, maintenance, and other set fees determine the baseline of the budget; additional funding might provide salaries for staff, and the rest of the operations depend on volunteers. Working with volunteers also solidifies the local community outreach of the station, effectively working within their mandate. Finances and noncompliance with radio regulations are most commonly the reasons for native, community, or campus stations to relinquish their license or have it revoked by the CRTC. Compliance is complicated in part by a reliance on volunteer staff and governance, which is frequently cited in renewal applications.

Community, campus, and native radio stations compete for space on the dial with each other, as well as with the CBC, and commercial radio stations. Juggling the needs of one station over the other can be seen in the license renewals and applications as well. In one case, Cobequid Radio and Hubbards Radio applied to start a community radio station located in Lower Sackville, just outside of Halifax. However, CKDU-FM Halifax, a campus station at Dalhousie University, expressed concerns that it would be not only similar but also close on the dial, 88.7 to their 88.1. The CRTC concluded that both stations could operate in the same market (CRTC, 2014c). In the case of the International Harvesters for Christ Evangelistic Association Inc., an application was submitted to change the terms of the licenses for CITA-FM Moncton, New Brunswick, CITA-FM-1 Sussex, New Brunswick, and CITA-FM-2 Amherst, Nova Scotia, to broadcast commercial messages. The CRTC approved the change but did need to assess whether the advertising was truly needed and whether it would interfere with other stations in the market (CRTC, 2015).

The regulatory framework for Canadian "Aboriginal" broadcasting began in the 1960s, but it accelerated its development when the Northern Native Broadcast Access Program (NNBAP) was established in 1983 (CRTC, 1990). The expansion of the network, employees, and stations followed in the wake of the formation of this program. The CRTC grappled with the development of a framework and definition for a "native program" that would satisfy the Canadian Association of Broadcasters as well as public and community/campus broadcasting. The CRTC defined the native program as "a program in any language directed specifically towards a distinct native audience, or a program about any aspect of the life, interests or culture of Canada's native people" (CRTC, 1990, p. 2). As early as 1988, over one hundred native community radio stations were rebroadcasting Indigenous language programming produced by NNBAP-funded networks (CRTC, 1990, p. 89). Indigenous programming figures heavily in the cultural preservation delivered by the native stations: the tradition of preserving Indigenous culture continues to be sustained by existing stations. In their 2013 application, Arrow Radio in Ohsweken, Ontario, provided a detailed accounting of the station's programming. Musical programming dominated the week's schedule, but 48 of the 126 hours in the week was spoken-word programming (CRTC, 2014d, para. 5). The application also noted that the broadcast week would include Mohawk, Seneca, Cayuga, Tuscarora, Onondaga, and Oneida languages. Located on the Six Nations Indian Reserve, the station is poised to feature distinctive local content "with on-air interviews, call-in shows and spotlights on Six Nation talent . . . local emerging Aboriginalists, with . . . 90 per cent Canadian Aboriginal artists" (CRTC, 2014d). Similarly, the Aboriginal Christian Voice Network in Prince Rupert, British Columbia, planned to feature an ambitious schedule of programming. While the plan for engagement with the Aboriginal community provided original programing, the application requested a reduction in the spoken-word requirement and increase in power (CRTC, 1994). However, at the station's request their license was revoked in 2016 (CRTC, 2016c). The requirements and desire to produce original programming are shared by community, campus, and native stations, but in every case these demands are considerable in a volunteer environment with limited finances and resources.

The burden of meeting the demands of radio regulations affects all radio stations. In the case of Aboriginal Voices, their license was rescinded by the CRTC in 2015 due to noncompliance, largely to do with the failure to file annual returns and programming obligations (Gignac, 2015). CKTP-FM Maliseet Nation Radio experienced similar difficulties with compliance, however was able to retain its license (CRTC, 2014b). Rather than maintaining a consistent application of the regulations, the CRTC has opted to evaluate each case on its own merits. Although the regulations might be administered unevenly, the CRTC provides additional chances to allow stations to survive despite individual deficiencies, such as an inability to keep up with form submission.

The CRTC promotes the production of "native" original spoken-word and music programming and has done so actively since the 1960s. Providing a high level of original content, complying with radio regulations, and dealing with other challenges, such as volunteers or finances, have produced the greatest obstacles to the survival of native stations. The ongoing efforts of the CRTC to encourage Aboriginal culture through radio programming are consistent with the recommendations of the Truth and Reconciliation Commission of Canada, including the steps toward reconciliation that include increased Aboriginal program and Aboriginal language speakers (Truth and Reconciliation Commission of Canada, 2015, pp. 9–10).

The ongoing challenges of community, campus, and native radio are consistent with the small, independent stations that have existed for decades in Canada. The expanded mandate to create local programming is frequently required with limited access to resources. The opportunity presented by the CRTC's *Three-Year Plan 2016–2019* and the revised plan allows the regulator to investigate the place of radio within the larger context of changing Canadian audiences and the new technologies for media use and consumption. The volunteer commitment and work of the community, campus, and native stations demonstrate that the impetus for local and original radio outside the confines of national public radio and commercial radio endures. The difficulties of producing radio with a high level of community commitment and limited resources while complying with radio regulations are the challenges that the CRTC can evaluate and perhaps find ways to alleviate.

Finally, the CRTC's *Three-Year Plan 2016–2019* creates an opportunity to reevaluate the role of community in the larger context of the changing broadcasting environment. Community, campus, and native radio stations are licensed to provide service to underserved communities or regions. Originally planned to provide more coverage across the country, these stations overlap with the regions where the CBC and commercial broadcasters operate. While campus stations have the stability of some financial support, usually through student fees, community and native stations are forced to operate on a smaller budget, but with a more permanent or stable group of volunteers. The regulations and paperwork that accompany the license are generally considered burdensome and are sometimes the primary reason cited for the demise of many stations. While the community, campus, and native stations operate independently as early Canadian stations did, they have regulatory obligations that the early stations did not. In the future, the CRTC and perhaps some government departments, such as Heritage Canada, could provide necessary assistance and funding to support the significant contributions community, campus, and native stations make to the culturally diverse Canadian broadcasting landscape.

## References

Armstrong, R. (2016). *Broadcasting policy in Canada* (2nd ed.). Toronto: University of Toronto Press.

Bredin, M. (2012). Indigenous media as alternative media: Participation and cultural production. In K. Kozolanka, P. Mazepa, & D. Skinner (Eds.), *Alternative media in Canada* (pp. 184–204). Vancouver, BC: UBC Press.

Canadian Radio-Television and Telecommunications Commission. (1990). *Public notice: Native broadcasting policy* (CRTC 1990-89). Ottawa, ON: Canadian Radio-Television and Telecommunications Commission. Retrieved from http://crtc.gc.ca

———. (2009a). *Broadcasting decision: Bonne Bay Cottage Hospital Heritage Corporation* (CRTC 2009-690). Ottawa, ON: Canadian Radio-Television and Telecommunications Commission. Retrieved from http://crtc.gc.ca

———. (2009b). *Campus and community radio sector-informal stakeholder meetings*. Ottawa, ON: Canadian Radio-Television and Telecommunications Commission. Retrieved from http://crtc.gc.ca

———. (2010). *Broadcasting Regulatory Policy CRTC 2010-499*. Ottawa, ON: Canadian Radio-Television and Telecommunications Commission. Retrieved from http://crtc.gc.ca

———. (2011). *A snapshot of volunteerism in Canadian campus & community radio*. Ottawa, ON: Canadian Radio-Television and Telecommunications Commission. Retrieved from http://crtc.gc.ca

———. (2012). *Broadcasting decision: Low-power community radio station in Salmon Arm* (CRTC 2012-450). Ottawa, ON: Canadian Radio-Television and Telecommunications Commission. Retrieved from http://crtc.gc.ca

———. (2013a). *Broadcasting decision* (CRTC 2013-362). Ottawa, ON: Canadian Radio-Television and Telecommunications Commission. Retrieved from http://crtc.gc.ca

———. (2013b). *CFRC: Application to renew a broadcasting licence to operate a campus or community radio undertaking (including low-power)—Form 110* (CRTC 2010-499). Ottawa, ON: Canadian Radio-Television and Telecommunications Commission. Retrieved from https://crtc.gc.ca/eng/archive/2014/2014-50.htm

———. (2013c). *CKUT: Application to renew a broadcasting licence to operate a campus or community radio undertaking (including low-power)—Form 110* (CRTC 2013-1603-4). Ottawa, ON: Canadian Radio-Television and Telecommunications Commission. Retrieved from https://crtc.gc.ca/eng/archive/2014/2014-50.htm

———. (2014a). *Volunteer Participation CHRY* (CRTC 2013-1498-9). Ottawa, ON: Canadian Radio-Television and Telecommunications Commission. Retrieved from http://crtc.gc.ca

———. (2014b). *Broadcasting decision: CKTP-FM Fredericton—Licence renewal* (CRTC 2014-184). Ottawa, ON: Canadian Radio-Television and Telecommunications Commission. Retrieved from http://crtc.gc.ca

———. (2014c). *Broadcasting decision Hubbards Radio Society* (CRTC 2014-279). Retrieved from http://crtc.gc.ca

———. (2014d). *Broadcasting Decision: Type B Native FM radio station in Ohsweken* (CRTC 2014-583). Ottawa, ON: Canadian Radio-Television and Telecommunications Commission. Retrieved from http://crtc.gc.ca

———. (2014e). *Broadcasting decision: Radio Ryerson Inc. English-language community-based campus AM station in Toronto* (CRTC 2014-644). Ottawa, ON: Canadian Radio-Television and Telecommunications Commission. Retrieved from http://crtc.gc.ca

———. (2015). CITA-FM Moncton and its transmitters—Licence amendment (CRTC 2015-429). Ottawa, ON: Canadian Radio-Television and Telecommunications Commission. Retrieved from http://crtc.gc.ca

———. (2016a). *Broadcasting decision: Centre communautaire "Bon Courage" de Place Benoît* (CRTC 2016-217). Ottawa, ON: Canadian Radio-Television and Telecommunications Commission. Retrieved from http://crtc.gc.ca

———. (2016b). *Broadcasting decision* (CRTC 2016-397). Retrieved from http://crtc.gc.ca

———. (2016c). *Broadcasting decision: CIAJ-FM Prince Rupert—Revocation of licence* (2016-454). Ottawa: Canadian Radio-Television and Telecommunications Commission. Retrieved from http://crtc.gc.ca

———. (2016d). *Three-year plan 2016–2019*. Ottawa, ON: Canadian Radio and Television Telecommunications. Retrieved from http://crtc.gc.ca

———. (2017). *Three-year plan 2017–2020*. Ottawa, ON: Canadian Radio and Television Telecommunications. Retrieved from http://crtc.gc.ca

———. (2018). *Let's talk TV: A conversation with Canadians*. Retrieved from http://crtc.gc.ca

Conseil de la Radiodiffusion et des Télécommunications Canadiennes. (2006). *Demande de renouvellement d'une licence de radiodiffusion pour une entreprise de programmation de radio communautaire*. Retrieved from http://crtc.gc.ca

Darling, A. J. (1994). *Decision* (CRTC 94-901). Ottawa, ON: Canadian Radio-Television and Telecommunications Commission. Retrieved from http://crtc.gc.ca

Defund Brock University student radio—yes or no? (2013, October 8). *Brock Press*. Retrieved from www.brockpress.com/2013/10/defund-brock-university-student-radio-yes-or-no/

Duffy, D. J. (1983). *Imagine please: Early radio broadcasting in British Columbia*. Victoria: Sound and Moving Image Division, Provincial Archives of British Columbia.

Fauteux, B. (2008). Campus frequencies: The "alternativeness" of campus radio broadcasting. *Canadian Journal of Media Studies, 3*(1), 131–141.

———. (2015). *Music in range: The culture of Canadian campus radio*. Waterloo, ON: Wilfrid Laurier University Press.

Gignac, J. (2015, July 25). *CRTC revokes Aboriginal Voices Radio license over non-compliance*. APTN National News. Retrieved from http://aptnnews.ca/2015/06/25/crtc-revokes-aboriginal-voices-radio-license-non-compliance/

Government of Canada. (1991). *Broadcasting Act, S. C 1991, c 11*. Ottawa, ON: Ministry of Justice. Retrieved from http://laws-lois.justice.gc.ca/PDF/B-9.01.pdf

Johnston, R. (1994). The early trials of protestant radio, 1922–38. *Canadian Historical Review, 75*(3), 376–402.

Karim, K. H. (2012). Are ethnic media alternative? In K. Kozolanka, P. Mazepa, & D. Skinner (Eds.), *Alternative media in Canada* (pp. 165–183). Vancouver, BC: UBC Press.

Kozolanka, K., Mazepa, P., & Skinner, D. (Eds.). (2012). *Alternative media in Canada*. Vancouver, BC: UBC Press.

Lewis, P. M., & Booth, J. (1990). The listener as participant: North America and Australia. In P. M. Lewis & J. Booth (Eds.), *The invisible medium: Public, commercial and community radio* (pp. 115–137). Washington, DC: Howard University Press.

Light, E. (2012). Public participation and community radio in Quebec. In K. Kozolanka, P. Mazepa, & D. Skinner (Eds.), *Alternative media in Canada* (pp. 145–164). Vancouver, BC: UBC Press.

MacLennan, A. F. (2001). *Circumstances beyond our control: Canadian radio program schedule evolution during the 1930s*. Unpublished doctoral dissertation, Concordia University, Montreal, QC.

———. (2011). Cultural imperialism of the north? The expansion of CBC's northern service and community radio. *Radio Journal, 9*(1), 63–81.

———. (2013). Learning to listen: Becoming a Canadian radio audience in the 1930s. *Journal of Radio and Audio Media, 20*(2), 311–326.

———. (2016). Transcending borders: Reaffirming radio's cultural value in Canada and beyond. *Journal of Radio and Audio Media, 23*(2), 197–198.

———. (2018). Private broadcasting and the path to radio broadcasting policy in Canada." *Media and Communication, 6*(1), 13–20. Retrieved from www.cogitatiopress.com/mediaandcommunication/article/view/1219

MacLennan, A. F., & Knezevic, I. (2012). *Radio broadcasting, community and culture: The official languages act, broadcasting act and the case of CBEF Windsor* (Final report). Retrieved from www.cmg.ca/en/wp-content/uploads/2011/06/CRTC-CBC-licence-renewal2012EN.pdf

Mastrocola, D. (2016). *Another one bites the dust? The transition from CHRY 105.5 FM to VIBE105*. Ottawa, Ontario: Canadian Radio-Television and Telecommunications Commission. Retrieved from https://crtc.gc.ca/eng/acrtc/prx/2016/mastrocola2016.pdf

McChesney, R. (1993). *Telecommunications, mass media, and democracy: The battle for the control of U.S. broadcasting, 1928–1935*. Oxford: Oxford University Press.

O'Neill, B. (2007). Digital audio broadcasting in Canada: Technology and policy in the transition to digital radio. *Canadian Journal of Communication, 32*(1), 71–90.

———. (2008). Digital radio policy in Canada: From analog replacement to multimedia convergence. *Journal of Radio and Audio Media, 15*(1), 26–40.

Raboy, M. (1990). *Missed opportunities: The story of Canada's broadcasting policy*. Montreal, QC: McGill-Queen's University Press.

Raboy, M., & Shtern, J. (2010). *Media divides: Communication rights and the right to communicate in Canada*. Vancouver, BC: UBC Press.

Skinner, D. (2005). Divided loyalties: The early development of Canada's "single" broadcasting system. *Journal of Radio Studies, 12*(1), 136–155.

———. (2012). Sustaining independent and alternative media. In K. Kozolanka, P. Mazepa, & D. Skinner (Eds.), *Alternative media in Canada* (pp. 25–45). Vancouver, BC: UBC Press.

Truth and Reconciliation Commission of Canada. (2015). *Truth and Reconciliation Commission of Canada: Calls to action*. Winnipeg: Truth and Reconciliation Commission of Canada. Retrieved from www.trc.ca/websites/trcinstitution/File/2015/Findings/Calls_to_Action_English2.pdf

Vipond, M. (1992). *Listening in: The first decade of Canadian broadcasting*. Montreal and Kingston, QC/ON: McGill-Queen's University Press.

———. (1994). The beginnings of public broadcasting in Canada: The CRBC, 1932–36. *Canadian Journal of Communication, 19*(2). Retrieved from www.cjc-online.ca/index.php/journal/article/view/806/712

# 13

## Revenge of the Nerds

•••••••••••••••••••

How Public Radio Dominated
Podcasting and Transformed
Listening to Audio

BRAD CLARK AND ARCHIE McLEAN

Public radio's place in popular culture as a bastion of dull, pseudo-intellectual programming is perhaps best illustrated in the iconic *Saturday Night Live* sketch known as "Schweddy Balls." The sketch opens with generic classical music, a still photo of a nondescript brick building emblazoned with the letters "NPR," and two nerdy hosts announcing in utterly noncommercial unison, "You're listening to the 'Delicious Dish' on National Public Radio." Their conservative hairstyles, garish festive sweaters, and discussion of their Christmas wish lists—featuring rat traps, a funnel, and a wooden bowl—reinforce their image as entirely uncool. Alec Baldwin famously delivers double entendres as Pete Schweddy, a guest chef hawking yuletide treats he refers to as his Schweddy Balls. The play on words drives the sketch, with his radio hosts interacting with the deliberate, egg-headed good humor associated with the public radio trope. One of those spoof NPR hosts, Ana Gasteyer, told the real NPR many years later that the parody was based on a real public radio cooking show and consistent with the genre: "You just need to take your time and explore a subject to the point that people want to weep with boredom" (*Rolling Stone*, 2014, para. 2).

Despite the perception that public radio is a bland alternative to commercial formats, in the twenty-first century public broadcasters dominate podcast charts globally. In Canada, where public broadcasting has played a much bigger role in the lives of media consumers, the Canadian Broadcasting Corporation (CBC) joins the top U.S. podcasters in capturing the biggest audiences for Canadian-produced audio content. Public broadcasters are the stars of the podcast world, as the genre has "arrived in the mainstream consciousness," heralding what some are calling a new "golden age of radio" (Markman, 2015, pp. 240–241). This chapter argues that public broadcasters have been well positioned to develop and advance the full technological attributes of the medium, relying on the best features of the radiogenic narratives they have been producing for decades, and in some cases "remediating" them for even deeper listener engagement. At the same time, the analysis reveals podcast norms are increasingly migrating into public radio programming as part of an evolving reciprocal relationship between audio formats.

The podcast's evolution from the terrestrial public broadcasting tradition is first described and then used to establish a baseline of radiogenic traits—those sublime qualities of mediated sound that engage the listener and gird the most popular podcasts. Those traits are represented as codes in a content analysis of the monthly twenty top-ranked podcasts in the United States and the top ten Canadian-produced podcasts, over a nine-month period in 2016–2017. The audio from a random sample of these podcasts is examined with a view to detailing the prevalence of the traits (codes) that appeal to podcast audiences. The analysis finds there is an upper echelon of "prestige podcasts" that draw huge listenership and incorporate the full range of radiogenic traits associated with public radio while advancing those elements to new heights of authenticity and intimacy. Public broadcasters have pioneered personal journalism and storytelling narratives that are well suited to the "hyper-intimacy" of headphones or earbuds, the method of consumption increasingly used by legions of podcast subscribers. The content analysis also helps to more clearly articulate other categories of podcast—some well established, some emerging—including a class of independently produced programs that do not have all the production values of public radio, but attract audience through radiogenic intimacy practices all the same. Across the spectrum of the thirty podcasts under analysis, it is clear that the best features of public radio form the foundation for a range of on-demand audio products featuring elements of documentary, radio drama, intimate one-on-one interviews, and live storytelling. The result is a range of content successfully designed to engage a mass audience of listeners at the most personal level, to the point where an article in *Gawker* declared in a headline, "Listening to the Radio Is Cool Again" (Evans, 2014).

## Radio's Broad Appeal and Public Broadcasting

In the age of digital convergence, scholars struggle with definitions of radio (see Crisell, 1994; Dubber, 2013), but where they tend to agree is the qualities of the medium that have appealed to audiences for decades, regardless of the technological format. It is these radiogenic qualities that form the foundation of public radio and its broad appeal. Lacey (2013) relates the etymology of the term with photogenic, drawing on the "poetical, uncanny or sublime properties of an image" to the artistry of the visual medium: "In the same way, the 'radiogenic' refers to those aspects that are only evident in the recording and broadcasting of sound and that reveal or express an encounter with some sort of truth" (p. 90). When King George V delivered the first Royal Christmas Message over the airwaves in 1932, there was delight among British subjects at hearing the regent's own voice and words. Radio pioneers recognized they were creating an "artificial reality" (p. 91) but a reality nonetheless.

"Liveness," whether the broadcast is prerecorded or not, is also part of the "realist aesthetic" associated with radio, delivering a sense of "being right there, right now" (p. 97). Crisell (1994) maintains that radio "seems to be a 'present-tense' medium, offering experiences whose outcome lies in an unknown future . . . it seems to be an account of what *is* happening rather than a record of what *has* happened" (p. 9, emphasis original). This is reflected in the radio script-writing convention that emphasizes using the present tense as much as possible (Papper, 2013, p. 46). Realism is further enhanced when the microphone leaves the studio environment to record the "actuality" of voices and noises of the real world, thereby conveying an "intensive and complex montage of sounds" (Lacey, 2013, p. 97). For example, the sounds of protesters chanting at a demonstration in Athens give listeners in Vancouver an authentic sense of the event as if it were unfolding right before their ears, even though it might well have been recorded hours earlier. For the audience, the voices and the sounds, even the emotional tension, are all real, however mediated the audio might be.

The sense of reality and authenticity in the auditory experience of radio is further conveyed by the human voice, so prominent in the talk-based content associated with public broadcasters. Radio studies scholars routinely interrogate voice, conversation, dialogue, intimacy, and the formation of bonds with individual listeners. Lindgren (2016) writes, "Voice is the intimate key to audiences' hearts. By listening to detailed personal experiences of 'others,' listeners become connected to the people whose stories they share" (p. 27). Presenters and hosts, she points out, "are informal and conversational in their presentation style and tone. They sound relaxed and personal—like real people, or friends engaging in a conversation with us." In fact, broadcast textbooks prescribe on-air personnel to "visual[ize] who you are speaking to" so that "each member of the audience receives your words as an individual" (Fleming, 2010, p. 92). If radio, as Crisell

(1994) suggests, is a "personal medium," then it is "the voices of presenters and newsreaders that we most respond to" (p. 85). U.S. president Franklin Roosevelt's "fireside chats" of the 1930s brought a homespun, conversational intimacy to political discourse over the radio. Celebrated public radio hosts such as Peter Gzowski in Canada and Ira Glass in the United States have derived some of their appeal in an informal, personal delivery whereby they sound "like real people, or friends engaging in a conversation with us" (Lindgren, 2016, p. 27).

The intimacy of the spoken word would undoubtedly hold little interest if the text behind it were, for example, the impersonal recitation of monthly wheat exports statistics for Saskatchewan. Public radio has firmly established storytelling as part of its traditional appeal. Dubber explains it well: "It's a useful cliché, repeated by practitioners and radio educators alike, that radio is 'theatre of the mind.' By telling stories using words, music and sound effects, radio can engage the imagination to communicate ideas and images that create a kind of narrative uniquely experienced by each individual listener . . . radio storytelling has the capacity to make personal connections, paint pictures with sound, and indeed create scenes that would be impossible in another context" (2013, p. 121). In fact, NPR aspires to create "driveway moments" for its listeners through its storytelling, where the report or interview is so strong that—according to one NPR executive—"the story keeps you pinned in your car, in a parking lot, in your driveway, or at the side of the road, as you wait to hear how the story will end" (Kern, 2008, p. 12). The arrival of the "selfie" culture on social media seems to coincide with a renewed popularity in personal narrative, which is a trend that extends to radio and now podcasting (Lindgren, 2016).

An additional and obvious radiogenic element is music. Very early on in radio's technological development broadcasters recognized the connection between music, "the most universal of all the arts," and radio, "this universalizing medium" (Lacey, 2013, p. 92). Music's aesthetic appeal forms the very backbone of a huge proportion of radio programming, but it also "performs an ancillary function in signifying something outside itself" (Crisell, 1994, p. 48) in content beyond the airing of songs and musical performances. In all other forms of radio content, music is deployed as a "'framing' or 'boundary' mechanism" (p. 50) to establish a whole range of meanings, styles, moods, and transitions—a somber track for a documentary on the Holocaust, or a lively, up-tempo theme for a comedy show. Radio producers rely on the associative meaning of music to intentionally signal characteristics about the content they have created.

These radiogenic traits are not unique to public broadcasters. Commercial radio in North America similarly relies on music, voice, personality, immediacy, and authenticity to connect with audiences. However, the remit of public broadcasters, freed to varying degrees from the existential demands of profitability, has required that they offer what the privates will not. In the United States, the Public Broadcasting Act of 1967 paved the way for noncommercial, educational television and radio to play a more vital role in information programming.

The National Educational Radio Network, "often perceived as dull, stuffy" (McCauley, 2005, p. 23), was replaced by NPR in 1970. With the emergence of commercial talk radio in the ensuing years, NPR evolved in a different direction, leaving behind the ponderous "Schweddy Balls" ethos satirized on TV, shifting "its mission from providing a more traditional definition of serious educational programming to presenting a diverse, in-depth alternative" (Hilmes, 2011, p. 342). It also experimented "with radio as a sound medium" focusing on the "aesthetic field of sound itself in a way that its commercial counterparts had given up long ago" (p. 342).

In Canada, the broadcast system developed as a government-supported model of a national network in recognition of the much bigger market south of the border. The slogan "the state, or the United States" helped compel parliament to establish the Canadian Radio Broadcasting Commission in 1932, the forebear of the CBC (Thompson & Randall, 2008, p. 117). Private radio stations sprang up alongside the public broadcaster, but CBC Radio dominated listenership in many communities. However, by the 1970s, CBC Radio was losing audience, at a tremendous rate. Former CBC executive Richard Stursberg, in his book on the crown corporation, admits it had grown into a "snobby, self-important, elitist service" described by one CBC Radio host as "ponderous, a sort of university of the air ... it talked down to people and was patronizingly intellectual" (2012, p. 218). Success would eventually come as a complete rebound in ratings, but not until CBC Radio adopted an approach that was "informal, populist and engaging ... intensely personal" (p. 219). In contrast to the private stations, CBC offered more than an ongoing cycle of news, weather, and traffic with strong journalism in the form of "local current affairs, documentaries, interviews and investigative pieces" (p. 216).

Public radio's success in the ensuing years stems from its embrace of radio's ability to engage audiences with the tools at its disposal: voice, music, and sound. Personal narrative, strong journalism, and intelligent production and sound design clearly set public radio apart from commercial competition in both countries. As a result, public broadcasters were well positioned to seize on the emergence of a liberating, new delivery system for audio production, the podcast in the early 2000s.

## From Radio to Podcast

In the waning years of the twentieth century, the music industry underwent a massive structural shift brought on by MP3s and the rise of peer-to-peer file-sharing services such as Napster. By 2004, it was radio's turn for a revolution in the creation and distribution of content. The same file formats, plus the launch of Apple's iPod, cheap editing software, and weblogs led producers to start creating and publishing their own audio content. Journalist Ben Hammersley noted this trend in an article in the *Guardian*, writing that "all the ingredients are there for a new boom in amateur radio" (Hammersley, 2004). The only question was what to call this new medium: "Audioblogging? Podcasting? GuerillaMedia?" (2004, para. 2).

Thankfully, GuerillaMedia didn't take off. Instead, the portmanteau "podcasting" became common usage and with the ubiquity of smartphones will now likely outlive the device for which it was named. The trends associated with Hammersley's "new boom" continued unabated, and just over a year later the cover of *Wired* magazine was predicting "The End of Radio." There was some early evidence that the arrival of the iPod had led to a decline in live radio listening by fifteen- to twenty-five-year-olds, but by 2008 data out of the United Kingdom showed podcasting was driving listeners to programs they had not listened to before and boosting overall listenership (Fleming, 2010, p. 55). The *Wired* cover notwithstanding, podcasting has flourished in tandem with its traditional precursor, adopting radiogenic traits while also pushing public broadcasters to adapt to changing distribution, production, and journalistic conventions.

Those early years of podcasting were marked by two distinct types of programming: independently produced shows, and public radio programs aired "live" and then posted, unaltered online. The rise of independent producers of audio on demand mirrored the earlier ascent of blogs, which had become a fixture of the digital information world by the early 2000s, especially in U.S. politics. Blogs freed writers from the tyranny of print deadlines, space limitations, and editors, while podcasts similarly freed producers from the constraints of terrestrial radio, including strict time limits and regulations around language. The *New York Times* documented the energy and enthusiasm of early independent audio producers, noting that the rawness was part of the appeal. A California insurance salesman who produced his own movie review podcast argued in the *Times* story that "it's more interesting to listen to someone who's not a professional but who has something genuine or interesting to say" (Zernike, 2005, para. 26).

At the same time indie producers were experimenting with the medium, public broadcasters began to test-drive the platform for their programming. In Canada, after a successful pilot in 2005, the CBC made its first real foray into podcasting by offering some of its popular radio shows—*The Current*, *Dispatches*, *Definitely Not the Opera*, *Ideas*, *Outfront*, and *As It Happens*, as well as some regional content—as podcasts (Cwynar, 2015). The podcasts, uploaded as exact radio copies, existed as paratexts for the source programs, not as distinct digital content. Indeed, one executive described the initiative as "like the VCR for radio" (p. 192). The BBC approached its early podcasts in similar ways (Berry, 2016), as did NPR (Zernike, 2005).

If we think of this era as podcasting's first wave, the second wave began in 2012 when a number of successful U.S. public radio producers began to break from their radio funding and financed themselves through listener support (Bonini, 2015). Among the first of these was *99% Invisible*, produced by Roman Mars for KALW public radio in San Francisco, which raised nearly a half million dollars in 2012 and 2013 through Kickstarter. But it was the launch of *Serial* in 2014 that truly heralded this new era. Produced by public radio icon Ira Glass and his team at *This American Life*, the murder-mystery series quickly became the most downloaded and certainly the most talked-about podcast series ever (Dredge, 2014). *Serial* introduced millions of people to podcasting and unexpectedly put the normally staid world of public broadcasting "at the whitehot epicenter of pop culture" (Chafin, 2015, para. 4). With public attention suddenly focused on podcasting, investment in the industry followed, and podcast companies (including Gimlet Media, Panoply, and even Spotify and Amazon) are placing bets that there's a profitable future for the medium. Gimlet, founded by *This American Life* alum Alex Blumberg and Matt Lieber, recently raised fifteen million dollars in venture capital, a vote of confidence in an industry that still makes up a tiny part of the commercial entertainment business (Kafka, 2017).

In concert with podcasting's second wave, public radio's strong journalistic tradition has also evolved in the shifting media landscape. Karlsson (2011) captures a change in journalistic ethics in which truth telling has been extended to include greater transparency, where journalists "disclose the methods of their newsgathering," revealing what goes on "back stage" and boosting accountability and legitimacy (p. 284). His argument is built on Goffman's (1990) dramaturgy theory, which breaks down social interaction to front- and backstage representations of self. Frontstage is the image individuals want others to see; backstage is where people let down their guard, relax, and show their true nature. Karlsson equates the backstage in journalism with the "gathering" and "processing" of news, while the frontstage is represented by "distribution/presentation" (p. 282). Under the traditional model of journalism the messy practice of rapidly determining news is "concealed from the audience," backstage, to maintain the apparent authority of news organizations. Consumers see only the frontstage: "TV news is more often than not presented by an anchor who reads the news—the audience is not shown the editing room and how news material has been cut" (p. 282). However, Meyrowitz (1985) postulates that changes in "communication technology" disrupt journalistic norms and undermine public perception of news producers, resulting in "moving old backstage performances to the frontstage, such as explaining how news is being produced" (cited in Karlsson, 2011, p. 284). The CBC podcast *Someone Knows Something* demonstrates this routinely. For example, in the third episode of season 2, the host/reporter David Ridgen incorporates audio of what amounts to a cold call with a source at the box store where she works.

RIDGEN  This is going to sound weird to you, you're Pamela Branton?
BRANTON  Yeah.
RIDGEN  Odette Fisher told me that you work here, she said you'd be a great
person to talk to about her daughter. Yeah, because we couldn't get a hold of

you, I sent you a Facebook message, I work for CBC, and she said you were a great friend of hers. (Rigden, 2016)

The foregrounding of the production process in public radio journalism is evident in the personal journalism increasingly associated with podcasting's second epoch. Lindgren (2016) notes the rise of "personal and subjective approaches to storytelling" among the most popular podcasts (p. 24). Lindgren suggests public radio producers in particular, building on radio's intimacy, have allowed audiences to see and understand the challenges and struggles of individual journalists: "Allowing audience access to hearing 'the real Sarah Koenig' became a hallmark style on *Serial*. She spoke directly with the listeners about the production challenges of the programme, guiding them through the twelve episodes by inviting them to share her ethical conundrums and journalistic personal narrative journalism and podcasting challenges. As Glass suggested, listeners heard her reactions on tape and her emotions" (Lindgren, 2016, pp. 36–37).

Production norms have also loosened to make more room for authenticity, so that the voice editing that might have occurred backstage in the past allows for a more intimate and honest representation of what was said in the finished product. Jay Allison, who produces *The Moth Radio Hour*, where people tell their personal stories on stage in front of a live audience, argues the imperfection can be engaging: "Part of the appeal is the mistakes and the moments when people stop, and go 'I ... um ... well, what I ... My father ...' that's when you pay attention. That stuff stays, I don't cut that out. That's the beauty" (Abel, 2015, p. 82). Free from the constraints of a limited air time in the broadcast schedule, podcast producers can afford to let their recorded audio stand on its own with fewer edits. In a similar vein, podcast content is not subject to the regulatory standards around explicit content and coarse language. This seems to afford another avenue to intimacy and authenticity. Psycholinguists observe that in some contexts swearing is "especially meant to communicate that the situation we are confronted with deeply affects us, as evidenced by the display of strong emotions" (Vingerhoets, Bylsma, & de Vlam, 2013, p. 290). The use of profanity in media is perhaps best represented by online news sites such as *Vice*, where a story on the last federal election campaign in the United Kingdom featured the headline "How the Tories Fucked the Country" (Beach, 2017). A review of *Vice*'s election coverage pointed to language that was "witty and sarcastic, comfortable with swearing," coverage that was "familiar as a pub discussion with your hilarious—maybe already tipsy—but still well informed mates" (Sampaio-Dias & Dennis, 2017, para. 6). All of this contributes to the evolution of an intimate medium, radio, into one of "hyper-intimacy," as described by Berry (2016, p. 14). He suggests there is a deeper bond that has emerged between audiences and many podcasts, "where listeners feel deeply engaged with both the process of listening and the material to which they listen" (p. 14). The analysis that follows demonstrates the extent to which podcast producers have advanced the established intimacy of public radio into something even more personal in many of today's most popular podcasts.

## The Study

There is little doubt that public broadcasters have pioneered spoken-word radio in North America and that their creative efforts are advancing audio productions in new ways with podcasting. At a time when independent and private entities are increasingly joining the fray, the authors sought to gauge the extent to which public radio dominates the podcast space, its influence on the genre, and potential differences between the state-sponsored (Canada) and hybrid (United States) models of public broadcasting.

The analysis takes a purposive sampling approach, that is, intentionally seeking a particular kind of podcast, in this case the ones that audiences seem to like the most. The researchers used ranking charts in both countries to identify the most popular podcasts over a nine-month period from September 2016 to June 2017. The sampling period is consistent with other media content analyses that avoid atypical programming associated with irregular listenership and summer vacation schedules (Hansen, Cottle, Negrine, & Newbold, 1998, p. 103). Arriving at precisely which podcasts and publishers are the most popular is problematic and an often discussed topic among podcast correspondents. Most of the data come from Apple, downloads are not the same as actual listening, and the potential for charts to be "gamed" to boost audience numbers is quit real (van Beinum, 2018, para. 2). Data are more readily available from the much bigger U.S. market. The monthly rankings from Podtrac are used for the American component of this analysis. Podtrac is described as a "decade-old podcast measurement and advertising company" and though its methodology is not perfect, it is well regarded for its "network-oriented, apples-to-apples comparison" (Quah, 2016, para. 4). The company's published ratings for each month were examined through the sample period. Table 13.1 shows the twenty U.S. podcasts the analysis identified as most consistently appearing on Podtrac's charts.

In Canada, where the media audience is about a tenth the size of that in the United States, data on podcast consumption are much less clear, and there are few organizations trying to measure podcast penetration. While public broadcasting and the CBC have a long tradition, "the Canadian podcasting industry is in its infancy" (Buck, 2016, para. 7). Any long list of top on-demand audio products would feature programs with insignificant audiences—as the founder of one Canadian podcast company points out—"If you have over 500 listeners to your podcast within the first 30 days of podcasting, you are in the top 5 per cent of iTunes" (Swartz, 2016, para. 12). Nonetheless, as part of this analysis, a top ten list of Canadian-produced podcasts was compiled over the sample period. There are no freely available monthly rankings in Canada, but iTunesCharts.net published daily podcast ratings. A random sample of those rankings was used to

### Table 13.1
### Top 20 U.S. Podcasts Based on Podtrac's Monthly Rankings, September 2016 to June 2017

| Rank | Podcast | Publisher |
| --- | --- | --- |
| 1 | This American Life | This American Life/Serial |
| 2 | Radiolab | WNYC Studios |
| 3 | Ted Radio Hour | NPR |
| 4 | Freakonomics Radio | WNYC Studios |
| 5 | Stuff You Should Know | HowStuffWorks |
| 6 | Planet Money | NPR |
| 7 | Fresh Air | NPR |
| 8 | NPR Politics Podcast | NPR |
| 9 | Wait Wait... Don't Tell Me! | NPR |
| 10 | The Joe Rogan Experience | Joe Rogan |
| 11 | 99% Invisible | PRX/Radiotopia |
| 12 | The Moth Podcast | PRX/Radiotopia |
| 13 | Hidden Brain | NPR |
| 14 | How I Built This | NPR |
| 15 | Serial | This American Life/Serial |
| 16 | Stuff You Missed in History Class | HowStuffWorks |
| 17 | S-Town | This American Life/Serial |
| 18 | The Daily | New York Times |
| 19 | Pod Save America | Crooked Media |
| 20 | Criminal | PRX/Radiotopia |

identify ten podcast that most consistently appeared on the charts. Table 13.2 shows the programs that make up that list.

The second part of the study is a content analysis in which those top podcasts were further analyzed series by series, episode by episode. The inductive approach of grounded theory was used to categorize and define established and emerging radiogenic traits in the content, namely those properties of audio production that most appeal to audiences. Grounded theory is an approach where findings are "'grounded' in data... rather than taken from the research literature" (Leedy & Ormrod, 2010, p. 144). The two key features of the method are "its development of theory out of data" and its "iterative approach... the data collection and analysis proceed in tandem, repeatedly referring back to each other" (Bryman & Teevan, 2005, p. 284). The first round of micro-analysis involved listening, identifying distinct audio elements, and review—the "constant comparative methods" associated with grounded theory—looking for "similarities and differences" to "establish analytic distinctions" (Charmaz, 2006, p. 54). At this level of analysis, patterns and contrasts started to emerge. For example, some programs had strong elements of journalistic practice, while others clearly sought to entertain; some involved sounds and scenes recorded in the field, while others were entirely produced in studio. There were also elements that seemed to surface more

### Table 13.2
**Top Canadian Podcasts and Publishers Based on a Random Sample of Rankings on iTunesCharts.net**

| Rank | Podcast | Publisher |
| --- | --- | --- |
| 1 | Someone Knows Something | CBC |
| 2 | Vinyl Cafe | CBC |
| 3 | Missing and Murdered: Who Killed Alberta Williams? | CBC |
| 4 | Canadaland | Canadaland |
| 5 | The Current | CBC |
| 6 | Under the Influence | CBC |
| 7 | The Colour Code | The Globe and Mail |
| 8 | Grownups Read Things They Wrote as Kids | Grownups Read Things They Wrote as Kids |
| 9 | This Is That | CBC |
| 10 | Ideas | CBC |

in programs that were offered only as podcasts compared to those that also aired terrestrially, such as the use of explicit language.

This initial analysis was followed by "focused coding" where the data were further synthesized according to the most "significant" or frequent codes (Charmaz, 2006, p. 57). As the content analysis proceeded it became clear additional characteristics needed to be considered in the analysis, such as if the program also aired on radio stations. Shows that air terrestrially face constraints that podcast-only programs do not, such as time limits, prescribed scheduling, and explicit language restrictions. As a result a "format" category was added to reflect these variables.

Categories and codes were retested and redefined, until a five-category coding schedule was arrived at: production values, journalistic approach, narrative structure, intimacy codes, and format. The coding variables associated with each category are described and listed in Table 13.3. Public radio storytellers use sound and voice to engage the listener and advance narrative, thus *production value* codes were identified for the use of sound/sound effects, interview clips, and audio from media or archival sources. The codes of the *journalistic approach*, so strongly associated with the public service remit, include evidence of verification/accuracy in the text, fairness and balance in the context of bias, and research/investigation as a feature of the content. *Narrative structure* is represented as codes of a sequence of chapters or acts, elements of plot and character development, and foreshadowing as a device to hold the attention of listeners. The *intimacy codes* are most closely associated with public radio's advancement of audio storytelling into the podcast genre. They include personal reflections on the part of the show's hosts or presenters, the use of coarse "explicit" language that would not ordinarily meet regulatory standards for terrestrial broadcasts,

### Table 13.3
### Coding Schedule Variables and Descriptions

| Coding variables | Descriptions |
| --- | --- |
| **Production values** | |
| Sound effects | Actuality ("wild sound") or produced sound effects |
| Interview clips | Edited segments of recorded interviews |
| Media clips | Edited segments from TV, radio, film, digital sources, private recordings, archives |
| **Journalistic approach** | |
| Accuracy/verification | References to efforts to substantiate facts |
| Fairness/balance | References to efforts to find alternate viewpoints, address bias |
| Research, investigation | Efforts to find and reveal information |
| **Narrative structure** | |
| Chapters/acts/segments | Content structured along story arc and/or clear segments |
| Plot/characters | Clear focus on story and character development |
| Foreshadowing/signposting | References or hints to upcoming content |
| **Intimacy codes** | |
| First person reflection | Regular hosts/presenters offer personal anecdotes, observations and/or clear expression of opinions or emotions |
| Unedited coarse language | Presence of explicit language as tagged by iTunes |
| "Backstage" transparency | Content reveals details, conversation, events left out of traditional radio production and journalism |
| **Format** | |
| Limited run | The podcast has limited runs; not produced on a regular schedule |
| Podcast only | The program does not air on terrestrial radio |

and "backstage" transparency (actuality or scripted references to the "gathering and processing" functions of media production) often taking the form of audio that would traditionally be cut from the final on-air product. These show up as side stories, off-mic exchanges, or recorded incidents that reveal something about the featured character, show producers, or hosts. Sometimes, the actuality includes a scripted segment to explain production or journalistic decision made in the field. The *format* codes help to delineate traits that fall outside the audio content, but appeal to certain audiences.

The researchers then coded the thirty individual podcast series listed in Tables 13.1 and 13.2. For the limited-run podcasts *all* episodes were coded. For podcasts running continually (typically weekly or daily) a random sample of 20 percent of the episodes was analyzed. The coding schedule was used to determine whether each variable appeared in the episode under examination. An additional step was added to more precisely measure for explicit language. For that variable, the iTunes store was accessed for each episode to see if the red "E" for explicit content was assigned. The totals for each podcast series were aggregated. To help further conceptualize the data the total scores for every podcast series were entered into a table. Variables associated with content (production values, narrative structure, journalistic approach, and intimacy) were assigned check marks on the following basis: one for appearances of the variable in less than one-third of the episodes coded, two if the variables show up in one-third to two-thirds of cases, and three if the variables are found in more than two-thirds of the sample. For the two format variables a single check mark simply indicates whether the podcast series was "limited run" and another if it was available as a "podcast only."

Constant comparative methods were applied again to evaluate these data and to identify patterns. The clusters of similar codes associated with different podcasts led the researchers to arrive at categories that reflect the influence of public broadcasters on podcasting's popularity. Those categories are described in the next section.

## Findings

In a familiar pattern seen in virtually all media and art forms (television, film, magazines, music) U.S. content dominates the Canadian audience for podcasts as well. With few exceptions, the most listened to podcasts in Canada are made in the United States: *This American Life*, *Freakonomics*, *S-Town*, *The Joe Rogan Experience*, *The Daily*, *Serial*, *Criminal*, and many others. The ten Canadian podcasts that most consistently showed up in the iTunes charts were almost entirely published by CBC, with three notable exceptions—*Colour Code* (from Toronto-based *Globe and Mail*), *Grownups Read Things They Wrote as Kids*, and *Canadaland*, the private, crowd-funded venture of media veteran Jesse Brown. Brown worked as a CBC radio producer before launching *Canadaland*, and *Grownups Read* started out as a series on CBC Radio. While the metrics for podcast popularity are not precise, public radio's ties to the most popular podcasts are well established.

The influence of public radio is obvious in the coding data for podcasts. Just over 70 percent, twenty-two out of the thirty top podcasts, are associated with public radio publishers, fifteen of the twenty U.S. shows and seven of the ten Canadian programs. In the United States, seven of the twenty are from NPR, three from *This American Life/Serial*, three from PRX/Radiotopia, two from WNYC Studios, two from HSW, and three from private entities. In the Canadian sample, seven of the ten are from CBC.

True to their established commitment to public broadcasting ideals, the public-radio-produced podcasts in the sample are more likely to incorporate production values and narrative structure in their content. Moreover, the public-radio-based podcast producers are more likely to build on intimacy codes

## Table 13.4
## Coding and Categorization of Podcasts

| Podcasts | Codes | | | | | |
|---|---|---|---|---|---|---|
| | Production values | Narrative structure | Journalistic approach | Intimacy | Limited run | Podcast only |
| **Prestige** | | | | | | |
| This American Life | ✓✓✓ | ✓✓✓ | ✓✓✓ | ✓✓✓ | | |
| Serial | ✓✓✓ | ✓✓✓ | ✓✓✓ | ✓✓✓ | ✓ | ✓ |
| S-Town | ✓✓✓ | ✓✓✓ | ✓✓✓ | ✓✓✓ | ✓ | ✓ |
| Someone Knows Something | ✓✓✓ | ✓✓✓ | ✓✓✓ | ✓✓✓ | ✓ | ✓ |
| Missing and Murdered... | ✓✓✓ | ✓✓✓ | ✓✓✓ | ✓✓ | ✓ | ✓ |
| **Top-tier public radio** | | | | | | |
| Radiolab | ✓✓✓ | ✓✓✓ | ✓✓✓ | ✓✓✓ | | |
| Criminal | ✓✓✓ | ✓✓✓ | ✓✓✓ | ✓✓✓ | | |
| Planet Money | ✓✓✓ | ✓✓✓ | ✓✓✓ | ✓✓ | | |
| Ideas | ✓✓✓ | ✓✓✓ | ✓✓✓ | ✓✓ | | |
| Freakonomics | ✓✓✓ | ✓✓✓ | ✓✓✓ | ✓✓ | | |
| How I Built This | ✓✓✓ | ✓✓✓ | ✓✓✓ | ✓✓ | | |
| Fresh Air | ✓✓✓ | ✓✓✓ | ✓✓✓ | ✓ | | |
| 99% Invisible | ✓✓✓ | ✓✓✓ | ✓✓✓ | ✓ | | |
| Under the Influence | ✓✓✓ | ✓✓✓ | ✓✓ | ✓ | | |
| Hidden Brain | ✓✓ | ✓✓✓ | ✓✓ | ✓✓ | | |
| The Moth | ✓✓ | ✓✓✓ | ✓✓ | ✓✓ | | |
| The TED Hour | ✓✓ | ✓✓✓ | ✓✓ | ✓ | | |
| **Intimate, moderate production value** | | | | | | |
| Canadaland | ✓✓ | ✓✓✓ | ✓✓✓ | ✓✓✓ | | ✓ |
| Pod Save America | ✓✓ | ✓✓ | ✓✓ | ✓✓ | | ✓ |
| Colour Code | ✓✓ | ✓✓ | ✓✓ | ✓✓ | ✓ | ✓ |
| Joe Rogan Experience | ✓ | ✓✓ | ✓ | ✓✓✓ | | ✓ |
| Stuff You Should Know | ✓✓ | ✓✓ | ✓✓ | ✓ | | ✓ |
| Stuff You Missed in History Class | ✓✓ | ✓✓ | ✓✓ | ✓ | | ✓ |
| **Immediate** | | | | | | |
| The Daily | ✓✓✓ | ✓✓✓ | ✓✓✓ | ✓✓✓ | | ✓ |
| The Current | ✓✓✓ | ✓✓✓ | ✓✓✓ | ✓✓ | | |
| NPR Politics | ✓✓ | ✓✓ | ✓✓✓ | ✓ | | ✓ |
| **Comedy/entertainment** | | | | | | |
| Wait Wait... | ✓✓ | ✓✓✓ | ✓✓ | ✓✓ | | |
| This Is That | ✓✓✓ | ✓✓✓ | | | | |
| Vinyl Cafe | ✓✓ | ✓✓✓ | | | | |

associated with podcasting, especially for programs that are not also aired on terrestrial broadcasts. At the same time, the independent podcast publishers are less likely to use production values associated with public radio narrative and journalism, though more likely to engage with podcast's deeper intimacy traits.

To better understand public radio's influence on podcasting, the thirty podcasts were grouped into categories based on the degree to which they incorporate the radiogenic codes. Table 13.4 shows the distribution of podcasts through the five categories and coding results. The categories are (1) prestige podcasts, (2) top-tier public radio, (3) intimate moderate production value podcasts, (4) immediate podcasts, and (5) comedy/entertainment. Each category is discussed at length below.

## Prestige Podcasts

The data demonstrate that some of the most popular podcasts in both countries are highly produced, intimate, and strongly journalistic programs in the documentary tradition of public radio. Four of the five identified here are offered exclusively as podcasts. They are both limited-run *and* serialized stories, that is, the programming has a fixed number of episodes, and the subject is one story with each installment advancing the narrative. These four include CBC's *Missing and Murdered: Who Killed Alberta Williams?* and *Someone Knows Something*, two of only four Canadian-made podcasts to top the iTunes charts in the sample. Joining the two CBC offerings are *Serial* and *S-Town*, among the most popular shows in both countries. *Serial*'s ongoing appeal is of particular note, as it remains near the top of the charts despite the fact that the last episode was released at the end of March 2016, almost six months before the beginning of the sample period. *This American Life* is included in this category despite the fact that it is not a stand-alone podcast. The two CBC podcasts both investigate cold cases, similar to the first season of *Serial*, though *Missing and Murdered* also focuses on the broader issue of Indigenous women as victims of crime and the associated apathy in Canadian society.

The programs in this category score the highest for characteristics related to the radiogenic traits associated with public broadcasting and the development of podcasting into a distinct media line. They are all strongly journalistic and pay careful attention to ethics as they seek to reveal deeper meaning in the stories they pursue; they use sound recorded in the field to create vivid scenes in the minds of their listeners and pay careful attention to narrative structure, engaging the audience with elements of foreshadowing and suspense. While *This American Life* is not focused on one story the way the other four are, it certainly has pioneered much of the strong character development and intimacy seen in the others. For example, *Missing and Murdered* features a retired Royal Canadian Mounted Police detective, Garry Kerr, "who is still haunted by the case" of Alberta Williams, a twenty-four-year-old Indigenous woman, whose body was found along the so-called Highway of Tears in Western Canada in 1989 (Luke, 2016). In the second season of *Someone Knows Something*, an exploration of the disappearance of Sheryl Sheppard in 1999, Sheryl's still grief-stricken mother Odette helps the reporter navigate the backstory and colorful people in Sheryl's life. In *S-Town* the focus of the story is John B. McLemore, an apparently brilliant and eccentric man who so despises his small town in rural Alabama that he calls it "Shit-town," the source of the series' title. The skilled storytelling around McLemore's character—critics called it "brilliant" and "unnaturally sophisticated" (Addley, 2017, para. 7)—is also intensely personal and intimate.

The *This American Life/Serial* brand behind *S-Town* is in some ways a pioneer of personal journalism, and so it is not surprising to see *S-Town* hit a new standard of intimacy. After the first two episodes introduce us to "John B," Bibb County, and an unsubstantiated murder conspiracy, the third installment starts with a phone exchange between reporter Brian Reed and Skyler, a close friend of McLemore's:

SKYLER  Well, we have some bad news to tell you.
BRIAN REED  OK.
SKYLER  John B. killed himself Monday night.
BRIAN REED  Are you kidding me?
SKYLER  No.
BRIAN REED  Oh my gosh.
SKYLER  With everything that happened, we weren't able to call yesterday. His body was found yesterday morning, and it happened yesterday morning. It happened between last Monday night and Tuesday morning.
BRIAN REED  Oh my God.
SKYLER  Yeah. So right now, his mother is OK.
BRIAN REED  Oh, Skyler.
SKYLER  Now we're just trying to get her taken care of and make sure she don't go to a nursing home.
BRIAN REED  Oh my gosh.
SKYLER  And the way he killed himself is he drank cyanide.
BRIAN REED  Oh my God. Oh, I'm so sorry. I—(Reed, 2017, para. 5).

Reed's voice cracks with despair through this exchange. The inclusion of this highly personal dialogue is consistent with other intimacy codes in this study such as personal reflection and backstage transparency. *Missing and Murdered* does not have any of the expletive-laced clips of *S-Town*, but there are instances where the journalist, Connie Walker, alludes to her personal discomfort with ambush interviews, and many of the journalistic decisions she and her producers make as they pursue the story. Walker references her own First Nations identity throughout the series, she explains she is Cree and grew up on a reserve in Saskatchewan, and she adds context with the authenticity of personal experience with this comment in Episode 7: "It's a truth that Indigenous women are disproportionally victims of violence, that 76 per cent of kids on reserves in the province of Manitoba live in poverty; that kids on reserves across the country get less money for education.... Indigenous people are over-represented in the criminal justice system, *our* infant mortality rate is higher, *our* life expectancy is lower" (Walker, 2016, emphasis added).

In both seasons of *Serial*, Sarah Koenig brought plenty of personal insight and reflection to her journalism and storytelling. In episode 5 of season 2, the story of Sergeant Bowe Bergdahl, she discusses the negative online comments she had seen in news stories of people who enter dangerous areas of the world and get kidnapped. She confesses that "I've thought things like this. I mean, it's great they're home, but also, it's their own damn fault. I admit it. And I'll wager we've all thought things like this, right?" (Koenig, 2016, para. 114).

That four of the five podcasts identified came out in limited runs is likely to have enhanced their appeal, as noted in the case of *S-Town*, "allowing listeners to gorge ... Netflix-style" (Addley, 2017, para. 6). During the sample period another serialized podcast, with only six episodes, also proved incredibly popular. *Missing Richard Simmons* featured many of the traits associated with this category, but fell just below the ratings of other programs in the sample.

## Top Tier Public Radio Podcasts

The twelve podcasts in this category represent the height of public radioness. They are popular in the digital space, but also as terrestrial broadcasts. For the most part, they represent the first wave of podcasting, in which radio content was simply made available for digital download. The majority are well-established radio programs with deep production values and strong interviewing; they privilege storytelling and thoughtful use of sound. Documentaries are regularly featured in shows such as *Radiolab*, *Planet Money*, *Freakonomics*, *Fresh Air*, and *Ideas*. The degree of intimacy might not be quite as high as in the prestige category, but the content is often presented personably and informally, and there are instances of heightened first-person experience. One of the best instances of this is *Freakonomics* host Stephen Dubner's exploration of his own intense disgust with the sounds emanating from the stalls of public restrooms and a quest for a solution (Dubner, 2014). The podcasts listed in this category in Table 13.4 are those that emerged from the data in our sample period; however, there are programs that are similarly highly produced and popular that did not quite meet our criteria but are worth mentioning. Some examples include *On the Media* and *Snap Judgement* from WNYC Studios, CBC's *Quirks and Quarks*, a long-running weekly science show, *As It Happens*, a daily current affairs show, and *Q*, an offering of pop culture interviews and discussions weekday mornings. These Canadian programs also routinely show up in the broadcast schedule of public radio stations across the United States.

The compelling interplay in this category is not the presence of well-established radio programs finding a digital audience, but rather a reverse or circular trend, where content developed as either a podcast or radio program evolves and transitions between the two. *How I Built This* is a clear example, originating as a podcast, while *Hidden Brain* and *99% Invisible* followed a more complex path involving both the podcast and public radio realms. According to its website, *Hidden Brain* began as a series on NPR's *Morning Edition* before becoming its own podcast in September 2015, then relaunching as a one-hour radio show in the fall of 2017 ("About Hidden Brain," 2017). In the case of *99% Invisible*, host Roman Mars began by producing short cut-ins related to the design world for San Francisco public radio station KALW, but "off the air waves—in the world of podcasts—the show was a blockbuster" (Kang, 2014, para. 13). Mars gave up his public radio job to work on the successful podcast full-time and also helped establish the podcast collective *Radiotopia* ("99% Invisible," 2017). However, the show is still broadcast over the airwaves by a few independent radio stations.

In this category, what seems to be important to both podcast and radio audiences is the strong narrative, the intimate discussion, and the use of sound to engage the audience. A simple example illustrates this point. In episode 257, "Reversing the Grid," of *99% Invisible*, an explanation of how an electricity meter works is narrated over the mechanical sound of dials spinning, apparently faster and faster, racking up the power consumption; the cadence of the host's presentation speeds up too: "5 kilowatt hours, 10 kilowatt hours, 20, 30, 40, 50. . . ." The segment lasts only about fifteen seconds, but the attention to production adds imagery and meaning for the listener and creates tension in the podcast narrative.

## Intimate, Moderate Production Value Podcasts

The six podcasts in this category are linked by a strong sense of intimacy, including first-person reflection, unedited coarse language, and backstage transparency to talk directly to the audience. While the content of these shows—*Canadaland*, *Pod Save America*, *Colour Code*, *Joe Rogan Experience*, *Stuff You Should Know*, and *Stuff You Missed in History Class*—is clearly diverse, the programs are all driven by a dynamic host or hosts who rely on their connection with the audience to drive listenership.

For a consumer, the question of whether to listen to these shows is often this: do I want to hang-out with these people for the duration of the show? For those who identify strongly enough with the host's personality and presence to download and listen, the connection is enhanced by the "hyper-intimacy" referenced throughout this chapter. For some listeners two-plus hours with Joe Rogan, a bombastic comedian and mixed martial arts commentator, might feel like getting trapped by a loudmouth at the end of the bar. However, his wide-ranging interests, celebrity guests, and contrarian opinions transform him into a friend or smart acquaintance (at least for some) who comes to visit each week.

Programs that trade heavily on this intimacy and host connection are often able to employ stripped-down production values more in line with early independent podcasts than the prestige shows discussed above. The simplest format involves hosts talking to each other, trading stories and information, where the listener acts as a sort of eavesdropper. For example, the *Stuff You Should Know* podcast incorporates very little public-radio-style production and instead trades on the talent and interplay of hosts Josh Clarke and Chuck Bryant to keep listeners engaged. But for listeners who do not find the hosts especially charming, the format does not offer much to keep them downloading and listening. Similarly, two episodes of *Stuff You Missed in History Class* devoted to comic radio stars Abbott and Costello do not contain a single clip from any of their classic routines. Interview-based shows such as *Colour Code*, *Pod Save America*, and *Canadaland* also feature strong, opinionated hosts alongside rotating guests and contributors. The additional voices offer more for listeners who don't connect with the hosts. However, the shows' aesthetics and politics are still largely host driven, so while Democrats might find the trio of former Obama administration staff utterly convincing, Donald Trump Republicans are not going to find much to like on the decidedly partisan *Pod Save America*.

## Immediacy

This category features programs that reflect a high-degree of immediacy, including *The Daily* from the *New York Times*, *NPR Politics*, and CBC's *The Current*. These shows display some overlap with other categories but are linked by a commitment to covering timely issues and events while maintaining strong journalistic traits such as accuracy and verification. *The Current*, for example, describes itself as a place to get both the latest news and new information about events in real time: "If major news breaks, we're on it, both on air and online. We shed new light on the stories we cover" (CBC, 2017b, para. 2). The show airs weekday mornings on terrestrial radio but is consistently among the most downloaded podcasts in Canada, partly a function of its daily schedule and reliable quality. *NPR Politics* follows a similar format, though typically running over a much shorter duration than *The Current*'s seventy-five minutes. The show's focus is on strong journalistic analysis and intelligent conversation on the major developments of the day by NPR's political correspondents.

Daily podcasts from big media companies are not new, but *The Daily* and other programs that did not show up in the sample, including Slate's *The Gist* and NPR's *Up First*, are breaking ground in creating high-quality productions that explicitly promise the latest news and information. These are relatively new stand-alone podcasts banking on an emerging pattern of late-breaking news consumption, and at the time of writing there is at least one other media company planning to enter the U.S. market for daily digital news (Quah, 2017). *The Gist* is uploaded for the East Coast afternoon commute, while *The Daily*'s host imagines people loading their smartphones in the morning and bringing the show along on the subway or in their car (Johnson, 2017). The opportunity to garner a consistent audience of daily subscribers has enormous appeal, and the efforts appear to be paying off. Though *The Daily* and *Up First* have been on offer only for less than a year, they have established that "there's a market for such an audio product—at least for one that's done smartly, thoroughly, and in a way that brings the weight of legendary newsrooms to bear" (Quah, 2017, para. 1).

## Comedy/Entertainment

The comedy podcasts share the obvious trait of having humor at or near the center of the show's mission. Comedy is, of course, subjective, but these shows clearly stand apart from the others in their attempts to entertain and, with one exception, their lack of journalistic pretext. NPR's *Wait, Wait Don't Tell Me* and CBC's *The Vinyl Café* and *This Is That* all score well on traditional public radio traits, including high-quality production values and narrative structure.

One of the shows, *This Is That*, does not just display public radio traits; it copies them verbatim for laughs. For example, the September 7, 2017, episode begins with this introduction from host Peter Oldring: "We are absolutely delighted to bring you another year of stories that are not only relevant to us as journalists but to all Canadians. And I'm also pleased to announce that Pat is wearing a fun yet tasteful cardigan and of course I'm wearing one of my favorite piano key ties. We carefully curate these outfits to make you feel at ease and to set a tone of trustworthiness" (Kelly & Oldring, 2017). Oldring is an improvisation comic not a journalist, but he clearly nods to the traits he knows radio journalists are supposed to display—trustworthiness, intimacy, and a desire to tell stories that resonate outside the newsroom. Like the *Onion* for public radio, the show uses fake interviews and documentaries to highlight the absurdity of the news and the sometimes overearnest CBC radio style. The show has managed to use these radio traits so effectively that it regularly features baffled and outraged calls from their listener talk-back line, people who believe the show to be real.

The *Vinyl Café* was a long-standing CBC storytelling and variety show hosted by Stuart McLean and featuring stories about Dave, a small-town record store owner, his wife Morley, and their family. The stories are often funny, but exist entirely in their own universe, detached from news and current events. On the other hand, *Wait, Wait Don't Tell Me* is a weekly quiz show about news and current events. Its humor flows from the host and contestants riffing on headlines and news clips. Unlike the other two shows in this category, it relies on truthful information to power the show's questions and humor. In this way it offers a chance for listeners to catch up on the week's events, in the way people often claim to receive their news from the *Daily Show*.

## Discussion

The analysis shows public radio not only has established the foundation for podcasting's mass appeal, but continues to engage and capture new listening audiences by playing to the radiogenic strengths of the spoken-word format it forged as an alternative to commercial radio. In its second century, audio content has been liberated from the linear, temporal, and regulatory constraints of conventional broadcasting. The result is experimentation, innovation, and critical and commercial success. The most popular podcasts in North America either are produced by or owe a lot to public broadcasters.

However, this study highlights the distinct digital landscape for on-demand audio in Canada and the United States. As noted, the top U.S. shows also dominate the Canadian charts. As a state-funded public broadcaster, CBC has committed to a digital-first strategy to offer multimedia content on all platforms, although the Canadian market remains but a fraction of that in the United States for both public and private broadcasters (CBC, 2017a). Though better supported, public broadcasting in Canada cannot match the output of both private and nonprofit media producers in the United States, where reliance on donor support is obvious in the preamble to so many of the top podcasts. It is beyond the scope of this study, but it might well be that the U.S. model of public broadcasting, with some federal government support but a heavy reliance on fund-raising campaigns, spurs the development of innovation of new programming at a rate not seen in countries with state-supported broadcast networks. Even though there are some Canadian-made podcasts attracting Canadian audiences, at this stage the slogan "state, or the United States" defines another cultural industry north of the border.

Many observers have linked the podcast's arrival in the mainstream with the debut of *Serial* as a spinoff of *This American Life*. Since the first episode aired in late 2014, two seasons of the show have been downloaded more than a quarter billion times (Spangler, 2017). The production team's investigation into the murder of Hae Min Lee, in Baltimore, and the 2000 murder conviction of her ex-boyfriend, Adnan Syed, was a clear hit and set the bar for slick podcast production and success. In fact, the show so captured the public's attention that *Saturday Night Live* once again turned its satiric attention to the realm of public broadcasters. "Christmas Serial" performed by the *SNL* cast investigated the mysterious arrival of presents every December 25, delivered to a young boy—as if by magic—by an elf named "Kris." The parody features the familiar, stark piano theme and an uncanny impersonation of *Serial* host Sarah Koenig, intimate with her audience, and transparent in her journalism as she shares, "I had to ask myself, Could Kris really have done this?" (Young, 2016). The contrast to the "Schweddy Balls" sketch almost thirty years earlier is stark. The *Serial* piece works because of its obvious familiarity with so many in the audience, as opposed to the geeky, niche listenership linked to the NPR of earlier decades. It is an obvious sign that public radio has outgrown its nerdy roots and—through podcasting—has earned recognition and respect in popular culture.

## References

99% Invisible. (2017, October 30). *The Show*. Retrieved from https://99percentinvisible.org/about/the-show/
Abel, J. (2015). *Out on the wire: The storytelling secrets of the new masters of radio*. New York: Broadway Books.
About Hidden Brain. (2017, September 3). NPR. Retrieved from www.npr.org/2015/09/03/437264048/about-hidden-brain
Addley, E. (2017, March 31). True-crime podcast S-Town even better than Serial, rave viewers. *Guardian*. Retrieved from www.theguardian.com/media/2017/mar/31/true-crime-podcast-s-town-even-better-than-serial-rave-viewers
Beach, B. (2017, June 7). How the Tories fucked the country. *Vice*. Retrieved from www.vice.com/en_uk/article/payg5b/how-the-tories-fucked-the-country
Berry, R. (2016). Podcasting: Considering the evolution of the medium and its association with the word "radio". *Radio Journal, 14*(1), 7–22. doi:10.1386/rjao.14.1.7_1
Bonini, T. (2015). The "second age" of podcasting: Reframing podcasting as a new digital mass medium. *QUADERNS DEL CAC, 18*, 21–30.
Bryman, A., & Teevan, J. J. (2005). *Social research methods* (Canadian ed.). Don Mills, Canada: Oxford University Press.
Buck, G. (2016, July 29). Why Canadian podcasters are being drowned out by American offerings. Retrieved from www.metronews.ca/life/technology/2016/07/29/canadian-podcasters-are-being-drowned-out-by-americans.html
CBC. (2017a). A space for us all. Retrieved from www.cbc.radio-canada.ca/en/explore/strategies/2020/
———. (2017b, June 5). The Current. Retrieved from www.cbc.ca/radio/thecurrent/about
Chafin, C. (2015, January 21). Since 2004, This small team has been crushing the podcasting competition. *FastCompany*. Retrieved from www.fastcompany.com/3041055/since-2004-this-small-team-has-been-crushing-the-podcasting-competition
Charmaz, K. (2006). *Constructing grounded theory*. London: Sage.
Crisell, A. (1994). *Understanding radio* (2nd ed.). Abingdon, UK: Routledge.
Cwynar, C. (2015). More than a "VCR for radio": The CBC, the Radio 3 podcast, and the uses of an emerging medium. *Journal of Radio and Audio Media, 22*, 190–199. doi:10.1080/19376529.2015.1083371
Dredge, S. (2014, November 18). Serial podcast breaks iTunes records as it passes 5m downloads and streams. *Guardian*. Retrieved from www.theguardian.com/technology/2014/nov/18/serial-podcast-itunes-apple-downloads-streams
Dubber, A. (2013). *Radio in the digital age*. Cambridge: Polity.
Dubner, S. J. (2014, December 18). Time to take back the toilet: A new Freakonomics radio podcast. *Freakonomics*. Retrieved from http://freakonomics.com/podcast/time-to-take-back-the-toilet-a-new-freakonomics-radio-podcast/
Evans, D. (2014, September 8). Listening to the radio is cool again: 8 smart podcasts you should hear. *Gawker*. Retrieved from http://gawker.com/listening-to-the-radio-is-cool-again-1619583911
Fleming, C. (2010). *The radio handbook* (3rd ed.). Abingdon, UK: Routledge.
Goffman, E. (1990). *The presentation of self in everyday life*. London: Penguin.

Hammersley, B. (2004, February 12). Audible revolution. *Guardian*. Retrieved from www.theguardian.com/media/2004/feb/12/broadcasting.digitalmedia

Hansen, A., Cottle, S., Negrine, R., & Newbold, C. (1998). *Mass communication research methods*. New York: New York University Press.

Hilmes, M. (2011). *Only connect: A cultural history of broadcasting in the United States* (3rd ed.). Boston: Wadsworth.

Johnson, E. (2017, October 28). Michael Barbaro explains why you love the New York Times' podcast, "The Daily." *Recode*. Retrieved from www.recode.net/2017/10/28/16561160/michael-barbaro-the-daily-new-york-times-podcast-journalism-nyt-recode-media-peter-kafka

Kafka, P. (2017, August 2). VCs don't love podcasting but Gimlet has raised another $15 million anyway. *Recode*. Retrieved from www.recode.net/2017/8/2/16079634/gimlet-media-podcast-funding-stripes-laurene-powell-jobs-advertising-crooked-media-the-daily

Kang, C. (2014, September 25). Podcasts are back—and making money. *Washington Post*. Retrieved from www.washingtonpost.com/business/technology/podcasts-are-back—and-making-money/2014/09/25/54abc628-39c9-11e4-9c9f-ebb47272e40e_story.html?utm_term=.223fe820fd64

Karlsson, M. (2011). The immediacy of online news, the visibility of journalistic processes and a restructuring of journalistic authority. *Journalism 12*(3), 279–295. doi:10.1177/1464884910388223

Kelly, P., & Oldring, P. (2017, September 7). This is that: Can-con Netflix, undercover gone wrong, national smokers museum. *CBC*. Retrieved from www.cbc.ca/radio/thisisthat/can-con-netflix-undercover-gone-wrong-national-smokers-museum-1.4274182

Kern, J. (2008). *Sound reporting: The NPR guide to audio journalism and production*. Chicago: University of Chicago Press.

Koenig, S. (2016, January 21). Episode 05: Meanwhile, in Tampa. Serial Podcast. Retrieved from https://serialpodcast.org/season-two/5/meanwhile-in-tampa/transcript

Lacey, K. (2013). *Listening publics: The politics and experience of listening in the media age*. Cambridge: Polity.

Leedy, P. D., & Ormrod, J. E. (2010). *Practical research: Planning and design* (9th ed.). Upper Saddle River, NJ: Pearson.

Lindgren, M. (2016). Personal narrative journalism. *Radio Journal, 14*(1), 23–41. doi:10.1386/rajo.14.1.23_1

Luke, M. (2016, December 20). CBC podcast uncovers new information in unsolved murder of Alberta Williams. *CBC*. Retrieved from www.msn.com/en-ca/news/canada/cbc-podcast-uncovers-new-information-in-unsolved-murder-of-alberta-williams/ar-BBxm1mG

Markman, K. M. (2015). Everything old is new again: Podcasting as radio's revival. *Journal of Radio and Audio Media, 22*(2), 240–243. doi:10.1080/19376529.2015.1083376

McCauley, M. P. (2005). *NPR: The trials and triumphs of National Public Radio*. New York: Columbia University Press.

Papper, R. (2013). *Broadcast news and writing stylebook* (5th ed.). New York: Pearson.

Podtrac. (2017, June 12). May 2017—Top Podcast Publishers. Retrieved from http://analytics.podtrac.com/blog/2017/6/8/may-2017-top-podcast-publishers

Quah, N. (2016, May 24). Hot pod: We now have new, free rankings to show how podcasts stack up against each other. *Nieman Lab*. Retrieved from www.niemanlab.org/2016/05/hot-pod-podcast-network-rankings-are-here-and-free/

———. (2017, August 22). The daily podcaster's choice: Try to fit in listeners' crowded mornings or tackle the evening commute? *Nieman Lab*. Retrieved from www.niemanlab.org/2017/08/the-daily-podcasters-choice-try-to-fit-in-listeners-crowded-mornings-or-tackle-the-evening-commute/

Reed, B. (2017, March 28). Chapter 3: Tedious and brief. S-Town Podcast. Retrieved from https://stownpodcast.org/chapter/3

Rigden, D. (2016, December 5). Episode 3: Blondie. *Someone Knows Something*. Retieved from https://www.cbc.ca/radio/sks/season2/episode-3-blondie-1.3876315

*Rolling Stone*. (2014, February 3). 50 Greatest 'Saturday Night Live' Sketches of All Time. Retrieved from www.rollingstone.com/tv/pictures/50-greatest-saturday-night-live-sketches-of-all-time-20140203/nprs-delicious-dish-schweddy-balls-0402572

Sampaio-Dias, S., & Dennis, J. (2017, July 7). Not just swearing and loathing on the internet: analysing BuzzFeed and VICE during #GE2017. *Election Analysis*. Retrieved from www.electionanalysis.uk/uk-election-analysis-2017/section-3-news-and-journalism/not-just-swearing-and-loathing-on-the-internet-analysing-buzzfeed-and-vice-during-ge2017/

Spangler, T. (2017, March 31). Podcast, "S-Town," tops 10 million downloads in four days. *Variety*. Retrieved from http://variety.com/2017/digital/news/s-town-podcast-10-million-downloads-serial-productions-1202020302/

Stursberg, R. (2012). *The tower of babble: Sins, secrets and successes inside the CBC*. Vancouver: Douglas and McIntyre.

Swartz, A. (2016, November 18). Podcasting is the new blogging. *Globe and Mail*. Retrieved from https://beta.theglobeandmail.com/report-on-business/small-business/sb-marketing/podcasting-is-the-new-blogging/article32876525/?ref=www.theglobeandmail.com&

Thompson, J. H., & Randall, S. J. (2008). *Canada and the United States: Ambivalent allies* (4th ed.). Athens: University of Georgia Press.

van Beinum, E. (2018, May 16). The kerfuffle about podcast charts. *Podcast Hotdog*. Retrieved from https://podcasthotdog.com/2018/05/16/podcast-charts.html

Vingerhoets, A., Bylsma, L. M., & de Vlam, C. (2013). Swearing: A biopsychosocial perspective. *Psychological Topics, 22*(2), 287–304.

Walker, C. (2016, December 15). Missing & murdered: Who killed Alberta Williams? With Connie Walker episode 7. *CBC*. Retrieved from www.cbc.ca/listen/shows/missing-murdered-who-killed-alberta-williams/episode/11141486

Young, M. (2016, December 16). Serial podcast's creator Julie Snyder talks of the fallout from Saturday Night Live parody: "It was shocking." Retrieved from www.news.com.au/entertainment/celebrity-life/serial-podcasts-creator-julie-snyder-talks-of-the-fallout-from-saturday-night-live-parody-it-was-shocking/news-story/0ae1da34eb68aa7e65bf1838e20b1c25

Zernike, K. (2005, February 19). Tired of TiVo? Beyond blogs? Podcasts are here. *New York Times*. Retrieved from www.nytimes.com/2005/02/19/technology/tired-of-tivo-beyond-blogs-podcasts-are-here.html?_r=0

# 14

# Reproducing Analog Pathologies in the Digital Radio Landscape

●●●●●●●●●●●●●●●●●●●●

The Case of Greece

MICHAEL NEVRADAKIS

In Greece there is a common saying to the effect of "nothing is more permanent than the provisional" (Papathanassopoulos, 1989, p. 37). This certainly can be said to be true in the case of Greek broadcasting. Deregulation of the airwaves occurred in a rapid and seemingly anarchic manner in the late 1980s, and since then a comprehensive and nationwide licensing procedure for radio stations has never been conducted. Instead, most Greek radio stations have operated under a haphazard and illogical mishmash of "temporary" permits or expired licenses whose terms have been repeatedly extended, or with no legal standing whatsoever. Furthermore, the definition of what is and what is not "legal" as it pertains to broadcasting has frequently shifted.

Scholars who have examined the mediascape in Greece in the past have described its development as an example of "savage deregulation" (Traquina, 1995) and the country's broadcasting model as fitting the "polarized pluralist" or "Mediterranean" model proffered by Hallin and Mancini (2004, p. 125; 2016, pp. 159–160). As Greek broadcasting transitions to a digital environment; however, whether such a transition will signify a fresh start for the

Greek mediascape or will merely result in the reproduction of the analog and offline mediascape in a digital and online environment remains an open question.

Drawing upon a longitudinal study I performed in Greece during the 2012–2017 time period (Nevradakis, 2018), which examined the potential impact of social and new media upon the public sphere, civil society, and the public discourse, this chapter examines the current status of and recent developments in the Greek radio landscape as well as the transition to digital transmission in various forms (broadcast, Internet, satellite). As will be argued, the offline and analog media landscape—characterized by clientelist relations and haphazard regulations—is being reproduced in the digital realm. This can be explained, at least in part, by a long history in Greece of the public sphere and public discourse being dominated by political interests, including media moguls who utilize the media to further their own business interests and political agendas as well as to influence public opinion. Furthermore, despite a growing credibility crisis toward the mainstream media on the part of the Greek public at large during the years of the economic crisis, an interesting aspect of the "digital transition" is the dearth of online-only radio stations focusing on news, information, and issues of social, political, or economic importance. Instead, the digital radio landscape in Greece, such as it is at the present time, is largely dominated by existing actors and by music-intensive programming, while over-the-air DAB programming remains limited and largely unknown to the Greek audience at large.

Qualitative research methods such as semistructured interviews were employed in this study, in addition to a historical-descriptive analysis of the development of the Greek mediascape. As illustrative examples, the cases of online stations such as Radiobubble and ERT Open will be examined to highlight both the successes and struggles faced by alternative media outlets in the digital sphere in Greece.

## Savage Deregulation?

While the saying "nothing is more permanent than the provisional" has been applied to many aspects of public and political life in Greece, it is an especially apt descriptor for the manner in which the broadcast landscape has developed since deregulation in the late 1980s. In defining the "polarized pluralist" or "Mediterranean" model prevalent in the countries of Southern Europe, Hallin and Mancini (2004) point to such characteristics as the existence of a low-circulation press, media outlets that tend to be economically marginal and in need of state subsidies, the predominance of electronic (broadcast) media, and a public broadcasting system that tends to be directly state controlled (p. 73). An additional characteristic is the frequent intervention of the state in media institutions—and the reverse as well, as media moguls use their outlets and their political connections to influence both policy and public opinion, cultivating strong political ties and gaining access to lucrative state contracts and projects (Hallin & Mancini, 2004, pp. 113–115, 134–135).

Also true of Greece is Hallin and Mancini's (2004) description of media regulation in countries fitting the "polarized pluralist" model. The authors include clientelism as a prevalent characteristic of such countries. Accordingly, adherence to legal norms is typically weaker in these national contexts: powerful actors in the media landscape utilize their political ties to avoid inconvenient regulations or to shape and tailor policy to their interests. A vicious cycle ensues where politicians threaten media owners with selective enforcement of the law while media owners, as well as prominent journalists and media personalities, pressure public officials by threatening to expose corruption and scandals (Hallin & Mancini, 2004, pp. 58–59). Such conditions are reflective of a concept that originates from the field of political science, "capture theory" or "regulatory capture," defined as "the view that regulators are influenced by the interests of the industries they regulate" (Danesi, 2009, p. 54; Etzioni, 2009, pp. 319–320).

Hallin and Mancini characterize the development of the commercial broadcast sector in countries such as Greece as examples of savage deregulation, a term initially introduced by Traquina (1995) to describe the phenomenon in Portugal. Under such conditions, privately owned commercial broadcasting was introduced in an uncontrolled manner, without the imposition of significant public service requirements or other regulations. According to Hallin and Mancini (2004), Greece closely fits this model due to the rapid proliferation of radio and television stations beginning in the late 1980s (p. 125).

Conversely, Vovou (2009) argues that the deregulation of broadcasting in Greece was *not* indicative of savage deregulation, as it occurred not under anarchic conditions but rather as the result of political battles that transpired in Greece during the late 1980s, a time of political instability and frequent changes of government in the country. Similarly, Kogen (2010), in an examination of broadcast deregulation in Greece and Thailand, has argued that the Greek case does *not* represent an example of savage deregulation. Instead, deregulation occurred due to the efforts of civilians and oppositional political actors who were previously excluded from the existing state-run broadcast landscape and who therefore sought a presence on the airwaves in order to fill this gap. Unlike the deregulation that occurred in countries such as Portugal and Italy, Greek deregulation did not take place within a legal framework.

Indeed, the deregulation of broadcasting in Greece was highly politicized from the beginning while the ineffectiveness of any regulations that were passed became immediately evident. The first radio stations that, in 1987, broke the state radio monopoly, were launched by the then mayors of major Greek cities, aligned with the New Democracy party, Greece's main opposition party at the time (Zaharopoulos, 2003, p. 234). This politicization is referred to in Greece as *diaploki*—a uniquely Greek word, defined as the "interplay between media owners and politicians . . . that determines who will influence public opinion and apply pressure in the political arena" (Sims, 2003, p. 203). Professor Alexandros Baltzis of the Aristotle University of Thessaloniki described *diaploki* in this way: "There are two main characteristics of media in Greece. One characteristic is the instability of the legal framework and regulation. The other is the close relation of the most mainstream media with the construction, banking, and shipping sector and with the political parties. This is what we call in Greece *diaploki*" (personal communication, February 23, 2013). For Augustine Zenakos, editor of *Unfollow* magazine, *diaploki* is synonymous with power: "The state in Greece is political power, is judicial power, is a very tight group of financial players that control the vast majority of the sectors of the economy: shipping, construction, mining, tourism.... They're in the hands of perhaps 10 people ... who also own the media" (personal communication, July 19, 2013).

Scholar Georges Contogeorgis of the Panteion University of Social and Political Sciences in Athens describes *diaploki* as a reproduction of the central state and political system: "Without a doubt, the central system reproduces itself at all levels, from local government, to the media, the political parties, the unions, the collectives, everywhere it reproduces itself, specifically its personality-driven and individualist character which produces clientelist politics.... [Broadcasting] is transformed into a space where politics is produced, it is the space where the political system is constructed and where it operates in reality ... determining the agenda, who will be represented, who will speak, who won't speak" (personal communication, December 19, 2016).

Kostas Vaxevanis, publisher of *Hot Doc* magazine, connects the *diaploki* system with the lack of enforceable broadcast regulation:

> The mass media landscape in Greece is anarchic, and this is intentional. It did not emerge as the result of some oversight. In Greece, to operate even a kiosk you need a permit, yet [broadcast] stations are unlicensed. They're illegal, their legal status is renewed each year [by the Parliament] ... and this happens because in this way, a hostage situation develops between the media moguls and the political system. Prior to elections, the government will blackmail ... stations that they will not receive a license, and for the next four years ... stations will blackmail the government as to whether they will provide it with support or not. (personal communication, March 6, 2013)

Following deregulation, a hodgepodge of legislation pertaining to broadcasting was enacted. This legislation was, however, ineffective in curtailing the mushrooming of new municipal and privately owned stations, while the National Radio-Television Council (ESR) was largely invisible during its first decade of existence. What is evident is that privately owned broadcasting was introduced in Greece under conditions not of uncontrolled anarchy but rather of *controlled* "anarchy." This legal vacuum seems to have been intended to create conditions in which vested interests could take advantage of the apparent confusion. Such an environment enabled powerful actors to commence broadcasting either without a license or as the result of tailored legislation. Within this context, such actors would not have to face competition from potentially more qualified applicants who would be discouraged from applying for a license due to the legal uncertainty. As was stated by journalist Nikos Andritsos of Skai 100.3 FM in Athens, "As with many things in Greece, [the broadcast landscape] developed without a specific context.... It developed upon a basis which was not defined by any specific framework, in order for specific standards to be set. This resulted in side effects which impacted the standards of public discourse" (personal communication, April 12, 2013). Ioannis Adamidis, an editor at co-owned Greek national broadcaster Skai TV, added, "The mass media in Greece developed in a paradoxical and illogical manner... the process was a bit backward. It began initially with radio. First the radio stations opened and then the law followed, and even then it was not fully enforced" (personal communication, April 10, 2013).

As described above, the radio stations came on the air first and the law followed, a clear example of "regulatory capture." Though comprehensive legislation governing broadcasting was passed in 1995 (Nomos 2328/1995, 1995) and 2007 (Nomos 3592/2007, 2007), these laws have only been partially enforced, as have been FM frequency allocation tables published in 1991, 1999, and 2008 (Nevradakis, 2014a). It was under the 1995 law that the only two instances of radio licensing tenders—the 2001 and 2002 bids for Athens-area licenses—were completed, generating great controversy and a sharp and likely unjustifiable reduction in the number of stations permitted to operate, on technical grounds. Furthermore, the licenses issued in 2001 expired in 2005, while the licenses issued in 2002 were invalidated by Greece's Council of State—the country's highest administrative court—in 2004 (Nevradakis, 2012, p. 137).

The aforementioned "permanent provisionality" of the Greek radio landscape is perhaps best embodied by law 2778/1999, which was passed in an effort to curtail the continued proliferation of radio stations (Nomos 2778/1999, 1999). This piece of "photographic" legislation legalized the stations that were on the air as of November 1, 1999 and which had previously submitted an application for a broadcast license. As of 2019, this law continues to provide the legal umbrella under which most radio stations nationwide—save for the Athens region—operate (Nevradakis, 2012, p. 132). Several stations are legalized each year under this "temporary" law, two decades after its passage. A similar piece of legislation, law 3310/2005 (Nomos 3310/2005, 2005), legalized all radio stations that were broadcasting without a license in Athens on December 31, 2004, as long as they were operating under the same name and same ownership as they were prior to being shut down in 2001 and with the precondition that they had previously applied for a license (Nevradakis, 2012, p. 137). Legalization falls under the purview of the ESR, which finally gained some tangible legal authority in 2001 following that year's constitutional revision (Kalogirou & Sourpi, 2006, p. 102).

Nevertheless, the ESR's ability to regulate the airwaves was, for a time, severely curtailed, as for much of 2015 and 2016 it remained inactive due to the expired terms of its members, resulting in an enormous backlog of cases. Indeed, some members' terms had expired years earlier, but until 2015 they remained in their positions while the ESR continued to issue regulatory decisions. This was despite two rulings of the Council of State that found this practice to be unconstitutional and called into question the validity of the decisions reached by the ESR during the period when some of its members' terms had already ended (Nevradakis, 2014a).

## The Broadcast Radio Landscape Today

Few aspects of the most recent comprehensive broadcasting law, 3592/2007, have come into effect, though the portions of the law that have been enforced have had a significant impact on the Greek radio landscape. One such impact is a marked increase in the concentration of ownership. The 2007 legislation formally allowed one entity to own multiple radio stations, a practice that had previously been done only by a few media moguls via proxies. A buying spree commenced, particularly in the years immediately preceding the onset of the Greek economic crisis, though the process of concentration has continued to the present time, with the ownership of radio stations transferring to a smaller number of industry players. Incumbent groups represent one set of beneficiaries of this change, but recently upstart groups such as Frontstage, which has acquired four stations in Athens, and 24 Media, with two stations in Athens, have also entered the marketplace (Alexandra Daskalopoulou, 2018). In Thessaloniki and in provincial cities, smaller media conglomerates have developed in recent years, in some cases establishing regional "franchises"—radio stations with the same format and branding operating in different markets—a first for the Greek radio industry. Nevertheless, the aforementioned purchasing spree drove many of these entities into unsustainable debt and eventual bankruptcy, as was the case with the Lymberis Media Group and the two radio stations it operated in Athens, one of which (VFM) has never returned to the airwaves (Nevradakis, 2014b, 2017a).

Another notable aspect of the 2007 law is the preferential treatment it afforded to radio and television stations that have been classified as "news stations" as opposed to "entertainment stations." Stations were mandated to classify themselves as one or the other, and face different legal obligations based on their categorization. For instance, "news stations" are required to employ a minimum number of journalists (Nomos 3592/2007, 2007). More significantly though, a 2014 law allowed "news stations" to change their classification to "entertainment" simply by submitting an application to the ESR. However, "entertainment stations" are not permitted under this law to change their classification to "news." In effect, this has created a closed broadcast news marketplace, and "entertainment stations" that have aired news programming have been fined (Nevradakis,

2014a). As a result of this law and the lack of opportunity to apply for a new license, the only way a potential broadcaster who wishes to air news programming can gain access to the airwaves is by purchasing an existing station and taking a risk that this station will be licensed if and when a bid is announced in the future. Furthermore, the limited number of "news stations" means that the purchase price of such stations is likely to be inflated, limiting the range of potential buyers to those with the deepest pockets.

Reflecting the rampant politicization of the media landscape that continues to this day, law 3592/2007 contains a provision—perhaps uniquely Greek—allowing radio and television stations owned by political parties with parliamentary representation to operate without a formal license. Two stations have been legalized under this provision: Sto Kokkino 105.5 FM in Athens, owned by the SYRIZA political party, which co-governed Greece between January 2015 and June 2019, and ART FM of the Popular Orthodox Rally (LAOS) political party. LAOS is no longer represented in either the Greek or the European parliament, but ART FM nevertheless remains on the air to this day (Nevradakis, 2014a).

Law 3592/2007 also included limited provisions for noncommercial broadcasting, specifically on the part of institutions of higher education. However, no clause for community or LPFM broadcasting exists in the law or in any other piece of legislation governing radio, while the number of stations that could be classified as such in Greece as a result of their programming or organizational structure is small (Nevradakis, 2017a). In an interesting contrast, while there is no coherent framework for noncommercial broadcasting, the *diaploki* system ensures that numerous commercial radio stations operate on a de facto "nonprofit" basis in that they are not financially viable nor intended to be, instead existing to serve the other political and business interests of their owners.

Further contributing to the regulatory troubles governing the radio landscape is the uncertainty surrounding the country's music licensing bodies. AEPI, the organization representing composers, authors, heirs, and music publishers, was dissolved in May 2018 following an investigation into impropriety within the organization. A new entity is legally obliged to be established by 2020 ("Anaklisi," 2018; Kanellopoulos & Psara, 2017). In recent years a new organization, GEA, representing musicians and singers, has also been established, and radio stations have been obligated to pay significant sums to both GEA and AEPI in order to legally air copyrighted musical works. In the midst of the economic crisis and declining advertising revenues, this has placed a heavy financial burden on radio stations. For instance, in 2010 Skai 100.3 FM ceased broadcasting copyrighted music due to high music licensing fees ("Skai," 2010), before later reinstating such music into its programming. The allegations against AEPI and its subsequent dissolution have created an uncertain environment for radio stations regarding their compliance with music licensing, and this has resulted in legal disputes. For example, a 2018 regional court ruling absolved a radio station in the city of Lamia from paying music licensing fees to AEPI ("Apofasi-stathmos," 2018).

Finally, even the ESR, despite a new slate of members who were appointed in 2016, may still be operating afoul of the law. Until his recent passing, the body's vice president, Rodolfos Moronis, was serving in his third (albeit nonconsecutive) term, although members are constitutionally limited to two terms. Nevertheless, his presence on the ESR was never challenged legally, nor were the decisions adopted by the body during this period ever disputed (Nevradakis, 2017a).

## Why Such Regulatory Sclerosis?

Explanations for the regulatory inertia that characterizes radio and broadcasting in Greece can be found in Greece's political and social history. According to Hallin and Mancini (2004), the development of a "polarized pluralist" media landscape is the result of the delayed development of liberal market institutions in Southern Europe and the ensuing importance of patronage and personal relationships (pp. 135–137). These countries were the last to transition to liberal democracy in Western Europe. Consequently, freedom of the press and the development of commercial media generally arrived later. Hallin and Mancini (2004) point out that the late development of liberal institutions in such countries is closely connected to the high degree of clientelism and the relatively slow emergence of rational-legal authority alongside a high degree of political parallelism, where the media system tends to parallel the political party system. Since the state is such an important actor in the economy due to the delayed development of market institutions, the media becomes a battleground for influence and for preferential access to state contracts, subsidies, relaxed regulations, and other advantages (pp. 135–136).

Contogeorgis (2013), in turn, argues that clientelism in Greece—within and beyond the media realm—serves the interest of party loyalists and specific interest groups, instead of targeting the society as a whole. He describes the clientelist system as one that has existed since the earliest days of the modern Greek state and a phenomenon that is the norm, not the exception, at the present time and a defining feature of the relationship between politics and society (pp. 55–56, 85). Contogeorgis further argues that Greece's partisan system has taken ownership of the political system and transformed public discourse into private discourse (Contogeorgis, 2012, p. 53).

According to journalist Aggeliki Boubouka, "The space of public discourse [in Greece] was very strictly constructed traditionally. It was controlled by the hegemonic powers in society, meaning political, economic, and business interests... much more so than in most other European countries" (personal communication, May 31, 2013). Similarly, Tasos Oikonomou, a journalist with the *Kathimerini* newspaper, stated, "[Pre-crisis] things were rather entrenched. The public sphere consisted of citizens acting within political parties, identifying with political parties . . . reflecting the positions of political parties in the public dialogue or being represented in the public dialogue via the positions of the political parties, in the press, the television stations, the radio stations. Pre-2008 where did the public sphere exist? Nowhere outside of the mass media" (personal communication, April 10, 2013).

A credibility crisis often results within such environments. This could be said to be the case in Greece, as evidenced by survey data that indicate particularly low levels of trust in journalists and the news media, and an extremely strong perception that the media are free of neither political nor economic influence. For instance, in the 2016 Reuters Institute report on digital news consumption, Greece was the country with the lowest levels of trust in mainstream news media across the twenty-six countries surveyed: only 20 percent of respondents in Greece said that they trusted the news media, 16 percent stated that they trust the mass media in general, 11 percent trusted journalists, 7 percent of respondents felt that the news media were independent of political influence, and 5 percent believed that the news media were free of influence from economic interests (Kalogeropoulos, Panagiotou, & Dimitrakopoulou, 2016, pp. 35–36). Similarly, in Eurobarometer's (2015) survey, Greece had the fifth lowest trust in the media overall (49 percent with low or no trust) and lowest level of trust in the EU for radio (37 percent). Low levels of trust in the mass media were also reflected in a Kapa Research survey conducted in October 2016, with only 6.5 percent of respondents stating that they trusted the mass media, a decline of 22 percent since 2003 (Kapa Research, 2016, p. 6).

Reflecting this sentiment, journalist Paris Karvounopoulos connects *diaploki* with the credibility crisis suffered by the mass media in Greece: "There is a huge credibility crisis, which is due to the fact that the citizens have become convinced, for years now, that the news and information they receive is part of the 'diaploki' system, which . . . they consider primarily responsible for the situation the country is in" (personal communication, June 28, 2013).

## What Has Changed?

Undoubtedly the biggest development in the Greek broadcasting landscape in recent years was the shutdown (and subsequent reestablishment) of national public broadcaster ERT. The sudden closure of ERT by the then government on June 11, 2013, serves as an emblematic example of the heavy-handed yet spasmodic government regulation of broadcasting in Greece (Psychogiopoulou & Kandyla, 2013, p. 142). The shutdown was justified by citing low ratings, corruption, waste, partisanship, and a lack of transparency (Nevradakis, 2014c). This action took ERT's five nationwide radio services, its regional radio stations, its shortwave transmitters, most of its medium-wave transmitters, and its online webcasts off the air (Nevradakis, 2014c).

ERT was initially replaced by an interim state-run broadcaster and later by a new, trimmed-down entity, NERIT, which nevertheless was beset by many of the same structural and operational problems as ERT (Iosifidis & Katsirea, 2015, p. 6). After the SYRIZA-led coalition government entered office in January 2015, ERT was reopened, but it again replicated the same anomalies, such as lack of independence from the state, as those of NERIT (Papathanassopoulos, 2015, p. 473). Furthermore, its radio services have never been fully reinstated, as its domestic foreign-language service was eliminated, most medium-wave transmitters were never restored, and shortwave broadcasts and regional programming were curtailed. Despite the role of many public service broadcasters in promoting domestic culture, ERT has no radio channel devoted exclusively to Greek music (while its *Kosmos* station solely airs world music), whilst coverage of "Europe" is emphasized, at levels perhaps disproportionately high compared to audience interest in such topics. This is likely reflective of government meddling. ERT, in the view of Vasilis Vasilopoulos, head of its multimedia department, "has not managed to become a public broadcaster in the ideal sense of the term . . . but it is not a state broadcaster" (personal communication, August 22, 2017).

As previously mentioned, recent years have also seen an increase in ownership concentration in the radio landscape. One of the developments associated with the increase in concentration is the entry of new media moguls into the radio marketplace, such as Dimitris Maris of 24 Media (Nevradakis, 2017b), signifying a reproduction of the existing system with new faces. At the other end of the spectrum, the aforementioned law 3592/2007 permitted the unpaid employees of radio stations that have gone bankrupt or run into financial difficulty to file a claim with the ESR, which would allow them to inherit the entity's broadcast permit (such as it is presently) and self-manage the station (Nomos 3592/2007, 2007). Employees at several stations in Athens, such as Best 92.6 FM of the bankrupt Lymberis Media Group, former leading news station Flash 96 FM, Nitro Radio 102.5 FM of the bankrupt IMAKO media group, and Xenios 94.3 FM, formerly of the Athens-area municipality of Ano Liosia, were able to successfully apply for self-management. In most cases, however, these stations were then absorbed by larger entities under leased management agreements: Nitro Radio, for instance, is now managed by the *Athens Voice* weekly free newspaper and has rebranded as Athens Voice Radio, while Best 92.6 is managed by the Star TV group. Flash 96, in turn, has gone off the air and its frequency commandeered by pirate stations, while Xenios FM has seen a revolving "musical chairs" of formats and name changes ever since its return to the airwaves—it now operates as Ellada FM—and has even collaborated with a pirate station (Nevradakis, 2017a). The employees at news station Vima FM 99.5, formerly of the powerhouse Lambrakis Press Group, which itself went bankrupt and was absorbed by oligarch Vangelis Marinakis (owner of Parapolitika 90.1 FM), seemingly have not even bothered with the process of applying for self-management. Since the

Marinakis takeover, the station has gone silent and its legality has been stripped ("Epistrefei," 2018). Its frequency is now occupied by a pirate station. In 2017, the previous government, despite its supposed left-wing orientation, announced that it was considering rescinding the legal clause allowing self-management ("E kivernisi," 2017).

In recent years, the haphazard legal framework has also resulted in numerous ex post facto "legalizations" of various radio stations, sometimes under dubious circumstances, even if their original shutdown (particularly those stations who were shuttered as a result of the 2001 and 2002 licensing processes in Athens) was itself questionable. In one instance, radio station Irodotos FM (now known as Nostos 100.6 FM) was legalized after it claimed it operated for four months that encompassed the December 31, 2004 date, even though the station, in its application, allegedly used the paperwork of another station that was licensed in the 2002 bid. In another case, Hristianismos FM, which was shut down after not being licensed in 2001 and 2002 and which in 2012 won a legal appeal against its closure, was finally issued an FM frequency in 2018 by the ESR. It then faced interference from pirates operating on the same frequency for the first few months of its return. Hot FM, which had been legalized under the aforementioned law 3310/2005 in 2007 but was shut down in 2010 after having reached second place in the Athens-area audience ratings (Nevradakis, 2012, p. 137), successfully appealed its decision and reopened in 2013, broadcasting without a name or advertisements for three years before the frequency was leased to another broadcaster. Atlantis FM, another station shut down in 2001 but which returned to the airwaves as a pirate before securing, in 2008, a court order prohibiting its closure, was finally legalized by the ESR in 2018 under the auspices of the 2005 law ("Dikaioma," 2018). This station—based in the port city of Piraeus, which comprises part of the Athens metropolis—was, for several years, affiliated with the Chinese-owned *GB Times* news service. Notably, Piraeus is home to significant Chinese financial interests, namely the port of Piraeus, which has been fully privatized and sold to Chinese-owned Cosco. After the *GB Times* affiliation was pulled from Atlantis FM, it moved to pirate radio station Astro FM, also based in Piraeus. Astro FM was one of the stations that had been shut down in 2001 but later reopened without a license. Following this change, rumors have circulated that Astro FM—now renamed Smooth 99.8—is in line to be legalized under the 2005 law ("Kainourios," 2018). Overall, even though in 2001 the government claimed that only twenty (and later twenty-eight, and later thirty-five) privately owned radio stations could operate in Athens without interfering with the aviation frequencies used by the city's then-new international airport, today forty-six privately owned radio stations have managed to secure the legal right to operate on the FM dial in Athens, in addition to at least three stations from adjacent regions with temporary permits of legality—and numerous pirates, some of which can be legalized at any time (Ethniko Symboulio Radiotileorasis, 2018).

In Athens and the rest of Greece, the economic crisis of the past decade has, as with other sectors of the economy, taken its toll on the radio industry. Dozens, perhaps hundreds, of radio stations have gone off the air throughout Greece in the preceding years. In some cases, the temporary permits of legality or (expired) licenses these stations possessed have been formally rescinded by the ESR. When this occurs, no legal provision exists for the frequency to be issued to any other party. Accordingly, recent years have seen a marked reduction in the total number of radio stations operating in Greece. Other stations have been placed at risk of running afoul of the law as a result of frequent and seemingly senseless changes in the regulations, often issued and then rescinded by ministerial decree. One such example has to do with permitting radio stations to operate from more than one transmitter site in their designated coverage area—a necessity for many stations considering Greece's mountainous terrain and numerous islands. This practice was formally prohibited until 2013 and has since been legalized, reversed, and reinstated on several occasions, creating headaches for stations that have invested in infrastructure to expand their signal, only to later be told they were again operating outside legal boundaries ("Radio Kriti," 2017). Many islands and rural areas of Greece have been left without domestic radio coverage as a result.

What should be evident is that in Greece's radio sector there is a very fine line between what is legal and what is not, a line that can shift at any time and under the flimsiest of pretexts. With numerous stations having been "legalized" after operating illegally, there is no incentive for pirate operators to cease their broadcasts. Furthermore, stations operating with the degree of legality which the current system provides are at risk of being shut down at any time for a multitude of reasons. It is here where many believe that digital broadcasting offers both radio stations and the Greek state an opportunity at a fresh start, a chance to right old wrongs and to develop a new legal framework that would govern digital radio without the pathologies of the analog-only era.

Interestingly, turning back to Hallin and Mancini (2016), the two authors have revisited their comparative models of media systems, highlighting the persistence of these models despite widespread predictions of a convergence toward the "liberal" model in the digital age. Replication of the existing system was discussed as one possibility, while other possibilities were that national online media might converge with global economic and media systems and undermine national media systems, or that they might remain nationally rooted while becoming distinct from the incumbent national media model (Hallin & Mancini, 2016, pp. 162–165).

## Digital Radio in Greece

It is likely that the Greek state has largely given up on explicitly regulating the analog FM landscape, while many have argued that digital radio can fill gaps that exist in the present-day radio landscape, such as providing a framework for noncommercial and community broadcasters. Reality, though, highlights a different story: until recently, no legal framework for digital audio broadcasting (DAB) existed in Greece, nor were there any such broadcasts.

This is not due to a lack of effort or interest. In 2004, just prior to the Summer Olympic Games, Kiss FM inaugurated experimental DAB transmissions in Athens (Kiss FM 92.9, 2004). This broadcast was promptly shut down by the authorities for operating illegally. In 2006, Kiss FM collaborated with the Technical Educational Institute of Piraeus to launch an experimental DAB signal, though this initiative was short-lived ("Xekina," 2006). The Technical Educational Institute of Piraeus followed up with further experimental broadcasts in 2009 (Bakogiannis, 2009). Since then, no known DAB broadcasts existed until 2018 as a result of the legal void, while the penetration of digital receivers in the Greek market remains at extremely low levels.

It was the relaunched ERT that brought digital radio back to the Greek airwaves, introducing experimental DAB+ broadcasts on channel 12C in Athens in January 2018 following ministerial decision 170/2018, featuring all of ERT's national radio services, plus audio of the parliamentary television station ("Dokimastikes," 2018; "Ypourgiki Apofasi," 2018). Broadcasts initially began from the primary transmission point for the Athens region, Mount Imitos, at low power (300 watts), and were soon launched from the city's secondary transmission point, Mount Parnitha (also on channel 12C) and from Mount Geraneia, outside of Athens, on channel 9C and at very low power (90 watts). In the first half of 2018, ERT's DAB test broadcasts were also launched in Thessaloniki via the city's secondary transmission point (Filippeio) on channel 5C, in the city of Patra on channel 7A from Mount Panahaiko, and in the city of Tripoli on channel 10C from Mount Assea. Reportedly, ERT utilized decommissioned VHF television antennas from the analog era, which were connected to new DAB transmitters. However, these digital broadcasts have barely been promoted by ERT, if at all. Since 2006, ERT's radio services are also available via its terrestrial digital television multiplex, a privilege Greek law does not afford to private broadcasters.

Some private broadcasters also launched experimental DAB transmissions in the first half of 2018. The most notable example comes from the city of Thessaloniki, which was also the city where Greece's first-ever radio station *and* first-ever television station were launched. A local engineering firm, Sigmacom Broadcasting, obtained a temporary license from the Hellenic Commission of Telecommunications and Post (EETT) to begin test broadcasts on channel 12B. These broadcasts operated between February and May 2018 and featured a rotating lineup of FM radio stations from Thessaloniki and the surrounding region, including Energy 88.3 (from the nearby city of Veria), Rainbow 89 FM, Arena 89.4 FM, Yellow Radio 92.8, Radio Thessaloniki 94.5, Cosmoradio 95.1 FM, Metropolis 95.5, Radio Ekrixi 99.8 FM, FM 100 (municipally owned), Kalamaria

FM 101.7, Plus Radio 102.6, More Radio 103.0, Fly 104.0, Praktoreio 104.9 FM, Rock 105.5 FM, Libero 107.4 FM. An online station, CityFaces, was also part of the lineup.

In June and July 2018, privately operated experimental DAB broadcasts also arrived in Athens, via an operator known as Digital Power, which was reportedly affiliated with a major FM radio station and received a temporary license from the EETT. Digital Power broadcast four separate music streams via its transmission, which operated on channel 11A from Mount Imitos. In early 2018, a group of privately owned radio stations in the city of Patra also launched short-lived experimental DAB broadcasts.

In January 2018, Greece's parliament passed, for the first time, legislation governing digital radio broadcasting. Law 4512/2018 includes a timeline for the licensing of the entity that will build and operate the national network of digital transmitters, as well as for the licensing of broadcasters themselves ("Tmima," 2018). The law also hints at the future possibility of a full digital switchover and abandonment of analog FM broadcasting, even though a firm deadline was not established ("Psifistike," 2018). Several days after the legislation was passed, an accompanying national frequency allocations table was publicized, including a provision for some privately owned broadcasters to receive national licenses, which were never foreseen for analog FM broadcasting. As was the case with television, local broadcasting is also eliminated in favor of "regional" stations ("Neos hartis," 2018). Should this change come to fruition, it will ignore radio's ability to provide localism and which will likely raise the cost of leasing a digital channel, perhaps to levels which are prohibitive for smaller local broadcasters. It is unclear how many of today's FM broadcasters would be legally permitted to make the switch to digital broadcasting or if they will receive preferential treatment in a future licensing bid, essentially replicating the existing FM band in the new digital environment. Nevertheless, and consistent with historical precedent, delays have already been noted in the digital radio licensing process, as only two entities submitted bids to operate digital radio transmission facilities in a licensing tender issued in early 2018. Their applications were deemed unsuitable and the initial bid was scrapped, with no clear indication as to when a new tender will be announced ("Kathisterei," 2018). Furthermore, reflecting the still-politicized nature of broadcasting and of media regulation in Greece, the new legislation governing digital radio was met with opposition by municipally owned radio stations, who have requested that they be exempted from the law, a position supported by the journalists' union of Athens (ESIEA) ("ESIEA," 2018).

Satellite radio likewise has hardly taken off in Greece. While two subscription-based satellite television services, Nova and Cosmote TV, offer some limited radio options, stand-alone satellite radio has never been launched in Greece. Furthermore, few Greek radio stations offer free-to-air satellite broadcasts of their programming ("Free Radio," 2019). This is despite the fact that Greece and Cyprus have jointly been allocated the 39°E orbital position, which is home to

Hellas Sat. Few Greek broadcast services utilize this "Greek" satellite, limited as of August 2019 to the Greek and Cypriot public broadcasters ("Hellas Sat 2/3," 2019). Indeed, the Hellas Sat consortium was sold in 2013 by the legacy Greek telecommunications giant OTE (itself owned by Deutsche Telekom) to Arab-Sat ("OTE," 2013).

On the other hand, online radio can be said to have boomed in Greece. Internet radio broadcasts from Greek radio stations date back at least to 1995, and today practically all of the country's FM radio stations, including all of ERT's radio services, plus thousands of online-only radio stations are in operation. Several major online radio portals, such as e-radio.gr, live24.gr, onradio.gr, and media.net.gr (operated by this author) are also in operation. The websites of Sport FM and sport24.gr (which encompasses Sport 24 Radio) rank in Alexa's top fifty most visited Greek websites as of the time of this writing, while skai.gr, athensvoice.gr, real.gr (encompassing Real FM), plus the e-radio.gr and live24.gr portals are included in Alexa's top hundred most visited websites operating within the .gr top-level domain ("Top Greek Sites," 2019; "Top Sites," 2019). Relatively few FM broadcasters have eschewed online webcasting, though a few radio stations have in past years ceased streaming as a result of music licensing fees levied by actors such as AEPI, such as Radio Enigma in the town of Florina ("To exontotiko," 2007). In an ironic twist of fate though, Radio Enigma ceased its FM broadcasts in October 2017, continuing exclusively as an online radio station (Radio Enigma, 2017).

Notably, despite the relatively low Internet penetration rate in Greece, which according to Eurostat (2018) was at 71 percent in 2018, ranking twenty-seventh out of twenty-eight EU members, Greece ranked first in the usage of online radio stations, while Greece ranked higher than the EU average in the usage of music-sharing websites and in accessing music in a digital/electronic format (European Commission, 2016). The keyword here, however, may be "music." A review of online radio portals shows that there exists a dearth of online-only radio stations that provide news and talk programming. Indeed, the vast majority of online-only radio stations feature musically oriented formats.

In recent years, a notable exception to this trend was an online station known as Radiobubble. Founded in 2007, just prior to the onset of the economic crisis, and initially operating from the residence of one of its founders, Radiobubble soon became known for its central Athens studio space, which doubled as a café, and for its "alternative" news and talk programming and its accompanying presence on social media, particularly Twitter.

Dora Oikonomides, a volunteer with Radiobubble, described the station as such:

> Radiobubble is a very strange animal in Greece, because it is an online community essentially. Radiobubble as a whole has many components. One of it is the news component, which I contribute to, there is one part which is about

music. . . . One part is blogs, where basically there is a team of people monitoring the Greek bloggers here and selecting what they find interesting. There is one section called "the community," where anyone can choose to create a radio show or a podcast and upload it to that section. The idea overall is user-generated content. (personal communication, December 17, 2012)

Panagiotis Oikonomou, a producer with Radiobubble, described the station as a second chance to create what is known in Greece as "free radio," as deregulated FM radio was known in its early years: "With the advent of privately-owned radio, the frequencies were taken over by certain businesspeople and 'free radio' could not develop. We've made an attempt, through the opportunity provided to us by new media, to establish a free Internet radio station," adding his belief that "traditional radio in Greece is dead" (personal communication, February 13, 2013). Regarding the station's programming, Oikonomides stated that "the basic rule is that there is no rule." The station imposed no editorial policy or musical restrictions. As stated by Oikonomides, "You have anything, from jazz, to Greek music, to Rock 'n' Roll, to Reggae, to anything you can imagine" (personal communication, December 17, 2012). As described by Radiobubble volunteer Petros Papathanasiou, "Producers have full freedom as to what they want to do. The station intentionally maintains an amateur feel. Even producers who are professionals maintain this amateurism" (personal communication, December 17, 2012).

For years though, the centerpiece of Radiobubble's programming was its news output, which acted as an alternative to mainstream news sources, especially in the midst of the Greek economic crisis. Papathanasiou outlined Radiobubble's news philosophy: "The news department does not invite political figures. Systematically though we invite ordinary people, people who are involved in activism, people who are involved in the health or education sectors, and we prefer to speak to them even about politics, rather than with government representatives" (personal communication, December 17, 2012).

Oikonomou, highlighting Radiobubble's achievements in the realm of news programming, said that it was the only radio station in Greece to provide full coverage of Barack Obama's reelection in 2012 and noted the station's connection with civil society, supporting via its newscasts initiatives such as food drives and the Gaza Flotilla while "using social media to create a social radio" (personal communication, February 13, 2013). Maria Kadoglou, founder of an activist initiative known as Antigold Greece, which opposes controversial gold mining activities in the Skouries region in the north of the country, stated that Radiobubble was one of the first two media outlets in Greece to draw attention to the cause (personal communication, July 4, 2013). Noting this activity, Oikonomides stated that Radiobubble earned a strong leftist reputation as a result of its news programming, but argued that the station welcomed other viewpoints: "We would like to have a bigger diversity of opinions to be presented here than what we already have" (personal communication, December 17, 2012).

Radiobubble's news programming was closely associated with the station's social media presence. According to Papathanasiou, in the midst of the riots transpiring in Athens in December 2008 following the shooting death of fifteen-year-old Alexandros Grigoropoulos by a police officer, the station's #rbnews Twitter hashtag was born, with immediate impact. Papathanasiou stated that "an ecosystem developed surrounding this hashtag, through which the individuals appeared who developed our news department" (personal communication, December 17, 2012). News posted via the #rbnews hashtag was cross-checked and curated by the Radiobubble news team prior to being reported on the air. Oikonomides cited #rbnews as the news department's most powerful tool: "The purpose of that hashtag is for people out there in the streets to be able to tweet information about important things that are happening in Greece: if there are demonstrations, if there is an important event in your neighborhood. Contributors to the hashtag [are] people from Radiobubble . . . but also people who might tweet using that hashtag once a year. . . . The hashtag is a relatively well-known and respected institution on Greek Twitter." (personal communication, December 17, 2012). The #rbnews feed even captured the interest of the *Guardian* before Greece's June 2012 follow-up parliamentary elections, after no winner emerged from the May 2012 polls: "The most interesting example was during the second elections in June [2012], when *The Guardian* bought our English language Twitter feed and embedded it in their live blog for two days, because they knew that after following it for so long, that it was a reliable source of information . . . we had already done the work verifying everything that is there" (personal communication, December 17, 2012). Radiobubble volunteer Panos Kounenakis noted that #rbnews was the most widely used hashtag in Greece in 2011 due to its prominence during the widespread "Indignants" protest movement (personal communication, June 13, 2017).

The Radiobubble café space in central Athens served as a hub for producers, activists, and listeners, as the studio was openly visible and accessible to the public. Christina Lardikou, a producer with Radiobubble and volunteer with the associated Tutorpool initiative, described the café as an advantage for Radiobubble: "You can hang around here, you can have your show, you can listen [to the station], but if you want, you can also come here and drink a coffee and be here . . . it's not something that is only in the Internet" (personal communication, February 20, 2013). Several civil society initiatives were borne out of the station's programming and its physical space, including Tutorpool, which used social media to connect volunteer tutors with families who could not afford paid tutoring for their children, and Hackademy, a training program for journalists on radio production and new media use. In highlighting Radiobubble's contributions to civil society and public discourse in Greece, Oikonomou characterized the Greek public sphere as a "televisual democracy... operating in lieu of the public," adding that society is closer to the rhetoric expressed on alternative mediums such as Radiobubble (personal communication, February 13, 2013).

According to Papathanasiou, anyone could produce a program as long as they loved radio and were willing to commit to a schedule (personal communication, December 17, 2012). Kounenakis described how he was able to join the station from afar: "I started my [radio show]... while I was in South Korea. I started back in 2009, remotely uploading shows, and in 2011 when I came back in Greece, I got to know the people and I started being more active in the community" (personal communication, June 13, 2017). Overall, the station averaged four thousand listeners per month as of late 2012 according to Oikonomides. Total listening hours ranged between seventy and ninety thousand hours per month (personal communication, December 17, 2012).

The station's visibility and the news programming that helped make it distinct did not last. Two major changes that occurred in recent years were the shutdown of the Radiobubble café and relocation of the studio to a less visible site inside a theater, and the restructuring of the station as a legally registered cooperative, after which a significant number of staffers departed. As a result, emphasis shifted away from news and Twitter, in favor of music and culture. Kounenakis described the station's adaptation of Mixcloud for asynchronous broadcasting: "We are looking for new ways. Mixcloud is one of these tools that we think it is the future, which is free, open. It's a broadcast that you can use it any time" (personal communication, June 13, 2017). As described by Radiobubble volunteer Ioanna Paraskevopoulou, "There is a greater emphasis being placed on radio rather than Twitter," adding that "radio was always the heart of Radiobubble. It was never social media, even if this impression always existed because it became widely known on Twitter" (personal communication, February 2, 2015).

Another example of online broadcasting with a news-based orientation is that of ERT Open, the protest station that emerged out of the shutdown of ERT in 2013. Operating out of occupied ERT facilities in Athens and Thessaloniki and later out of the offices of ERT's administrative employee union, ERT Open initially had access to a significant portion of ERT's network of transmitters. However, the heart of its operations was the Internet, where it streamed radio and television programming continuously until ERT was relaunched in 2015. ERT Open featured programming that likely never would have been aired on the official ERT, including live newscasts free of state oversight, and roundtable discussions with activists, bloggers, representatives of worker-run collectives, and economists presenting alternatives to austerity.

Today, ERT Open remains on the air in Athens as a union-run radio station, utilizing ERT's Mount Parnitha transmission facilities and a frequency (106.7 FM) allocated to ERT, even if the station's legal status is dubious. Its signal does not effectively cover all of Athens, however, and as such its online stream remains central to the station's operations. Vasilopoulos notes that ERT Open is managed by administrative and technical staff of ERT and "provides an alternative voice" (personal communication, August 22, 2017), while Aris Tolios, a member of the political council of the Popular Unity political party, described ERT Open as "the greatest achievement [of the protest movement] . . . embraced by pretty much every party, every political organization of the left spectrum . . . and by grassroots movements in general" (personal communication, February 22, 2017).

Another notable online-only station that features some live news, talk programming, and a large air staff is NGradio.gr (New Generation Radio), which also maintains a deep archive of interviews and audiovisual content on its website. The station's air staff are mostly in their twenties, and the station maintains a professional appearance despite operating out of a basement apartment in the Athens suburb of Glyfada. Certain political parties, ranging from the former parliamentary party To Potami ("The River") via its Potami Web Radio service, to the extra-parliamentary EPAM ("United People's Front") via the e-roi.gr web radio station, also maintain an online radio presence. However, the quantity and consistency of live broadcasts and the availability of programming that is archived digitally varies. Some highly professional music-oriented web radio efforts have also launched, including offradio.gr, joinradio.gr, and boemradio.com, which maintain a live air staff throughout the day. Other stations though have not been as successful. For instance, idradio.gr, a station that emphasized live interviews and programming oriented toward social issues and civil society, has ceased operating. Prominent online music station Mango Radio has also stopped operating, despite sponsorship from Vodafone's "CU" pay-as-you-go mobile phone service. Even Hot FM, at one time the top-rated FM music station in Athens prior to facing legal tumult, operated as a web radio station during the 2010–2013 period that is its certificate of legality for FM broadcasting was rescinded, and again beginning in 2016 when the station's FM frequency was leased. As of 2018 though, Hot FM's online website had vanished, although the station continues to stream via major web radio portals. Athens International Radio, launched with a "temporary" permit during the 2004 Olympics and operated by the Municipality of Athens, also moved online after its FM signal was shut down by the authorities in 2010—but has since ceased operations. Conversely, some terrestrial radio broadcasters, such as Easy 97.2 FM and Rythmos 94.9 FM of the Antenna Group, have invested in the creation of niche online radio stations, which serve to complement their FM offerings and have similar branding as their on-air counterparts. For instance, Easy 97.2 has launched "Easy Rock," "Easy 80s," and "Easy Love Ballads" ("Web Radios," 2019).

Notably, podcasting is not particularly widespread in Greece. This is not due to a lack of demand. According to the Reuters Institute Digital News Report 2019, 36 percent of Greeks polled stated they had listened to a podcast in the preceding month, mirroring the overall average among the countries included in the sample (Newman et al., 2019, pp. 61, 88). Nevertheless, most major broadcasters, including ERT, have not yet embraced this technology. Instead, YouTube is a preferred method for disseminating archived radio programming. A review of the top hundred podcasts in the Greek iTunes store in August 2019 revealed that the most popular podcasts in Greece are non-Greek. Prominent exceptions include podcasts produced by major Greek broadcasters such as Skai 100.3 FM, Real FM 97.8, and Easy 97.2 FM, as well as by online radio station offradio.gr, independent journalist Aris Chatzistefanou, political figures such as former prime minister George Papandreou, and offerings from independent producers.

## Online Replication of the Offline Media System?

In their recent, revised look at comparative models of media systems, Hallin and Mancini (2016) warned that replication of the incumbent media system in the digital world is one of three possibilities going forward, as national media systems continue the digital transition. This possibility is thus far emerging as the new digital reality in Greece.

The primary reason for this is the same issue that has plagued the analog broadcast environment ever since deregulation: regulatory sclerosis and haphazard, uneven policy making and enforcement. The previous legal framework in Greece governing radio broadcasting did not make accommodations for digital radio, recently passed legislation has yet to be implemented, with no firm timeline in place for its implementation. As a result, only ERT has officially launched DAB+ broadcasts as of this writing—and only on a limited basis.

Interestingly, one key distinction with the deregulation of analog broadcasting in the late 1980s in Greece is that there has not been an anarchic "land grab" of vacant frequencies. This is likely due to the very low penetration of digital radio receivers in Greece and the familiarity and ease of using FM radio by both listeners and broadcasters alike. Therefore, while pirate broadcasts remain widespread, they remain confined to the analog FM and medium-wave bands.

Nevertheless, this regulatory sclerosis may be hastening broadcast radio's decline in Greece. As seen earlier, online radio in Greece, at least as a source of *music*, is more popular in Greece as compared to other EU member states. But even in the online realm, there is a great degree of replication with the offline world: despite a large number of web-only music stations, existing FM broadcasters remain key players online. Their stronghold is even more firm in the area of news programming, where few online-only radio stations that offer news, talk, or other informative programming exist.

At the same time, should the licensing of digital radio broadcasters proceed, the country's new legal framework for digital radio provides a clear advantage to today's major broadcasters of the *diaploki* system through the provision foreseeing nationwide licenses, the continued legal distinction between "news" and "entertainment" radio stations, the fees for leasing a channel on a digital multiplex, and the elimination of local licenses. These factors, individually or when combined, may force many smaller broadcasters off the air. Indeed, a similar trend has been noted with digital broadcast television in Greece, where the number of stations operating today is *smaller* than in the analog era. A reduction in stations or a further increase in concentration will benefit the same media moguls of the existing system of *diaploki*, as was the case with the Athens radio licensing bids of 2001 and 2002, and such a reduction can have a tangible societal impact. As Greece's economy entered into crisis, news stations in Athens—all oligarch owned—provided largely uniform, pro-austerity reporting while alternative viewpoints and oppositional voices were habitually excluded. As of today, indications are that a similar process is in the process of developing in Greece's fledgling digital radio landscape.

## References

Alexandra Daskalopoulou, e nea dinami sto radiofono [Alexandra Daskalopoulou, the new power in radio]. (2018, June 29). Retrieved from www.e-tetradio.gr/Article/16282/alexandra-daskalopoyloy-h-nea-dynamh-sto-radiofwno

Anaklisi tis adeias tis AEPI—dimiourgia neou forea apo tous kallitehnes [AEPI license revoked—creation of new entity by artists]. (2018, March 22). Retrieved from www.radiofono.gr/node/46172

Apofasi-stathmos gia idioktites radiofonikou stathmou / Kerdisan tin mahi me tin AEPI [Landmark decision for owners of a radio station: They won their battle with AEPI]. (2018, June 14). Retrieved from www.lamianow.gr/lamia-apofasi-stathmos-gia-idioktites-radiofonikoy-stathmoy-kerdisan-tin-quot-machi-quot-me-tin-aepi/

Bakogiannis, B. (2009, March 20). DAB in Greece: Martios 2009 [DAB in Greece: March 2009]. YouTube. Retrieved from www.youtube.com/watch?v=pPwGOoJEooE

Contogeorgis, G. (2012). *Kommatokratia kai dynastiko kratos: Mia ermineia tou Ellinikou adiexodou, tetarti ekdosi* [Partyocracy and the dynastic state: One interpretation of the Greek dead end, fourth edition]. Athens: Ekdoseis Pataki.

———. (2013). *Oi oligarhes: I dinamiki tis ypervasis kai i antistasi ton sigkatanevsifagon* [The oligarchs: The ability to overcome and the resistance of the yes-men]. Athens: Ekdoseis Pataki.

Danesi, M. (2009). *Dictionary of media and communications*. Armonk, NY: M. E. Sharpe.

Dikaioma ekpompis ston Atlantis FM [Atlantis FM gains right to broadcast]. (2018, March 30). *Typologies*. Retrieved from www.typologies.gr/dikeoma-ekpobis-ston-atlantis-fm/

Dokimastikes ekpompes DAB+ apo tin ERT stin Athina [DAB+ transmissions by ERT in Athens]. (2018, January 5). *Digital TV Info*. Retrieved from www.digitaltvinfo.gr/news/media-news/item/21310-dab

E kivernisi katargei tin aftodiaheirisi sta radiofona [The government is abolishing the self-management of radio stations]. (2017, July 24). Retrieved from www.e-tetradio.gr/article/15069/I-kubernisi-katargei-tin-autodiaxeirisi-sta-radiofona

Epistrefei sto dimosio e syxnotita 99,5 [99.5 frequency returning to the state]. (2018, June 18). *Typologies*. Retrieved from www.typologies.gr/epistrefi-sto-dimosio-i-sychnotita-995/

ESIEA: To nomoshedio gia to psifiako radiofono plittei tous dimotikous radiofonikous stathmous [ESIEA: Draft legislation on digital radio harms municipal radio stations]. (2018, January 12). *Athens-Macedonia News Agency*. Retrieved from www.amna.gr/mobile/articleen/220731/ESIEA-To-nomoschedio-gia-to-psifiako-radiofono-plittei-tous-dimotikous-radiofonikous-stathmous

Ethniko Symboulio Radiotileorasis. (2018). Leitourgontes radiofonikoi stathmoi ana nomo [Radio stations operating in each prefecture] [Data file]. Retrieved from www.esr.gr/wp-content/uploads/bnl.xls

Etzioni, A. (2009). The capture theory of regulations—revisited. *Society, 46*(4), 319–323.

Eurobarometer. (2015, Autumn). Media use in the European Union [Data file]. Retrieved from http://ec.europa.eu/COMMFrontOffice/publicopinion/index.cfm/ResultDoc/download/DocumentKy/72667

European Commission. (2016, September). Flash Eurobarometer 437 Report: Internet users' preferences for accessing content online [Data file]. Retrieved from http://ec.europa.eu/commfrontoffice/publicopinion/index.cfm/ResultDoc/download/documentky/74564

Eurostat. (2018, March). *Digital economy and society statistics—Households and individuals.* Retrieved from http://ec.europa.eu/eurostat/statistics-explained/index.php/Digital_economy_and_society_statistics_-_households_and_individuals

Free radio from Greece. (2019). *Lyngsat.* Retrieved from www.lyngsat.com/freeradio/Greece.html

Hallin, D. C., & Mancini, P. (2004). *Comparing media systems: Three models of media and politics.* New York: Cambridge University Press.

———. (2016). Ten years after *Comparing Media Systems*: What have we learned? *Political Communication, 34*(2), 155–171.

Hellas Sat 2/3 at 39.0°E. (2019). *Lyngsat.* Retrieved from www.lyngsat.com/Hellas-Sat-2-3.html

Iosifidis, P., & Katsirea, I. (2015). Public service broadcasting in Greece: Back to the future or point of no return? *Global Media Journal: Mediterranean Edition, 10*(1), 1–12.

Kainourios 99,8 FM anatellei kai fainetai pos kati kalo ginetai ekei [A new 99.8 FM is born and it looks like something good is happening there]. (2018, April 2). Retrieved from www.e-tetradio.gr/Article/15842/kainoyrgios-998-fm-anatellei-kai-fainetai-pws-kati-kalo-ginetai-ekei

Kalogeropoulos, A. (2019). Reuters Institute digital news report 2019: Greece. In Newman, N., Fletcher, R., Kalogeropoulos, A., & Nielsen, R.K., *The Reuters Institute & The University of Oxford.* Retrieved from https://reutersinstitute.politics.ox.ac.uk/sites/default/files/2019-06/DNR_2019_FINAL_1.pdf

Kalogeropoulos, A., Panagiotou, N., & Dimitrakopoulou, D. (2016). *Reuters Institute erevna gia tis psifiakes eidiseis 2016* (Ellada) [Reuters Institute survey on digital news 2016 (Greece)]. Athens: iwrite.gr Publications.

Kalogirou, S., & Sourpi, A. (2006). Anaptixi radiofonou kai rythmistiko plaisio [Growth of radio and legal framework]. In O. Kleiamaki (Ed.), *To radiofono stin Ellada* [Radio in Greece]. Athens: Institouto Optioakoustikon Meson.

Kanellopoulos, D., & Psara, A. (2017, February 9). Plousioi oi metohoi AEPI, ftohoi oi kallitehnes [AEPI shareholders wealthy while artists are poor]. *Efimerida ton Syntakton.* Retrieved from www.efsyn.gr/arthro/ploysioi-oi-metohoi-aepi-ftohoi-oi-kallitehnes

Kapa Research. (2016, October). I krisi ton thesmon kai i apohi [The crisis of the institutions and abstention] [Data file]. Retrieved from www.kaparesearch.com/index.php?option=com_k2&view=item&task=download&id=76_841eb312a5e458cbd1cec8bf65ba7928&Itemid=137&lang=el

Kathisterei e adeiodotisi tou psifiakou radiofonou [Digital radio licensing delayed]. (2018, July 5). Retrieved from www.radiofono.gr/node/47227

Kiss FM 92.9. (2004). Press release: Digital Audio Broadcasting. Kiss FM 92,9: The innovator in technology presents DAB in Greece [Data file]. Retrieved from www.radiofono.gr/files/KissFM-brings-DAB-to-Greece.pdf

Kogen, L. (2010). Savage deregulation in Thailand: Expanding Hallin and Mancini's European model. *Media, Culture & Society, 32*(2), 335–345.

Neos hartis psifiakou radiofonou: Posa radiofona "horane" ana perioxi [New digital radio allocations map: How many stations "fit" in each region]. (2018, January 19). *Radiofono.gr*. Retrieved from www.radiofono.gr/node/45332

Nevradakis, M. (2012). Government-sanctioned anarchy: Greece's chaotic airwaves. In J. A. Hendricks (Ed.), *Palgrave handbook of global radio* (pp. 131–160). New York: Palgrave Macmillan.

———. (2014a, October 11). Setting a bad example: Flouting legal requirements in Greek broadcasting. *Truthout*. Retrieved from www.truthout.org/articles/setting-a-bad-example-flouting-legal-requirements-in-greek-broadcasting/

———. (2014b, October 25). Greek mainstream media: Economic interests come before the law. *Truthout*. Retrieved from www.truthout.org/articles/greek-mainstream-media-economic-interests-come-before-the-law/

———. (2014c, November 3). "I have just been ordered not to speak": Reasons for Greek public broadcasting shutdown. *Truthout*. Retrieved from www.truthout.org/articles/i-have-just-been-ordered-not-to-speak-the-real-reasons-behind-the-ert-shutdown-in-context/

———. (2017a, September 28). Adeiodotiseis MME: O proanaggeltheis thanatos ton aftodiaheirizomenon (meros 3o) [Media licensing: The forewarned death of self-managed stations (part 3)]. *To Periodiko*. Retrieved from www.toperiodiko.gr/αδειοδοτήσεις-μμε-ο-προαναγγελθείς-θ/

———. (2017b, October 10). How to become a Greek oligarch in seven easy steps. *Mint Press News*. Retrieved from www.mintpressnews.com/how-to-become-a-greek-oligarch-in-seven-easy-steps/232971/

———. (2018). *From the polis to Facebook: Social media and the development of a new Greek public sphere*. Unpublished doctoral dissertation, University of Texas at Austin.

Nomos 2328/1995 [Data file]. (1995). Retrieved from www.synigoroskatanaloti.gr/docs/law/gr/N2328-1995.pdf

Nomos 2778/1999. (1999). Retrieved from www.taxheaven.gr/laws/law/index/law/366

Nomos 3310/2005 [Data file]. (2005). Retrieved from www.mou.gr/elibrary/N3310_140205_fek30.pdf

Nomos 3592/2007. (2007). Retrieved from www.wipo.int/wipolex/en/text.jsp?file_id=226574

OTE: Symfonia gia tin polisi tis Hellas Sat. (2013, February 7). *Naftemporiki*. Retrieved from www.naftemporiki.gr/finance/story/605803

Papathanassopoulos, S. (1989). The "state" of "public" broadcasting in Greece. *InterMedia*, *17*(2), 29–35.

———. (2015). Deregulating the Greek broadcasting system. In N. Georgarakis & N. Demertzis (Eds.), *To politistiko portraito tis Elladas: Krisi kai i apodomisi tou politikou* [The cultural portrait of Greece: Crisis and the deconstruction of the politician] (pp. 456–475). Athens: Ekdoseis Gutenberg.

Psifistike to nomoshedio gia tin adeiodotisi tou psifiakou radiofonou [Legislation for the licensing of digital radio passed]. (2018, January 15). Retrieved from www.radiofono.gr/node/45256

Psychogiopoulou, E., & Kandyla, A. (2013). Media policy-making in Greece: Lessons from digital terrestrial television and the restructuring of public service broadcasting. *International Journal of Media & Cultural Politics*, *9*(2), 133–152.

Radio Enigma. (2017, October 9). Titloi telous [The end]. Retrieved from www.facebook.com/Radioenigmaflorina/posts/841992759294040

Radio Kriti: Nomoi pou den tirountai, exontosi ton radiofonon tis eparhias [Radio Kriti: Laws that are not followed, extermination of regional radio stations]. (2017, June 19). Retrieved from www.radiofono.gr/node/35190

Sims, J. R. (2003). Politicians and media owners in Greek radio: Pluralism as diaploki. *Journal of Radio Studies, 10*(2), 202–215.

Skai: Tora horis pnevmatika dikaiomata [Skai: Now royalty free]. (2010, September 8). Retrieved from www.radiofono.gr/node/2265

Tmima ST' nomou 4512/2018: Adeiodotisi idiotikon radiofonikon stathmon psifiakis evriekpompis eleftheris lipsis [Excerpt of 6th article of law 4512/2018: Licensing of free-to-air digitally transmitted private radio stations]. (2018, February 1). Retrieved from www.radiofono.gr/node/45506

To exontotiko kostos tis AEPI apokleiei radiofono tis Florinas [The prohibitive fees of AEPI shut out a Florina radio station]. (2007, July 5). Retrieved from www.radiofono.gr/node/1055

Top Greek sites by Alexa traffic rank. (2019). *Top GR*. Retrieved from www.topgr.gr

Top sites in Greece. (2019). *Alexa*. Retrieved from www.alexa.com/topsites/countries/GR

Traquina, N. (1995). Portuguese television: The politics of savage deregulation. *Media, Culture & Society, 17*, 223–238.

Vovou, I. (2009). Stoixeia gia mia meta-istoria tis Ellinikis tileorasis: To meso, i politiki kai o thesmos [Evidence for a meta-history of Greek television: the medium, politics, and the institution]. In I. Vovou (Ed.), *O kosmos tis tileorasis: Theoria, analysi programmaton kai Elliniki pragmatikotita* [The world of television: Theory, analysis of programming and Greek reality] (pp. 93–135). Athens: Irodotos.

Web radios. (2019). *Easy 97.2*. Retrieved from www.easy972.gr/el/webradio-list/

Xekina to psifiako radiofono stin Ellada! [Digital radio to begin in Greece!]. (2006, April 10). Retrieved from www.radiofono.gr/node/91

Ypourgiki Apofasi 170/2018: Ekhorisi fasmatos epigeias psifiakis radiofonikis evriekpompis stin "Elliniki Radiofonia, Tileorasi Anonimi Etaireia (E.R.T. A.E.)" [Allocation of terrestrial digital radio broadcast spectrum to Hellenic Radio Television Anonymous Corporation (E.R.T. A.C.)]. (2018, January 18). Retrieved from www.radiofono.gr/node/45507

Zaharopoulos, T. (2003). The rise and fall of municipal radio in Greece. *Journal of Radio Studies, 10*(2), 231–245.

# 15

# Almost 100 Years of Women in Radio

Where Are We Now?

SIMON ORDER

## Women and Early Radio

The early days of radio were fraught for women who wanted to get their voice heard. Anne McKay (2000) has documented some of the struggles would-be female announcers faced. Mrs. Giles Borrett, the first ever female presenter at the BBC, was highly praised by managers during her three-month trial in 1933 but was abruptly removed from her position amid alleged listeners' complaints about the unsuitability of the female voice for radio. In addition, one suggestion stood out: that she was, as a married woman, taking a man's job (Kamarae, 1984). Similarly, across the Atlantic in the United States in 1935, NBC's first female announcer among twenty-six men, Elsie Janis, received listener complaints that a "woman's voice was inappropriate," and her employer responded by stating she will "read no more Press-Radio news bulletins" (Radio Announcer, 1935, p. 24).

Debate about the woman's broadcast voice also appeared in the pages of the North American *Radio Broadcast*, a popular North American magazine for early radio enthusiasts (Brown, 1998, p. 69). Jennie Irene Mix wrote a column titled "The Listener's Point of View." One reader, a retailer of phonographic records, whose letter was published, stated that "the public will not pay to listen to the talking record of a woman's voice" (McKay 2000, p. 23). However, Mix responded, stating, "Some of the highest paid women in vaudeville are the women only heard in monologues" (Mix, 1924a, p. 332). The discussion continued in the *Radio Broadcast* magazine, receiving further contributions from various male station associates:

> I have nothing against a woman announcing, but really do believe that unless a woman has the qualifications known as "showman's instinct," it really does become monotonous ... a woman's voice is considerably higher pitched than a man's voice and sometimes becomes distorted. In no case does the female voice transmit as well as that of the man ... it does not carry the volume of the average male voice. As far as women announcers are concerned, we have never used them with the exception of Miss Bertha Brainard, who occasionally broadcasts theatrical material. [A] woman speaker ... is rarely a success ... their voices do not carry the appeal ... few women have voices with distinct personality ... their voices are flat or shrill, and they are usually pitched far too high to be modulated correctly ... [they] don't seem able to become familiar with their audiences, to have that clubby feeling toward the listeners. (Mix, 1924b, pp. 391–393)

Clearly, women were not welcomed by their male colleagues in the early days of radio. The various reasons given appear overly technical, rather than based on research, and women's societal equality was far from apparent. Has much changed in the intervening ninety years?

## Gender Equality in and through the News Media

The Global Media Monitoring Project (GMMP), run by the World Association for Christian Communication (WACC), is the longest running and largest research and advocacy initiative for gender equality. The objective is to "assess how far the vision for media gender equality has been achieved over the past two decades, and identify persistent and emerging challenges" (WACC, 2015, p. 1). Some of their findings serve as pertinent background for this chapter because they highlight the global state of gender parity in the news media. In 2015

> women make up only 24% of the persons heard, read about or seen in newspaper, television and radio news, exactly as they did in 2010. Only 37% of stories in newspapers, television, and radio newscasts are reported by women. The overall proportion of stories focussing on women has held relatively steady at 10% since 2000. Women as news reporters are most present on radio, at 41% and least in print news, at 35%. Women's relative invisibility in traditional news media has crossed over into digital news delivery platforms: Only 26% of the people in Internet news stories and media news Tweets combined are women. (WACC, 2015, p. 1)

The GMMP commenced in 1995, and although there have been some small increments in media gender parity for women as receivers and producers of information, key findings indicate the rate of progress has "almost ground to a halt over the past five years" (WACC, 2015, p. 1). For radio, gender parity is slightly better than the overall media picture. The percentage of radio news presented by women remained fairly constant at around 41 percent from 2000 to 2015, but stories reported by women improved from 28 percent in 2000 to 41 percent in 2015 (WACC, 2015, p. 1). For people in the news, on radio there has been some change: 15 percent of news radio broadcasters were female in 1995 and 21 percent in 2015 (WACC, 2015, p. 1). The GMMP paints an unbalanced gender parity picture for those participating in the production of the media and also those represented in the media. Gender parity has improved since the early days of radio, but globally there is a ways to go. This chapter, as directed by the literature, focuses on the United Kingdom, Australia, and India as sites for further enquiry.

## Radio at the BBC

Radio at the BBC has bucked the global trend, at least between 1985 and 1999. Millington (2000) gives an overview of female employment at BBC Radio that points toward achieving a better gender balance. In 1985, Monica Sims was the most senior woman in BBC Radio, the "number 2" to the managing director (Millington, 2000, p. 212). Her task before she left her position was to write what became known as the "Sims Report." The "Sims Report" made recommendations focused on achieving a "better balance of staffing at all levels of the BBC and to recognise women as equal colleagues" (Sims, 1985, p. 37 cited by Millington, 2000, p. 212). According to Millington, the BBC took the recommendations seriously: they increased the number of women in management courses and provided courses specifically for women. Later in 1996, the BBC World Service launched the Women's Development Initiative (WDI), which sought to help women compete with men at the management level within the BBC (Millington, 2000, p. 213). The impact of the "Sims Report" was significant. In 1985, females composed 3.6 percent of senior executives, 10.3 percent of senior managers, 8 percent senior middle managers, and 13 percent junior middle managers (Sims, 1985, p. 5 cited by Millington, 2000, p. 213). In 1999, a BBC Corporate Human Resources Planning Report (BBC, 1999, cited by Millington, 2000, pp. 213–24) showed a breakdown of women in management across production, broadcast, news, world service, and resources. The collated figures in Table 15.1 show a clear increase in women across the management spectrum, although men still dominate the senior executive positions.

More recent controversial gender issues at the BBC overall have been highlighted by a public report from the BBC Remuneration Committee showing employees who are paid more than £150,000 (BBC, 2017). Only one-third of the BBC's highest paid are women. The pay differences between men and women at

### Table 15.1
### Women in Management at BBC Radio in 1999

|  | Production (%) | Broadcast (%) | News (%) | World service (%) | Resources (%) |
|---|---|---|---|---|---|
| Senior executives | 31.8 | 35.4 | 29.6 | 26.7 | 11.5 |
| Senior managers | 41.6 | 37.5 | 29.7 | 39.2 | 12.9 |
| Middle managers and senior professionals | 52.7 | 43.2 | 43 | 34.9 | 16.1 |

all levels of the pay ladder were significant. One particular example cited by the *Guardian* considered the top-earning woman, Claudia Winkleman, in comparison to Chris Evans, the top-earning man in a similar position. Winkleman earned one-fifth of the £2.2 million per year that was paid to Evans (Ellis-Petserson & Sweney, 2017). Following the publication of the report, forty female BBC employees sent an open to letter to BBC director general Lord Tony Hall, inviting him to "discuss ways in which you can correct this disparity so that future generations of women do not face this kind of discrimination" ("Female BBC," 2017, para. 6). Hall responded by saying, "I want the BBC to be one of the best performers when comparisons are made ... I want the BBC to be regarded as an exemplar on gender and diversity" (Kirton, 2017, para. 12). Hall indicated that the BBC would be consulting over the issue in the coming months (Kirton, 2017). In terms of the number of female positions, the BBC appears to have improved the gender parity balance, but their own public document (BBC, 2017) shows remuneration is far from equal.

## Radio in Australia

Does Australia fare any better? Peter Saxon (2017), a key Australian radio commentator, provided an overview of the broader picture of gender in Australian radio and surveyed the gender ratios on radio group boards. This followed a radio interview between Mark Levy (2GB presenter) and Elizabeth Proust, chairman of the Australian Institute of Company Directors, on Sydney station 2GB. Their discussion portrayed some of the typical gender parity arguments in Australian media. Proust told listeners that Australia's largest companies were not meeting a suggested target of 30 percent women in the boardroom, with Ms. Proust suggesting a gender quota system be implemented. In response, Levy stirred the "merit" pot by stating, "I just think it's another example of the world going mad as far as political BS, if you ask me. If you've got 5–10 people, vying for that position on the board or that job, you give it to the person best suited to the job—not because she's a woman—not because he's a bloke. I can't come into that argument [quotas]. It doesn't wash with me" (Levy, cited in Saxon, 2017, para. 5).

The merit argument has its own issues. Saxon suggests that there are good reasons why one does not see company directors recruited through the normal advertised channels. He describes a typical process: "Some names are thrown in the ring at a board meeting and it is agreed that those people will be 'sounded out' over lunch to see if they would be interested in joining the board should the opportunity arise. Often it's a case of someone on the board having gone to a private school (usually all boys) with 'Binky,' 'quite a sound chap, if I recall. A handy wicketkeeper for the First XI'" (Saxon, 2017, para. 12). Although this may be a little disparaging and humorous, this process seems quite normal. People who are recognizable business leaders who bring with them reputation, shares in the company, or a financial commitment to buy their seat are likely to be approached. They will also need to be known to interact well with the existing board. All of these above trends, as Saxon notes, "conspire against women getting a shot at a directorship" (Saxon, 2017, para. 14).

Where does radio stand in this picture? To offer a national benchmark, the average number of women on boards in the ASX200 companies is 25.4 percent (Saxon, 2017). In the commercial radio industry, Southern Cross Austereo has nine board members, two of whom are women. Australian Radio Network's parent company, Here, There and Everywhere (HT&E), has six board members, of whom two are women. Macquarie Media Limited has seven board members, three of whom are women. Pacific Star Network has six board members, no women. In total, twenty-eight board members, of whom seven, or 25 percent, are women—this is just a smidgen below the national average of 25.4 percent. Commercial Radio Australia, the peak body for commercial radio in Australia, has eleven board members, of whom three are women. Bucking the trend, the Australian Broadcast Corporation, Australia's public service broadcaster, has seven board members, three of whom are women (Saxon, 2017).

Overall, the above data show women are significantly underrepresented as managers of radio. Commercial radio in Australia offers the least gender parity. The situation is, however, improving in some quarters, notably the public broadcasters at the BBC and the Australian Broadcast Corporation. Outside of the public and commercial radio broadcasters, what stands out in the literature concerning radio and gender is the strong preference for women turning to community radio as a vehicle for their gender empowerment. Additionally, ethnic minorities, the poor, and the disabled suffer from limited media visibility (Gallagher, 2001; Malik & Bandelli, 2012, p. 5). In particular, in countries where women's participation in civil life is far from parity with that of their male counterparts, the flow of information about women and produced by women is lacking. In India, where women are excluded from the public sphere, scholars point to the need for systemic inclusion of women's voices to move toward gender equality and empowerment of women (Connelly, Murray Li, MacDonald, & Parpart, 2000; Guijt & Shah, 1998; Pavarala & Malik, 2010; Riano, 1994). The literature supporting community radio as a cultural empowerment opportunity for women is strongly bound up with the overarching theory of the public sphere. Community radio theorists resonate strongly with this body of ideas.

## The Potential of Community Radio to Contribute to Progress toward Gender Equality

The value of community radio has been analyzed by Order (2013, 2015, 2017; Order & O'Mahony, 2017). Two of the primary themes to come from Order's work are the adequate representation of all segments of society and the wide-ranging diversity of voices possible via community radio. Order's work draws significantly on Habermas's theory of the public sphere and other community radio theorists. Drawn together, they focus the potential for furthering gender parity in the media, specifically community radio.

Habermas's (1989) theory of the public sphere resonates strongly with the theoretical values of community radio and opportunity for gender parity in the media. Habermas proposes a social environment that would enable a "rational-critical debate about public issues conducted by private persons willing to let arguments and not statuses determine decisions" (Calhoun, 1992, pp. 1–2). In Habermas's view, the public sphere was an opportunity for citizens, women included, individually or as groups, to express themselves publicly and hence exert some influence on political events. For the first time, public opinion or a "public of *private* individuals" had the potential to challenge and impact state authority (Calhoun, 1992, p. 7). In the modern context, there is an assumption that the public sphere can be animated by "democratic" mass media and that citizens can be represented in some way by the media. The theory of the public sphere suggests that media should be accessible to citizens as producers, not just as consumers (Zhao & Hackett, 2005, p. 11). Downey and Fenton (2003), in an analysis of Habermas's later work, discuss community radio, community television, community newspapers, and restricted service licenses, which "seek to intervene in the mass media public sphere or to develop a counter-public sphere" (p. 187). This rings true for women equally as a channel for gender parity in the media.

Habermas was, however, critiqued for offering little specific attention to women. Focusing the discussion closer to gender, Fraser's (1992) revised public sphere history includes consideration of members of "subordinated social groups—especially women, workers, people of colour, and gays and lesbians . . . subaltern counter-publics" (p. 123). These groups form their own discursive forums to formulate their own identities and interests, which offer oppositional stances to the mainstream. In the case of a male-dominated media, women can be considered a subaltern counterpublic, whose voices and interests can potentially be advanced in a movement toward gender parity. Community radio is one natural home for subaltern counterpublics. Forde, Meadows, and Foxwell (2002) expand on Fraser's concept of *subaltern counterpublics* and suggest, "Community radio can be thought of as a cultural resource that plays a central role in the formation of a community public sphere.... Community radio is a cultural resource that is used to facilitate citizenship in ways that differentiate it from other media.... We need to think in terms of a series of parallel and overlapping public spheres—spaces where participants with similar cultural backgrounds engage in activities concerning issues and interests of importance to them" (pp. 56–57). This notion is close to Rodriguez's (2001) concept of citizens' media in *Fissures in the Mediascape: An International Study of Citizens' Media*. Her work on community media resonates strongly with Habermas and is also an important touchstone for women's participation. The classic notion of participatory communication tends to concentrate on its role of informing and influencing general publics. However, Rodriguez (2001, p. 3) instead proposes that participation in media production promotes social interaction and political empowerment at a personal level, a valuable opportunity for promoting gender parity within the mass media and wider society. As Rodriguez (2001) explains of the value of participation in media production, "It implies having the opportunity to create one's own images of self and environment; it implies being able to recodify one's own identity with the signs and codes that one chooses, thereby disrupting the traditional acceptance of those imposed by outside sources; it implies becoming one's own storyteller, regaining one's own voice; it implies reconstructing the self-portrait of one's own community and one's own culture" (p. 3).

Alternative communications theory aside, what is happening to implement this kind of thinking at the operational and international levels? Is there any kind of translation to action that may improve gender parity within community radio? The World Association for Community Radio Broadcasters (AMARC) published "Gender Policy for Community Radio," in conjunction with the Women's International Network (AMARC WIN, 2008). The authors state that community radio has an "obligation to redress the imbalance; facilitate women's involvement at all levels of decision-making and programming.... [The gender policy] will serve as a tool to implement gender equality in stations" (AMARC WIN, 2008, p. 2). The policy identifies six areas of importance: women's access to the airwaves, women's representation on air, the special needs of minority women, women's representation at all levels of station management, the use of appropriate technology and the funding and capacity building for women's radio (AMARC WIN, 2008, pp. 2–7). AMARC, as the international peak body for community radio, have offered their ideal policy objectives toward achieving gender parity in the radio space. However, even a cursory glance at the developing world indicates that the imbalance of gender access and representation on radio can signify deeper cultural challenges.

A review of recent scholarly work on community radio and gender highlights the Indian perspective. The Indian perspective exemplifies community radio's role in increasing female empowerment and is prominent in the recent scholarly literature. The Indian context also strongly highlights deeper cultural issues that are at play in increasing the representation of women in radio. How can community radio improve gender parity in the media or more significantly in the wider Indian public sphere? For Indian women, access to their own voice is the first challenge.

## Access to a Voice in the Indian Perspective

### Empowering Women

Empowering women is a process for women who become aware of the gender power relations in their lives and through that awareness wish to participate in their social development. The traditional sociocultural maternal fabric of Indian society is being confronted by women who are seeking personal or group empowerment. Empowering women means challenging family values, community norms, caste identity, religion, patriarchy, and long-term male bias within society. From the household level to the local community and the state, national, and international levels, empowered Indian women are gradually increasing their strength and awareness to challenge long-term gender inequalities (Kumar & Varghese, 2005, p. 57).

Empowerment can refer to various activities: personal or group assertion, collective resistance to gender inequity, or challenging gender power relations. Ultimately, women want to gain more control over their own lives, be that political, social, cultural, sexual, personal, and managerial (Nirmala, 2015, p. 43). Empowerment can be the redistribution of gender power (Nirmala, 2015, p. 43).

According to Joseph and Sharma (1994), the rebalancing of gender inequality in India is an "accepted social goal of the country" (p. 17). Poverty, especially among rural women, is a major issue, as are dowry abuse, domestic violence, and the normalization of rape. These have been concerns of the Women's Movement in India since independence from the United Kingdom. The efforts of the Women's Movement have seen changes to the "rape law" in 1983 (UNFPA, 2009, p. 17) and the Protection of Women from Domestic Violence in 2005 (Saxena, 2015). In addition, one-third of the Panchayat seats have been reserved for women and other disadvantaged groups (Malik & Bandelli, 2012). However, discrimination remains a challenge. Inability to access quality health care, poor nutrition, sex-selective abortions, and female infanticide are said to be the cause of death for forty-two million women per year (Kapur, 2010). Sharma also suggests that although there are now women in the Panchayat, women's voices are still not being heard (Sharma, 2008) and politics remains dominated by informal networks of male power (Kotwal, 2008, p. 220).

As Malik and Bandelli (2012) indicate, third world media scholars are emphatic that little will change until women are able to voice their experiences and needs in a public way. Women must talk back and escape their voice poverty; this is an essential act of female empowerment articulated by feminist writer bell hooks (1989): "Moving from silence into speech is for the oppressed, the colonized, the exploited, and those who stand and struggle side by side a gesture of defiance that heals, that makes life and new growth possible. It is that act of speech of 'talking back' that is no mere gesture of empty words; that is the expression of our movement from object to subject- the liberated voice" (p. 9). Without access to a public voice to contribute to discussions that affect lives, one has "voice poverty" (Tacchi & Kiran, 2008, p. 31). An effective voice that is given attention by a listener is a "basic dimension of human life" (Couldry, 2010, p. 7), providing communication, leading to life development outcomes. Lister (2004) asserts, "One of the most striking developments in the contemporary politics of poverty is the growing demands for poverty to be understood as powerlessness and a denial of fundamental rights and for the voices of those in poverty to be heard in public debates" (p. 10). The potential for change through listening and content production is theorized as "conscientization" (Freire, 1972). The unrepresented or marginalized can discuss their status and through communication begin the development process toward their personal or group empowerment (Rodriguez, 2001, p. 3). In the communication experience, "to have one's voice heard can be an imposing experience of self-worth" (Malik & Bandelli, 2012, p. 4). Community radio is one medium of mass communication where local and diverse voices have the potential to be heard in the wider Indian society. There is also the potential for dialogue, for and about women to be heard.

## Community Radio in India

India's third media sector was enshrined in legislation in 2006 after the long-term advocacy of the Community Radio Forum (CRF). Similar to groups in other countries (ACMA & CBAA, 2008; AMARC, 2007, p. 51; Atton, 2007, p. 18), the CRF felt the need for an alternative to cater to audiences/producers not currently served by state-run or commercial radio (Parthasarathi & Chotani, 2010; Pavarala & Malik, 2007). Outside of community radio, India has a history of national state-run radio working in the developmental communications sphere, with All India Radio providing some support with their network of local stations. They have been critiqued, however, as unable to address local and grassroots community's needs (Pavarala & Malik, 2007) because of their large national remit. Therefore, there is a need for community radio as another avenue for citizens to access the airwaves and increase the range of voices represented.

India's community radio sector is now thriving, with 132 operating stations and a further 267 license applications in process. Stations and nongovernmental organizations (NGOs) are beginning to involve women in programming and decision-making roles. In the state of Maharashtra, there are community stations run by women and for women (Malik & Bandelli, 2012, p. 8). One example is the station Mann Deshi Tarang Vahini, which is broadcast in 102 villages in the

Satara district. Chetna Sinha, founder of the station and NGO Maan Vikas Samajik Sanstha, says, "The reason we collaborated with these women volunteers is that since they are from the Maan Deshi community, they are aware of the issues faced by the community. They convey these problems to us and that helps us organise an expert discussion around it on the radio. The very aim of launching the radio station was to enhance access to information, build local capacity and empower women to improve their lives and those of their families through creative programming" (cited by Poorvi, 2017, para. 6). Stations like Mann Deshi Tarang Vahini are slowly helping to give voice to marginalized rural women and women whose societal role has traditionally been defined by feudal, class, and caste social structures (Malik & Bandelli, 2012, p. 8). In mixed-gender stations, the story is slightly different, where those preexisting social norms are hindering women's participation (Thomas, 1994). There are a range of discriminatory cultural gender norms that inhibit Indian women's engagement with the public sphere of community radio.

Bandelli's (2012) studies at Radio Namaskar and Radio Dhadkan reveal that the control of radio receiving devices is largely dominated by men, where women are expected to fulfil traditional gender and cultural roles such as caring for children and conducting household tasks. Women, as radio talent or reporters, are not culturally available late at night and not expected to mix with male outsiders such as other reporters or male talent. Once women are married, their freedom is largely determined by their husbands and their in-laws. There are obstacles to both participation in producing content and even listening to female-oriented content (Bandelli, 2012). Similar sentiments are expressed by Pavarala and Malik (2009) in their study of Chala Ho Gaon Mein radio station in Jharkhand. Women are not able to listen as much as men, women's issues are not covered significantly compared to issues relevant to male listeners, and involvement by women in content production is minimal. The number of female reporters is small compared to men because sociocultural norms dictate that women should be protected in society. Traveling to interviews, mixing with strangers, and independent work by women are seen as contrary to the notion of women's safety. Interestingly, this has been described by Malik and Bandelli (2012, p. 9) as typical of the "NGOisation" of an Indian community radio station, where local cultural norms are at odds with the NGO's gender parity agenda of programming/participation and women's developmental communications objectives. Although the rebalancing of gender inequality in India is described as an "accepted social goal of the country" (Joseph & Sharma, 1994, p. 17), at the grassroots, village level of community radio operation, empowerment for women is making slow progress.

Yalala Nirmala's (2015) approach to empowerment focuses on the mass media as the main actors that stereotype women's roles in India. Most women are depicted in their traditional role and appear more often as decoration in advertising. Her belief is that women managing media will be able to challenge these stereotypes. All India Radio, the state-run, national broadcaster, has policy objectives that include serving the interests of women, promoting their welfare and development. Similarly, from 2006, when community radio was officially borne in India, as a third sector, its primary objective has been the development of the community and indirectly the women in the community (Nirmala, 2015, p. 43).

There are some success stories in relation to community radio in India. The Namma Dhwani (Our Voices) station of Karnataka was started as India's first cable community radio station with funding from UNESCO in 2003. The village of Budikote harnessed the power of their community to produce programs for the many illiterate women in the region who would normally have no access to information. The station functions as a multimedia center for local people, is financially self–sustaining, and offers significant support for women. Information about health, sanitation, education, finances, food health, and family is broadcast, and that awareness is enhancing the life of rural women (Singh, Kumar, Yadav, Dan, & Singh, 2010).

Another community radio success story relates to a community radio station for the Dalit Caste. Sangham Radio was launched in 2008, the southern Indian state of Telangana, by the Deccan Development Society, who work with the poorest women of the Dalit caste. Dalit means "oppressed" in Sanskrit and "broken/scattered" in Hindi. They are the "untouchables" in Indian culture (Gorringe, 2005). The word *Sangham* indicates the women's village collectives, who solely operate the station for the marginalized rural women of the Dalit caste. They cover fifty thousand people over one hundred villages in a twenty-five-kilometer radius (Nirmala, 2015, p. 44).

Anna FM at Anna University in Tamil Nadu was documented by Kar (2010). It is the oldest community station in India and broadcasts to the local, urban, low and middle classes. Kar's study indicated that for women listeners the radio station played an important role in enhancing their social and political empowerment, allowing them to discuss local issues and vote in an informed way. They learned new skills, became more employable, and subsequently found freedom to spend money. Kar argues that the voice and empowerment now available to marginalized women via Anna FM are significant (Kar, 2010).

Holy Cross Community Radio, Tamil Nadu, started broadcasting in December 2006 and specifically targeted the women of Dharmanathapuram and Jeevanagar, the slum areas of the Trichy city. They broadcast eight hours a day. Researchers surveyed 170 listeners about the station. Of those listeners, 27 percent stated that programming improved their self-confidence and helped in their personality development and awareness about pollution and health. Pertinently, 44 percent suggested that programming raised awareness about child health and epidemics, while 22 percent agreed that they were better informed about AIDS and cancer (Ankit, 2008).

Puduvai Vaani, community radio at Pondicherry University, was launched in 2008 as a committed "ideological framework for carrying community voices"

(Balan Siva & Norman, 2012, p. 20). The students at the university are able to utilize the participatory communication to develop their voices. Women and children are a focus, and the station offers training courses for "empowering their skills and economic status" (Balan Siva & Norman, 2012, p. 20). Balan Siva and Norman (2012) were keen to discover the influence of this community radio on the development of rural women. They chose the nearby village of Pillaichavady and spoke to one hundred random women. From that group, 20 percent were keen to hear programs related to education, children, health, and nutrition, while 12 percent were keen to hear content for women and youth. Pertinently, 67 percent were interested in broadcasting on community radio. There is an appetite for female-centric broadcasting.

While these success stories from the Indian community radio perspective offer plenty of hope for gender balance, the journey of women to gender parity in radio is not a condition dependent on radio. The change must come from a grassroots societal evolvement toward women's overall equality. Societal change may be generational, but women in community radio can potentially quicken the pace by their participation and example.

## Conclusion

In a broadest sense, the literature points to gender parity in radio as a two-speed discussion, one in the developed world and one in the developing world. However, cultural legacy is at the center of both broadcast media worlds, rather than radio occupying any special position.

That representation is reflected in media generally. At the international level of news media, the GMMP shows a low representation of women delivering news media, managing media, and being talked about in the media. Radio news achieves a slightly better gender parity than other mediums. Some small increments in gender parity have been made since 1995, but progress has stalled over the last five years (WACC, 2015, p. 1). The GMMP data can also be viewed by broadcast topic and by region.

Interestingly, drawing on the GMMP topic data (WACC, 2015, p. 49,) one of the cover articles on the World Radio Day 2018 website (UNESCO, 2018, paras. 2–3) summarizes the alarming situation in global sports broadcasting. Only 12 percent of sports stories are reported by women, while 7 percent of athletes featured are women, and the numbers are worse for radio. Sports broadcasting is a powerful medium that shapes cultural norms for men and boys, "not just how they view women, but how they think about themselves" (UNESCO, 2018, para. 6). There are few institutions with as much influence on the values and behaviors of young men (UNESCO, 2018, para. 6). Sports broadcasters have a significant opportunity here to reshape cultural gender parity norms. From a purely financial perspective, advertisers could have more access to the female market if sports broadcasting demonstrated more gender parity.

Drilling down into the GMMP's regional results (WACC, 2015, pp. 117–120) indicates Asia and Africa are often the least balanced across the spectrum of gender parity measurements. Heading the charge in radio for balancing gender parity, the BBC and the Australian Broadcast Corporation are significantly closer to a balanced picture at all levels of the industry. However, there are still significant issues.

In the United Kingdom and Australia, what jumps out of recent debates indicates gender parity has been publicly focused first on the significant differences in remuneration between male and female media employees and second on the gender imbalances in media company board membership. In 2017, the BBC found itself embroiled in a remuneration scandal, where female employees were shown to be earning a fifth of males in similar positions (Ellis-Petserson & Sweney, 2017, para. 6). In Australia, female board membership of commercial radio companies is averaged at 25 percent (Saxon, 2017, para. 17). In context, however, in Australia the national average for all types of companies is 25.4 percent (Saxon, 2017, para. 17). That statistic indicates a cultural gender parity imbalance rather than something specific to radio.

Cultural traditions are also at the heart of gender parity in radio in India, where the gender parity discussion is at a different stage. In the early days of radio in the developed world, women faced fundamental challenges, struggling to be accepted as broadcasters and negotiating the male disparaging of the female voice in sonic and cultural terms. In India today, women are in a similar situation, struggling to be heard; their voices, their topics, and their opinions are only beginning to be acknowledged. Community radio is highlighted in the recent literature as the primary medium of empowerment for Indian women.

Women as producers and listeners in India have started to reflect on their abilities and aspirations. Radio can develop leadership qualities among women, improve their confidence in speaking in public, highlight awareness around education, health, pollution, hygiene, the rights of women, maternity, violence, and nutrition, and offer social, economic, and political empowerment. There is significant evidence that community radio in India is powerful developmental communication that can identify and address local needs for local women (Nirmala, 2015, pp. 45–46). Radio also remains easily accessible as a tool for mass communication for listeners and producers; the technology is easy and cheap to master, and literacy is not a barrier (Balan Siva & Norman, 2012). Community radio is potentially a powerful tool for grassroots development via participatory communication.

The intention of this chapter was to discover, through a review of the literature, what had been written about radio and gender parity in recent years and highlight significant trends. Globally, gender parity in the production of broadcast media and the content of media, including radio, has improved but still has a significant way to go. The issues of unequal remuneration within the media and unbalanced media company board memberships are still cultural challenges. By a similar token, the Indian perspective of community radio starkly reminds us that culture is far more pervasive than any individual medium or topic. Radio or media generally says little about gender parity; rather, it seems to reflect culturally accepted norms of unbalanced gender parity globally. The privilege of mass communication carries responsibility. How will we use that privilege, perpetuating unbalanced cultural gender parity or animating gender balance for the future, in the production and content of broadcast media?

## References

ACMA & CBAA. (2008). *Community radio broadcasting: Codes of practice*. Sydney: CBAA.
AMARC (World Association of Community Radio Broadcasters). (2007). *Community Radio Social Impact Assessment: Removing Barriers, Increasing Effectiveness*. Montreal: World Association of Community Radio Broadcasters.
AMARC WIN. (2008). Gender policy for community radio. Retrieved from www.amarc.org/documents/Gender_Policy/GP4CR_English.pdf
Ankit. (2008). Case study: Holy Cross Community Radio, Trichy, Tamil Nadu, India. *i4d*. Retrieved from http://i4d.eletsonline.com/case-study-holy-cross-community-radio-trichy-tamil-nadu-india/ Retrieved from http://i4d.eletsonline.com/case-study-holy-cross-community-radio-trichy-tamil-nadu-india/
Atton, C. (2007). Current issues in alternative media research. *Sociology Compass, 1*(1), 17–27.
Balan Siva, K. C., & Norman, S. J. (2012). Community radio (CR)—Participatory communication tool for rural women development. *International Research Journal of Social Sciences, 1*(1), 19–26.
Bandelli, D. (2012). Indian women in community radio: The case studies of Radio Namaskar in Orissa and Radio Dhadkan in Madhya Pradesh. *Journal of South Asia Women Studies, 13*(1). http://asiatica.org/jsaws/13-1/indian-women-community-radio-case-studies-radio-namaskar-orissa-and-radio-dhadkan-madhya-pradesh/
BBC. (1999). *BBC corporate human resources planning report*. London: BBC.
———. (2017). *BBC pay disclosures July 2017*. London: BBC.
Brown, M. (1998). Radio magazines and the development of broadcasting: Radio broadcast and radio news, 1922–1930. *Journal of Radio Studies, 5*(1), 68–81. doi:10.1080/19376529809384530
Calhoun, C. (1992). Introduction: Habermas and the public sphere. In C. Calhoun (Ed.), *Habermas and the public sphere* (pp. 1–48). London: MIT Press.
Connelly, M. P., Murray Li, T., MacDonald, M., & Parpart, J. L. (2000). Feminism and development: Theoretical perspectives. In J. L. Parpart, M. P. Connelly, & E. Barriteau (Eds.), *Theoretical perspectives on gender and development* (pp. 51–159). Ottawa, ON: International Development Research Centre.
Couldry, N. (2010). *Why voice matters: Culture and politics after neoliberalism*. London: Sage.
Downey, J., & Fenton, N. (2003). New media, counter publicity and the public sphere. *New Media and Society, 5*(2), 185–202.
Ellis-Petserson, H., & Sweney, M. (2017, July 21). BBC women "furious but not surprised" by gender pay gap. *Guardian*. Retrieved from www.theguardian.com/media/2017/jul/21/bbc-women-furious-and-not-surprised-by-gender-pay-gap
Female BBC stars' letter to Tony Hall demanding equal pay in full. (2017, July 22). *Telegraph*. Retrieved from www.telegraph.co.uk/news/2017/07/22/female-bbc-stars-letter-demanding-equal-pay-tony-hall-full/

Forde, S., Meadows, M., & Foxwell, K. (2002). Creating a community public sphere: Community radio as a cultural resource. *Media International Australia Incorporating Culture and Policy, 103*(1), 56–67.

Fraser, N. (1992). Rethinking the public sphere: A contribution to the critique of actually existing democracy. In C. Calhoun (Ed.), *Habermas and the public sphere* (pp. 109–142). London: MIT Press.

Freire, P. (1972). *Pedagogy of the oppressed*. Harmondsworth: Penguin.

Gallagher, M. (2001). *Gender setting: New agendas for media monitoring and advocacy*. London: Zed Books.

Gorringe, H. (2005). *Untouchable citizens: Dalit movements and democratisation in Tamil Nadu*. London: Sage.

Guijt, I., & Shah, M. K. (1998). Waking up to power, conflict and process. In I. Guijt & M. K. Shah (Eds.), *The myth of community: Gender issues in participatory development* (pp. 1–23). London: Intermediate Technology Publications.

Habermas, J. (1989). *The structural transformation of the public sphere*. Cambridge, MA: MIT Press.

hooks, b. (1989). *Talking back: Thinking feminist, thinking black*. Boston: South End Press.

Joseph, A., & Sharma, K. (1994). *Whose news? The media and women's issues*. New Delhi: Sage.

Kamarae, C. (1984). Resistance to women's public speaking. In S. Tromell-Plotz (Ed.), *Gewalt durch Sprache* (pp. 203–228). Frankfurt: Fischer Taschenbuch Verlag.

Kapur, N. (2010). *Everyday equality*. South Asia: UNIFEM/UNWOMEN.

Kar, E. S. (2010). *Social impact of community radio stations in India: Enhancing participatory development and women's empowerment*. Unpublished PGPPM dissertation, Indian Institute of Management, Bangalore, India.

Kirton, H. (2017). Female stars call on BBC to "act now" to end gender pay row. *People Management,*. Retrieved from www.peoplemanagement.co.uk/news/articles/gender-pay-row-bbc-female-stars-call-act-now

Kotwal, L. M. (2008). Contesting power in Panchayats. In V. Kalpagam & J. Arunachalam (Eds.), *Rural women and development in India: Issues and challenges* (pp. 219–237). New Delhi: Rawat Publications.

Kumar, H., & Varghese, J. (2005). *Women's empowerment, issues, challenges and strategies: A source book*. New Delhi: Regency.

Lister, R. (2004). *Poverty*. Cambridge: Polity.

Malik, K., & Bandelli, D. (2012). *Community radio and gender—Towards an inclusive public sphere*. Paper presented at the India Media Symposium: Public Spheres, the Media & Social Change in India, University of Queensland.

McKay, A. (2000). Speaking up: Voice amplification and women's struggle for public expression. In C. Mitchell (Ed.), *Women and radio: Airing differences* (pp. 15–28). London: Routledge.

Millington, C. (2000). Getting in and on: Women and radio management at the BBC. In C. Mitchell (Ed.), *Women and radio: Airing differences* (pp. 209–218). London: Routledge.

Mix, J. I. (1924a, August). The listener's point of view. *Radio Broadcast*, p. 332.

———. (1924b, September). The listener's point of view. *Radio Broadcast*, pp. 391–393.

Nirmala, Y. (2015). The role of community radio in empowering women in India. *Media Asia, 42*(1–2), 41–46.

Order, S. (2013). *Community radio in western Australia: Notions of value*. Doctoral dissertation, Murdoch University. Retrieved from http://researchrepository.murdoch.edu.au/view/author/Order,_Simon.html

———. (2015). Towards a contingency-based approach to value for community radio. *Radio Journal, 13*(1–2), 121–138.

———. (2017). All the lonely people, where do they all belong: Community radio and social connection. *Radio Journal, 15*(2), 243–258.

Order, S., & O'Mahony, L. (2017). Building a purposeful identity in the older adult volunteer space: A case study of community radio station 6RPH (radio print-handicapped). *Communication Research and Practice, 3*(1), 1–14. doi:10.1080/22041451.2017.1271971

Parthasarathi, V., & Chotani, S. (2010). *A tale of two radios: Tracing advocacy in a deregulatory milieu*. McGannon Center Research Resources, Working Paper 7. New York: Donald McGannon Communication Research Center. Retrieved from https://fordham.bepress.com/cgi/viewcontent.cgi?referer=www.google.com/&httpsredir=1&article=1003&context=mcgannon_research

Pavarala, V., & Malik, K. (2007). *Other voices: The struggle for community radio in India*. New Delhi: Sage.

———. (2009). *Community radio for social change: Evaluating Chala Ho Gaon Mein in Jharkhand*. New Delhi: National Foundation for India.

———. (2010). Community radio and women: Forging subaltern counterpublics. In D. Rodriguez, D. Kidd, & L. Stein (Eds.), *Making our media: Creating new communication spaces* (pp. 95–113). New York: Hampton Press.

Poorvi, G. (2017, May 15). Women run community radio in this Maharashtra village. *SheThe PeopleTV*. Retrieved from www.shethepeople.tv/women-run-community-radio-in-this-maharashtra-village/

Radio Announcer. (1935, December 1). The "sweetheart of the AEF" joining NBC. *Newsweek*.

Riano, P. (1994). *Women in grassroots communication*. London: Sage.

Rodriguez, C. (2001). *Fissures in the mediascape: An international study of citizens' media*. Cresskill, NJ: Hampton Press.

Saxena, T. (2015). *Indian protection of women from domestic violence act: Stumbling or striving ahead?* Doctoral dissertation, Australian National University, Canberra. Retrieved from https://openresearch-repository.anu.edu.au/bitstream/1885/104291/1/SaxenaThesis%202015.pdf

Saxon, P. (2017, October 30). Why I want to throw a brick through my radio when they talk about gender equality. *RadioInfo*. Retrieved from www.radioinfo.com.au/news/why-i-want-throw-brick-through-my-radio-when-they-talk-about-gender-equality

Sharma, K. (2008). (Re)negotiating power and spaces. In V. Kalpagam & J. Arunachalam (Eds.), *Rural women and development in India: Issues and challenges* (pp. 264–280). New Delhi: Rawat.

Sims, M. (1985). *Women in BBC management*. Retrieved from London: BBC.

Singh, B. K., Kumar, R. K., Yadav, V. P., Dan, S., & Singh, H. L. (2010). Social impact of community radio in Karnataka. *Indian Research Journal of Extension Education, 10*, 10–14.

Tacchi, J., & Kiran, M. S. (2008). *Finding a voice: Themes and discussions*. New Delhi: UNESCO.

Thomas, P. (1994). Participatory development communication: Philosophical premises. In S. White, K. S. Nair, & J. Ascroft (Eds.), *Participatory communication: Working for change and development* (pp. 49–59). New Delhi: Sage.

UNESCO. (2018). Is sports broadcasting "dropping the ball" on gender equality? *News*. Retrieved from www.diamundialradio.org/2018/news/sports-broadcasting-dropping-ball-on-gender-equality.html

UNFPA. (2009). *Programming to end violence against women. 8 case studies*. Retrieved from http://unfpa.org/webdav/site/global/shared/documents/publications/2009/violence.pdf

WACC. (2015). *The global media monitoring project 2015*. Retrieved from http://cdn.agilitycms.com/who-makes-the-news/Imported/reports_2015/highlights/highlights_en.pdf

Zhao, Y., & Hackett, R. (2005). Media globalization, media democratization: Challenges, issues, and paradoxes. In Y. Zhao & R. Hackett (Eds.), *Democratizing global media* (pp. 1–33). Lanham, MD: Rowman & Littlefield.

# Acknowledgments

The editor conveys appreciation to all of the contributors to this scholarly monograph for their thoughtful studies and their willingness to assist at all stages of the editing and publishing process. This book would not have come to completion without their interest in and desire to learn more about the twenty-first-century radio industry.

Lisa Banning, editor at Rutgers University Press, deserves sincere acknowledgment for her support of this project from its beginning. Lisa's patience and guidance throughout the evolution of the book are especially appreciated. Moreover, the editor expresses gratitude to the external reviewers who provided prudent input and wise guidance on the project: Michael Brown (University of Wyoming) and Christopher H. Sterling (George Washington University).

Angela Piliouras and Joseph Dahm, at Westchester Publishing Services, did a wonderful job guiding the project through its final stages. Westchester conducted the final copyediting and typesetting for the book. Twin Oaks Indexing created the book's index in a timely fashion and their good work deserves recognition, too.

Stephen F. Austin State University, in Nacogdoches, Texas, is acknowledged for its continued support of the editor's research. The university understands and supports a healthy balance between teaching, research, and administrative responsibilities. Notably, this book is the beneficiary of financial support from the SFA Research Enhancement Program. Additionally, Dr. Hendricks expresses appreciation to his two graduate assistants, Milad Chizari and Melissa Hutchens, both of whom provided conscientious and meticulous assistance throughout the editing process.

As always, the editor is grateful to his wife, Dr. Stacy Hendricks, whose words of encouragement remain steadfast and her advice is always wise.

## About the Editor

JOHN ALLEN HENDRICKS (PhD, University of Southern Mississippi) has served as chair of the Department of Mass Communication and professor at Stephen F. Austin State University in Texas since 2009; he teaches courses in communication theory, research methods, and First Amendment law and ethics. He has authored/edited more than eleven books on the broadcasting industry, social media/new media technologies, and media/politics. He is coauthor of *The Radio Station: Broadcasting, Podcasting, and Streaming* (with Bruce Mims), *The Palgrave Handbook of Global Radio*, and *The Twenty-First-Century Media Industry: Economic and Managerial Implications in the Age of New Media*. He is past president of the Broadcast Education Association (BEA) and served on the BEA Board of Directors from 2009 to 2017. He is the past president of the Oklahoma Broadcast Education Association (OBEA) and past chair of the Southern States Communication Association's (SSCA) Political Communication and Mass Communication divisions. He serves as founding editor of the book series *Studies in New Media* for Lexington Books, a scholarly imprint of Rowman & Littlefield.

# Notes on Contributors

**JOHN F. BARBER** (PhD, Indiana University of Pennsylvania) convenes with the faculty of Creative Media & Digital Culture at Washington State University Vancouver. His scholarship, teaching, and creative endeavors arise from the collision of art, humanities, and technology, with a focus on digital scholarship and radio art-performance-research. His work regarding the latter has been published in *Digital Humanities Quarterly*, *Digital Studies/Le champ numérique*, *ebr*, *Hyperrhiz: New Media Cultures*, *Leonardo*, *MATLIT (Materialities of Literature)*, *Scholarly Research and Communication*, and others, featured in juried exhibitions in America, Brazil, Canada, England, Germany, Ireland, Italy, Lithuania, Macedonia, Northern Ireland, Portugal, Spain, and United Arab Emirates, and broadcast as part of several international radio art programs. A focus of his research in digital scholarship has been American author Richard Brautigan. His direction of *The Brautigan Library* was featured on the NPR radio program *This American Life*.

**JOSEPH R. BLANEY** (PhD, University of Missouri) has published seven books and dozens of articles largely related to image restoration of political, religious, corporate, and athletic persons and organizations. His book *Putting Image Repair to the Test* helped lead the evolution of image restoration research from a critical approach to a social scientific paradigm. A former radio morning personality, program director, production director, and promotions director, he has been at Illinois State University since 2000 and is currently professor of communication and associate dean of the College of Arts and Sciences.

**ANJULI JOSHI BREKKE** (PhD candidate, University of Washington) is an advanced doctoral candidate in communication at the University of Washington. She is a fellow and research assistant with the Center for Communication, Difference and Equity and a member of the Communication and Difference Research Group as well as a Mortar Board Alumni/Tolo Foundation scholar. Her research focuses on the potential and politics of listening and interweaves conversations from a number of traditions including cultural studies, rhetorical studies, and new media studies. Her doctoral research explores the power and limitations of sharing personal narratives, both online and within situated communities, to facilitate listening across difference. She proposed and led an oral history and digital storytelling project to record and share stories of racial discrimination from the larger Seattle area. From this research, she is currently collaborating on a paper as lead author on the challenges and possibilities of community-based digital humanities projects.

**MICHAEL BROWN** (PhD, University of Utah) is emeritus professor with the Communication and Journalism Department at the University of Wyoming, where he taught since 1993. Although officially retired in 2018, he continues to research media history and focuses on periods of transition in radio and visual communication, particularly in the early twentieth century. His most recent work includes a partnership with faculty at the Kazakh National University to examine the media in Kazakhstan, with a particular interest in the influence and legacy of the Soviets. In addition to his research he produced a series of radio documentaries exploring the music of a variety of American ethnic communities.

**BRAD CLARK** (PhD, University of Wales) is associate professor and chair of Broadcast Media Studies and Journalism at Mount Royal University in Calgary, Alberta, Canada. Before entering the academy in 2006, he worked as a journalist for twenty years, including six as a national radio reporter for the Canadian Broadcasting Corporation (CBC). His doctoral dissertation examined network television news representations of Indigenous peoples and ethno-cultural minorities in Canada, and he has disseminated his work in this area in both academic and professional settings. His other research interests include professional ideology and ethics, curriculum, Indigenization, and audio narrative.

**DAVID CRIDER** (PhD, Temple University) is the author of *Performing Personality: On-Air Radio Identities in a Changing Media Landscape*. His doctoral dissertation—from which his book was adapted—was the recipient of the 2015 Kenneth Harwood Dissertation Award from the Broadcast Education Association. His previous study of localism in talk radio was published in the *Journal of Broadcasting and Electronic Media* in 2012. His research has also been published in the *Journal of Radio and Audio Media*. His research interests include the presentation and promotion of identity through radio, including issues of local and gender identity, as well as programming and industry concerns related to consolidation and localism. He has been an adjunct professor of broadcasting in the School of Communication, Media & the Arts at SUNY Oswego since 2014.

JOHN MARK DEMPSEY (PhD, Texas A&M University) is an associate professor of radio-television at Texas A&M University–Commerce. He has published five books, *The Jack Ruby Trial Revisited: The Diary of Jury Foreman Max Causey*; *The Light Crust Doughboys Are on the Air!*; *Eddie Barker's Notebook: Stories That Made the News (and Some Better Ones That Didn't)*; *Sports Talk Radio in America: Its Context and Culture*; and *Always Connected: The Power of Broadcasting and Social Media*. His primary research interests are broadcasting history, and local and regional history. He previously served on the journalism faculties of the University of North Texas and Texas A&M University. He has worked as a radio news anchor and producer for the Texas State Network in Dallas since 1998. He also produces a daily program, the "Blacklands Café," for Texas A&M–Commerce's public radio station, KETR, which has won awards from the Broadcast Education Association and the Texas Associated Press Broadcasters.

EMILY W. EASTON (PhD, University of Illinois at Chicago) has been studying, working in, and generally hanging around underground music scenes since 2001. Her academic work focuses on how individuals build cultural and subcultural capital, with a special emphasis on the collaboration (not competition) that fuels smaller scenes with passionate fans. She is also a co-founder of Girls Rock! Chicago and former DJ at WHPK in Chicago, Illinois, and she will never be able to own enough records.

RACHEL SUSSMAN-WANDER KAPLAN (PhD, Duquesne University) is a part-time assistant professor at Point Park University in Pittsburgh, Pennsylvania. She has published several articles on integrated marketing communication, precarity, and internal branding. Her most recent project includes exploring the connection between rhetoric and the opioid crisis.

ANNE F. MACLENNAN (PhD, Concordia University) is an associate professor and chair of the Department of Communication Studies at York University and editor of the *Journal of Radio and Audio Media*. She has over twenty years of experience teaching communication studies, media studies, history, methodology, and other interdisciplinary topics. She is curating a show of historical radios and radio advertising with Michael Windover, accompanied by their coauthored book, *Seeing, Selling, and Situating Radio in Canada, 1922–1956*. Her ongoing work includes a book on early Canadian radio programming; SSHRC-funded research, "Remembering Radio: The Canadian Radio Audience in the 1930s"; and a Canadian Media Research Council–funded project, "First Person Plural: Transcribing the Perspectives of Canadian Broadcast Pioneers for a Digital Age" with Paul Moore. Her next project is "Programming, Practices, Production and Policy: Canadian Community Radio." She has published in *Media and Communication*, *Journal of Radio and Audio Media*, *Women's Studies: An Interdisciplinary Journal*, *Radio Journal*, *Relations Industrielles/Industrial Relations*,

*Urban History Review*, and other collections. She works on media history, community radio, broadcasting, popular culture, Canadian history and Canadian studies, women, social welfare, poverty, and cultural representations in the media.

ARCHIE McLEAN (MA, Columbia University) is assistant professor of journalism at Mount Royal University in Calgary, Alberta, Canada. He joined the faculty at Mount Royal in the fall of 2016, after working for most of the previous four years as the managing editor for the Canadian Broadcasting Corporation's media operations in the Arctic and Northern Quebec. Under his leadership, CBC North's newsroom was nominated for a Canadian Journalism Foundation Innovation Award and was recently nominated for the Michener Award, the country's highest journalistic honor. Prior to joining CBC News, he was an editor and political reporter at the *Edmonton Journal*. He also served as Canwest News Service's Afghanistan correspondent in 2009. His research interests include Indigenous language broadcasting, multimedia pedagogy, and hyperlocal journalism.

BRUCE MIMS (PhD, University of Southern Mississippi) is professor emeritus of mass media at Southeast Missouri State University (1989–2018). He is coauthor (with John Allen Hendricks) of *The Radio Station: Broadcasting, Podcasting and Streaming* (10th ed.). His research has also been published in the *Journal of Radio Studies*, *Journalism and Mass Communication Educator*, *Radio World*, and *Billboard*. His research interests include programming history and broadcast technology.

MICHAEL NEVRADAKIS (PhD, University of Texas at Austin) is an instructor in communication at Deree–The American College of Greece. His dissertation, titled "From the Polis to Facebook: Social Media and the Development of a New Greek Public Sphere," drew upon multiyear research performed in Greece studying the impact of social and new media on the public sphere, civil society, and public discourse during the Greek economic crisis. He was a Fulbright scholar and has received scholarships from the Alexander S. Onassis Foundation, the Greek State Scholarships Foundation, and the Erasmus+ program, in addition to a dissertation grant from Phi Kappa Phi. Currently, he is working on publishing his first book, based on his dissertation, and continues to perform research pertaining to social and new media and the public sphere, and to the Greek media landscape. His other research interests encompass media and telecommunications policy, alternative and community media, global and international media, the media industry, communications technology, radio studies, and diaspora media. He produces and hosts Dialogos Radio, is an independent journalist contributing to *Mint Press News* and other outlets, and is general manager and program director of LPFM station WCSQ-LP 105.9 FM in New York.

SIMON ORDER (PhD, Murdoch University) works at the School of Arts in Murdoch University, Western Australia, within the creative media disciplines. His teaching, research, and creative outcomes are primarily from across the areas of sound, music, and radio. Community Radio in Australia is one of his strong foci, while creativity and music technology also figure strongly in his research. In the world of electronic music, as a production practitioner, his alter-ego, *Liminal Drifter*, is globally known for his immersive and ambient dreamtronica. His music and interviews appear regularly on PBS's radio program *Echoes* (United States) and SBS Chill in Australia, among many others. His professional background includes audio production roles in the U.K. television and music industry, radio station manager, and professional photographer. As former academic director of media and mass communications for Murdoch University in Dubai, he developed the United Arab Emirates' premier tertiary media education center. He now teaches radio broadcasting, sound production, and music technology at Murdoch University in Australia.

DANIEL RIFFE (PhD, University of Tennessee) is Richard Cole Eminent Professor at the UNC–Chapel Hill School of Media and Journalism. His teaching and research areas include research methodology, broadcast news, political communication, mass communication and environmental risk, international news, and government-press relations. He has published three books or monographs, eighty-five refereed journal articles, and ninety-two refereed conference papers.

MARK WARD SR. (PhD, Clemson University) is associate professor of communication at the University of Houston–Victoria, Texas. His research on American evangelical culture and popular media has been published in numerous books, journals, and chapters (for a bibliography, see markwardphd.com), and he has been quoted by the *New York Times*, *Politico*, Bloomberg, Religion News Service, Associated Press, and other media outlets. He is a winner of the Clifford G. Christians Ethics Research Award for his multivolume series *The Electronic Church in the Digital Age: Cultural Impacts of Evangelical Mass Media* and of the David R. Maines Narrative Research Award and Religious Communication Association Article of the Year Award for his ethnographic research on evangelical culture. His books include two histories of religious broadcasting, *The Lord's Radio: Gospel Music Broadcasting and the Making of Evangelical Culture, 1920–1960* and *Air of Salvation: The Story of Christian Broadcasting*. In 2018, he was named his institution's scholar of the year.

LU WU (PhD, University of North Carolina at Chapel Hill) is an instructor and the Associated Program chair at University of Colorado Denver and International College Beijing. Her primary research focuses on digital transformation of news production and processes and journalism sustainability in the digital environment. Her research also explores how digital technologies adopted by news outlets are changing audiences' usage experiences and how new experiences can translate to uses and gratifications, audience loyalty, and engagement. Her work has been published in various peer-reviewed journals, including *Mass Communication & Society*, *Newspaper Research Journal*, *Electronic News*, and *Journal of Mental Health*.

LAITH ZURAIKAT (MA, Upper Iowa University) has primarily had his work published in the realm of news media, having written for multiple newspapers over the last several years. He also has a background in the field of art and photography, having had his work shown in multiple juried shows. This is his first academic publication to date. His main research interests in the field of communications media focus on social media, modern cinema, media marketing, and the intersection between athletics and the media. He is currently pursuing his PhD in communications media and instructional technology at Indiana University of Pennsylvania.

# Index

AAA (adult album alternative) commercial stations, 158
ABC Radio, 77, 140
"Aboriginal" broadcasting regulations, Canada, 202–203. *See also* Indigenous radio, Canada
Aboriginal Christian Voice Network, 202
Abumrad, Jad, 177, 178, 179, 180
accessing content. *See* content delivery means
Adamidis, Ioannis, 235
Ad Council, 11
advertising, 53–63; copyright law and, 10–11; on freeform radio, 123; listenership trends and, 53–54, 55; NPR and, 158, 167, 168; NTR and, 55–56; on podcasts, 5, 48–49; price drop in, 69–70; replaces radio network sponsorship, 113; satellite radio operates commercial-free, 11; television, 48; on Top 40, 121; traditional spots, 55. *See also* commercial radio; funding; revenue
AEPI (intellectual property administration organization, Greece), 237–238
African Americans: black podcasting networks, 176–177; NPR and, 155, 156, 168; religious radio and, 143
age of listeners. *See* listener demographics
Ahlkvist, J., 126
Air1, 143
*Air Raid* (1938 radio drama), 97, 107, 114, 115
Akron, Ohio, 79

album-oriented rock (AOR) format, 124, 125
Allen, M., 50
All India Radio, 263, 265
Allison, Jay, 214
Allport, Gordon, 97, 114
*All Songs Considered* (NPR program), 158, 159
*All Things Considered* (NPR program), 154, 157, 159, 163, 165
Alpha Media, 70
alternative music, 125. *See also* freeform radio
AMARC (World Association for Community Radio Broadcasters), 261
Amazon Music, listenership statistics, 13–14
American Family Radio, 142–143
American Federation of Television and Radio Artists (AFRA), 11
American Radio Act (1927), 194
American Society of Composers, Authors, and Publishers (ASCAP), 9, 121
AM/FM radio. *See* terrestrial radio
AM/FM receivers, 4, 5, 7. *See also* content delivery means
*Amos 'n Andy* (radio program), 140
AM radio, 122, 166; FM radio, 122, 123, 124–125, 127
analog technology. *See* digital technology; terrestrial radio
Andritsos, Nikos, 235
Ang, Ien, 100

283

Anna FM (Indian radio station), 265
Antigold Greece, 246
appeal of radio, 209–211
Apple iPods, 15, 211, 212
Apple Music, 12, 13–14
apps, 6, 17–18, 145. *See also* content delivery means
Arbitron, 7
Arrow Radio, 202
ART FM (Greece), 237
*As It Happens* (CBC program), 163, 212, 223
Associated Press, 105
Association, the, 123
Association of College and University Radio Stations (later National Association of Education Broadcasters), 156
Astro FM (Greece), 241
Athens International Radio, 249
Atlantis FM (Greece), 241
Audible, 159
audience building, format stations and, 119, 121, 126–127, 131–132. *See also* listeners, number of
audience building, freeform radio and, 120–132; college stations, 120, 125; community stations, 120, 125–126, 127–131; corporatization and, 124; female DJs, 124; financial challenges, 121, 122; introduction to unfamiliar music, 122, 123, 126, 130, 131; listener numbers, 120, 124, 127–131, 132; satellite radio and, 126–127; WLPN, 120, 127–131. *See also* freeform radio
audience fragmentation, religious radio, 145–146
audience statistics. *See* listener demographics; listeners, number of
"audio," as medium, 4–6
Audion (the "tube"), 3
"aural imaginary" theory, 175, 177, 185
Australia, 258–260, 267
Australian Broadcast Corporation, 259
automobiles, 5, 6, 16, 48, 54
Ayyaz Bhunnoo, Seth, 175, 182

backstage transparency, 213, 214, 218, 222, 224–225. *See also* intimacy
*Back to the Bible* (radio program), 140
Bailey, George, 157
Baker, M. B., 173
Baker, Nick, 103

Bakker, Jim, 145
Balan Siva, K. C., 266
Baldwin, Alec, 207
Baltimore, Maryland, 86
Baltzis, Alexandros, 234
Bandelli, D., 262, 264
Barnhouse, Donald Grey, 140
Barrett, B., 17–18
Bartos, Adrian, 160
Batey, Dick, 194
BBC Radio 2, 164–165, 168
BBC World Service, 257
Beam, R. A., 36
"beautiful music" stations, 122
Beck, Glen, 83
Bergdahl, Bowe, 223
Berkman Center for Internet & Society (Harvard), 15
Berlin Funkstunde (Germany), 104
Berman, Doug, 161
Berry, R., 15, 214
Biagi, S., 4
*Bible Study Hour* (radio program), 140
Billboard awards, Stern and, 85
Billy Graham Evangelistic Association, 149
binge listening, 223
black podcasting networks, 176–177
"black voice," 176
blogs, 212
Blumberg, Alex, 213
Bogdanovich, Peter, 110, 111
Boilen, Bob, 158, 159
Booth, J., 195
Borrell, Gordon, 18
Borrett, Mrs. Giles, 255
Boubouka, Aggeliki, 238
Brady, Frank, 107, 108, 110–111
break-in news announcements, 114; in *Broadcasting the Barricades*, 99, 101–103; in *Death Triangle*, 97; in *Minister Is Murdered!*, 104; in *War of the Worlds*, 96, 97, 98, 105, 108–109, 112. *See also* news reporting narrative style
Briggs, Asa, 112
British Broadcasting Corporation (BBC): BBC Radio 2, 164–165, 168; *Broadcasting the Barricades* on, 99–103; funding for, 164, 165, 168; history of, 100; podcasting, 212; RTE, compared, 167; women at, 255, 257–258, 259
British General Post Office, 100

BroadcastAmerica.com, 7, 8
Broadcast.com, 7, 8
Broadcast Education Association, 62–63
*Broadcast Hysteria: Orson Welles's War of the Worlds and the Art of Fake News* (Schwartz), 111
broadcasting, legal distinction, 10
Broadcasting Act (Government of Canada, 1991), 196, 198, 203
*Broadcasting the Barricades* (1926 radio drama), 97, 99–103, 110, 114, 115
broadcast integration concept, 138, 146
Broadcast Music, Incorporated (BMI), 9
broadcast radio. *See* terrestrial radio
Brock University, 200
Brooks, Arthur, 70
Brown, A., 83
Brown, Jesse, 219
Brown, R. R., 139
BRS Media, 7, 8
Bryant, Chuck, 225
Bush, George H. W., 141

Calvary Episcopal Church, 139
campus radio. *See* Canadian campus/community radio; college radio
Canada: broadcasting history, 193–195, 211; commercial radio in, 193–195, 197, 201, 203; funding for programming in, 164, 196, 197–201, 202, 203, 215, 227; podcast ratings data, 215–216, 217; regulations in, 193, 194–196, 197, 199, 201–203; U.S. podcasts popular in, 219, 227. *See also* podcasting, Canadian-produced
*Canadaland* (podcast), 219, 224, 225
Canadian Broadcasting Corporation (CBC), 163, 194, 203; digital-first strategy, 227; elitism reputation, 211; northern service expansion, 195, 196; podcasts by, 208, 212, 213–214, 215, 217, 219, 221
Canadian campus/community radio, 193–203; Broadcasting Act outlines mission of, 196, 198, 203; CRTC *Three-Year Plan 2016–2019*, 196–197, 203; dial frequency competition, 201; digital media and, 195, 197, 203; early history of, 193–195, 197; funding and support for, 196, 197–201, 203; grassroots action and, 196, 197; Indigenous radio, 196, 197, 201, 202–203; license renewal data, 195, 197–200, 201–203; localism and, 194, 196, 197, 198, 203; volunteers in, 198–200, 201. *See also* college radio; community radio
Canadian Radio and Television Commission (CRTC; later Canadian Radio-Television and Telecommunications Commission), 195, 196–203; dial frequency competition decisions, 201; Indigenous radio, 196, 197, 201, 202–203; license oversight by, 197–200, 201–203; *Three-Year Plan 2016–2019*, 196–197, 203; volunteers, findings about, 198–200
Canadian Radio Broadcasting Commission, 194, 211
Cantril, Hadley, 97, 110, 114
Carnegie Commission, 156, 167
Carr, David, 160
*Car Talk* (NPR program), 161
Carter, Jimmy, 141
*Casablanca* (film), 108
CBC. *See* Canadian Broadcasting Corporation (CBC)
CBS Radio, 9, 70, 76, 77, 140; Canadian station affiliates, 194; Welles and, 98, 111
Central Intelligence Agency, 177
CFRC (Kingston), 199
Chaffee, S. H., 24
chain broadcasting, 140
Chala Ho Gaon Mein (India), 264
Chatzistefanou, Aris, 250
*Chicago Sunday Tribune,* 106
*Children's Hour* (radio program), 101
Chipmunk Punk, 130
Christian radio. *See* religious radio
Christian Satellite Network, 143
"Christmas Serial" (*Saturday Night Live* sketch), 227–228
CHRY (Toronto), 199–200
churches: electronic, 142, 145, 149; service broadcasts, 139. *See also* religious radio
Church of the Foursquare Gospel, 139
*Citizen Welles* (Brady), 107, 108, 110–111
CKDU-FM (Halifax), 201
CKUT (Montreal), 199
Clarke, Josh, 225
classical music, 158
Clear Channel, 23, 88, 126. *See also* iHeartMedia (formerly Clear Channel Communications)
Clinton, Hillary, 154
CMJ New Music Report, 125
Cobequid Radio and Hubbards Radio, 201

college radio, 9, 84, 120, 125; early "educational" radio and, 156, 162–163. *See also* Canadian campus/community radio; freeform radio
Collins, Ray, 107, 108
*Colour Code* (podcast), 219, 224, 225
*Columbia Journalism Review,* 70, 168
*Columbia Workshop, The* (radio program), 105, 107
*Comedy of Danger, A* (1924 radio drama), 112
commercial radio: in Australia, 259, 267; BBC, competition, 164, 167; in Canada, 193–195, 197, 201, 203; consolidation in, 27; copyright law and, 10, 11; educational broadcasting and, 156; format radio, 126; freeform radio, 125; in Greece, 233, 237, 238; in India, 263; music and, 210; news-oriented, 154; radiogenic elements, 210; satellite radio, competition, 11; streaming content by, 7, 9; talk radio, 211. *See also* advertising; public radio; terrestrial radio
commercial radio, localism and. *See* localism, American talk radio study
commercial radio, religious. *See* religious radio
commercial radio, social media analytics for. *See* social media analytics
Communications Act (1934), 113
community, genre audiences building, 138
community radio, 125–126; grassroots movements and funding, 196, 197, 267; NPR member stations, 163–164; WLPN, 120, 127–131; women and, 259–262, 263–266. *See also* Canadian campus/community radio
Community Radio Forum (CRF), 263
Community Radio Fund of Canada, 201
*Complete Television, Radio & Cable Industry Directory,* 28, 30
composition copyrights, 9
Connolly, B., 10
conscription model, 11
consolidation, 9, 55; after Telecommunications Act, 27, 69; in Canada, 194; effects on local programming, 67, 69–70, 80; effects on religious radio, 138, 139, 142, 143, 144, 150; in Greece, 236; satellite radio, 11–12, 89–90. *See also* station ownership

content delivery means, 4–6; automobiles, 5, 16, 48, 54; mobile devices, 6, 12–13, 45–46, 47, 53, 179; NPR and, 157, 158–159; phones, 6, 179; podcasting and, 46–47; receivers, 4, 5, 7, 11; religious radio and, 139, 144–145, 149; satellite radio, 11. *See also* Internet radio; streaming; terrestrial radio
Contogeorgis, Georges, 234, 238
Copyright Act (1976), 9
copyright law, 9–11
Corporation for Public Broadcasting, 154, 155, 156, 159, 164. *See also* Public Broadcasting Act (1967)
*Criminal* (podcast), 219
*Crimson Wizard, The* (1938 radio drama), 97, 106–107, 114, 115
Crisell, A., 209–210
Cronbach's alpha reliability coefficient, 30, 33
crusade evangelism, 139
Cumulus, 18
*Current, The* (CBC program), 212, 225
Curtius, Julius, 105

*Daily, The* (podcast), 219, 225–226
Daystar Television Network, 145
*Death Triangle, The* (1937 radio drama), 97
*Decision* magazine, 149
*Definitely Not the Opera* (CBC program), 212
demographics of listeners. *See* listener demographics
deregulation: religious radio and, 139, 142, 144; Telecommunications Act, 27, 69, 126, 142. *See also* consolidation; regulation(s)
deregulation, Greek broadcasting and. *See* regulation(s), Greek broadcasting and
designingsound.org, 180
Detroit, Michigan, 85
Devine, T., 178
*diaploki* (political/media interplay in Greece), 233–234, 237, 239, 250–251
Dibble, J. L., 41–42, 44
digital audio broadcasting (DAB), 243–244, 250
Digital Millennium Copyright Act (DMCA), 10–11
Digital Performance Right in Sound Recordings Act (1995), 10
Digital Power (Greece), 244

digital radio. *See* Internet radio; podcasting; satellite radio; streaming
digital technology, development and proliferation, 3–18; "audio" classification, 4–6; in Canada, 195, 197, 203; in Greece, 243, 244, 250; listener statistics and, 6, 25, 54; on-demand listening, 5–6, 25, 158–161, 178, 208, 215, 227; religious radio and, 138, 144–145, 149. *See also* Internet radio; podcasting; satellite radio; social media; streaming; terrestrial radio
Digity, 70
disc jockeys (DJs): on college and community stations, 125–126; female, 124; first use of term, 121; freeform radio, 119–120, 123, 124, 125–126, 128–132; live playing by, at bars and clubs, 129–130; Top 40, 121, 124–125; underground rock, 123; at WLPN, 128–131
*Dispatches* (CBC program), 212
Dobson, James, 141, 142, 148, 149
Donahue, Tom, 123
Donkinson, William, 100
*Do's and Don'ts of Radio Writing* (Rogers), 97
Douglas, Susan, 97, 112, 114, 115
Downey, J., 260
downloading, 12–13, 54, 144, 145. *See also* streaming
downloading podcasts, 14–15, 45, 49; evolution of technology, 15, 46–47; ratings based on download numbers, 46–47, 176–177, 213, 215, 225, 227. *See also* podcasting
*Dracula* (1938 radio drama), 108
Drakakis, John, 112
dramaturgy theory, 213
"driveway moments," 210
Dubber, A., 210
Dubner, Stephen, 223
Duffy, Dennis, 194
Dunbar-Hester, C., 70

earphones, 49. *See also* intimacy
Ebermeyer, Erich, 104–105
Eckstein, J., 178, 185, 186
Edison Research, 13, 15–17
education: Broadcast Education Association, 62–63; level of NPR listeners, 155, 156, 157, 160, 161, 163, 168

Educational Media Foundation, 143
"educational" radio, 156, 162–163
Ejnes, S., 180
elitism reputation: of CBC, 211; of NPR, 155, 160–162, 167–168
Ellenberger, Kurt, 157–158
empowerment, 262–263
engaging storytelling, 210, 214, 217; history of experimentation with, 99–103, 112, 113–115. *See also* radiogenic elements; *War of the Worlds, The* (1938 radio broadcast)
Engelman, Ralph, 162
Entercom, 7, 9, 70
entertainment stations, Greece, 236–237
Entrepreneur.com, 55
Erickson, D., 69, 80
ERT Open (Greek online station), 232, 239–240, 243, 248–249, 250
ESR (National Radio-Television Council, Greece), 234–236, 238, 240, 242
*Essays in Satire* (Knox), 103
evangelical Christians: early distrust of radio, 139; evangelical mass culture, 138, 140–141, 146, 149; fragmentation of movement, 138, 146; fundamentalism, 147–148; network airtime purchased by, 140, 141; number of, 137, 138; as voting bloc, 141, 149. *See also* religious radio
Evans, Chris, 258
Experience of Parasocial Interaction (EPSI) scale, 42

Facebook, 56, 60, 61, 185–186
face-to-face interactions, 39–40. *See also* parasocial interactions
"Fact of the Matter, The" (*Radiolab* episode), 174. *See also* "Yellow Rain" (*Radiolab* story)
Fairness Doctrine, 141–142
fake news, *War of the Worlds* considered, 96, 97–98, 99, 110–112, 115
*Fall of the City, The* (1937 radio drama), 97, 105, 107, 114, 115
Falwell, Jerry, 141
fandom of *Howard Stern Radio Show*, 82–87, 91–94
fandom scholarship, 83–84
Fass, Bob, 123
Fauteux, Brian, 195

Federal Communications Commission (FCC): creation of, 113; Fairness Doctrine decision, 141–142; Main Studio Rule, 80; programming duplication restriction, 123; public radio and, 162; religious radio and, 140, 141–142; station ownership regulations, 126; Stern and, 82–83, 84. *See also* regulation(s)
Federal Council of Churches, 140
Federal Radio Commission, 139
feminism, evangelicalism and, 148
Fenton, N., 260
Fessenden, Reginald, 3, 139
field recording, 209, 221
Fioravanti, Dom, 86
*Fissures in the Mediascape: An International Study of Citizens' Media* (Rodriguez), 261
Flegel, R. C., 24
Flesch, Hans, 104
Florini, S., 176–177
FM radio, 122, 123, 124–125, 127; AM radio, 122, 166
Focus on the Family, 145
*Focus on the Family* (radio program), 141, 148
*Forbes,* 18
Ford, Gerald, 141
Forde, S., 260–261
Ford Foundation, 156
Forest, Lee de, 3
"Forgotten Interlude, A" (*Broadcasting the Barricades* script, Knox), 103
format radio, 158; audience building, 119, 121, 126–127, 131–132; defined, 121; on FM stations, 122, 124–125, 127. *See also* freeform radio; religious radio
Fox, Justin, 156
Fox News, 155
Foxwell, K., 260–261
Fraser, N., 260–261
*Freakonomics* (podcast), 219, 223
freeform radio, 119–132; college stations, 120, 125; community stations, 120, 125–126, 127–131; DJs, 119–120, 123, 124, 125–126, 128–132; evolution of, 120–127; funding for, 120, 121, 122, 124; gender and, 124; genre-based and genre-spanning programming, 130; listenability, 129; musicologists philosophy to programming, 126; streaming services and,

126–127, 132; underground rock and, 123–124; WFMU, 128, 131; WLPN, 120, 127–131. *See also* audience building, freeform radio and
free radio (Greece), 246
frequencies, competition, 201–202
*Fresh Air* (podcast), 160, 223
Front de Libération du Québec (FLQ), 195
Frontstage (media group), 236
Fuller, Charles, 140, 141, 148
Fuller, Grace, 148
fundamentalism, religious, 147–148
funding: for BBC, 164, 165, 168; for Canadian community/campus radio, 196, 197–201, 203; for Canadian content, 164, 196, 197–201, 202, 203, 215, 227; by Corporation for Public Broadcasting, 154, 155, 156, 159, 164; for early radio programming, 104; freeform radio and, 120, 121, 122, 124; for Greek content, 249; for Indian content, 261, 265; for Indigenous programming, 202; listener donations, 122, 167, 212–213, 219; NTR and, 53, 55–56; for podcasts, 48–49, 212–213, 219; radio network sponsorship, 113, 121, 123; for religious radio, 139, 140, 141, 145–146; for RTE, 167, 168. *See also* advertising; grassroots movements and funding; public broadcasting, funding for; revenue
funding, for NPR: listener support, 167, 212–213; Public Broadcasting Act and, 154, 155, 156, 159, 164; underwriting, 161, 167, 168. *See also* National Public Radio (NPR)

Garcia, Robert, 160
Garden, Mary, 120
Garment, Charles, 165
Gasteyer, Ana, 207
Gaudet, Hazel, 110
*Gawker,* 208
*GB Times* news service, 241
gender: freeform radio and, 124; religious radio and, 143, 144; "Yellow Rain" reactions and, 186–187, 188
Gender Policy for Community Radio (AMARC WIN), 261
geographical distribution of listeners, 69, 155, 195, 196, 197, 242

index • 289

George Newnes, Ltd., 100
George V, King of England, 209
Germany, 97, 104–105
Gimlet Media, 213
Giovanni, David, 157
*Gist, The* (podcast), 225
Gladstone, Brooke, 179
Glass, Ira, 210, 213, 214
GlobalMedia.com, 7, 8
Global Media Monitoring Project (GMMP), 256–257, 266–267
Goffman, E., 213
Goldhoorn, C., 40–41, 42, 50
Goldthwaite, M., 5
Google Analytics settings, 61
Google Play All Access, listenership statistics, 13–14
Google Podcasts, 17–18
Graham, Billy, 141
grassroots movements and funding: in Canada, 196, 197; community radio and, 196, 197, 267; freeform radio and, 121; in Greece, 249; in India, 263, 264, 265; local NPR member stations, 163; podcasting and, 176. *See also* funding
Great Britain, 164, 168. *See also* British Broadcasting Corporation (BBC)
Great Recession, 70
Greece, 231–251; clientelist relations, 232, 233, 238; DAB in, 243–244, 250; economic crisis, 232, 242; ERT Open, 232, 239–240, 243, 248–249, 250; ESR in, 234–236, 238, 240, 242; Internet radio in, 245; podcasting in, 249–250; "polarized pluralist" model, 232, 233, 238; political/media interplay *(diaploki)*, 232–234, 237, 238–239, 244, 249; privately-owned broadcasting introduced in, 234–235; research methods, 232; satellite radio in, 244–245; self-management station status, 240–241; station classifications as news or entertainment, 236–237, 239, 246–249. *See also* regulation(s), Greek broadcasting and
Gregg, P. B., 50
Grigoropoulos, Alexandros, 247
Grossberg, L., 83–84, 92
grounded theory method, 216
*Grownups Read Things They Wrote as Kids* (podcast), 219
Grundmann, Anya, 159–160

*Guardian, The,* 15, 211–212, 247, 258
Gzowski, Peter, 210

Habermas, Jürgen, 67–68, 69, 260, 261
Hall, Tony, 258
Hallin, D. C., 231, 232–233, 238, 242, 250
Hammersley, Ben, 15, 211–212
Hand, Richard J., 112
Haraway, D., 183
Harris, M., 12, 13
Hart, Dennis, 165–166
Hartford, Connecticut, 84–85
Hartmann, T., 40–41, 42, 50
Harvard University, 15
*Have You Had Your Breakfast Yet?* (KAXE program), 163
headphones, 49. *See also* intimacy
Hellas Sat consortium, 244–245
Hellenic Commission of Telecommunications and Post (EETT, Greece), 243
Hertz, Heinrich, 3
Herzog, Herta, 110
*Hidden Brain* (radio program/podcast), 224
Hispanics, NPR and, 156, 168
Hitler, Adolph, 105
Hmong narrative in "Yellow Rain," 174, 175, 177–178, 180–185, 186–187. *See also* "Yellow Rain" (*Radiolab* story)
"Holiday" (Madonna), 129, 131
Holmes, D., 146–147
Holy Cross Community Radio, Tamil Nadu (India), 265
"Holy Terror: The First Great Radio Hoax" (Slade), 110
hooks, bell, 263
Horton, Donald, 40, 83–84
*Hot Doc* magazine, 234
Hot FM (Greece), 241, 249
*Hour of Decision* (radio program), 141
Houseman, John, 108, 111
*Howard Stern Radio Show, The:* calls in, 84, 92, 94; fandom, 82–87, 91–94; FCC and, 82–83, 84; Infinity Broadcasting and, 86, 87, 88; interviews, 85, 87–88, 91; on NBC, 86–87; Norris and, 85; Quivers and, 83, 85, 86; ratings, 84, 87, 90–91; on satellite radio, 82, 88, 89–91; show segments, 85–86; Stern's on-air reflections on his early life, 84; Wack Pack on, 85, 92; on WXRK, 86, 87. *See also* Stern, Howard

*How I Built This* (radio program/
   podcast), 224
Hristianismos FM (Greece), 241
Hughes, Richard, 112
*Hyphen Magazine,* 178, 185, 187

*Ideas* (CBC program), 212, 223
identity presentation, on social media, 185–186
iHeartMedia (formerly Clear Channel
   Communications), 18, 23; localism study
   and, 76–77, 79
iHeartRadio, 7, 13–14, 15, 23
imagination: aural imaginary, 175, 177, 185;
   early radio experimentation and, 97, 111,
   112, 114, 115; intimacy and, 210; parasocial
   interactions and, 50, 93
income level of listeners, 155, 157, 161, 163
India, 259, 261–266, 267–268
Indigenous people, *Missing and Murdered*
   and, 221, 222–223
Indigenous radio, Canada, 196, 197, 201,
   202–203
*Indivisible America* (radio program), 169
industry consolidation. *See* consolidation
*Infinite Dial 2018* (Edison Research study),
   13–14, 15–16
Infinity Broadcasting, 7, 86, 87, 88
*Insight for Living* (radio program), 141, 148
Instagram, 56
intellectual property law, 9–11, 237–238
International Harvesters for Christ
   Evangelistic Association Inc., 201
Internet Advertising Bureau (IAB), 14, 16
Internet radio, 6–11, 245; copyright law
   and, 9, 10–11; media network providers
   list, 7, 8; news organizations and, 22–23;
   podcasts, compared, 45; program
   scheduling, 25, 35; terrestrial radio
   programming as, 6, 7–9, 22–23, 25, 29;
   terrestrial radio revenue through, 54.
   *See also* digital technology, development
   and proliferation; streaming; terrestrial
   radio
Internet Talk Radio, 55
interpretive community, concept, 138, 146
intimacy: earphones and, 49; terrestrial
   radio and, 49, 209–210, 214
intimacy, parasocial interactions and, 41, 49,
   51–52; podcasts and, 43, 44, 48; Stern
   and, 93. *See also* parasocial interactions

intimacy, podcasts and: analysis coding for,
   217–218, 220, 221; backstage transparency,
   213, 214, 218, 222, 224–225; host connection and, 224–225; parasocial interactions
   and, 43, 44, 48; parody of, 227; prestige
   podcasts, 208, 214, 220, 221–223; public
   radio-based production and, 208,
   214–215, 219–221, 221–225; through
   narrative sound design, 179, 187. *See also*
   podcasting
*In Touch* (radio program), 141, 148
*Invisibilia* (NPR program), 159, 161–162
iPhones, 17–18
iPods, 15, 211, 212
Ireland, 166
Irodotos FM (Nostos FM, Greece), 241
iTunes charts, 176–177, 215–216, 221

Jacobs, Fred, 17
Jacobs, Paul, 17
Jacobs Media, 5, 17
Jacobson, T., 68, 69
Janis, Elsie, 255
*Jay Sekulow Live* (radio program), 145
jazz music, 157–158
Jeremiah, David, 142, 149
*Jeremy Vine Show, The* (BBC program), 165
*Jesus Calling* (devotional book and
   associated media), 145
job loss in industry, 70
*Joe Rogan Experience, The* (podcast), 219,
   224
Johnson, Lyndon, 156
Joseph, A., 262
journalism, 24, 186–187, 208; podcasts and,
   213–214, 217–218, 220, 221. *See also*
   British Broadcasting Corporation (BBC);
   Canadian Broadcasting Corporation
   (CBC); National Public Radio (NPR);
   news

KABL (San Francisco), 122
Kadoglou, Maria, 246
KALW (San Francisco), 212, 224
Kamen, Jeff, 157
Kar, E. S., 265
Karlsson, M., 213
Karvounopoulos, Paris, 239
Kassner, Minna F., 113
Katz, Donald, 159

Katz, E., 40
KAXE-KBXE FM (Grand Rapids, Michigan and Bemidji, Minnesota), 163–164
KCBS (San Francisco), 4
KDKA (first radio station, Pittsburgh), 4, 76–77, 139
Keefe, Dylan, 180
Kennedy, D. James, 141, 142
KFAB-AM (Omaha), 74
KFSG (Los Angeles), 139
Khan, G. F., 56
Kheshti, R., 175, 179, 185
"King Schmaltz Bagel Hour" (Stern's first comedic talk show), 84
Kiss FM (Greece), 243
Kittross, J. M., 4
KKXT (Dallas), 158
K-LOVE, 143
KMPX (San Francisco), 124
Knox, Ronald Arbuthnott, 99–103
Koch, Howard E., 108
Koenig, Sarah, 214, 223, 227
Kogen, L., 233
KOIL-AM (Omaha), 74–75
Kounenakis, Panos, 247, 248
KOWH (Omaha), 121
Kozolanka, K., 195
KQW (San Jose), 4
Krippendorff's alpha reliability coefficient, 73
Krulwich, Robert, 177, 178, 183–184; apologizes for tone in "Yellow Rain," 186, 187; K. Yang's response to, 185
Kumanyika, C., 176
KYW (Chicago), 120

Lacy, S., 26, 71, 209
Lamb, Marcus, 145
Lardikou, Christina, 247
Larsen, Roy Edward, 97
Larson, Sara, 162
Leaming, Barbara, 111, 114
Lee, Robert M., 106
legislation. *See* regulation(s)
leitmotifs, 179–183
*Let's Talk TV: A Conversation with Canadians* (CRTC), 197
Levy, Mark, 258
Lewis, P. M., 195
licenses, operations and broadcasting: BBC and, 164; in Canada, 193–194, 195, 197–200, 201–203; FCC and, 113, 139, 140; in Greece, 231, 235, 237, 242, 251; RTE and, 168. *See also* regulation(s)
Lieber, Matt, 213
*Light and Life Hour, The* (radio program), 140
Limbaugh, Rush, 74, 83
Lind, R. A., 6–7
Lindgren, M., 209, 214
Lindlof, T. R., 138, 146–147
LinkedIn, 56
listener demographics, 5; BBC, 164–165; education and income level, 155, 156, 157, 160, 161, 163, 168; gender, 263–264, 265–266, 267; geographic distribution, 69, 155, 195, 196, 197, 242; music streaming services, 13; NPR, 154–160, 168; podcasting, 15–16, 46, 160, 176; political ideology, 69; race, 155, 156, 160, 168, 176; religious radio, 143–144; terrestrial radio, 46, 53–54. *See also* National Public Radio (NPR), audience inclusivity issues
listener demographics, age, 5, 53–54; BBC, 164–165; music streaming services, 13; NPR, 154, 155, 156, 158–160, 168; podcasting, 15–16, 160, 212
listeners, as active agents, 174–175, 185, 188
listeners, number of: advertising and, 5, 53–54, 55; CBC, 211; freeform radio and, 120, 124, 127–131, 132; Internet radio, growth, 6, 7, 23, 25; music streaming services, 13–14; NPR, 154, 157–158, 159, 160–161, 168; podcasting, 15–17, 25, 46–47, 160, 176, 208, 212; religious radio, 144; satellite radio, 12, 25; terrestrial radio, 15–16, 46, 53–54, 121, 159, 168; Top 40 stations, 121
listener support. *See* funding
*Live from the Poundstone Institute* (podcast), 160
"liveness," as radiogenic quality, 209
Local Community Radio Act, 127
localism: Canadian broadcasting and, 194, 196, 197, 198, 203; "educational" radio and, 156; local content, 27; NPR member stations and, 162–164, 168–169; religious radio and, 141, 142, 143
localism, American talk radio study, 67–80; data analysis, 73–77; declining localism, 69–71, 79; market size, 71, 72, 73–76, 78–79

localism, American talk radio study (cont.) nationalism trend, 69–70; public sphere theory and, 68–69; research methods, 72–73; station ownership, 71, 72, 73, 79, 80; syndicated programming category in, 70, 72–78, 80
Louisville, Kentucky, 76
low power FM (LPFM) stations, 127
Lowrey, W., 35
*Lutheran Hour, The* (radio program), 140
Lydon, Christopher, 15
Lymberis Media Group, 236

MacArthur, John, 141, 142
MacDougall, R. C., 43, 45, 179
MacLeish, Archibald, 97, 105, 107
Madonna, 129, 131
Madsen, V., 179
Magliozzi, Ray, 161
Magliozzi, Tom, 161
Maier, Walter, 140
Main Studio Rule (FCC), 80
Malamud, Carl, 55
Malik, K., 262, 264
Mancini, Henry, 122
Mancini, P., 231, 232–233, 238, 242, 250
Mango Radio (Greece), 249
Mann Deshi Tarang Vahini (India), 263–264
*March of Time, The* (radio program), 96–97, 98, 105
Marconi, Guglielmo, 3
Maria's Community Bar, 129, 130
Marinakis, Vangelis, 240–241
Maris, Dimitris, 240
market size, 58, 60–62, 121, 126, 142, 201; localism and, 71, 72, 73–76, 78–79
Mars, Roman, 212, 224
Marshall, George L., 99, 101, 103
Marszewski, Ed (WLPN station director), 129
Mastrocola, Daniela, 200
Maxwell, James Clark, 3
Mazepa, P., 195
McCauley, Michael P., 156, 157, 167–168, 169
McCourt, Tom, 167
McIntyre, H., 12
McKay, Anne, 255
McLean, Stuart, 226
McLemore, John B., 222
McPherson, Aimee Semple, 139

Meadows, M., 260–261
Media-Com, 79
media gender equality: community radio and, 259–262, 263–266; GMMP and, 256–257, 266–267. *See also* women
media genre audience, 138
media theory, 146–147
Medoff, N. J., 6–7
Mercury Theatre (drama company), 108
*Mercury Theatre on the Air, The* (radio program), 98, 105, 108, 111
mergers and acquisitions. *See* consolidation
Merzbow, 129, 131
Meselson, Matt, 181, 182
Metaxas, Eric, 149
Meyrowitz, J., 213
*Microphone Check* (NPR program), 159, 160
*Mike Gallagher Show* (radio program), 145
Miller, Larry, 18
Millington, C., 257
*Minister Is Murdered!, The* (*Der Minister ist ermordet!*, 1930 radio drama), 97, 104–105, 114, 115
*Missing and Murdered: Who Killed Alberta Williams?* (CBC podcast), 221, 222–223
*Missing Richard Simmons* (podcast), 223
Mitchell, Jack, 156, 164
Mix, Jennie Irene, 255–256
Mixcloud, 248
mobile devices, 6, 12–13, 45–46, 47, 53, 179. *See also* content delivery means
Mohn, Jarl, 160
*Monitor* (NBC radio program), 165–166, 168
*Monitor, the Last Great Radio Show* (Hart), 165
Moody, Dwight Lyman, 147–148
Moody Bible Institute, 139
Moody Radio, 143
*Morning Edition* (NPR program), 154, 159, 224
Moronis, Rodolfos, 238
Morris, J. W., 173
Moscote Freire, A., 173
*Moth Radio Hour, The* (podcast), 214
movies, 4
MP3 technology, podcasting and, 15
music: industry revenue, 54; leitmotifs in podcasting, 180–182; musical work copyrights, 9–10; peer-to-peer file-sharing and, 211; radiogenic element of,

210; streaming services, 4, 5, 12–14, 54, 126–127, 132
musicologist philosophy to programming, 126
music programming, 210–211; BBC, 165; format radio, 122, 158; freeform radio, 122, 123, 125, 126, 130, 131; Greek online radio, 237–238, 245, 249, 250; NPR, 157–158, 159, 162. *See also* freeform radio
Mutual Broadcasting System, 140, 194

Najoo, Farhad, 162
Namma Dhwani (Our Voices), 265
National Association of Broadcasters, 54, 62–63
National Campus and Community Radio Association, 201
National Educational Radio Network, 211
national programming, 67, 69–70. *See also* localism
National Public Radio (NPR), 15, 154–169; "driveway moments" and, 210; evolution and creation of, 156–157, 211; female journalists on, 124; listener demographics, 154–160, 168; listener numbers, 154, 157–158, 159, 160–161, 168; local member stations, 162–164, 168–169; music programming, 157–158, 162; parodied on *Saturday Night Live,* 207–208, 227–228; promotional media, 155, 167. *See also* funding, for NPR; public radio; public radio, podcasting and
National Public Radio (NPR), audience inclusivity issues, 154–156, 157–168; advertising and, 158, 167, 168; age, 154, 155, 156, 158–160, 168; alternative programming possibilities, 164–167; BBC as model for addressing, 164–165, 167, 168; education and income levels, 155, 156, 157, 160, 161, 163, 168; efforts to address, through local station programming, 162–164, 168–169; efforts to address, through podcasts and streaming content, 158–160, 161–162, 168; elitism reputation, 155, 160–162, 167–168; geographic location, 155; *Monitor* as model for addressing, 165–166, 168; music programming, 157–158, 159, 162; news-talk format, 155–156, 158; Public Broadcasting Act's inclusivity directive, 154, 155, 157, 167, 169; race, 155, 156, 168; RTE as model for addressing, 166–167, 168; sound quality, 160–161, 162, 165. *See also* listener demographics
National Radio-Television Council (ESR, Greece), 234–236, 238, 240, 242
National Religious Broadcasters association, 141, 143
"Native radio" stations, Canada, 195, 201, 202–203
NBC, 86–87, 140, 165–166, 194, 255
*NBC Magazine* (TV program), 86
NBS, 194
NERIT (Greek state-run broadcaster), 240
networks, religious radio and, 138, 140, 141, 142, 148, 149
new media. *See* digital technology, development and proliferation; Internet radio; podcasting; satellite radio; social media; streaming
*New Oxford American Dictionary, The,* 15
news deserts, 70
news-oriented radio stations study, 22–36; audience feedback measures, 22, 25, 29–30; competition level and, 22, 26, 28, 30, 32, 33–34, 35, 71; economic goals, 27, 28, 33, 35; "engagement" strategies, 25; local programming, 27; organizational characteristics, 26–27, 28, 30–31, 32, 33–34, 35; ownership, 26–27, 28, 30, 31, 32, 33–34, 71; research deficit, 24–26; research findings, 29–36; research methods, 27–29; social media activity measures, 30; survey questions and responses, 29–31; websites, 29–30, 31–32, 33–35
newspapers, 24, 106; competition between radio and, 97, 100, 102
news programming: BBC, 165; news-talk format, NPR, 155–156, 158; ratings, 154. *See also* National Public Radio (NPR)
news reporting narrative style, 114; in *Air Raid,* 107; in *Broadcasting the Barricades,* 100, 103; in *Death Triangle,* 97; in *Fall of the City,* 105; in *March of Time,* 97; in *War of the Worlds,* 97, 98–99, 107. *See also* break-in news announcements
news stations, Greece, 236–237, 239, 246–249
New York City, New York, 86
*New Yorker,* 162
*New York Times,* 70, 160, 212, 225

NGradio.gr (New Generation Radio, Greece), 249
nichecasting, 54
niche programming, 120–127; religious radio as, 138–139, 149. *See also* freeform radio
Nielsen, 5, 72, 155–156
*99% Invisible* (radio program/podcast), 212–213, 224
Nirmala, Yalala, 264–265
Nitro Radio (Athens Voice Radio, Greece), 240
noncommercial radio. *See* freeform radio; public radio
nontraditional revenue (NTR), 53, 55–56
Norman, S. J., 266
Norris, Fred, 85
Northern Community Radio (NCR), 164
Northern Native Broadcast Access Program (NNBAP), 202
NPR. *See* National Public Radio (NPR)
NPR Music division, 158
NPR One, 158
*NPR Politics* (podcast), 225
NTR (nontraditional revenue), 53, 55–56
Nuzum, Eric, 159

Oikonomides, Dora, 245–246
Oikonomou, Panagiotis, 246–248
Oikonomou, Tasos, 238–239
*Old Fashioned Revival Hour* (radio program), 140, 141, 148
Oldring, Peter, 226
*Old Time Gospel Hour* (radio program), 141
Olympic Games, in Greece, 243
Omaha, Nebraska, 74–75
"on-demand" listening, 5–6, 25, 158–161, 178, 208, 215, 227. *See also* digital technology, development and proliferation; podcasting; streaming
online streaming. *See* streaming
*On the Media* (NPR program/podcast), 179, 223
Order, S., 260
organization of stations, 26–27, 28, 30–31, 32, 33–34, 35
*Orson Welles' Sketch Book* (radio program), 110
OTE (Greek telecommunications company), 245

*Outfront* (CBC program), 212
ownership. *See* station ownership

paid religious programs, 140, 141. *See also* religious radio
Pandora, 12, 13–14, 126–127
Papandreou, George, 250
Papathanasiou, Petros, 246, 247, 248
parasocial interactions, 39–52; history of, 39–40; intimacy and, 41, 43, 44, 48, 49, 51–52, 93; mindreading in, 42–43; parasocial relationships, measuring, 41–42; parasocial theory, evolution of, 40–41; Stern and, 84, 93; television and, 39, 40, 42–43, 47, 48; terrestrial radio and, 39, 40, 42, 43, 45–47, 48, 49. *See also* intimacy, parasocial interactions and
parasocial interactions, podcasts and, 43–52; future research possibilities, 51–52; hosts' role in, 44, 50; intimacy and, 43, 44, 48; listeners' role in, 43–44; mindreading in, 43; other media, compared, 47–50; quantifying and measuring, 51, 52; terrestrial radio broadcasts, compared, 45–47. *See also* podcasting
Parasocial Interaction (PSI) scale, 41–42
participant observation research, 128
Pavarala, V., 264
Pear, Tom, 114
people of color: podcast networks and, 176–177; in public radio, 176; "Yellow Rain" reactions, 186, 187. *See also* listener demographics; race
performing rights society (PRS), 9
Perkins, Tony, 149
Pesca, Mike, 162
Peters, J. D., 43–44
Petty, Tom, 130
Pew Research Center, 56, 155, 158
phones, 5, 179
Pinterest, 56
pirate radio, 240, 241
Pittsburgh, Pennsylvania, 76–77
*Planet Money* (NPR program), 160, 223
podcasting, 14–18, 173–188; advertising and, 5, 48–49; black networks of, 176–177; content delivery, 46–47; as disruptive technology, 15, 18, 173; early history of, 15, 211–213; engaged storytelling and, 214, 217; funding for, 48–49, 212–213, 219;

Google Podcasts, 17–18; in Greece, 249–250; growth in, 16–17, 25; headphones and, 49; hosts, 44, 50, 224–225; independently-produced, 212; Internet radio, compared, 45; lack of restrictions in, 48; listener demographics, 15–16, 46, 160, 176, 212; listener numbers, 15–17, 25, 46–47, 160, 176, 212; mobile aspect of, 45–46, 47; news-oriented radio stations study and, 29; NPR, 158, 159–160, 161–162, 168, 212; people of color and, 176–177; prestige podcasts, 214, 220, 221–223; regulations avoided in, 212, 214, 217, 227; release schedules, 44, 218, 219–220; religious, 145; specialized and diverse content, 44–45; streaming *vs.* downloading, 46–47; term, 15, 212; terrestrial radio, compared, 43, 45–47, 160; terrestrial radio content presented as, 212; UK listenership, 212. *See also* intimacy, podcasts and; parasocial interactions, podcasts and; production value, podcasts; public radio, podcasting and

podcasting, Canadian-produced, 219–222, 227; by CBC, 208, 212, 217, 219, 221; coding and categorization of, 220, 221–222, 223, 224, 225, 226; ratings data, 215–216, 217

podcast ratings, 208; based on download numbers, 46–47, 176–177, 213, 215, 225, 227; Canadian shows, 215–216, 217; iTunes charts, 176–177, 215–216, 221

Podcast app (Apple), 17–18
*Pod Save America* (podcast), 224, 225
Podtrac Inc., 15, 215–216
Poindexter, M., 68–69
"polarized pluralist" media landscape, 232, 233, 238
policy. *See* regulation(s)
political context for Greek mediascape, 232–234, 237, 238–239, 244, 249
political news coverage, presidential *vs.* local, 67, 70
politics, evangelical Christians and, 141, 149
Pondicherry University, 265–266
Potts, J., 179
Poundstone, Paula, 160, 162
Prebbenow, Merle, 180, 181, 182–183
present-tense script writing convention, 209

presidential election, 1980, 141
presidential election, 2016, 67, 149, 154
presidential politics, 67, 70
prestige podcasts, 208, 214, 220, 221–223
print media, evangelicalism and, 147–148
*Private Parts* (Stern), 83, 84
production value, podcasts, 173, 217–218, 219–220; comedy/entertainment programs, 220, 221, 226; immediacy programs, 220, 221, 225–226; intimate, moderate production value programs, 220, 221, 224–225; prestige podcasts, 208, 214, 220, 221–223; top-tier, 220, 221, 223–224. *See also* podcasting
production value, religious radio, 142
profanity, 214, 217, 219, 222
programming, centralized strategies, 119
programming, freeform. *See* freeform radio
programming, Indigenous radio, 202
programming, music. *See* music programming
programming, news. *See* news programming
programming, NPR. *See* National Public Radio (NPR)
programming, religious. *See* religious radio
Protestant broadcasts, 140
Proust, Elizabeth, 258
proximity effect, 179
public broadcasting, funding for, 167, 168; in Canada, 227; by Corporation for Public Broadcasting, 154, 155, 156, 159, 164; podcasts, 212–213. *See also* funding
Public Broadcasting Act (1967), 156–157, 159, 161, 210; inclusivity directive, 154, 155, 157, 167, 169; public radio and (*vs.* podcasting), 162
Public Broadcasting Service (PBS), 154, 161, 168
public radio: history of, 113, 156–157, 162–163; music and, 210–211; people of color working in, 176; radiogenic elements of, 208, 209; *Saturday Night Live* parody, 207–208. *See also* British Broadcasting Corporation (BBC); Canadian Broadcasting Corporation (CBC); commercial radio; National Public Radio (NPR)
public radio, podcasting and, 207–208, 211–228; backstage transparency, 213, 214, 218, 222, 224–225; BBC, 212; CBC, 208,

public radio, podcasting and (cont.)
212, 213–214, 215, 217, 219, 221; coded analysis of top-ranked podcasts, 208, 215–219; comedy/entertainment programs, 220, 221, 226; evolution of, 208, 223; format type, 218, 220; funding and financing for, 212–213; hosts, importance of, 224–225; immediacy programs, 220, 221, 225–226; intimacy construction and, 208, 214–215, 219–221, 221–225; intimate, moderate production value programs, 220, 221, 224–225; journalistic approach, 217–218, 220, 221; journalistic norms disrupted in, 213–214; limited-run, 221, 223; narrative structure, 217–218, 219, 220, 221; NPR, 158, 159–160, 161–162, 168, 212; prestige podcasts, 208, 214, 220, 221–223; radiogenic narrative techniques for listener engagement, 208, 221, 223; reciprocal relationship between formats, 208; release schedule, 220, 221, 223, 225–226; research methods for study, 215–219; second wave, 212–214; sound use, 223, 224; top-tier public radio programs, 220, 221, 223–224. *See also* National Public Radio (NPR); podcasting; production value, podcasts; *Serial* (podcast)
public service announcements (PSAs), 11
public sphere theory, 68–69, 260–261
Puduvai Vaani (India), 265–266
pureplay webstreaming, 12

*Q* (CBC program), 223
Quebec, 195
*Quirks and Quarks* (CBC program), 223
Quivers, Robin, 83, 85, 86

race: listener demographics, 155, 156, 160, 168, 176; of producers, 143, 176–177. *See also* whiteness
race, podcasting and: white male voices in, 173–174; "Yellow Rain" reactions and, 186–187, 188. *See also* sonic whiteness; "Yellow Rain" (*Radiolab* story)
"race music," 121
racial auralities, 176
racialized soundscapes, 175
Rader, Paul, 139
*Radio Bible Class* (radio program), 140

*Radio Broadcast* (magazine), 255–256
Radiobubble (Greece), 232, 245–248
*Radio Chapel Service* (radio program), 139
Radio.com, 9
radiogenic elements, 208, 209–210, 221, 226; etymology of term, 209. *See also* intimacy; podcasting
radio hoaxes. *See* War of the Worlds
*Radiolab* (podcast), narrative sound design of, 223; leitmotif use, 179–183; sonic whiteness, 174–175, 177, 178, 179, 186–188. *See also* "Yellow Rain" (*Radiolab* story)
Radio-locator.com, 28
radio news. *See* news
Radio Online, 72
Radio Ryerson Inc., 199
*Radio Times* magazine, 100
*Radiotopia* (podcast collective), 224
Radio Unnamable (radio program), 123
RadioWave.com, 7, 8
Rathenau, Walter, 104, 105
ratings and charts. *See under individual format*
RBM.com, 7, 8
RDG.com, 7, 8
Reagan, Ronald, 141–142, 177, 181
Reagan administration, 177, 178, 179, 184
received pronunciation (RP) speaking style, 100
receivers: satellite radio, 11; terrestrial radio, 4, 5, 7
Recording Industry Association of America (RIAA), 10
record labels, copyright law and, 10
*Red Lion Broadcasting Co. v. FCC* (1969), 141
Reed, Brian, 222
"Refugee" (Petty), 130
regulation(s): of BBC, by British General Post Office, 100; in Canada, 193, 194–196, 197, 199, 201–203; of early radio, 100, 104, 113, 138; equipment operations, 139; intellectual property law, 9–11, 237–238; podcasts avoid, 212, 214, 217, 227; public sphere theory and, 68; regulatory capture, 233, 235; religious radio and, 138, 139, 140–141, 142; satellite radio avoids, 83, 88; Stern and, 83, 86, 88; *War of the Worlds* and, 109, 111. *See also* Canadian Radio and Television Commission (CRTC;

later Canadian Radio-Television and Telecommunications Commission); Federal Communications Commission (FCC); licenses, operations and broadcasting; Public Broadcasting Act (1967)
regulation(s), Greek broadcasting and: DAB transmissions, 243, 244, 250; *diaploki* and, 233–234, 237, 239, 250–251; ERT shutdown, 239–240; ESR and, 234–236, 238, 240, 242; Hallin and Mancini on, 231, 232–233, 238, 242, 250; haphazard operations, 231, 232, 241–242, 250; music programming and, 237–238; "polarized pluralist" media landscape, 232, 233, 238; Radiobubble as "free radio", 246; "savage deregulation", 231, 232–236. *See also* Greece
Reith, John, 100, 164
religious radio, 137–150; as bellwether to evolution of radio, 137–138; Canada and, 194; chain broadcasting and, 140; current state of, 142–146; deregulation and, 139, 142, 144; digital technology and, 138, 144–145, 149; evangelical divide between religious television and, 138, 146; FCC and, 140, 141–142; funding for, 139, 140, 141, 145–146; future of, 146–150; growth in station numbers, 141; history of, 138–142; homogenized ownership and perspective in, 138, 143; listener numbers, 144; listener response, 139, 140; localism and, 141, 142, 143; music programming, 143; networks and, 138, 140, 141, 142, 148, 149; Protestantism and, 138, 140, 144; regulations and, 138, 139, 140–141, 142; Salem Media Group and, 142, 143, 144–145. *See also* evangelical Christians
Reneau-Wadeen, Zack, 17
"Requiem for the Masses" (the Association), 123
Resnikoff, Paul, 162
Reuters, 11, 100
revenue: advertising price drops, 69–70; commercialization of early radio, 113; nontraditional (NTR), 53, 55–56; satellite radio operates at a loss, 11, 90; trends, 53–55. *See also* advertising; funding; social media analytics
Ridgen, David, 213–214
Riffe, D., 26, 28

*Riot That Never Was, The* (2005 re-creation of *Broadcasting the Barricades*), 103
Roberts, Oral, 142
Robson, William N., 107
Rockefeller Foundation, 156
Rodriguez, C., 261
Rogan, Joe, 224
Rogers, Adrian, 142, 149
Rogers, Ralph, 97
Roosevelt, Franklin D., 210
Rosaen, S. F., 41
Rosso, John, 4–5
Rothenbuhler, E. W., 125
Royal Canadian Corps of Signals, 195
royalty payments, 9–11, 121
RTE (Radio Telefís Éireann; Radio Television Ireland) Radio 1, 166–167, 168
Rubber City Radio, 79

SAG-AFTRA, 11
Salem Media Group, 76; religious radio and, 142, 143, 144–145
Sangham Radio (India), 265
satellite radio, 4; freeform radio and, 126–127; in Greece, 244–245; regulations avoided on, 83, 88; Sirius Satellite Radio, 11–12; SiriusXM Satellite Radio, 12, 82–83, 126, 145; Stern on, 82, 88, 89–91; XM Satellite Radio, 11–12
*Saturday Night Live* (television show), 207–208, 227–228
"savage deregulation," 231, 232–236. *See also* deregulation; regulation(s), Greek broadcasting and
Saxon, Peter, 258–259
Scannell, Paddy, 113–114
Schadow, Karl, 106
Schiappa, E., 50
Schiller, Vivian, 160, 161
Schwartz, Brad, 105, 111
"Schweddy Balls" (*Saturday Night Live* sketch), 207, 227
Screen Actors Guild (SAG), 11
Seacrest, Ryan, 83
Seeley, Tom, 182
Sekulow, Jay, 145–146
self-management status (Greece), 240–241
*Serial* (podcast), 15, 25, 213, 219, 221, 223; backstage transparency and, 214; parodied on *Saturday Night Live*, 227–228

SESAC (formerly Society for European Stage Authors and Composers), 9
Settel, Irving, 107
sexism, 124
*Shadow, The* (radio broadcast), 97, 98
Shakespeare, William, 112
Sharma, K., 262
Shaw, E. F., 28
Shulman, M., 176
Siemering, Bill, 157, 162
Silverman, Art, 163
Simon, P. M., 70
Simonson, P., 43–44
Simpson, K., 124
Sims, Monica, 257
"Sims Report, The," 257
Sinfield, Bob, 103
Sirius Satellite Radio, 11–12
SiriusXM Satellite Radio, 12, 25, 82–83, 126, 145
Six Nations Indian Reserve, 202
Skai 100.3 FM (Athens, Greece), 235
Skinner, D., 195
Slade, Paul, 100, 103, 110
*Slate* online magazine, 159, 162, 225
smartphones, 5, 179
smart speakers, 5, 17
Smith, F. L., 4
Smith, Fred, 96
Smith, Margaret Low, 161
SmithGeiger (consulting firm), 161
*Snap Judgment* (radio program/podcast), 223
Snoddy, Ray, 103
Snyder, Thomas James "Tom," 110
social integration approach to media theory, 146–147
social media: Facebook, 56, 60, 61, 185–186; Greece and, 232; listeners as active agents through, 174–175, 185, 188; news-oriented radio stations study and, 30; NPR member stations on, 163; NTR and, 56; personal narrative and, 210; Radiobubble and, 247; reactions to "Yellow Rain" on, 174, 177, 178, 185–187; religious radio and, 145; Twitter, 22, 56, 163, 247
social media analytics, 53, 56–63; interviews, 60–62; "seven layers" typology of data, 56; surveys on, 58–62, 63; tone monitoring, 57, 58, 59, 60, 62

*Someone Knows Something* (CBC podcast), 213–214, 221, 222
*Sonic Color Line: Race and the Cultural Politics of Listening, The* (Stoever), 176
sonic orientalism, 174, 182, 183, 188; defined, 175. *See also* "Yellow Rain" (*Radiolab* story)
sonic rationality, 182–185, 187. *See also* "Yellow Rain" (*Radiolab* story)
sonic whiteness, 173; defined, 175; history of, 176–177; *Radiolab* curates, 174–175, 177, 178, 179, 186–188. *See also* "Yellow Rain" (*Radiolab* story)
sound, early radio experimentation, 100, 112
sound, use in podcasts, 223, 224; intimacy and, 179, 187. *See also* intimacy; production value, podcasts; *Radiolab* (podcast), narrative sound design of
SoundCloud, 13–14, 132
SoundExchange (RIAA organization), 10
sound quality, of NPR broadcasts, 160–161, 162, 165. *See also* vocal sound qualities
sound recording copyrights, 9–10
SoundWorks Collection, 180
southern U.S., NPR and, 155
spoken-word radio. *See* National Public Radio (NPR); news; public radio
sponsorship, 113, 121, 123. *See also* advertising; funding
sports programming, 72, 73, 75, 78, 162, 266
Spotify, 12, 13–14, 126
Stanley, Charles, 141, 142, 148
station affiliations, 122, 124, 194
station organization, 26–27, 28, 30–31, 32, 33–34, 35
station ownership: Clear Channel, 23, 88, 126; concentration, in Greece, 236; FCC regulations, 126; local, 71, 72, 73–78, 79, 80, 141; news-oriented radio stations study, 26–27, 28, 30, 31, 32, 33–34, 71; religious, 138, 141, 142, 143; Salem Media Group, 76, 142, 143, 144–145. *See also* consolidation; *individual network/owner*
Staver, Mat, 149
Sterling, C. H., 4
Stern, Ben, 84
Stern, Howard, 82–94; early life and career, 84–87; earnings, 83, 85; fandom, 82–87, 91–94; FCC battles, 82–83, 84; games with listeners, 85–86; gay and lesbian

community advocacy by, 86; parasocial interactions and, 84, 93; *Private Parts,* 83, 84; Quivers and, 83, 85, 86; regulations and, 83, 86, 88. See also *Howard Stern Radio Show, The*
Stern, Ray, 84
Sterne, J., 173
Stoever, J., 173–174, 176
Sto Kokkino 105.5 FM (Athens, Greece), 237
storytelling. *See* engaging storytelling
Storz, Todd, 121
*S-Town* (podcast), 219, 221, 222, 223
streaming, 31–32; commercial radio and, 7, 9; *vs.* downloading, 12–13, 54, 144, 145; legal distinctions, 10; measuring podcasts consumed by, 46–47; music streaming services, 4, 5–6, 12–14, 54, 126–127, 132; "on-demand" listening, 5–6, 25, 158–161, 178, 208, 215, 227; of religious content, 145; of unaltered terrestrial programming, 6, 7–9, 22–23, 25, 29. *See also* downloading podcasts; Internet radio
*Stuff You Missed in History Class* (podcast), 224, 225
*Stuff You Should Know* (podcast), 224, 225
Stursberg, Richard, 211
subaltern counterpublics theory, 260–261
Sunday, Billy
Supreme Court, 141
Swaggart, Jimmy, 142
Swindoll, Chuck, 141, 142, 148
syndicated programming, 69, 72–78, 80, 148–149

*Takeaway, The* (radio program), 168–169
talk radio, commercial, 211. *See also* localism, American talk radio study; news
Taylor, Marlin, 12
*Tech Survey* (Jacobs Media), 5
Tech Terms, 6
*TED Radio Hour* (podcast), 160
Telecommunications Act (1996), 27, 69, 126, 142
televangelism, 141, 145
television, 4, 140; parasocial interactions and, 39, 40, 42–43, 47, 48; PBS, 154, 161, 168; religious, 138, 141, 145, 146; visual experience and, 49–50
*Televisory* (radio industry blog), 18
Terkel, Studs, 122

terrestrial radio: competition between newspapers and, 97, 100, 102; copyright law and, 10; early history and evolution, 4–6, 18, 112–113, 156–157, 162–163, 255–256; intimacy and, 49, 209–210, 214; listener demographics, 46, 53–54; listener numbers, 15, 46, 53–54, 121, 159, 168; NTR and, 55–56; parasocial interactions and, 39, 40, 42, 43, 45–47, 48, 49; podcasts, compared, 43, 45–47, 160; social media analytics and, 53, 56–63; sonic whiteness and, 176; station websites, 6–7, 27, 29–30, 31–32, 33–35, 55; unaltered content available for streaming online, 6, 7–9, 22–23, 25, 29; unaltered shows presented as podcasts, 212. *See also* Canadian campus/community radio; commercial radio; consolidation; digital technology, development and proliferation; freeform radio; localism, American talk radio study; National Public Radio (NPR); news; public radio; religious radio; *War of the Worlds, The* (1938 radio broadcast); *individual program; individual station*
terrestrial radio, regulations for. *See* regulation(s)
*This American Life* (podcast), 219, 221, 222
*This American Life/Serial* (podcast). *See Serial* (podcast)
*This Is Orson Welles* (Welles and Bogdanovich), 110
*This Is That* (CBC program), 226
Thompson, M., 175
*Three-Year Plan 2016–2019* (CRTC), 196–197, 203
*Time* magazine, 96–97
*Today* (television show), 110–111
Tolios, Aris, 249
*Tomorrow Show, The* (television show), 110
Top 40 stations, 121, 123, 124–125
traditional radio. *See* terrestrial radio
Traquina, N., 233
Traynor, Mary, 112
Trillium Foundation, 201
Triton Digital, 4, 5
Trump, Donald, 145, 149, 154
*Truth about Father Christmas, The* (1922 radio drama), 112

Truth and Reconciliation Commission of Canada, 203
TuneIn, 7, 9
Tutorpool initiative, 247
24 Media (media group), 236, 240
Twitter, 22, 56, 163, 247
2GB (Australian station), 258

underground rock radio, 123–124. *See also* freeform radio
*Unfollow* magazine, 234
United Kingdom: podcasting data and, 212; women and, 255, 257–258, 259, 267. *See also* British Broadcasting Corporation (BBC)
United States: podcasting data, 215, 216, 219, 223; U.S. podcasts popular in Canada, 219, 227
University of Omaha, 121
unpredictable programming. *See* freeform radio
*Up First* (podcast), 160, 225, 226
USA Radio, 143

Valpy, Edmund George (E. V.), 103
*Variety* magazine, 18
Vasilopoulos, Vasilis, 240, 249
Vaxevanis, Kostas, 234
Verma, Neil, 97, 114
*Vice* (online news site), 214
Vietnam War, 177
Vima FM 99.5 (Greece), 240
*Vinyl Café, The* (CBC program), 226
vocal sound qualities: intimacy and, 209–210; on NPR, 162, 165; racial auralities, 176; received pronunciation style, 100. *See also* sonic whiteness; sound
voice-activated devices, 5, 17
volunteers, Canadian community/campus radio and, 198–200, 201
Vovou, I., 233

*Wait, Wait Don't Tell Me* (NPR program), 160, 226
WAKR-AM (Akron), 79
Walker, Connie, 222–223
Walker, David, 99
Walliser, Blair, 106
Walters, Pat, 178, 180, 181–182
Ward, Mark, Sr., 146

*War of the Worlds,* influences on: *Air Raid,* 97, 107, 114, 115; *Broadcasting the Barricades,* 97, 99–103, 110, 114, 115; *The Crimson Wizard,* 97, 106–107, 114, 115; *The Fall of the City,* 97, 105, 107, 114, 115; *The Minister Is Murdered!,* 97, 104–105, 114, 115
*War of the Worlds, The* (1938 radio broadcast), 96–99, 107–115; break-in news announcements used in, 96, 97, 98, 105, 108–109, 112; considered engaging storytelling, 96–97, 98, 99, 111; considered fake news, 96, 97–98, 99, 110–112, 115; considered radio hoax, 96, 97–98, 99, 110, 111–112; plot, 108–109; reactions to, 98–99, 110–111, 112. *See also* Welles, Orson
*War of the Worlds, The* (Wells), 107–108, 109
WarpRadio.com, 7, 8
Washington, D.C., 85–86
*Washington Blade* (newspaper), 86
*Washington Post,* 145, 155
Waugh, Evelyn, 100, 103, 110
WBAI (New York), 123
WBGG-AM (Pittsburgh), 76–77
WBUR (Boston), 161
WCCC (Hartford), 84–85
WEAE-AM (Pittsburgh), 77
Weaver, Sylvester L. "Pat," 165, 166
web radio and webcasting. *See* Internet radio
WebRadio.com, 7, 8
websites, terrestrial radio stations', 6–7, 27, 55; for news-oriented radio stations, 29–30, 31–32, 33–35
Weissberger, Arnold, 111
Welles, Orson: *Air Raid* and, 107; apologizes after *War of the Worlds* reaction, 99, 109–111, 112; *Citizen Welles* (biography of), 107, 108, 110–111; in *Fall of the City,* 97, 105, 107; in *March of Time,* uncredited, 97, 98; *Mercury Theatre on the Air* and, 98, 105, 108, 111; press conference with, 98–99, 104, 105, 109–111, 112; in *The Shadow,* 97, 98; in *War of the Worlds,* 96, 108–109. *See also War of the Worlds, The* (1938 radio broadcast)
Wells, H. G., 107–108, 109
Wertheimer, Linda, 157
Westinghouse, 4, 120

WFMT (Chicago), 122
WFMU (New Jersey), 128, 131
WFUV (New York), 158
WGN Radio (Chicago), 106
WGTK-AM (Louisville), 76
WHA (Madison), 4
WHAS-AM (Louisville), 76
*What's Good with Stretch & Bobbito* (podcast), 160
"white aurality" theory, 175
whiteness: white men, podcasting and, 173–174; white men, religious radio and, 143; "white voice," 176; "Yellow Rain" reactions, of white people, 186–187. *See also* race; sonic whiteness
WHLO-AM (Akron), 79
Will, George, 161
Williams, Juan, 155
Wilson, J. L., 12
Winchester, Simon, 158, 163, 164
Winer, Dave, 15
Winkleman, Claudia, 258
Winzenburg, Stephen, 146
*Wired* magazine, 212
*Wireless and Aviation News*, 194
wireless telegraphy research, 3
WJBC-AM (Bloomington, Illinois), 54
WJBT (Chicago), 139
WKJK-AM (Louisville), 76
WKRD-AM (Louisville), 76
WLPN (Chicago), 120, 127–131
WMBI (Chicago), 139
WNBC-AM (New York), 86
WNIR-FM (Akron), 79
Wohl, Richard, 40, 83–84
Wolfenden, H., 51
women, 255–268; in Australian media employment, 258–260, 267; at BBC, 255, 257–258, 259; career and pay differences, 257–258; community radio and, 259–262, 263–266; as DJs, 124; in early radio history, 255–256; female-oriented content, 263, 264; in Indian media employment, 259, 261–266, 267–268; at NBC, 255; at NPR, 124; public sphere theory and, 260–261; in UK, 255, 257–258, 259, 267; "Yellow Rain" reactions of, 186
Women's Development Initiative (WDI), 257

Women's International Network (WIN), 261
Women's Movement in India, 262
Woo, C. W., 35
*Word of Life Hour, The* (radio program), 140
WOR-FM (New York), 123
World Association for Christian Communication (WACC), 256–257, 266–267
World Association for Community Radio Broadcasters (AMARC), 261
*World Café* (NPR program), 158, 163
World Radio Day, 266
WPLJ-FM (New York), 124–125
WUNC (Raleigh), 155
WWDC (Washington, D.C.), 85–86
WXPN (Philadelphia), 158
WXRK-FM (New York), 86, 87

Xenios FM (Greece), 240
XM Satellite Radio, 11–12

Yahoo! News site, 24
Yang, Eng, 177–178, 180, 181, 182, 183–185
Yang, Kao Kalia, 178, 180, 181, 182, 183–185, 186–187
"Yellow Rain" (*Radiolab* story), 177–188; analysis of, 179–185; Hmong narrative in, 174, 175, 177–178, 180–185, 186–187; Krulwich apologizes for tone, 186, 187; leitmotifs in, 179–183; reactions, on social media, 174, 177, 178, 185–187; reactions, race and gender and, 186–187, 188; sonic orientalism in, 174, 175, 182–183, 188; sonic rationality and, 182–185, 187; sonic whiteness in, 174–175, 177, 178, 179, 186–188; story synopsis, 177–178; Yangs, interviews with, 177–178, 180, 181, 182, 183–185, 186–187. *See also* sonic whiteness
York University, 200
*Young People's Church of the Air* (radio program), 140
YouTube, 56, 250

*Zauberei auf dem Sender: Versuch einer Rundfunkgroteske (Wizardry on the Air: Attempt at a Radio Grotesque)* (1924 radio drama), 104
Zenakos, Augustine, 234

Printed in the United States
By Bookmasters